Luke the Interpreter:
Of Jesus' story and of Israel's scriptures

Peter Doble

vii

Bibliographical abbreviations

AnBib	Analecta biblica
BDAG	A Greek–English Lexicon of the New Testament and Other Early Christian Literature
BZNW	Beihefte zur ZNW
CBQ	*Catholic Biblical Quarterly*
D05	*Codex Bezae*
EvQ	*Evangelical Quarterly*
ExpTim	*Expository Times*
HTR	*Harvard Theological Review*
JBL	*Journal of Biblical Literature*
JETS	*Journal of the Evangelical Theological Society*
JSNT	*Journal for the Study of the New Testament*
JSNTSup	*Journal for the Study of the New Testament, Supplement Series*
JSOTSup Supplement	*Journal for the Study of the Old Testament, Supplement* Series
JTS	*Journal of Theological Studies*
NovT	*Novum Testamentum*
NovTSup	*Novum Testamentum*, Supplements
NTD	Das Neue Testament Deutsch
NTS	*New Testament Studies*
NTTS	New Testament Tools and Studies
ProcIrBibAssoc	*Proceedings of the Irish Biblical Association*
RB	*Revue biblique*
ResQ	*Restoration Quarterly*

SBLDS	SBL Dissertation Series
SBLMS	SBL Monograph Series
SBT	Studies in Biblical Theology
SJT	*Scottish Journal of Theology*
SNTSMS	Society for New Testament Studies Monograph Series
TDNT	*Theological Dictionary of the New Testament*
THNTC	Two Horizons New Testament Commentary
WUNT	Wissenschaftliche Untersuchungen zum Neuen Testament

Foreword

by Naomi, Peter's granddaughter

Before passing away in January 2023, Peter Doble had spent the last four of his ninety-three years working on Luke the Interpreter, although the ideas had certainly been brewing for far longer – arguably since the publication of The Paradox of Salvation in 1996 (Cambridge University Press). Unfortunately, this culmination of decades dedicated to Lukan scholarship was only in the early stages of publication when Peter died, and the publisher was unable to continue the project without the author's input.

Peter's own preface details many people for whom Luke the Interpreter was a point of great interest, and I cherish having become one of those involved in the conversation, entrusted with updating the manuscript during revisions and therefore in possession of the final copy. With no shortage of interested parties in seeing this work come to light, the family, especially Peter's children (Martin, Jonathan and Petra), has decided to self-publish the manuscript in the full certainty that doing so best honours his memory.

I offer this foreword as an explanation of the book's stage in its preparation for publication. Peter's main concern was that Part III (Two Witnesses) was too long. However, while these chapters could almost work as stand-alone articles, he was adamant that Stephen's speech and Paul's sermon were integral to his argument and their substance must hold a key place in the book. For Peter, this book was a summation of his multi-disciplinary understanding of Luke. He sought to reach not only scholars, but also politicians, economists and citizens, by shining light on Luke as an interpreter of meaning. Towards the end of his life and work, Peter's already-rich thoughts and sentences became richer and perhaps more intense. Presented herein is an unusually unedited volume so that his message might still reach a broad audience.

That said, I must mention Kate Sotejeff-Wilson's skilful proofreading and Kathryn O'Donoghue's prompt and thorough indexing: thank you for your valuable contributions to the completion of this project. Thanks also to Daniel Doble for the apt cover design. I am also grateful to Dr Susan Doherty and Dr Mary Hayward for their encouragement and suggestions as to how best to go about this task. Lastly, I must acknowledge the unswerving support of Peter's wife, Gwyneth, who shared a substantial amount of her husband's time with Luke and continues to ask after the book's progress even now. For your commitment to this work, Nanna, no one is more deserving of a copy in their hand than you.

It's a shame we will never know what Peter's next book, Luke among the Economists, was shaping up to be, but we hope that both current and future scholars will benefit from his insights into Luke the Interpreter.

Preface

One of the principal features of this book, and an important one, is its Analytical Diagram that maps Luke-Acts' fifty-two chapters, a substantial element of a canonical New Testament. My first discipline was economics, where I learned to value 'modelling' for giving visual shape to concepts and formulating problems. Like the nature of the subject itself, this aspect of economics has been the focus of much discussion, which I have transferred to Luke's "narrative" – *his* diegesis, not our narratology. That first discipline also made me increasingly aware of the interrelatedness of 'things': one focal problem interacts with and entails reckoning with other, consequent problems.

At the very heart of this diagram is the block sited in Jerusalem (Luke 19.41-Acts 8.3), marked by conflict – Jesus' speaking truth to power - and the setting for the two focal, disputed texts (Luke 24.25-27, 44-49) that are this book's sharp focus. Over many years my engagement with economics was increasingly spurred on by Luke's retelling of Jesus' story. The 'dark' side of that story, its conflict-narrative leading to Jesus' brutal execution, speaks clearly and at many levels to a world that repeatedly fails to learn from its history.

Luke-Acts' narrative integrity really does depend on how a reader understands those two disputed texts: a Luke who is allegedly mistaken has a different standing from a Luke who is arguably purposefully committed. There is much in this book that invites dialogue with other interpreters, and its heart is the much-discussed concept of interpretation. This book's core chapters (1-9) trace how *this* interpreter arrived at its conclusion – or, rather, its conclusions.

Every writer has debts beyond repaying. My principal thanks must go to those giants at Cambridge who in the early Fifties led me through the course for Part II of the Theological Tripos, and who then encouraged me into Part III in New Testament Studies. I owe a particular debt to W F Flemington, who unstintingly gave of his time, wisdom and friendship.

Then, in Bangalore, Anthony Hanson spurred me into a deeper engagement with Jewish non-canonical scriptures, an engagement nourished in later years particularly by the 'Hawarden Seminar,'[1] many colleagues focused on the relationships between Jewish and Christian scriptures, canonical and non-canonical, and their interpretations. Becoming an interpreter is a well-trodden, uphill road.

The British New Testament Society has been another forge in which understanding emerged though dialogue that hammers out ideas. Its Acts seminar long-since became by default a Luke-Acts (or Luke and Acts) seminar, and I owe much to countless friends there – particularly to Paul Ellingworth, Howard Marshall,[2] and Matthew Sleeman. Interpretation and collegiality belong together; my thanks go to its innumerable participants who have nurtured me in both. Among them are a number of American erstwhile postgrads whose lively and continuing engagement with *Interpreter*'s questions is welcome encouragement. To one of these, Dr Josh Mann, I owe especial thanks: now a family friend, Josh continues our dialogue about things Lukan.

Another forge includes the many non-specialist groups with whom I have worked. One, the Tuesday Fellowship of the York Methodist Circuit worked through Luke-Acts over a period of two years – during which Mrs Sylvia

---

[1] See North, J. L., *KAINA KAI PALAIA:* 'An Account of the British Seminar on the Use of the Old Testament in the New Testament' in Moyise, S. (ed.) (2000), *The Old Testament in the New Testament,* JSNTS 189, Sheffield: Sheffield Academic Press.

[2] Both of whom, also much indebted to W. F. Flemington, are now gathered to their fathers.

Bunting began the process of making my hand-sketched diagram accessible, and willingly commented on style. The Revd David Priestnall has discussed revisions of the text and checked its footnotes.

I offer especial thanks to four others. *Interpreter* is a sequel to my earlier *The Paradox of Salvation,* since when Dr Mary Hayward has readily continued her encouraging editorial dialogue and has overseen the coherence of the headings in this volume. My *Doktorvater*, and friend, Professor Keith Elliott, has remained a supportive consultant. I remain grateful to both for their companionship on this long way. In this present project they are joined by Mrs Naomi Teles Fazendeiro of Coimbra, a classicist, now an English lecturer at the University of Coimbra; Naomi, my granddaughter, has painstakingly transformatted my manuscript for publication, involving frequent and welcome digital discussions.

Finally, my thanks go to Gwyneth, my wife for sixty-five years, to whom I dedicate this book. She might well echo Dylan Thomas's: "Luke! Luke! I'm a martyr to that Luke!" But she welcomed Luke and 'his' great train of books and papers into our home and made possible the commitment without which scholarly work cannot exist. For this, Gwyneth, and for far more than can be told, my deepest thanks: this book is yours.

Introduction

This monograph focuses primarily on two disputed Lukan passages, Luke 24:25–27 and 24:44–49; their message is "according to the scriptures"; their content is that the Messiah must suffer and be raised from the dead or enter into his glory. Focusing on these passages entails a far wider discussion.[3] Luke's relationship with Israel's scriptures is structural; his retelling of Jesus' story is embedded within those scriptures and cannot be told without them. His story's structure comprises a reference-frame enclosing a narrative whose lexical palette is drawn from scriptural models or patterns, and whose purpose is to show how its events are "the things fulfilled among us" (Luke 1:1–4). According to Luke, who is Jesus? Which scriptures speak of his death and resurrection? What does Luke mean when he uses the word "fulfilment"?[4]

Addressing these focal verses, many commentators note that Israel's scriptures know nothing of a Messiah who must suffer and be raised from the dead;[5] some seek Luke's synthesis of Messiah with another descriptor,[6] e.g.,

---

[3] Throughout, the New Testament Greek text is NA28, except where otherwise noted; "Septuagint," or LXX, commonly refers to Rahlfs (1979). Variants from Rahlfs' edition are almost always to Vaticanus and noted in the text. OGT (Old Greek Text) signifies a Greek version that Luke used, not unlike the LXX.

[4] This last is a long-standing question in relation to the canonical gospels. Posed by Dodd (1952), it was re-focused by Hays (2015).

[5] E.g., Bock (2012); Caird, (1963); Conzelmann (1960); Creed (1950); Cunningham (1997); Ellis (1974); Evans (1990); Fitzmyer (1981, 1985); Franklin (1975); Grayston (1990); Green (1990, 1997); Johnson (1991); Kurz (1993); Mallen (2008); Manson (1930); Miura (2007); Moessner (2016); Nolland (1989; 1993a and 1993b); Pao (2000); Plummer (1922); Schweizer (1993); Strauss (1995); Talbert (1988); Tannehill (1996); Wiefel (1988). Others, like Carroll (2012); Marshall (1978); Parsons (2015) and Wolter (2017) remain uncritical of Luke, but open to a wider and vaguer reading of Luke's "scripture."

[6] Throughout, I use "descriptor" rather than "title," e.g., Bock (2012: 185–209), or "name," e.g., Taylor, V. (1953). Borrowed from information technology, "descriptor" works as a category index-name to access underlying texts: e.g., Son of Man takes readers primarily to Daniel; "Prophet" to Deuteronomy;

1

"suffering servant" or "prophet," who suffers according to the scriptures.[7] But what if Luke's critics are mistaken and he wrote Luke-Acts from his post-resurrection perspective to demonstrate retrospectively what he understood that scripture said? Luke attributes both of these passages to Jesus himself, who in Luke 24 clarifies for his followers those scriptures that constitute this claim, which in turn becomes the heart of their preaching.[8]

Neutestamentler tend to be alert to a scholar's personal perspective in her or his writing. My perspective emerges from continuing engagement with a still emerging global thought-world that highlights the complex organic interactions that constitute human living in its givenness. Economists, climatologists, naturalists and others have embarked on radical transformations of their disciplines as humans gradually articulate their renewed awareness of the organic, complex inter-relatedness within (a) the small blue planet that around 8 billion of us share; (b) the politico-socio-economic and philosophical systems we have inherited and developed; (c) the complex, frequently conflicting noospheres within which humans shape their varied experiences of being, from natality to mortality. In this age, when dissection is giving way to an age of exploring "wholes," Luke's whole statement of his case (διήγησις) to give assurance (ἀσφάλεια) to Theophilus needs to be heard and understood.

A suitable catch-term for this perspective is "holistic." My "method" is a synergistic amalgam of three distinct but interrelated approaches: (a) literary narrative; (b) via *la Problématique*; and (c) abductive reasoning. This amalgam

---

"Righteous One" to Psalms or Wisdom; "Servant" to texts about Abraham, Moses and David. Luke presents Jesus as God's agent whose life and work evoke diverse hopes and patterns mapped by descriptors from Israel's scriptures.

[7] See Doble (2006a). *Interpreter* (abbrev. for this work's title) results from my affirming that Luke's focus is on Jesus' resurrection rather than on his suffering, which itself resonates with Wisdom's δίκαιος and Daniel's Son of Man models and evokes Ps. 2:1–2.

[8] E.g., Luke 24:45–49; Acts 17:2–3 and 26:22–23.

is indebted to generations of scholarly dialogue in many areas of study, among which discourse analysis,[9] dialogical intertextual interpretation[10] and macro-economic theory figure significantly. My debt to Markus Bockmuehl's seminal *Seeing the Word* will be clear to all who know and value his work.[11] In this monograph we address the problem of two disputed Jesus-*logia* in a widely-used, critical-eclectic Greek text – and in a changing scholarly context.[12]

First, Luke chose to call his work a narrative (διήγησις, Luke 1:1) and *Interpreter*'s conclusions confirm that his two volumes constitute one continuous, developmental, narratival shaping. Consequently, I argue that a *specific* problem in Luke-Acts is normally best resolved narratively, for that problem constitutes one element in Luke's architectural word-building. Why is the element there, where is it, and how does it work in the whole text?

Second, the text we use has a long ancestry. It emerged from a Graeco-Roman literary world at the hands of a Jewish author skilled in handling Jewish literature.[13] Over the past seventy-five years, however, scholarly discussion of that long ancestry has shifted from its default setting – a relentlessly literary model that sometimes reduced Luke to a cut-and-paste editor of texts – to a growing recognition that Jesus' story remains a living tradition whose interpretation is crucial but variable, and that literary texts are not permanent fixtures.[14] Significant developments in our understandings of memory, of scribal

---

[9] I am much indebted to conversations with Jenny Read-Heimerdinger and acquaintance with her writings for my dealing with structural and other issues.

[10] Steve Moyise has long been a kind mentor and the Hawarden Seminar a rich source of shared learning in matters of interpretation and intertextuality.

[11] Bockmuehl (2006); see my review article, Doble (2007).

[12] NA[28] itself indicates much of the long "textual" ancestry of this common scholars' working and research text.

[13] See, e.g., Adams (2020).

[14] See, e.g., Dodd (1952); Bockmuehl (2006); Dunn (2013); Kirk, A. (2018); Kelber & Byrskog (eds) (2009).

practices and of manuscript medium now ensure that we view our text in a new way. I have concluded that Luke-Acts' inferred purposes determine its genre – *apologia*;[15] that its core is expanded apostolic proclamation (*kerygma*) that the scriptures are fulfilled; and that its story of Jesus, rooted in oral/aural tradition, is re-interpreted for Theophilus' re-assurance. Luke's two volumes are the memory of Jesus' story as a living tradition fixed for Theophilus.[16] Once Luke's "text" is "heard" it cannot be easily shoe-horned into Graeco-Roman literary genres.

As every French student well knows, any formulated problem itself becomes *la Problématique* – essentially that constellation of problems entailed by their initial formulation and leading to a reasonable hypothesis. In this monograph, that "leading" is an abductive process. The major problem entailed by claims that Luke is mistaken in his reported Jesus-*logia* is that his narrative-theology is thereby rendered incoherent to both his earliest and latest readers.[17] The architectural metaphor of a word-building embodied in my analytical diagram directly following this introduction reveals that and how the two disputed passages are load-bearing features; fracture these and Luke's entire structure collapses.

To resolve that problem, I identified a constellation of three related problems that must be resolved before one can decide whether Luke is or is not mistaken: (a) how does Luke understand the word Messiah; (b) is Luke's perspectival focus Messiah's death or resurrection; (c) how does he understand

---

[15] I have chosen this plain descriptor rather than offer a qualifier – which might possibly have been "a narrative-theological apologia" rather than the "biographical" or "historical" apologia of ongoing vigorous genre discussion. Luke himself describes his work for Theophilus as a "narrative of the things fulfilled among us" (Luke 1:1). My task is to read Luke-Acts to grasp how two problematic Jesus-*logia* function within Luke's *whole* work. The question of his work's genre is affected by what his theological narrative proves to be, and the readers(hip) for whom it was probably written.

[16] παρέδοσαν ἡμῖν οἱ ἀπ' ἀρχῆς αὐτόπται καὶ ὑπηρέται γενόμενοι τοῦ λόγου, (Luke 1:2).

[17] Luke is alleged to have been mistaken in affirming that scripture knew of a suffering Messiah whom God would raise up. See Doble (2006: 267–83).

4

phrases kin to "according to the scriptures"? Answers to this constellation of problems lead not only to whether Luke was mistaken or not, but to how he understood the phrase in his preface "things fulfilled among us" (διήγησιν περὶ τῶν πεπληροφορημένων ἐν ἡμῖν πραγμάτων, Luke 1:1).

Abductive reasoning is inference from assembled evidence to the simplest and most probable conclusion, so the evidence assembled from that constellation of problems suggests hypotheses concerning Luke's purposes, structures, themes, and convictions – the inferential process leading to my account of Luke's coherent narrative world. My approach to Luke's two disputed Jesus-*logia* has also been to identify and organize his whole narrative's principal features – structural,[18] thematic, perspectival, lexical, and narratival – before framing a simple and coherent account of its "message" to Theophilus, Luke's dedicatee. This "organized account" necessarily comprises the intersection of two time-distanced thought-worlds: first, a multi-disciplinary understanding of Luke's complex, unstable world, and of his narrative within it; then, a critical awareness of "our" current, complex, unstable, still emerging thought-world and its ways of thinking – what did Luke want to say, and how can a reader best hear him?

From this study Luke emerges as both an interpreter of Jesus' story and of Israel's scriptures, very different from the cut and paste editor of an earlier age's imagining, for a relentlessly literary approach to the gospels is yielding to newer insights from many disciplines.

Interpreter is a monograph, not a commentary. By its clearly indicated method and strategy, this work argues its positive case for dealing with a *crux interpretum*. Here, many of the problems that *Neutestamentler* regularly encounter and hover nearby do not need to be addressed. I return to some of them in the final chapter. Meanwhile, where I want to indicate my awareness of

---

[18] See the analytical diagram.

and acquaintance with such hovering issues I write of "bracketing out" or "prescinding from" discussing it.

A recent incident has convinced me that these procedural terms needed to be clarified: I have been alerted to the possibility that a hostile reader might claim that I use these expressions to avoid evidence "that tells against my case." While my experience of working among *Neutestamentler* has been one of pleasure in their friendly, cooperative ambience, I must affirm that *Interpreter* is *not* a commentary but a monograph arguing for Luke's narrative coherence. To that case we briefly turn.

As the front matter indicates, the case argued in *Interpreter* falls into four parts. Part I, on Luke's problem dissected, occupies three chapters. Chapter 1, having clarified this work's focal issue, sets out its logical, conceptual, intertextual case. It first offers a proposed threefold purpose for Luke's writing his *apologia* for Theophilus to assure him on those three counts;[19] then a narrative structure shaped by Luke's Davidic reference-frame and an outline of Luke's scriptural subtext that underlies it. Finally, a cumulative argument, focused by this sect's deeply problematic foundational event – Jesus' resurrection – and by four scriptural passages associated with resurrection,[20] affirms God's "I will raise up" (ἀναστήσω), retrospectively reinterpreted bivalently. This case is developed first in Chapter 2 that posits Luke's base-text, the David-promise, and through a triptych portrays its fulfilment; then Chapter 3 resolves this volume's "unparalleled shift" from Son of Man to Messiah and Luke's preparation for his second volume's "witnessing."

---

[19] (a) How did we (the Jewish world) get to where we are, divided over Israel's hope; (b) was this work's Paul a genuine representative of the Jesus movement; (c) were Christian claims about Jesus truly grounded in Israel's scriptures?

[20] 2 Sam. 7:11b–14 (esp. 12); Ezek. 34:11–25 (esp. 23); Amos 9:11–12 (esp. 11(*bis*)); Deut. 18:15–19 (esp. 18).

In Part II, on Peter and exegesis, an overview and three chapters reveal Peter's hinge role (Luke 22:31–34) as Jesus' principal witness and hermeneut. In a sequence of exegetical speeches that both "mirror" Jesus-*logia*[21] embedded within tradition's account of the conflict in Jerusalem and forge a firm link between Luke's two volumes, Peter "explains" Pentecost and a lame man's "saving" to pilgrim crowds and the Sanhedrin. His hermeneutic key is consistently that "you killed him but God raised him (ἀνέστησεν) from the dead." These speeches confirm the first part's proposals.

Then, in Part III, Luke's programme moves from eyewitnesses to "ministers of the Word" and from crisis in Jerusalem to witnessing to the ends of the earth, from Rome. First, Stephen's speech clarifies what divides Jesus-followers from Jerusalem's elite and their adherents. Refuting the false charges brought against him and Jesus, Stephen's exegetical defence completes a Son of Man *inclusio* in his vision of the raised and exalted Jesus (Luke 22:69/Acts 7:55–56). By his careful rehearsing of Israel's story, Stephen highlights his accuser-hearers of themselves following those Israelites at Sinai's covenant who demanded from Aaron a portable, visible god – their Mammon (Acts 7:51–52). Conforming to the Prologue's Davidic reference-frame, the climactic core of Luke-Stephen's scripture-reasoning (Acts 7:45–50) is that God had raised up David's fallen house: Jesus was David's obedient son; Solomon, the wise, disobedient fool. Stephen's is not an anti-Temple speech; it is his reasoned defence against false charges brought by religious leaders unfaithful to the covenant.

Second, Paul's sermon in Pisidian Antioch's synagogue is Acts' sole example of Christian exegetical witness in a synagogue, and presumably represents what Luke wanted his readers to understand was typical – that God

---

[21] Luke 20:9–26, cf. Ps. 117:22; Luke 20:37–38, cf. Exod. 3:6; Luke 20:41–44, cf. Ps. 109:1. See Doble (2014: 193–196).

has brought a Saviour to Israel (13:23). Conforming to the Prologue's Davidic reference-frame, this sermon's core is that God has fulfilled "for us" what he promised to "our fathers" (13:32–33). His scripture-reasoning is firmly rooted in the bivalence of "raise up" (ἀνίστημι) fulfilled in what God had done in and through Jesus, both bringing him on to history's stage (13:33–34) and raising him from death and corruption (13:34–37). In this reasoning Luke's Paul clearly disambiguates that bivalence, demonstrating the "authenticity" of my appeal to such reasoning in the earlier exegetical speeches.

Apparently, it is not wrong-headed to seek where "it is written";[22] that is what Luke set out to do, and he affirmed that it was by Jesus himself that this Christian hermeneutic tradition was established (Luke 24:44–49). Consequently, the heart of my reading of our focal verses is that Luke's base-text and its extensions constitute those scriptures that speak of the Messiah's resurrection,[23] and that principally through David's psalms God spoke of a Messiah who suffered.[24] Luke's narrative needs no Christological synthesis.[25]

In Part IV, Chapter 9 addresses the heart of this monograph's principal issue by crystallizing what chapters 1–8 have disclosed of Luke's innumerable quotations, allusions and echoes. I conclude that from Luke's resurrection-perspective he was not mistaken: that his Davidic reference-frame with its promise "I will raise up" (ἀναστήσω); his triptych; and controlling Jesus-descriptors are determinative for interpreting what follows. I hypothesized his narrative shaping within that frame by abductive reasoning from Luke's whole narrative, supported by discourse analysis. This shaping has been developed diagrammatically (at the end of this introduction). At its heart is the volume-

---

[22] Cf. Green (1997: 857).

[23] See esp. Acts 13:16–41 on Nathan's and Ezekiel's oracles; cf. Acts 2:14–36 for an implied argument.

[24] Acts 4:23–31 and Ps. 2:1–2; note the introductory formula at 4:24b–25.

[25] Contra e.g., Strauss (1995: 343); Bock (1987: 148–154; 2012: 177–209); Green (1997: 848–849, cf. 857, 827).

bridging conflict narrative in Jerusalem. That conflict portrays both the Son of Man's fate and, for Luke, completes the multivalent Exoduos that Jesus had to complete in Jerusalem. This conflict's inter-textual dimensions, stretching before and after it, are explored in this chapter. Luke's range of Jesus-descriptors and their functions belong to such inter-textual dimensions. The chapter ends with a discussion of issues that my proposals have raised in seminars. Chapter 10 briefly summarizes *Interpreter*'s completed and uncompleted business before suggesting further research in a number of areas of human concern.

I have clarified *Interpreter*'s focal issue: the perceived coherence of Luke-Acts depends on its reader's engagement with two disputed and narratively focal Jesus-*logia*. I have then highlighted the distinctive holistic method undergirding this monograph, establishing the *Problématique* with which *Interpreter* is concerned: essentially, what is Luke's concept of Messiah and of his role in Israel's story?[26] Characterizing Luke-Acts as *apologia*, I have proposed a threefold purpose for the narrative.

To answer Theophilus' questions and confirm their trustworthiness (ἀσφάλεια), Luke's *apologia* is his whole narrative, as I argue in Chapter 1. Having established his concept of Messiah in the Prologue, Luke deploys witnesses in his "main narrative," rooting his Jesus-story in Israel's scriptures, especially through "exegetical speeches" that focus essentially on God's having raised from the dead the rejected and killed Jesus. This event is his narrative's dynamic, demonstrated in Parts II and III. Part II sets out Peter's scriptural reasoning, while Part III offers essays on Stephen's defence before the Sanhedrin and Paul's synagogue sermon, which are also called in evidence in Part IV, Chapter 9 to crystallize *Interpreter*'s case. *Interpreter*'s aim is to let Luke

---

[26] That complex matrix of issues and questions surrounding my focal concern Luke 24:25–27, 44–49. I have spelled out those issues systematically by indicating my standpoint and approaches to their solution(s).

be Luke, its thesis generated by many readings of Luke-Acts as a single narrative.

Analytical Diagram

Luke-Acts: Analytical Outline

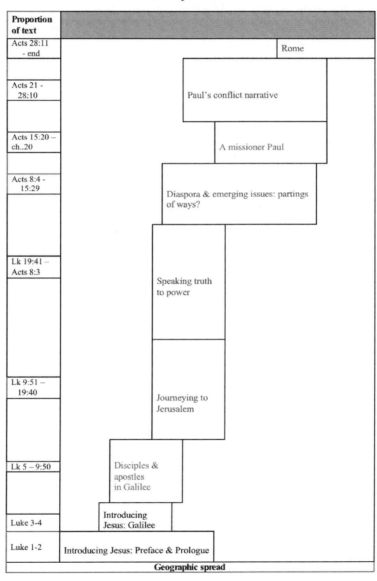

Proportion of text	
Acts 28:11 - end	Rome
Acts 21 - 28:10	Paul's conflict narrative
Acts 15:20 – ch..20	A missioner Paul
Acts 8:4 - 15:29	Diaspora & emerging issues: partings of ways?
Lk 19:41 – Acts 8:3	Speaking truth to power
Lk 9:51 – 19:40	Journeying to Jerusalem
Lk 5 – 9:50	Disciples & apostles in Galilee
Luke 3-4	Introducing Jesus: Galilee
Luke 1-2	Introducing Jesus: Preface & Prologue
	Geographic spread

Part I. Luke's problem dissected

Chapter 1. Interpreting Luke

This monograph focuses on two Lukan passages, Luke 24:25–27 and 24:44–49.[27] Their message is "according to the scriptures"; their content is that the Messiah must suffer and be raised from the dead, or enter into his glory. According to Luke, who is Jesus? Which scriptures speak of his death and resurrection? What does Luke mean when he uses the word "fulfilment"?[28]

Many commentators addressing these verses, often remarking that Israel's scriptures know nothing of a Messiah who must suffer and be raised from the dead,[29] then seek Luke's synthesis of Messiah with another

---

[27] Throughout, the New Testament Greek text is NA[28], except where otherwise noted; "Septuagint," or LXX, commonly refers to Rahlfs (1979). Variants from Rahlfs' edition are almost always to *Vaticanus* and noted in the text. OGT (Old Greek Text) signifies a Greek version that Luke used, "not unlike the LXX."

[28] This last is a long-standing question in relation to the canonical gospels. Posed by Dodd (1952), it was re-focused by Hays (2015).

[29] E.g., Bock (2012); Caird, (1963); Conzelmann (1960); Creed (1950); Cunningham (1997); Ellis (1974); Evans (1990); Fitzmyer (1981, 1985); Franklin (1975); Grayston (1990); Green (1990, 1997); Johnson (1991); Kurz (1993); Mallen (2008); Manson (1930); Miura (2007); Moessner (2016); Nolland (1989; 1993a and 1993b); Pao (2000); Plummer (1922); Schweizer (1993); Strauss (1995); Talbert (1988); Tannehill (1996); Wiefel (1988). Others, like Carroll (2012); Marshall (1978); Parsons (2015) and Wolter (2017) remain uncritical of Luke, but open to a wider and vaguer reading of Luke's "scripture."

descriptor,[30] e.g., "suffering servant" or "prophet," who suffers according to the scriptures.[31] But what if Luke's critics are mistaken and he wrote to demonstrate that what Luke-Acts reports is what he understood that scripture said? Luke twice attributes a form of this saying to Jesus himself, who then clarifies for his followers those scriptures that constitute this claim, which in turn becomes the heart of their preaching.[32]

---

[30] Throughout, I use "descriptor" rather than "title," e.g., Bock (2012: 185–209), or "name," e.g., Taylor, V. (1953). Borrowed from information technology, "descriptor" works as a category index-name to access underlying texts: e.g., Son of Man takes readers *primarily* to Daniel; "Prophet" to Deuteronomy; "Righteous One" to Psalms or Wisdom; "Servant" to texts about Abraham, Moses and David. Luke presents Jesus as God's agent whose life and work evoke *diverse hopes and patterns* mapped by descriptors from Israel's scriptures.

[31] See Doble (2006a). *Interpreter* (*abbrev.* for this work's title) results from my affirming that Luke's focus is on Jesus' resurrection rather than on his suffering, which itself resonates with Wisdom's δίκαιος and Daniel's Son of Man models and evokes Ps. 2:1–2.

[32] E.g., Luke 24:45–49; Acts 17:2–3 and 26:22–23.

13

A. Why this focus?

Principally because Luke-Acts remains a storm centre in New Testament studies.[33]

These focal verses in Luke 24 are central to any understanding of Luke's narrative and to the way that one reads his text to give an account of its Christology. Readers are commonly impressed by the narrative siting, density, and significance of references to scripture in these few verses and by the varieties of ways in which they have been interpreted. Their significance lies in how they are linked with Luke's protagonist, Jesus, and with his commonest descriptor, "Messiah," and how in Acts these verses relate to the apostles and their preaching. Luke's concept of Messiah in these verses is much-disputed. Notably, narrative self-referents by Jesus, these verses raise important questions about Luke's uses of scripture and the narrative function of kerygmatic-exegetical speeches in Acts.[34]

Luke says, however, only what early tradition said. For example, in Rom. 1:1–4 Paul's summary of "his gospel" focuses on the resurrection of

---

[33] While *Interpreter* is substantially different from the position proposed in JSNT (2006), my earlier critique of Luke's critics still stands.

[34] *Interpreter* does not ignore Paul's defence speeches, esp. Acts 26 – See Alexander (2005) on apologetic – it dissents from Soards (1994: 201): "The citation of scripture in the speeches *proves* very little indeed; rather, the citations illuminate the points the various speakers mean to make. One should recognize that Luke is not Matthew, and one should allow Luke to be Luke." Having missed the point of some of Acts' major exegetical speeches, Soards misread Jesus' commissioning the apostles (Luke 24:44–49).

14

David's seed, God's Son, as the prophets had said.[35] At the heart of his scripturally-based discussion of Israel's role in God's economy of salvation, Paul's "confession" highlights Jesus as "Lord" and a core trust that "God raised him from the dead" (Rom. 10:6–11). In another appeal to "tradition" (1 Cor. 15:3–11), Paul reports Messiah's death ("for our sins") and resurrection from the dead, both "according to the scriptures." He then emphasizes the centrality to tradition's proclamation of Messiah's "resurrection from the dead" (1 Cor. 15:12–19), before turning first to his long exposition of what such proclamation might mean within their shared eschatological timescale (1 Cor. 15:20–34), then to his explanation of the kind of body that God might give those who are "made alive in Messiah" (1 Cor. 15:35–58). Given such Pauline appeal to "tradition" it makes doubtful sense to speak of Paul's "emphasis" on the Messiah's suffering.[36]

These focal verses are central to that form of retelling Jesus' story that Luke deemed appropriate to Theophilus's need of assurance (Luke 1:1–4) – in that story *God has fulfilled promises*.[37] So what might have prompted Luke to

---

[35] See Whitsett (2000).

[36] Such alleged emphasis underlies much of the search for a Lukan synthesis.

[37] This italicized phrase summarizes *Interpreter*'s differences from Hays (2015), whose title for his account of Luke's reading scripture is *The One Who Redeems Israel*. Beginning from differing narrative positions, proposing differing structural intertextualities, we finally reach nuanced differences in the accounts offered of Lukan Christology. Hays continues to be a pioneer among international expositors, rescuing Luke from the creeping Marcionism of some of his contemporaries. *Interpreter* builds on this "fulfilled" sense of πεπληροφορημένων (Luke 1:1), Luke's "heavy" or sonorous equivalent for πληρόω; for Luke, size

15

write to Theophilus as he did?[38] All comment on Luke-Acts presupposes some purpose or purposes for Luke's having produced his work.

1. Luke the apologist: a proposal

What follows is a working "purpose" derived from my having reflected on multiple, detailed readings of Luke-Acts. This proposed purpose accounts for principal features of Luke's narrative,[39] and leads to its conceptual framework. This proposal can be verified only by the coherence of a reading of Luke-Acts from the perspective proposed here – Luke's reasoned focus on Jesus' resurrection.

Theophilus is possibly a person.[40] Probably Jewish and a Sadducee,[41] personally interested in the Jesus movement, Theophilus is Greek-speaking, at

---

sometimes strengthens sense. This verb's passive form conveys both the completeness of what God did in and through Jesus *and* its persisting effects into an unknown yet determined future. Contra Cadbury (1922: 496), *Interpreter*'s case is that what "has been fulfilled" by Jesus' story is indeed scripture. See, e.g., Alexander (1993: 111–112); Fitzmyer (1981: 292–293); Marshall (1978: 41).

[38] For *Interpreter*'s restricted purposes, I have bracketed out Luke's distinctive presentation of Jesus' focal proclamation of the Kingdom of God that entailed socio-economic, political and spiritual re-visioning and renewal; prophets and psalmists enriched Jesus' call.

[39] Cf. e.g., Doble (1996, 2000, 2004, 2013, 2014); unpublished seminar papers include studies relating to Luke's Passion Narrative.

[40] Cf. the Anderson proposal, noted above, strongly supported by Read-Heimerdinger and Rius-Camps (2002). I hesitate: would Luke have told Joanna's grandfather that she was the wife of Herod's steward (Luke 8:3)? Should "Theophilus" prove a group rather than a person, then the characteristics noted here are those of that group.

[41] Stephen's speech directed my thought in this direction; notice the role of the Sanhedrin, of rulers, in Luke-Acts. Note also Luke's handling of Jesus' own *gezerah shewa'* (Luke 22:69).

home in Israel's scriptures and possibly still resident in Jerusalem.[42] He has been "instructed" about "the things fulfilled among us," but is uncertain about that instruction, eliciting from Luke a systematic narrative offering of "security" (ἀσφάλεια). From Luke's narrative we may infer three related strands within Theophilus's need for security:

1. How did we (the Jewish world) get to where we are, divided over Israel's hope (e.g., Acts 28:16–28)? Luke begins and ends here: his prologue is a Jewish world filled with hope and expectation, with good people, yet with hints of upheaval to come.[43] His final scene is of that world further divided.

2. Was this Paul a genuine representative of the Jesus movement (that is everywhere spoken against) (Acts 28:22)? Paul's prominence in the final quarter of Luke-Acts, and the apparently divisive nature of his activity,[44] together with the narrative force of his Antioch sermon, suggest this question hanging over this former persecutor's work.

3. Were Christian claims about Jesus truly grounded in Israel's scriptures?[45] Luke's "things fulfilled among us" (Luke 1:1–4) assume a

---

[42] Commentators often note Luke's attention to Jerusalem.

[43] E.g., Mary's *Magnificat*; Simeon's word to Mary (2:34–35).

[44] E.g., Acts 13:42–14:7; 18:5–7, 12–17; 19:8–10; ending at 28:23–28.

[45] How may one most appropriately describe this group of Jesus-followers? Discussion revealed dislike of my preferred descriptor, "Jesus movement." Luke most commonly spoke of "brothers," a word the NRSV regularly transforms into the gender-neutral, misleading "believers." These brothers are of "the Way" (e.g., Acts 9:2; 18:25; 19:9, 23; 22:4; 24:14, 22), clearly a Jewish "sect" (αἵρεσις; Acts 24:5, 14), as Pharisees

17

new perspective in the presence of six exegetical speeches in Acts; his drawing attention to scriptural debates, particularly with synagogues; and his focus in Paul's Antioch sermon on God's fulfilled promises. Luke-Acts sends readers to Israel's scriptures as its context for Jesus' story.

Dodd (1952) crystallized such issues for scholars by pointing out that in the diversities of the NT's major writings, their shared tradition about the Jesus-event has come to us ready-wrapped in Israel's story. *Interpreter*'s problem is to identify and understand Luke's packaging of it.[46]

Offering "security," Luke's work is a whole narrative (διήγησις), a reasoned *apologia* for Theophilus concerning "the things fulfilled among us," not a patchwork from sources.[47] A "Christian" writer, Luke is indebted to oral and

---

(15:5) and Sadducees (5:17) were sects; a sect, however, "everywhere spoken against" (28:22). There is upheaval in the Jewish community, but, in Acts, these sects' ways have not yet parted: Paul has left the scene; the Jewish War may have begun; Jerusalem and its Temple are yet to suffer their predicted fate. Frequently, these brothers are called "disciples," but only twice does the word "Christian" feature in Acts (11:26; 26:28). With much reluctance, but for consistency and clarity, *Interpreter* uses "Christian" to parallel Pharisee and Sadducee, a sect within the Jewish family. Cf. Arnal (2011).

[46] Borrowing a Luther trope, Hays (2015: 1–16) writes of scripture as the manger in which Christ lies. In Chapter 2, I identify those scriptures as Nathan's (2 Sam. 7; Luke 1:26–38) and Ezekiel's (Ezek. 34; cf. Luke 2:8–20), oracles bracketing Luke's manger scene (2:1–7). The swaddling bands that Hays seeks to unwrap themselves evoke yet other scriptures. See Doble (2000).

[47] Given Luke's purposes, proposed above, I choose this genre rather than that of βίος or of history; see, e.g., Sean Adams, in Adams and Pahl, (2012), 97–120. My reflecting on Luke-Acts owes much to Loveday Alexander (2005), 183–206, from whose paper on Acts as apologetic text my careful dissent will be

18

written traditions about Jesus;[48] to his story's rootedness in Jewish history and scripture; to concerns about this sect raised through continuing debates with synagogues;[49] to traditions of Jewish arguing from the scriptures;[50] these are all elements implied by Luke's narrative. Luke is a creative theologian and writer who presents his distinctive, coherent account of "the things fulfilled among us" – in and through the person of Jesus of Nazareth, and witnessed to by Paul.

Interpreter's aim is to let Luke be Luke, its thesis generated by multiple readings of Luke-Acts.

2. Luke's argument

Given that proposal for Luke's purposes, and with such resources for his work, Luke wrote to reassure Theophilus on at least three counts.[51] First, what Christians were claiming about Jesus was supported by witnesses and rooted in scripture;[52] from beginning to end, Luke's story is about Jesus, his narrative's focal event. Through six exegetical speeches in Acts 1–15,[53] Luke

---

apparent. I address those elements of Luke-Acts affected by *Interpreter*'s research focus; these are substantial, structural elements.

[48] Note especially Rom. 1:1–6; 10:5–13; 1 Cor. 15.

[49] Debates about "this sect" (Acts 28:22) and about Paul himself characterize Acts 22–28, where this final scene is Luke's climax: Paul, in Rome, Jesus' witness interpreting from scripture what God has done.

[50] 4Q174 and Luke-Acts interpret a shared 2 Sam. 7; Ps. 2 and Amos 9.

[51] Luke's ἀσφάλεια is the goal of his opening sentence.

[52] Exemplified by the summaries preserved in Rom. 1:1–6 and 1 Cor. 15:3–8.

[53] Three by Peter, and the assembled apostles' prayer are examined below; those by Stephen to the Sanhedrin and Paul at Antioch are in chapters 7 and 8.

demonstrates the "things fulfilled among us." Second, it was indeed written that the Messiah must suffer and be raised. Paul's strategically sited Antioch sermon (Acts 13:16–41) exemplifies Luke's understanding of how Paul might have defended his gospel,[54] "proving" that God's raising Jesus from the dead was, in fact, "written." Here, the manner of Paul's arguing, as well as his choice of intertexts, was in the interest of "fulfilment."[55] Third, Israel's hoped-for Messiah was truly Jesus, David's seed.[56] Luke's Messiah-concept is controlled by his reading of Nathan's oracle (2 Sam. 7), his base-text from which many developments of the David-promise had emerged, e.g., Miura (2007: chs 2–6); Strauss (1995: Ch. 2).[57] Consequently, my approach places great weight on Luke's two Jesus-centred angelophanies in his Prologue.[58]

3. Luke's base-text

To boost Theophilus's confidence, Luke's implied foundational argument is that God fulfilled the ancient, often reworked promise to David through Nathan – of Messiah. That promise, Luke's base-text, shapes the thought-world, the

---

[54] Crystallized by Rom. 1:1–5.

[55] Explored in Ch. 8.

[56] E.g., Acts 13:23; NRSV's use of "descendants' often obscures scriptural reasoning based on the singular "seed."

[57] See Brooke (1998). *Interpreter* understands Luke's base-text to be 2 Sam. 7:12–14, his principal subject of thematic and systematic exegesis throughout Luke-Acts. This text is suggestive both of exegetical possibility and of being extended or supplemented by enriching texts.

[58] Luke 1:26–38; 2:8–20. See Ch. 2.

reference-frame, within which he retells Jesus' story, a shaping clarified for readers by four distinctive narrative moments.

i. Luke's Infancy Gospel

My argument takes seriously Luke's distinctive way of introducing Jesus to readers, sharply distinguishing him from John.[59] Gabriel's words to Mary evoke Nathan's oracle (Luke 1:26–38; 2 Sam. 7:11b–16), and the angelophany to the shepherds echoes Ezekiel's oracle to Israel's shepherd-rulers.[60] Each annunciation implies the fulfilment of a David-promise.[61] In his Prologue's three-scene introduction of Jesus,[62] Luke offers Theophilus the appropriate reference-frame within which to read his following narrative. For Luke, this is who Jesus is, fulfilling two versions of God's David-promise.

ii. God's anointing of Jesus

Luke's distinctive narrative of Jesus' anointing as Son of God is programmatic (Luke 3:21–22),[63] recalled at significant moments in Acts.[64] The genealogy, appended to Luke's account of Jesus' anointing (Luke 3:23–38), indicates that

---

[59] See Ch. 2; cf. Luke 16:16.

[60] Luke 2:8–20; Ezek. 34:11–24 (25).

[61] This case is summarized in Ch. 2.

[62] The third, central scene depicts Jesus' birth (Luke 2:1–7).

[63] Diff. Mark 1:9–11, Matthew 3:13–17; Luke offers no account of Jesus' baptism.

[64] e.g., Acts 4:27; 10:38.

while, like everyman, Jesus is a son of God (3:38), his familial descent is through David (3:31) but not through Solomon.[65] He is tested as Son of God (Luke 4:1–13).

His anointing then governs one's reading of Jesus' inaugural sermon at Nazareth.[66] This decision marks my distance from many other interpreters. Luke's Christology undoubtedly lives within a thought-world where the David-promise is re-shaped by the hopes of the Exilic prophets,[67] rather than by the Servant who introduces himself.[68]

Reflecting on Paul's Antioch sermon,[69] I argue the case for an *inclusio* formed by

(a) Luke's distinctive portrayal of God's anointing Jesus and proclaiming him as Messiah, in words drawn from Ps. 2:7,[70] and

---

[65] That Jesus, a Jew, is also of Abraham's seed is axiomatic; Luke, however, also identifies him as that "seed" through whom earth's families will be blessed (Acts 3:25–26; cf. Gen. 22:15–18). See Doble (2000). That Jesus is *not* of Solomon's "seed" is crucial to Stephen's speech; see Ch. 7.

[66] Luke 4:16–30. Luke's Messiah concept, drawing on Nathan's oracle and Ps. 2, includes "Son of God" as one of its boundary markers.

[67] For the role of Isa. 55–66 in Luke's conflict narrative (Luke 19:41-Acts 8:3) see Ch. 7; on Ezekiel, see Ch. 2.

[68] It also marks my distance from Hays's approach; in the anointing he understands "Son" to carry echoes from Gen. 22 and Isa. 41 (2015:60); perhaps they do, but given Luke's introductory triptych with its clear focus on God's David-promise, the *bat qol*'s "You are my Son" places Ps. 2:7 more sharply in focus than Hays allows; cf. Dodd (1952: 31–32). See Doble (2014) and Ch. 2 below.

[69] See Ch. 8.

[70] Luke 3:21–22; for Luke, "Son of God" primarily refers to Nathan's oracle and its David-promise: "I will be a father to him, and he shall be a son to me" (2 Sam. 7:14; cf. Ps. 88). Contra Hays (2015: 60–62).

(b) Luke's summary of the scriptural promise for raising up the Messiah in Israel and from the dead.[71] For Luke, God first fulfils the David-promise by bringing Jesus on to Israel's stage in words that evoke both David's story and Nathan's oracle. From his anointing forward, Jesus, David's seed, is God's Messiah.

iii. Resurrection: Luke's hermeneutic key

Chapter 3 examines Luke's distinctive resurrection narrative (Luke 24). Many have noted that Luke highlights Jesus' resurrection[72] rather than the death of the Messiah; we shall return to this observation.[73] Here, we simply note that in Theophilus's world, as in ours, the report of God's having raised Jesus from the dead would have met with scoffing: by Gentiles, as at Athens;[74] by Jews who looked to a resurrection of the dead at the End,[75] and by those who, like Sadducees, altogether refused the notion.[76] Everyone dies; death is our

---

[71] Acts 13:32–37; 2 Sam. 7:12.

[72] See Marshall (1988a), 29–32, 35–36, 41–44, 46–47, 50–52, 161–165; my debt to Marshall is immense, especially where our conclusions differ.

[73] I greatly doubt that Paul emphasizes Messiah's suffering; qualitatively, his accent is that God's decisive act in salvation history is his having raised Jesus from the dead (e.g., Rom. 1:1–6; 10:5–13; 1 Cor. 15:12–20).

[74] Acts 17:32.

[75] e.g., 1 Cor. 15:12–34. The final exchange among Paul, Festus and Agrippa (Acts 26:22–28) encapsulates this scepticism: on hearing Paul's affirmation of Jesus' resurrection (26:23, cf. 25:19), Festus thinks Paul mad; Agrippa disengages from the discussion.

[76] See, e.g., the internal evidence from Luke 20:27–40; Acts 23:8.

expected event. Stories of a dead man raised, however, are beyond human experience, so tend to be rejected. Consequently, Luke needed to argue this case – that it is written that the Messiah must suffer and be raised from the dead.[77] Wright (2003) on the uniqueness of this "event" is basic to my argument;[78] this event is Luke's hermeneutic key, particularly to the unprecedented transition in Luke 24 from Son of Man to Messiah,[79] and to Paul's Antioch sermon. It is this hermeneutic key, God's ἀναστήσω, that *Interpreter* seeks to verify.

iv. Paul's Antioch sermon

This key, ἀναστήσω, is good reason for paying particular attention to Paul's Antioch sermon (Acts 13:16b–41).[80] Its essence is that God has now fulfilled what was promised to the fathers (13:32). Luke-Acts' final argument from scripture – forming an *inclusio* with Luke 1–3 – re-interprets the David-promise in the light of God's having brought Jesus to Israel as Saviour and raised him from the dead (Acts 13:30, 37). This sole example of Paul's characteristic activity crystallizes Luke's essential case for Theophilus. Paul's sermon

---

[77] We distinguish resurrection from resuscitation: the latter is a temporary release from death, while resurrection conceives of a transformed life in a renewed creation where death is no more. That is a key point of Paul's reasoning at Antioch (Acts 13:32–37).

[78] See also Dunn (2003: 825–879); Bockmuehl (2001a).

[79] "This shift [from Son of Man or prophets to Messiah] is without direct and explicit precedent in the OT, for which "a suffering Messiah would be an oxymoron." Green (1997: 848, 857).

[80] See Ch. 8.

exemplifies where and how "it is written" that the Messiah must suffer and be raised from the dead forever.[81] Luke is thus responsible for readers' being able to grasp how, for those who followed Jesus, early belief in and proclamation of God's having raised Jesus from the dead transformed their re-interpretation of long argued-over scriptural material about David.

v. Summary

What binds together those four narrative moments is their rootedness in David's story. As I noted in an earlier study,[82] Luke's retelling resembles a comparative biography of David and Jesus. His retelling, however, is not simply *synkrisis*, but a demonstration of "things *fulfilled* among us," especially those of his base-text, which in an Old Greek Text (OGT) twice bears God's promise, ἀναστήσω. Like others, I am wary of reading too much into what may be coincidence. However, taking heart from Wright (2003: 149),[83] and weighing coincidence against authorial purpose, I re-read Luke-Acts' narrative, recording enough evidence to explore further possibilities presented by Luke's hermeneutic key – Jesus' resurrection. This word-group, ἀναστήσω, appeared significant for him.

---

[81] Luke dealt with Messiah's "suffering" in Acts 4:23–30; See Ch. 5.

[82] See Doble (2004; 2006a).

[83] "We should be wary of reading too much into verses like [e.g., 2 Sam. 7 and Ezek. 34]; equally, we should be wary of reading too little. Who can tell, at this remove, what overtones second-Temple Jews and first-generation Christians might not have detected?" Cf. Wright (2003: 80–82). It is gratifying to see that Wright currently appears to agree with *Interpreter*'s reading of ἀναστήσω; Wright (2015: 33–36).

25

Luke stands in a Jewish interpretative tradition,[84] not a twenty-first century critical tradition.

---

[84] I do not *know* whether Luke knew Hillel's "rules." Luke tells us that Paul was a pupil of Gamaliel (Acts 22:3), Hillel's grandson. Within those limits, alert to Hillel's norms, I have read Luke's exegetical speeches, following Luke's leading. His text is primary; Hillel's rules are auxiliary. *Interpreter*'s focus on Luke's "building up a family" from two or more texts that share the promise ἀναστήσω takes Hillel's followers into a diaspora setting, where we are still in dispute rather than at the partings of the ways, as Luke's final scene makes clear (Acts 28).

B. Luke and ἀναστήσω

My "sufficient evidence" lies primarily in the structure of Luke's argument that comprises four distinct and distinctive examples of God's ἀναστήσω ("I will raise up") promises,[85] culminating in Paul's Antioch sermon. Interestingly, two of them parallel the 4Q174 sequence,[86] suggesting that before drafting his work Luke possibly had in mind a range of scripture that already crystallized Israel's hope.[87] Luke never directly cites any of those promises.[88] Cumulatively, however, the effect of these four resembles that of a synagogue sermon whose text is obvious but never quoted.[89]

1. Luke's Infancy Gospel

Two of Luke's four examples appear in his Infancy Gospel; each an angelophany, each pointing to God's fulfilling a David-promise. First, Gabriel's announcement to Mary (Luke 1:26–38) *before* Jesus' conception evokes Luke's base-text (2 Sam. 7): καὶ *ἀναστήσω* τὸ σπέρμα σου μετὰ σέ. Heaven's

---

[85] 2 Sam. 7:5b–16; Ezek. 34:20–25; Deut. 18:18; Amos 9:9–12. The structure of Luke's argument makes no appeal to the two-fold ἀναστήσω of Jer. 23:4–5, for Luke 19:10 appears to seal the Ezekiel links with the Prologue's Jesus-triptych. Pss. Sol. 17:21–25 offers evidence for a contemporary 2T worldview with a David-based hope.

[86] 2 Sam. 7:12–14 and Amos 9:11.

[87] Cf. Dodd (1952: 28–60); Luke's substructure is wider, as both Brooke (1998) and Whitsett (2000) make clear.

[88] This proves difficult for many; *Interpreter* addresses this issue throughout the body of this work.

[89] Cf. Mann, J. (1971); Doeve (1954).

announcement to shepherds following the birth of the Saviour (Luke 2:8–20) evokes Ezekiel's David-oracle (Ezek. 34:11–31) with its vision of a covenant of peace:[90] καὶ ἀναστήσω ἐπ' αὐτοὺς ποιμένα ἕνα […] τὸν δοῦλόν μου Δαυιδ.

The siting and the function of Luke's distinctive triptych give Luke's introduction of Jesus great narrative weight, the Tel Aviv school's primacy effect.[91] Together, these two scenes form Luke's reference-frame, his pact with his reader.[92] Luke's framing is very different from that in Matthew – save for its David reference.[93] Notably, Ezekiel reworks the Davidic base-text to include God's initial promise, ἀναστήσω, and roots Jesus, Luke's protagonist, in God's purpose to seek and to save.[94]

2. James at Jerusalem

Luke's third example of an ἀναστήσω-promise concludes both Luke's David-trajectory (Luke 1:27 – Acts 15:16)[95] and his arguing from scripture – the "raising up" of David's fallen house.[96] This extract features also in 4Q174. Adapted from OGT, it serves a very different function in Luke-Acts "so that all other peoples

---

[90] Luke 2:13–14; cf. Ezek. 34:25.

[91] Luke 1:26–38; 2:1–7; 2:8–20. See Ch. 2.

[92] I have borrowed from Gerber (2008) on expression of the Prologue's function.

[93] Cf. Rom. 1:3 – περὶ τοῦ υἱοῦ αὐτοῦ τοῦ γενομένου ἐκ σπέρματος Δαυὶδ κατὰ σάρκα.

[94] Luke 19:10 is the distinctive, culminating statement of Jesus' self-understanding as Saviour; cf. Luke 2:8–10.

[95] See Doble (2004).

[96] Amos 9:11–12; Acts 15:13b–18.

may seek the Lord – even all the Gentiles over whom my name has been called" (Acts 15:17).

At this point, Luke has completed his theological-scriptural narrative for Theophilus. David's fallen house has been "raised up"; that is where Luke began (Luke 1:27) and where his promise-reasoning ends (Acts 15:18). I discuss later the detail of Luke's adaptation of Amos's oracle, which, in the OGT, reads:

> ἐν τῇ ἡμέρᾳ ἐκείνῃ *ἀναστήσω* τὴν σκηνὴν Δαυιδ τὴν πεπτωκυῖαν
>
> καὶ *ἀνοικοδομήσω* τὰ πεπτωκότα αὐτῆς
>
> καὶ τὰ κατεσκαμμένα αὐτῆς *ἀναστήσω*
>
> καὶ *ἀνοικοδομήσω* αὐτὴν καθὼς αἱ ἡμέραι τοῦ αἰῶνος[97]

By evoking three prophets' oracles Luke has distinctively introduced, then concluded his David-trajectory.[98] Each oracle affirms God's promise, "I will raise up," the bivalent ἀναστήσω.[99] Additionally, Paul's Antioch sermon exemplifies

---

[97] Amos twice parallels ἀναστήσω with ἀνοικοδομήσω, reminding readers that the point of Nathan's oracle is that David's seed ensures the stability of David's house; for Luke, without resurrection there is no rebuilding. Luke definitively reasoned the resurrection case in Paul's Antioch sermon; the house case in Stephen's speech; it is left to James to recognize that Gentile "Pentecosts" confirm that God's David-promise is fulfilled.

[98] See Luke 24:44.

[99] Bivalent, having two values; this term expresses both the "not only [...] but also" logical-interpretative principle that underlies, e.g., Hillel's grasping that a single lexical unit carries more than one "meaning,"

Jesus-followers' arguing from Luke's base-text's ἀναστήσω, rooting it in Luke 1–3, and it becomes clearer that there is more here than initially appears to modern ears and eyes. Luke offers even more than this David-matrix.

3. Stephen and Torah

A fourth example of an ἀναστήσω-oracle culminates in Stephen's speech[100] that becomes a trial of his accusers and the Sanhedrin.[101] His defence offers sceptical Sadducees and Sanhedrin evidence from Moses of God's plan to "raise up" a prophet like Moses.[102] While Luke-Acts addresses its case to those whose world-view has resurrection as its horizon, Luke does not forget Israel's sceptics to whom Jesus offered his scriptural argument for resurrection.[103] Further, this Sanhedrin comprised scripture's rulers who figure prominently in Luke's conflict-narrative (Luke 19:41 – Acts 8:3) and subtext.[104] Climactically, however, Stephen's speech concerns both David's house, the subject of

---

and the principle of George Caird (1980) that "meaning" derives from "use." Nathan was right (2 Sam. 7:12; cf. Ezek. 34:23), and Luke's Paul was right (Acts 13:34): neither replaces the other; each illuminates the other. That is why Acts 13:33–34 is a crux for interpreters: Paul placards this "both [...] and," setting each sense of ἀνίστημι in its Lukan narrative context, both anointing (Luke 3:21–22) and resurrection (Acts 13:30).

[100] See Ch. 7.

[101] It previously formed a part of Peter's reasoning in Solomon's Colonnade (Acts 3:13–26), itself resonating with Jesus' argument from the Bush for resurrection (Luke 20:34–38). See Doble (2013).

[102] See Luke 24:44.

[103] Luke 20:27–40; see Ch. 4 for discussion of this passage's role in Luke-Acts.

[104] See the analytical diagram. Rulers feature in Luke's subtext that culminates in Ps. 2:1–2 (Acts 4:24b–28); see Ch. 7.

Isaiah's oracle,[105] and the raised and exalted Jesus, Son of Man. Luke does indeed highlight Jesus' role as the prophet. Johnson's insights remain,[106] but Luke's prophet-theme proves to be as subsidiary to his David-matrix as is his use of Isaiah's oracles. Again, a narratively significant unit features a twice-used ἀναστήσω-oracle[107] leading to clearer understanding of God's plan that included resurrection – hence Stephen's vision of the vindicated Jesus, Son of Man, now standing, ἑστῶτα at God's right hand.[108]

4. Argument from interpretation

My argument (and Luke's) has a broader foundation. Luke's forms of scriptural reasoning offer evidence of his implied appeal to the bivalence of his base-text's ἀναστήσω. For example, in Luke 24, the implied presence of God's promise to David "I will raise up" (ἀναστήσω) makes sense of Luke's unprecedented move from Son of Man to Messiah.[109] Peter's Pentecost proclamation depends on his arguing that David's son (seed) is David's Lord, because God raised up (ἀνέστησεν) (Acts 2:24, 32) Jesus. God's promise to David – "I will raise up (ἀναστήσω) your seed after you" has been uniquely fulfilled in two senses.[110]

---

[105] The role of Isa. 66 in Stephen's speech (Acts 7:49) has been developed from Doble (2000; 2013).

[106] Johnson (1991; 1992).

[107] Deut. 18:15 features earlier in Peter's scriptural arguing (Acts 3:22); see Ch. 5.

[108] Acts 7:55–56; cf. Luke 22:69. See Doble (2013); see also Ch. 7.

[109] See Ch. 3.

[110] See Ch. 4.

31

Then to identify Luke's reasoning in Peter's address in Solomon's Colonnade, I have argued that Luke's reference to Samuel as the first of the prophets to speak of these things (Acts 3:24) implies for readers what they have known from Luke's first introducing Jesus: He is David's promised seed (τὸ σπέρμα σου) with all that that entails, and also Abraham's, now ἀναστήσας (Acts 3:25–26).

Consequently, supplementing the four narrative-moments noted earlier, there is evidence of the interpretative influence of Luke's base-text's ἀναστήσω within exegetical speeches other than his major example at Antioch. Chapter 9 crystallizes that evidence as part of *Interpreter*'s cumulative case.

5. A cumulative case

The cumulative effect of Luke's distinctives takes my case beyond coincidence and into serious exegetical possibilities. Together, Luke's hermeneutic key – God's having raised Jesus from the dead – and his structural use of four prophets' ἀναστήσω-oracles are Luke's entry into reinterpreting God's promises, especially those concerning David. This accumulation comprises an:

1. ἀναστήσω-triptych introducing Jesus to readers (Luke 1:26–38; 2:1–7; 2:8–20);

32

2. ἀναστήσω-narrative leading to, then concluding Luke's David-story (Acts 15:12–21);[111]

3. ἀναστήσω-focused Pauline argument crystallizing that God's has fulfilled those promises (Acts 13:16b–41);

4. ἀναστήσω-centred case from Torah for understanding the resurrection and vindication of the Jesus the Sanhedrin had condemned (Acts 7:37; cf. 3:22);

5. ἀναστήσω-focused scriptural interpretative techniques identifiable in key narratives. Here we also recognize the force of attention to a "common combination of scriptural passages" (Brooke 1998) shared by Luke, 4Q174, and in part by Hebrews.[112]

Identifying Luke's structural argument then allows us to assess Luke's wider uses of scripture – one of *Interpreter*'s three focal concerns.[113]

---

[111] Where Amos 9:11 is adapted to the rebuilding (ἀνοικοδομήσω) of David's fallen dwelling (σκηνὴν) as a result of the Jesus-event that fulfilled Amos's ἀναστήσω that James omits; Stephen's case parallels this (see Ch. 7).

[112] 4Q174 and Luke-Acts share a David-concern with 2 Sam. 7; Ps. 2 and Amos 9.

[113] See Ch. 7.

C. Luke's hermeneutic key and Luke-Acts

Fulfilment of God's David-promise is arguably the principal narrative thread that contributes to the shaping of Luke's narrative; this complicates *Interpreter's* reporting of his argument. For example, Luke clearly demonstrates that the prophet Jesus' words were also fulfilled by the events of his life. Tradition's reports of Jesus' own uses of scripture during his final week in Jerusalem find their explanations or answers in Peter's exegetical speeches (Acts 2–4, chs 4–7) and in Stephen's climactic vision and preceding speech (Acts 7:2–8:1a).[114]

Again, this rejected prophet, Jesus, had engendered a counter-cultural sect everywhere spoken against and opposed by authority. Luke's account for Theophilus of the continuing conflict between this sect and authorities – particularly the Sanhedrin – sets his long conflict-narrative (Luke 19:41 – Acts 8:3) firmly within a context of internal Jewish dissension over "the righteous" and their opponents. We track this thread primarily through the Sanhedrin's confrontations with Jesus, with Peter and with the apostolic band. Climactically the Jerusalem-conflict ends with Stephen.[115]

However, Jesus' resurrection and its unexpectedly fulfilling God's David-promises remain *Interpreter's* focus throughout. That event is foundational for this counter-cultural Jewish sect (1 Cor. 15:13–16). Many

---

[114] See Ch. 7.

[115] See Ch. 7: Stephen places Jesus firmly as the culmination of this retelling of Israel's story.

commentators tend to focus on a search for a suffering Messiah that presented a problem for the early communities' *kerygma*.[116] But Luke is not Luther, and Luke's urgent concern was manifestly with the problem of Jesus' resurrection:[117] Jesus' resurrection was simply incredible, standing outside the conceptual frame of both Luke's hearers and Israel's scriptures.[118]

Who then is this Jesus? For Luke, he is primarily David's seed whom God raised from the dead and exalted to his right hand, until that time of restoration implied by Ps. 109:1b and Acts 3:19–26. Luke's eschatological timetable is not very different from that sketched in 1 Cor. 15:20–28. Consequently, given the kinds of devotion accorded Jesus by his earliest followers,[119] and the unique role that Luke attributes to him in God's saving plan,[120] Luke's Jesus is more than an inspired prophet.[121] For reasons that will emerge, I cannot agree when Rowe (2009) identifies this "more than" as *Verbindungsidentität*;[122] nor am I sure that the final sentence (and only the final sentence) of the magisterial section on

---

[116] See, e.g., Bock (1987; 2012); Green (1988; 1990; 1995b; 1997); Miura (2007) and Strauss (1995).

[117] Hence Luke's emphatic argument against Jesus' David-like "decay," a problem posed by Ps. 88:49–50 for the classical David-promise.

[118] Luke *tends* to use two verbs in relation to Jesus' resurrection, ἐγείρω to affirm its eventness, ἀνίστημι to highlight that event's fulfilling a David-promise, or a variant (e.g., Deut. 18:15, 18). See the evidence uncovered by the following chapters.

[119] See, e.g., Hurtado, L. (1988; 2003); cf. North, J.L. (2014) who offers valuable insight into assessing the textual evidence for and history of 1 Cor. 8:6.

[120] E.g., Acts 26:22–23; cf. 17:1–4.

[121] Cf. Hays (2015: 57).

[122] See my review of Rowe (2009), JSNT (2010), 32:5, 56–57.

Jesus' resurrection as God's act in Wright (2003: 731–736) quite fits Luke's narrative theology. What I can say is that Luke assured Theophilus that those who encountered Jesus understood that in and through this Jesus God was fulfilling Israel's hopes and ancient promises – their Messiah and Saviour, they confessed this Jesus as the risen, ascended Lord.[123]

How does all of this address *Interpreter's* focal Lukan verses?[124] Multiple readings of Luke-Acts prompted five chapters (2–6) based on two interlocking elements.

1. *Interpreter's* basic case

The first is the logical, conceptual, intertextual case established to this point, summarized as:

0. a proposal for Luke's writing for Theophilus (assurance);

1. a narrative structure shaped by David-promises;

2. an outline of Luke's scriptural subtext;

3. a cumulative argument focused on this sect's deeply problematic foundational event – Jesus' resurrection – and on four scriptural

---

[123] See Ch. 7.

[124] Luke 24:25–27, 44–49.

36

passages associated with resurrection,[125] each affirming God's "I will raise up," ἀναστήσω, now reinterpreted bivalently.

This element is developed in chapters 2 and 3; Luke's uses of scripture are assessed in Chapter 9.

2. Mirroring and culminations

The second element is argued throughout chapters 4 to 6, later drawing on additional evidence freely available on the website – Luke's embodying and exemplifying his "assurance" for Theophilus in Jesus-followers' exegetical speeches.[126] This strand emerges from Luke 24:44, "that everything written about me in the Torah of Moses, the Prophets and the Psalms must be fulfilled," where "me" is that Jesus who has just shifted his talk of Son of Man (Luke 9) into talk of the Messiah (Luke 24:26, 44–46). Luke 24:44 is then modified by 24:46, "Thus it is written, that the Messiah is to suffer and to rise from the dead on the third day." Notably, between these two verses Luke describes Jesus opening his followers' minds to understand the scriptures.[127] It is they who then, in Acts, make exegetical speeches that "place" Jesus' suffering and resurrection in Israel's scriptures, and who demonstrate where and how Moses' Torah, the

---

[125] 2 Sam. 7:11b–14 (esp. 12); Ezek. 34:11–25 (esp. 23); Amos 9:11–12 (esp. 11(*bis*)); Deut. 18:15–19 (esp. 18).

[126] See Ch. 7 for Stephen and Ch. 8 for Paul.

[127] Luke 24:25; cf. Mann, J. L. (2016).

Prophets and the Psalms speak of the Messiah's suffering and his being raised.[128] In three speeches, examined in chapters 4 to 6, Luke first shows Peter explaining puzzling events by interpreting from his post-resurrection perspective Jesus' own intertext-*logia*.[129]

Then, in a further three speeches,[130] we encounter apostles,[131] Stephen,[132] and, climactically, Paul engaged in scriptural reasoning that demonstrates for Theophilus how in Psalms, Deuteronomy and Samuel it was certainly written that the Messiah must suffer and rise from the dead.[133] Apparently, it is not wrong-headed to seek where "it is written";[134] that is what Luke set out to do, and he affirmed that it was by Jesus himself that this Christian hermeneutic tradition was established (Luke 24:44–49). Consequently, the heart of my reading of our focal verses is that Luke's base-text and its extensions constitute those scriptures that speak of the Messiah's

---

[128] Chapter 7 discusses the nature of this mutual interpretation that does violence to neither text; intertextuality proves a weasel word; I am happy with the dialogical intertextuality of Moyise (2000b); Hays (2015) offers figural reading to account for Luke's practices. Whatever Luke's practice is called, it is not well described by "prophecy and fulfilment," as Dodd well knew (1952: 127–131).

[129] Luke 20:9–26, cf. Ps. 117:22; Luke 20:37–38, cf. Exod. 3:6; Luke 20:41–44, cf. Ps. 109:1. See Doble (2014: 193–196).

[130] The culmination of a thematic or narrative thread.

[131] Ch. 7; Acts 4:24b–28, Culmination 1: apostles together strengthened for witness.

[132] Ch. 7; Acts 7:2–60, Culmination 2: Luke's Jerusalem conflict-narrative culminates.

[133] Acts 13:16b–41, Culmination 3: Paul's κήρυγμα.

[134] Cf. Green (1997: 857).

38

resurrection,[135] and that through David's psalms God spoke of a Messiah who suffered.[136] Luke's narrative needs no Christological synthesis.[137]

---

[135] See esp. Acts 13:16–41 on Nathan's and Ezekiel's oracles; cf. Acts 2:14–36 for an implied argument.

[136] Acts 4:23–31 and Ps. 2:1–2; note the introductory formula at 4:24b–25.

[137] Contra e.g., Strauss (1995: 343); Bock (1987: 148–154; 2012: 177–209); Green (1997: 848–849, cf. 857, 827).

D. Summary

This chapter has set out the *Problématique* with which *Interpreter* is concerned: essentially, what is Luke's concept of Messiah?[138] The perceived coherence of Luke-Acts depends on its reader's engagement with two disputed and narratively focal Jesus-*logia*. To proceed, I have proposed a threefold purpose for Luke-Acts, characterizing it as *apologia* primarily addressing: (a) how did we (the Jewish world) get to where we are, divided over Israel's hope; (b) was this work's Paul a genuine representative of the Jesus movement; (c) were Christian claims about Jesus truly grounded in Israel's scriptures?

To answer these questions, confirming their trustworthiness (ἀσφάλεια) for Theophilus, Luke's *apologia* is his whole narrative. Having established his concept of Messiah in the Prologue, Luke deploys witnesses in his main narrative, rooting his Jesus-story in Israel's scriptures, especially through six exegetical speeches that focus essentially on God's having raised from the dead the rejected and killed Jesus. This event is his narrative's dynamic, demonstrated in Part II, which will set out Peter's scriptural reasoning, while Stephen's defence (Chapter 7) and Paul's synagogue sermon (Chapter 8) are also called in evidence in Chapter 9 to present *Interpreter*'s case.

---

[138] That complex matrix of issues and questions surrounding my focal concern Luke 24:25–27, 44–49. I have spelled out systematically those issues by indicating my standpoint and approaches to their solution(s).

Luke's foundational argument is that in and through Jesus, God had fulfilled Israel's long-hoped-for, often reworked promise to David of the Messiah. That promise becomes Luke's reference-frame within which he retells Jesus' story, shaped by the ἀναστήσω of four distinctive narrative moments – Luke's Infancy Gospel; God's anointing of Jesus (Chapter 2); James at Jerusalem and Stephen's speech.[139] The Nathan promise (2 Sam. 7:8b–14a) uncovered three other such promises (Ezek. 34:20–25; Deut. 18:18; Amos 9:9–12) and led Luke to focus on ways in which Luke reasoned from scripture by means of their common, bivalent ἀναστήσω.

---

[139] Amos 9:11; Acts 15:16. See Ch. 7.

41

Chapter 2. Luke introduces Jesus

In the previous chapter, we identified *Interpreter*'s focal problem as both Luke's concept of Messiah and the identity of those scriptures where it is written that the Messiah must suffer and be raised. *Interpreter*'s approach to that problem is that Luke was re-reading scriptures shared with fellow Jews, but from his perspective that God uniquely raised from the dead the Messiah whom he had anointed and Jerusalem and her rulers had killed. For Luke, event interprets scripture,[140] the fundamental reason why Luke's "I will raise up" (ἀναστήσω) criterion should be taken seriously and why, in this chapter, I argue that Luke's Prologue introduces Jesus based on that criterion.[141]

To find a way through the Prologue's forest of allusions to and echoes from scripture, we focus sharply on the vivid scenes by which Luke, a consummate literary artist, introduces Jesus to readers – as David's promised seed, Saviour, Messiah, Lord. To these scenes we add one other, Luke's distinctive cameo of God's anointing Jesus: "You are my son." Two appended notes extend this introduction: the first acknowledges Luke's debt to tradition's Jesus-descriptor, Son of Man, and notes its distinctive Lukan developments. The second note alerts readers to ways in which Luke's closing of his Prologue prepares them for Luke-Acts' core conflict-narrative in Jerusalem.

---

[140] See Chapters 3–7.

[141] On Luke 1–2, see Strauss (1995: 76–129); Kilgallen (2013: 9–27); cf. Brooke (2000b); Moyise (2013: 25–44); Barker (2008: 50–92).

A. Prologue

We need first to clarify a structural issue: how do Luke's opening two chapters relate to the remainder of Luke-Acts? The problem is complex but simple: Luke 3:1–20 reads like a grand opening. That opening accords with early tradition's position that Jesus' story began in and around the activity of John the Baptist:

> You know the message he sent to the people of Israel, preaching peace by Jesus Christ—he is Lord of all. That message spread throughout Judea, beginning in Galilee after the baptism that John announced: how God anointed Jesus of Nazareth with the Holy Spirit and with power; how he went about doing good and healing all who were oppressed by the devil, for God was with him. We are witnesses to all that he did both in Judea and in Jerusalem. They put him to death by hanging him on a tree; but God raised him on the third day and allowed him to appear, not to all the people but to us who were chosen by God as witnesses, and who ate and drank with him after he rose from the dead. He commanded us to preach to the people and to testify that he is the one ordained by God as judge of the living and the dead. All the prophets testify about him that everyone who believes in him receives forgiveness of sins through his name.
>
> (Acts 10:36–43; cf. 13:23–25).

In one sense, John's presence in Israel is where all four canonical gospels begin. Like Luke, Matthew and the Fourth Gospel offer pre-John material, though each is distinctive to its gospel. But no existing manuscript of Luke lacks these two chapters,[142] and there is a strong sense in which they amplify Paul's

---

[142] I have bracketed out discussion of Tyson (2006), who proposed Luke's relation to Marcion's "gospel." My own contention is that the Prologue is just that, not afterthought. Further, questions about the dating of

43

opening statement to the Romans (Rom. 1:1–6).[143] Conzelmann (1960) ignores these chapters, which cannot remain an acceptable position, this section summarizes my position with respect to them.[144] I call Luke's opening two chapters his Prologue with Franklin (2001: 926), who says that these chapters "are best understood as the prologue to Luke's whole work, summing up its message, proclaiming it, and giving it a firm basis in Israel's story."

With Gerber (2008: 13–97), I understand these chapters as Luke's "pact with the reader," where the "things fulfilled among us" are mapped before Jesus' appearance on history's stage, focusing attention on his life and work, not simply on his death and resurrection. Gerber's fine study roots Luke's distinctive telling of Jesus' story in these infancy narratives. With Aletti (1989), I take seriously Luke's work's genre as narrative, (*récit*); his detailed work on analepses exercised a powerful influence on my reading and on my responses to narratology.[145] That Luke's is good news in every sense of the term (cf. Luke 2:10) fits well with my hypothesis that Luke is answering Theophilus's uncertainties about the scriptural bases of Christian tradition's claims for Jesus.

Crystallizing Luke's message, his pre-story pact with his reader, his Prologue is where Luke re-orients Jesus' story. Before the curtain rises, we are familiar with his main themes – themes recalled from Israel's long story of hope; and we are at home in the key he has announced. This is what his story is about.

Luke-Acts must await firmer answers until Luke's work's structural and narratival dimensions are clarified. On Marcion's gospel see also Roth (2008, 2015); Vinzent (2014).

[143] See Whitsett (2000).

[144] For Conzelmann (1960), see especially pp. 18 n.1, 22 n.2, 24–5, 75 n.4, 172, 174 n.1, 193 n.5.

[145] A readerly recall of earlier events or exchanges within the narrative, or from narrative sources shared by the author and the reader.

1. Introducing Jesus

As its heading indicates, this chapter is a not a study of his Prologue but of Luke's introducing Jesus to his readers.[146] We explore the Prologue's Jesus-nativity material first, before turning to the Anointing-narrative (Luke 3:21–22), isolating and focusing on these scenes for three principal reasons. First, Luke's volumes for Theophilus focus on his re-telling of Jesus' story, so what he tells readers about Jesus in his introduction is critically important for reading his narrative.

Second, Christian tradition – that Luke respected – univocally related John to Jesus' story in two ways:

- John was the Baptist, from whose activity that of Jesus emerged. Four canonical gospels agree on that, though their narratives vary in detail.[147] Luke's second volume also acknowledges that emergence,[148] and indicates the persistence of a Baptist tradition.[149]

- Equally importantly, John was a prophet[150] whose authority Jerusalem's rulers were unwilling to discuss – was it from heaven or from men?[151] Consequently, for the avoidance of readers' doubt, before

---

[146] Other scenes relating to Jesus and the Temple are (a) Jesus' Presentation and his evaluation by Simeon and Anna (2:25–38), and (b) Jesus' Passover visit when aged twelve and his encounter with "teachers" (2:41–52). Each plays a significant role in Luke's thematic preview of his narrative; each develops insights implied by Luke's triptych, but, constrained by word limits, I focus here on Luke's base-text and its extension.

[147] Luke 3:1–20 has much in common with Mk 1:1–11 and with the perspective of Jn 1:6–8, 19–29. Mt. 3:1–17 and Luke 3:21–22 stand in stark contrast; Mark and Matthew overtly attribute Jesus' baptism to John. It is this that prompts *Interpreter*'s focus on Luke's account of God's *anointing* Jesus rather than John's baptizing him.

[148] E.g., Acts 10:37–38; 13:23–25 (see Ch. 8).

[149] E.g., Acts 18:24–28; 19:1–7.

[150] Affirmed by the Dual tradition; e.g., Luke 7:24–35; Mt. 11:7–19.

[151] E.g., Luke 20:1–8 et par.

45

recounting Jesus' birth (Luke 2:1–7), and plainly establishing whence Luke believed both John's and Jesus' authority came, Luke offers parallel announcements of their origins in God's plan.

Third, and more importantly, Luke programmatically distances the Baptist from Jesus (Luke 1:68–79; cf. 16:16), and in the Infancy Prologue he makes a sharp structural division at 2:1–7, where, taking up his earlier angelophany to Mary, he briefly recounts Jesus' birth before another angelophany setting that birth firmly in God's plan for David's house. Luke's programmatic distancing accords with a Jesus-saying known to both him and Matthew: "The law and the prophets were in effect until John came; since then the good news of the kingdom of God is proclaimed, and everyone tries to enter it by force."[152] This traditional distinction, rooted in a Jesus-*logion*, probably underlies Luke's distinctive focusing on Jesus' anointing, leaving readers to infer that John baptized him. Even within Luke's Prologue, John's father's *Benedictus* maps the two infants' respective roles in God's plan.[153]

2. Luke's triptych

For those reasons I liken Luke's Prologue's scenes introducing Jesus to a triptych. Each panel brings to mind what Luke wants a reader both to understand and to remember about Jesus throughout the narrative ahead. Henceforward, the word triptych encapsulates Luke's distinctive concept of who this Jesus *is*. Luke's first panel portrays Mary and Gabriel (Luke 1:26–38); a second briefly presents Jesus' birth in Bethlehem (Luke 2:1–7, 12, 16); the third, portraying shepherds hearing heaven's announcement of that birth, depicts earth bathed in God's glory and peace (Luke 2:8–30). Retaining the language of this visual imagery, we return to the literary artistry of Luke's text.

---

[152] Luke 16:16; cf. Mt. 11:12 – in very different contexts.

[153] On Jesus, 1:68–75; on John, 1:76–79.

Interpreter's case is that Luke's reason for choosing the elements of each side-panel is that they bring God's promise "I will raise up" (ἀναστήσω) to focus on the centre-panel's "babe in the manger," David's "seed."[154]

The Jesus of Luke 24 and its alleged oxymoron is the Jesus introduced by Luke's Infancy Gospel. That narrative identity needs to be affirmed. Luke 1–2 is Prologue, Luke's pact with the reader, his pre-drama scene-setting. Luke's Jesus is David's promised seed. In this brief discussion, I have bracketed off all discussion of Luke's careful separation of John the Baptist's from Jesus' panels.[155] That separation's significance is signalled in Zechariah's canticle by "his" distinction between 1:67–75 (concerning Mary's child) and 76–79 (addressed to his son John). These boys serve different eras, fulfilling differing purposes (Luke 16:16; cf. Acts 19:1–7).

By isolating and assessing the Lukan panels allotted to Jesus, we clarify his role as the protagonist of Luke's narrative, where his naming becomes important. Luke makes clear that it is through this particular person (1:31; 2:21), born in this setting (2:4, 11), to this family (1:27, 69; 2:4), at this juncture in Israel's story (3:1–20), that God has chosen to act to fulfil the promise (Acts 13:23, 32) that had come to stand at the core of Israel's hope (2 Sam. 7:8–16; cf. Ezek. 34:11–25a).[156]

---

[154] It is this case that distances my work from that of Koet (1989) on Luke's uses of scripture. Like Koet in his fine studies, I want only to offer building blocks for the study of Luke-Acts (20). If Koet had done for Jesus what he has done for Paul – discuss what made him who he is (73–96) – then he might have asked, "Who is it who interprets Isaiah in Luke 4:16–30?" Is it not the Saviour whom Simeon meets, introduced earlier by Luke 2:11? Luke's Isaiah quotation then illuminates this Saviour's programme.

[155] This is briefly discussed in the chapter on Paul's Antioch sermon. (cf. Luke's edits in 3; John the Baptist in Acts).

[156] Ch. 8.

3. "Using" scripture

That summary raises questions of Luke's using scripture and of my reading it, two activities that belong inextricably together. *Neutestamentler* still vigorously debate how to read Luke-Acts and how to grasp the significance of the presence in Luke's narrative of so extensive and so varied an engagement with Israel's scriptures. Traditionally, interpreters have attended to citation, allusion and form – a literary paradigm. Study has enabled the emergence of surer ways of working in that setting. For example, the groundbreaking work of Richard Hays (1989, 2015) proposed criteria by which one might be confident of the presence and function of Israel's scriptures; his criteria are widely used. But George Brooke (1998), coming from a different direction, studying the Dead Sea Scrolls, had already explored the different path of recognizing when scripture is in play in a Jewish setting, and the possibilities implied by incipit phrases, understood as labels rather than initial phrases.

Further, Dunn (2013a) on orality in the making of Christianity draws our attention to the kinds of readers for whom Luke retold this living tradition – readers and hearers whose involvement in a liturgical tradition within a shared worldview and cultural memory ensured their familiarity with swathes of remembered psalms, interpreted prophets and horizons of expectation.[157] Luke's intertextuality is his literary expression of a living oral tradition in dialogue with an ongoing interpretative tradition. His retelling of Jesus' story begins with

---

[157] Dodd (1952: 126) had earlier concluded that "at a very early date a certain *method* of biblical study was established [...] largely employed orally, and found literary expression only sporadically and incompletely." Dunn's insights, and those of Gerhardsson, have been developed and enriched in the essays in Kelber and Byrskog (2009), and by the work of Kirk, A. (2018).

the way in which he introduces Jesus: the clustering of "evocations" of scripture in the triptych's panels.[158]

i. Reference-frames

My approach focuses on both frames of reference and horizons of expectation. Litwak (2005) convinced me of the significance of reference-frames – though I dissent from his conclusions.[159] This approach highlights my dissent from the reading of Luke's Prologue in Joel Green (1997) as Luke's oxymoron; my reading sees not an oxymoron but Luke's solidarity with apostolic proclamation and early tradition (e.g., Rom. 1:1–6). We clearly agree on the significance of scripture for reading Luke-Acts – we differ in how we read its use in Luke. I sharply distinguish Jesus' story from John's and see a triptych that prepares a reader for who Jesus is. For Luke, David's house is focal; he presents Jesus as David's promised heir; apostolic proclamation is that the Messiah is Jesus.[160] Then, Green's discussion of sonship derives from his reading of Jesus' conception; mine from Luke's reference-frame where Jesus is of David's house,[161] fulfilling God's promises.

ii. David's house

In what follows, I briefly justify the importance for Luke's narrative development of a Jesus-triptych focused on God's promises to David by clarifying the

---

[158] See, e.g., Oropeza and Moyise (2016) Part II for a range of strategies discussed between 2008 and 2013 at SBL's *Intertextuality and the New Testament* sessions; Part I is a useful collection of essays on established techniques. A substantial bibliography (273–299) enriches this volume's value.

[159] See also Litwak (2012: 147–169).

[160] E.g., Acts 2:36; 5:42; 9:22; 17:3; 18:5, 28; cf. 28:31; Rom. 1:1–7.

[161] E.g., Luke 1:27, 32–33, 69; 2:4, 11.

conceptual and lexical features shared by Luke's two annunciatory side-panels with their scriptural originals.

First, I note that throughout Luke's triptych one finds a focus on David, both conceptually and lexically. Then, in the context of Luke-Acts, the name "David" offers a trajectory from Luke 1:26 to Acts 15:16; David is a significant presence in Luke (thirteen occurrences) and Acts (eleven). This "presence" reaches a climax in Paul's Antioch sermon, where one finds both an accent on David and "the promise," exegeted by a focal midrash on God's having fulfilled "the promise" (Acts 13:22–23, 32–39). That is, this narratively significant sermon addresses the very triptych with which this present chapter is concerned.[162]

Finally, the section of Acts characterized by engagement with Israel's scriptures (1–15) ends with James's midrash on Amos 9:11, another prophetic reflection on Luke's base-text and its "I will raise up" (ἀναστήσω), Nathan's oracle, this time in the light of Peter's and Paul's encounters with Gentiles.[163] Luke systematically explores his hermeneutic matrix.

Consequently, my reading of Luke's introductory triptych does not depend on two passages only, but is part of a much larger narrative shaping concerning David. Neither side-panel cites either oracle;[164] but their presence throughout Luke's narrative is palpable. Basically conceptually, though sufficiently lexically, each panel is connected to its originating oracle by grouped ties without which this story could not be told. Further, if we recall that Luke's

---

[162] Its significance is examined in Ch. 8; cf. Doble (2014).

[163] We discuss this ending in *Interpreter*'s final chapter.

[164] At BNTS, 2013, my drawing attention to this "absence" elicited considerable alarm from some participants. It is, however, an absence only in a relentlessly literary paradigm; and logically the absence of evidence is not evidence of absence, particularly where the oracles' effects are visible. In his narrative, Luke makes readers well aware of Israel's horizons of expectation. When a treasured text is so clearly marked and effective, has one need of citation? See Ch. 7.

earliest readers probably shared Israel's hope based on God's ancient, often reworked, promise to David, then Luke's promise of "things fulfilled among us" (Luke 1:1), together with the opening words of his first panel – "house of David" – would alert readers to a significant shift in Israel's story. We focus on the two side-panels of Luke's triptych framing Luke's depiction of Jesus' birth (Luke 2:1–7), for they tell readers who the babe in the manger really is.

B. Nathan and Mary: panel 1 (Luke 1:26–35)

This first panel's effect is to alert readers that Nathan's oracle to David will be fulfilled in the person of Jesus. Two actors, Gabriel (Dan. 8:15–16, TH; 9:21, OG; TH) and Mary,[165] play out Luke's introduction of his protagonist, Jesus.

1. Gabriel

Gabriel, an "angel of the Lord," appeared earlier in Luke's narrative about John: "I am Gabriel. I stand in the presence of God, and I have been sent to speak to you and to bring you this good news"[166] – reverential periphrasis for "God sent me [...] with this message." Gabriel now brings to Mary news of what will happen; his is a pre-conception announcement, about futures, about the not yet, but shortly to be. Gabriel's news for Mary is that she will be an agent in God's fulfilling that promise made to David through Nathan (2 Sam. 7:12–14), a scriptural reference-frame known to have been "in the air."[167] For example, this promise, of one "born of David's seed," introduced Paul's gospel for the Romans (Rom. 1:1–6);[168] Luke made the promise the centre-piece of Paul's synagogue sermon at Antioch (Acts 13:16b–41); earlier, it had formed the base-text for a

---

[165] Interpreter prescinds from discussing this name's possible evocation of Dan. 8:15–17 (TH) and 9:20–27(OG). Two Greek translations of Daniel exist. The Old Greek (OG) was that familiar to earlier readers of versions of the LXX; Theodotion, who wrote in the C2nd CE produced a version of Daniel (TH) that became popular among Christians. Luke could not possibly have known TH (see Ch. 8), but a developing scriptural tradition, evidenced in the Jewish Pseudepigrapha and in writings discovered at Qumran stretches between LXX and TH. Matthew's gospel also names Gabriel as one who reveals events that uncover scripture's meanings. Luke the interpreter inhabited a rich scriptural interpretative tradition (see Ch. 1).

[166] Luke 1:19; cf. 2:10; εὐαγγελίσασθαί σοι ταῦτα.

[167] Cf. Dunn (2013a: 54) on "horizons of expectation"; we earlier noted 4Q174.

[168] See Whitsett (2000) and his discussion partners.

pesher,[169] and we shall see later that this same base-text underlies Paul's "hope of Israel" (Acts 28:20). This David-promise certainly dominated Ps. 88, which figures large in *Interpreter's* reading of Luke-Acts. In their own ways, Isaiah and Jeremiah had built on this David-promise, but neither features in these panels.[170] And of course, we recall Luke's own David-trajectory, solid evidence of his interest.

2. Mary

Of Mary, a reader knows first that she is betrothed to Joseph who is of David's house.[171] While the notion of "house" remains ambiguous throughout Nathan's oracle 2 Sam. 7:6, 13), the transgenerational body of Davidic descendants remains its focus. Gabriel's message for Mary is that she will conceive and bear a son (Luke 1:31) who will be named Jesus (cf. 2:21). Luke's whole narrative from that point until 2:21 is centred on Jesus' being the fulfilment of God's promise to David – "I will raise up your seed after you, who shall be from your

---

[169] Here used of an interpretative technique that finds events concerning specific people in one's own time to be fulfilments of words found in scripture; see, e.g., 4Q174; Acts 4:24b–28.

[170] E.g., Isa. 9:1–7; 11:1–9 37:33–35 (Δαυιδ τὸν παῖδά μου); 55:1–5 (Acts 13:34). No Isaianic David-promise opens with ἀναστήσω. Jer. 23:4–5 twice has God's promise ἀναστήσω, and 23:5 is arguably echoed in Luke 1:78, and in the John element, but otherwise playing no discernible part in Luke's Jesus-story.

[171] Luke 1:27; cf. 2 Sam. 7:11, 16. Provisionally, I bracket out all discussion of whether or not this is a virginal conception. Readers should note, however, the radical physicality of both Nathan's oracle and Gabriel's announcement to Mary. Joseph, not Mary, is Jesus' link with David. Can a Jesus who is not Joseph's *physical* descendant be David's seed? And Paul's περὶ τοῦ υἱοῦ αὐτοῦ τοῦ γενομένου ἐκ σπέρματος Δαυὶδ κατὰ σάρκα (Rom. 1:3) has to be taken seriously. But that is a discussion to be continued elsewhere. See, e.g., Brooke (ed.) (2000b), especially Peacocke's essay "DNA of our DNA"; Lincoln (2013). Both Green (1997: 184), and Hays (2015: 60) treat this passage as a miraculous conception and relate this to Luke's use of "Son of God." *Interpreter's* view is that Luke's accent falls not on Jesus' conception, but on his embodiment and resurrection. For "embodiment" I am indebted to Jantzen (2000).

gut, and I will establish his kingdom" (2 Sam. 7:12).[172] Gabriel's message to Mary then continues this Davidic story:

> He will be *great* [2 Sam. 7:9], and will be called the *Son* [2 Sam. 7:14] of the Most High, and the Lord God will give to him the *throne* [2 Sam. 7:13, 16] of *his father David* [2 Sam. 7:5, 8, 15]. He will reign over the house of Jacob *forever* [2 Sam. 7:13, 16], and of his *kingdom* [2 Sam. 7:12, 13, 16] there will *be no end* (Luke 1:32–33).[173]

In his Prologue, Luke's "house of David" proves an incipit phrase that labels the whole David-promise complex of material. The lexical and conceptual triggers italicized in the extract above confirm that Zechariah eventually rightly discerned what was going on:

> [The Lord God of Israel] has raised up a horn of
> salvation for us
> In the house of his servant David (Luke 1:69).[174]

This first side-panel of Luke's introductory triptych portrays who the Jesus of his story is; it opens Luke's much longer narrative trajectory. We read this panel as a whole, as Luke's reference-frame to the basic promise underlying Israel's

---

[172] καὶ ἔσται ἐὰν πληρωθῶσιν αἱ ἡμέραι σου καὶ κοιμηθήσῃ μετὰ τῶν πατέρων σου, καὶ ἀναστήσω τὸ σπέρμα σου μετὰ σέ, ὃς ἔσται ἐκ τῆς κοιλίας σου, καὶ ἑτοιμάσω *τὴν βασιλείαν αὐτοῦ*, αὐτὸς οἰκοδομήσει μοι οἶκον τῷ ὀνόματί μου, καὶ ἀνορθώσω *τὸν θρόνον αὐτοῦ ἕως εἰς τὸν αἰῶνα*. ἐγὼ ἔσομαι αὐτῷ εἰς πατέρα, καὶ αὐτὸς ἔσται μοι εἰς *υἱόν* (2 Sam. 7:12–14). This promise came with its problem – who on earth can live for ever? See Ps. 88:47–58.

[173] A fuller study of Luke's Prologue will engage with Brooke (2000b: 25–27) on Luke 1:32–37; 4Q246; Dan. 2:44, 7:27.

[174] Luke 1:69. Echoing Ps. 88:25b? Note the connection between David and salvation; David and "servant" (Δαυὶδ παιδὸς αὐτοῦ). This will be resumed in *Interpreter*'s final chapter where we discuss James's use of Amos 9:11.

54

hope, one "born of David's seed": "I will raise up your seed after you." (2 Sam. 7:12–14). This introduction is distinctively Lukan; neither Gabriel nor Mary uses the word Messiah;[175] her son, identified as Jesus, will be called Son of God, a pointer to Luke's distinctive account of Jesus' anointing (3:21–22).[176] That, however, like Jesus' conception and birth, still lies in Luke's narrative future.

Before that anointing, Luke offers readers a birth announcement on the grandest of scales to the humblest of audiences (2:8–20). A clutch of conceptual and lexical signals suggests that Luke's second side-panel of his triptych specifically evokes Ezekiel's reworking of Nathan's as yet unfulfilled promise-oracle to David. That unfulfilled-ness lay at the heart of Ps. 88's despairing questions to God,[177] questions Israel had repeatedly sung:

> Who can live and never see death?
> Who shall rescue his being from the power of Hades?[178]
> *Diapsalma*
> Lord, where is your steadfast love of old,
> which you swore to David by your faithfulness? (Ps. 88:49–50).

But in exile, Ezekiel had also recalled God's promise – and reaffirmed his conviction that God would act through David, to save and restore Israel.

---

[175] Nor did Nathan.

[176] See the discussion at the end of this chapter on Jesus' anointing and Luke's use of "Son of God." In an essay on Paul's Antioch sermon I have argued that at Luke 3:21–22, the D05 reading is to be preferred; see Doble (2014), cf. Dodd (1952: 31–32).

[177] Contrast these verses with the celebration of that promise in Ps. 88:2–5, 20–38.

[178] τίς ἐστιν ἄνθρωπος, ὃς ζήσεται καὶ οὐκ ὄψεται θάνατον, ῥύσεται τὴν ψυχὴν αὐτοῦ ἐκ χειρὸς ᾅδου.

C. Ezekiel and shepherds: panels 2 (Luke 2:1–7) and 3 (Luke 2:8–30)

This panel portrays heaven's proclamation of Jesus' birth. The scene comprises an angel and a group of shepherds. The angel chorus are heaven's off-stage confirmation of the on-stage angelic message.

The scene's structure in panel 2

In Luke 2:1–7,[179] the central panel of the triptych, Luke briefly portrayed what had happened, a scene echoed in 2:12 and 16: Joseph and Mary and the babe (βρέφος) lying in a manger.[180] Again, Joseph is named first (2:4a) and identified as a *Davidid* (2:4b); it is his familial descent that takes him to David's city, Bethlehem. Of Mary, Luke reports three things: she was betrothed (ἐμνηστευμένην) to Joseph;[181] she was pregnant (οὔσῃ ἐγκύῳ), as Gabriel had announced she would be (2:5b; cf.1:31); she accompanied Joseph from Nazareth to Bethlehem on his journey to register his Davidic descent, where her son was born (2:7; cf. 1:31).[182]

---

[179] See Ch. 7.

[180] See Doble (2000: 183–186).

[181] Luke 1:27; cf. 2:5, τῇ ἐμνηστευμένῃ αὐτῷ; we note Luke's twofold affirmation of their relationship.

[182] καὶ ἔτεκεν τὸν υἱὸν αὐτῆς τὸν πρωτότοκον cf. Ps. 88:20–28, where sonship, πρωτότοκος, and the David-promise belong together.

2. Ezekiel reworked Luke's base-text in panel 3

We note the interconnectedness of 2:1–21 with 1:26–38; Luke's triptych is a unity. But we earlier identified four words that *together* suggest that Luke's scene is designed to evoke another David-oracle, this time Ezekiel's reworking (Ezek. 34:1–31) for a later age of the basic promise made through Nathan. We note each word separately.

i. Shepherds

This angel's audience comprises shepherds getting on with shepherding, at night, in fields. Here, Luke's apparently faithful shepherds contrast strikingly with the shepherds addressed by another messenger of the Lord, Ezekiel, exploiting an established metaphor for rulers, one itself rooted in Nathan's oracle (2 Sam. 7:7–8). Ezekiel's oracle is addressed to shepherds who had exploited their status for power, ruthless greed and selfish concern (Ezek. 34:1–16). Luke will later, and distinctively, highlight the role of Israel's rulers in Jesus' story.[183] But Luke also knows that God's promised salvation from the mess of Exile will be through one shepherd – David (Ezek. 34:23–25a).[184] Ezekiel addressed shepherds and promised a shepherd; the angel addresses shepherds and announces – a Saviour.

---

[183] See Ch. .

[184] We note, and reserve for discussion, Ezekiel's "word": καὶ ἀναστήσω ἐπ᾽ αὐτοὺς ποιμένα ἕνα καὶ ποιμανεῖ αὐτούς, τὸν δοῦλόν μου Δαυιδ, καὶ ἔσται αὐτῶν ποιμήν. Cf. Jer. 37:8–9; 23:4–5; Pss. Sol. 17:21; Acts 4:25–28 and Ch. 4.

57

ii. Saviour

Mary had hymned "God, my Saviour" (1:47); Zechariah also had recognized that in David's house God had raised up "a horn of salvation."[185] From its outset, Luke's narrative theology is being shaped by the promises celebrated in these two panels. Ezekiel's oracle had set out God's purpose – not only to judge Israel's oppressive shepherds, but also to save his flock: καὶ σώσω τὰ πρόβατά μου (34:22a). This saving entailed seeking out those scattered and lost (34:11–16); David, though long since dust when Ezekiel was speaking out,[186] was to be God's agent in this reconstituted flock (34:23–24).

Unsurprisingly, then, to awe-struck shepherds the angel announced the birth of a "Saviour." This word's Lukan trajectory closes in Acts 13:23,[187] where it is a focal word in Paul's sermon,[188] but its root, "save," is a strong and distinctive Lukan thread, climaxing in Luke 19:10,[189] where Luke definitively reformulates the purpose of Jesus' ministry: "for the Son of Man came to seek and to save what was lost."[190]

"Saviour" is qualified first by "Messiah." This is the word's first appearance in Luke-Acts, conforming to popular usage concerning the David-

---

[185] Luke 1:69, probably echoing the David-focused Ps. 88:25; καὶ ἐν τῷ ὀνόματί μου ὑψωθήσεται τὸ κέρας αὐτοῦ.

[186] Luke also firmly makes this point: see, e.g., Acts 2:29; 13:36.

[187] Cf. especially, Acts 5:29–32 – But Peter and the apostles answered, "We must obey God rather than any human authority. The God of our ancestors raised up Jesus, whom you had killed by hanging him on a tree. God exalted him at his right hand as Leader and Saviour that he might give repentance to Israel and forgiveness of sins. And we are witnesses to these things, and so is the Holy Spirit whom God has given to those who obey him."

[188] This final use of "Saviour" (and Paul's message of salvation, Ps. 106) is examined in Ch. 8. Cf. Acts 28:28.

[189] See Aletti (1989: 17–38).

[190] This is plainly Luke's radical transformation of Mk 10:45 in line with Jesus' role established by the second panel of this diptych. On Luke and "salvation" see esp. Marshall (1988a).

promise (e.g., Luke 20:41–44), then by "Lord" (again, Luke 20:41–44 etc.). This panel completes for Theophilus the Davidic concept-cluster – including Son of God – that will characterize Luke's story of Jesus.[191]

iii. Peace

Ezekiel's vision of David's rule includes the promise of a covenant of peace (Ezek. 34:25–31; cf. 37:26). Unsurprisingly, then, Luke's angelic chorus ascribes glory to God, and peace among men (2:14) – an oracle fulfilled. In its Lukan context, echoing Ezekiel's hope, this angelic hymn celebrates the inauguration of that hoped-for era in which David's offspring is Israel's shepherd-ruler. Peace is a distinctive Lukan theme; the word appears fourteen times in Luke's first volume and seven times in his second.[192] Peace becomes the characteristic first word of Jesus' missioners, and later Jerusalem's great want is the recognition of what coheres with shalom (Luke 10:5, 6; 19:41–44). It is the risen Lord's first word to his gathered followers (24:36b) and, for Cornelius, Peter summarizes what God had done in and through Jesus:

> You know the message he sent to the people of Israel, preaching peace by Jesus Messiah—he is Lord of all (Acts 10:36).

For shepherds, this new-born Saviour from David's house is the harbinger of God's peace, shalom; he is their peaceable Messiah, their Lord.

---

[191] See Brooke (2000a); he discusses Luke 1:32–35, John's Gospel and 4Q246. Age note (b) on Luke's version of Jesus' anointing will argue the linking of "Son of God" with Luke's base-text. Cf. Hays (2015: 60–62).

[192] Contrast Matthew, x4; Mark, x1.

iv. David

καὶ *ἀναστήσω* ἐπ' αὐτοὺς ποιμένα ἕνα καὶ ποιμανεῖ αὐτούς, τὸν δοῦλόν μου Δαυιδ, καὶ ἔσται αὐτῶν ποιμήν. For Ezekiel, God's agent in his saving activity is David. The angel's "In David's city" (Luke 2:11) sustains the Davidic connection already made strongly in 2:1–7 – and is reinforced indirectly by associated concepts. This is the child spoken of by Gabriel (1:26–38); recognized by the devout and righteous Simeon as God's Messiah (2:26–32), God's promised salvation. This coherence of salvation with the David-promise undercuts those who think primarily of Isaiah; we leave discussion of that position until Chapter 10.

3. Summary

From his story's opening, Luke has sharply distinguished Jesus from John the Baptist. In each panel of his triptych, Luke's focus is Jesus. Luke offers two side-panels, each a David-promise evoking Nathan's oracle, then Ezekiel's. Lexical and conceptual evidence strongly supports the claim that Luke has introduced Jesus to readers as the Saviour, Lord and Messiah of the David-promises. We pursue this link vigorously in Chapter 8. Luke introduced Jesus to Theophilus via two David-promises, each of which carries God's promise "I will raise up" (ἀναστήσω). Narratively, the significance of Luke's selection of these two from among various David-promises remains unremarked until that event about which Theophilus, like many others, remained doubtful – Jesus' resurrection.[193] It is this Jesus of whom Luke writes in Luke 24.[194] Essentially, his introductory triptych depicting Jesus "defines" Luke's concept of Messiah; it is found within his narrative and not in abstractions from a generalized Second Temple context.

---

[193] See the discussion below of Isa. 55 in Paul's Antioch sermon.

[194] Bart Koet's evidence for an implied reference to Isa. 53:7–8 at Luke 24:26 results from misguided parallelism with Acts 8. See Ch. 3.

60

A problem remains, unresolved until Chapter 10, that is of crucial importance in NT studies – how may a critical approach weigh a reference-frame against a clear quotation? Bart Koet (1989: 140) partly saw that problem, but had already committed himself to a quotation principle that led him to identify "crucial" quotations from Isaiah as a major factor in Luke's presentation of Jesus. Koet (1989: 144) has in fact pushed back before Jesus' debut (*sic*) with its extended quotation (Luke 4:16–30), recognizing an earlier quotation (Luke 2:32), "which seems to be even more programmatic for Jesus' meaning in the whole of Luke-Acts and may even be a 'device' of this work." What might "programmatic" now mean here? My decision was to place narrative "sense" and Jewish interpretative tradition before theoretical commitment. We pursue this decision later; first, we "return" to Luke's distinctive introduction of Jesus' public activity.

D. Anointing: a Lukan distinctive

Anointing is distinctive to Luke.[195] We noted above that Gabriel's word to Mary was that her son's name was to be Jesus, a thread completed at 2:21, and that "he will be called (κληθήσεται) "son of God'" (υἱὸς θεοῦ)" (1:35), or "son of the Most High" (1:32). Luke's twofold use of the future κληθήσεται invites reflection on distinctions between a name and a descriptor, and between a present state and a future way of talking about someone. As a descriptor of Jesus, "Son of God" is deep rooted in pre-Lukan, and pre-Pauline, tradition.[196] Two comments illuminate this future way of talking about Jesus.

---

[195] See Kilgallen (2013: 29–49).

[196] See, e.g., Rom. 1:3–4; on this tradition, note esp. the discussion in Whitsett (2000); see also the other Synoptists' and John's accounts of John's baptizing Jesus – and of events beyond that.

1. Anointing in Luke-Acts

First, given Luke's David reference-frame, his base-text's wording is notable: "I *will be* a father to him, and *he shall be* a son to me" (2 Sam. 7:14), a relatedness picked up by Ps. 88:26–27,[197] and celebrated by Ps. 2:7, traditionally David's own verbalizing of that father-son relationship.[198] Second, once the Prologue has ended and the curtain has gone up on Luke's drama (Luke 3:1–2) at the beginning of John's prophetic activity, Luke-Acts' adapting the Jesus-tradition is soon in full flow.

i. Luke

John obliquely but clearly denies that he is the awaited Messiah before his narrative, on-stage presence abruptly ends (Luke 3:15–17, 18–20). Unlike the other canonical gospels, Luke offers no account of Jesus' baptism, noting simply that he had been baptized; Luke offers instead, a brief account of Jesus at prayer, of the Spirit's descent, of God's assuring him, "You are my son."[199] Luke crystallizes this account by the concept of anointing.[200] Here, for the first time in Luke's narrative, Jesus is obliquely called "Son of God," (= "my Son"). This descriptor then becomes a thread through to the opening of Jesus' widening ministry; I have argued elsewhere for reading the D05 text at 3:22, but the descriptor "Son of God" is the implied, traditional common element.[201]

---

[197] αὐτὸς ἐπικαλέσεταί με Πατήρ μου εἶ σύ, θεός μου καὶ ἀντιλήμπτωρ τῆς σωτηρίας μου, κἀγὼ πρωτότοκον θήσομαι αὐτόν, ὑψηλὸν παρὰ τοῖς βασιλεῦσιν τῆς γῆς. Here, "father" and "firstborn" describe the same relationality; we note that Luke describes Jesus as Mary's πρωτότοκον (2:7) – καὶ ἔτεκεν τὸν υἱὸν αὐτῆς τὸν πρωτότοκον.

[198] So e.g., Acts 4:24–26.

[199] σὺ εἶ ὁ υἱός μου, Luke 3:21–22.

[200] See, e.g., Acts 4:27 (in context of 24–26); 10:38.

[201] See Doble (2014: 175–199).

Beginning with Gabriel's word to Mary, κληθήσεται, Luke's Son of God thread takes this symbol of the David-promise through Jesus' anointing, into his genealogy that passes through David (3:31), Abraham (3:34) and Adam, ultimately to God (3:38). People might suppose Jesus to be Joseph's son,[202] but, post-anointing, he was really Son of God. Luke's account of Jesus' wilderness testing (Luke 4:1–13) raises questions for this Son of God (4:3, 9) who is filled with Holy Spirit (4:1, 14), another clear narrative thread from the anointing's *bat qol*.[203] In Nazareth, continuing his Galilean ministry, Jesus read a passage from Isaiah that opened:

> The Spirit of the Lord is upon me,
>
> because he has anointed me (Luke 4:18).[204]

His hearers question who he is – is he not Joseph's son (Luke 4:22–23)? Yes, but, as readers know, he is also the anointed "Son of God," a thread that Luke continues through the Galilee story. There, Jesus' healing ministry leads demons to recognize him as Son of God and Messiah (Luke 4:40–41), descriptors from the Davidic concept-cluster. Luke's account of Jesus' transfiguration continues that thread: "This is my Son, my Chosen; listen to him" (Luke 9:35).

ii. Acts

That Jesus was anointed by God remains a Lukan thread in Acts, an affirmation of Jesus' authorization by God to act as he did. We shall see below how,

---

[202] E.g., his hearers at Nazareth, (Luke 4:22).

[203] See Ch. 8.

[204] *Πνεῦμα κυρίου ἐπ᾽ ἐμὲ / οὗ εἵνεκεν ἔχρισέν με,* where **χρίω**, "anoint," refers to the Jewish cultic practice of anointing kings, such as David, or High Priests. Luke-Acts' narrative tells of Jesus of David's line, announced as Saviour, Messiah and Lord, and of his being anointed (e.g., Acts 4:27). Χριστὸς (Englished as "Christ") is rendered by NRSV as Messiah at Luke 2:11.

reflecting in prayer on Ps. 2:1–2, Jesus' followers described him as "whom you anointed" (ὂν ἔχρισας, Acts 4:27). Later, Peter, briefly explaining the Jesus-story for Cornelius, distinguished John's baptism from God's anointing Jesus (10:37–38): "how God anointed Jesus of Nazareth with the Holy Spirit and with power" In the synagogue at Antioch, Paul also carefully separated John from Jesus: Jesus' entry on stage (εἴσοδος) followed John's exit (13:24–25), and Jesus is announced as David's promised seed (13:23, 32–37) through whom God has fulfilled that promise – initially through the words of Ps. 2:7 – "You are my son; this day I have begotten you" (Acts 13:33b).

2. Where does the narrative begin?

How Luke introduces Jesus is clearly important: via the Nazareth debut, or Luke's Prologue? I have urged that Luke's Prologue should be taken seriously as a statement of his scriptural reference-frame. The fact of his distinctively introducing Jesus afresh in this anointing cameo should alert readers to the narrative thread running from Luke 3:21–22 to Paul's sermon at Antioch (Acts 13:23, 32–37), where Luke's David focus is very sharp. Read from *Interpreter's* perspective, "The Spirit of the Lord is upon me, because he has anointed me" (Luke 4:18–19; Isa. 61:1–2) signals how Luke shapes the David-Messiah's ministry. God's anointing of Jesus controls Isaiah's oracle. Luke begins not with Isaiah, but with Jesus, the Jesus of his Prologue and of the anointing narrative. Consequently the focus here is on Jesus the Messiah, not a suffering servant Jesus, as also at Luke 2:32 and Acts 13:47.[205]

---

[205] Contra Koet (1989: 112–114).

E. Summary

This chapter establishes the evidence on which I based the first chapter's case for Luke-Acts' Davidic reference-frame. The Prologue's role is just that – a Euripidean device, giving context for an author's main narrative, adapted by Hellenistic Judaism,[206] as in John's Gospel. Luke-Acts' prologue is integral to the whole not an afterthought; it offers this author's understanding and using of the word "Messiah."

Luke's distinctive introducing of Jesus to readers by means of a triptych and by writing of Jesus' anointing rather than of his baptism indicate that Luke's controlling scriptural frame is the now-fulfilled David-promise. This device enables him firmly to distinguish, while validating, the ministries of both John the Baptist and Jesus. We examined the side-panels of Luke's triptych, identifying the Nathan and Ezekiel oracles from which I initially inferred both Luke's reference-frame and his sharp focus on the ἀναστήσω-promise.

Luke's base-text, "I will raise up (ἀναστήσω) your seed after you" (2 Sam. 7:12) remains Luke's hermeneutic key throughout his whole narrative. Extended first by the Ezekiel panel with its accompanying resonances, God's promise through Nathan to David is celebrated in the Prologue's canticles and in its closing scene.[207] The Prologue's focus, like that of the ensuing narrative is Jesus the *Davidid*; its final scene, set in Jerusalem's Temple and highlighting Jesus, previsions Luke-Acts' core, bridging conflict-narrative (Luke 19:41 – Acts 8:3) that is its driver.[208] Luke's distinctive narrative opening of Jesus' public ministry introduces him as the one whom God called "my Son" at his anointing with Holy Spirit (Luke 3:1–22). This Jesus is the Messiah of Luke 24 and of its

---

[206] See Tobin (1990).

[207] See the appended note to this chapter.

[208] See the analytical diagram.

two problematic Jesus-*logia*. God had promised David: "I will raise up (ἀναστήσω) your seed after you."

Appended Note: Luke's Prologue and

Jerusalem's Temple

Luke's introduction to Jesus points not simply backwards to the basic David-promise and its extension in Ezekiel, but also forward to Jesus' destiny. Before the curtain rises on his drama, Luke has alerted readers to Luke-Acts' significant thematic issues and threads. The Prologue prepares them especially for Luke's concern with Jerusalem's Temple, where Jesus will later in the narrative return to be among and speak truth to its teachers, and its rulers. Following his account of Jesus' birth, and before Jesus' public ministry opened, Luke offers four notes of Jesus' age:

> (a) eight days (Luke 2:21) – Jesus was circumcised and named.
> (b) forty days (2:22–40) – the infant grew in wisdom and with grace.[209]
> (c) twelve years (2:41–52) – on the brink of manhood, Jesus' growth in wisdom with grace is again featured.[210]
> (d) thirty years (3:23) – matured,[211] and roughly David's age when he began to rule, this note opens Luke's genealogy of Jesus.

Notes (b) and (c) are located in Jerusalem and associated with the Temple, both indicating that Jesus' parents were Torah-observant Jews and that their child, a true son of Abraham,[212] circumcised and presented, was growing in wisdom.[213] These two scenes prepare readers for the nature of Luke-Acts'

---

[209] Τὸ δὲ παιδίον ηὔξανεν καὶ ἐκραταιοῦτο πληρούμενον *σοφία*, καὶ *χάρις* θεοῦ ἦν ἐπ' αὐτό.

[210] Καὶ Ἰησοῦς προέκοπτεν [ἐν τῇ] *σοφία* καὶ ἡλικίᾳ καὶ *χάριτι* παρὰ θεῷ καὶ ἀνθρώποις.

[211] Καὶ αὐτὸς ἦν Ἰησοῦς ἀρχόμενος ὡσεὶ ἐτῶν τριάκοντα, ὢν υἱός...*usw*.

[212] E.g., Luke 1:46–55, 69–79; 3:34; cf. Acts 3:25–26; 6:8–8:3.

[213] Luke 2:21, 23, 24, 27, 39, 41.

conflict-narrative in Jerusalem, especially for Jesus' role as a *Davidid* in that story.

A. Age note (b). Jesus' presentation in the Temple and Mary's purification

Apart from Joseph and Mary whose piety is highlighted, three people command attention here: Jesus, Simeon and Anna.

We learned earlier that Mary gave birth to Jesus, her first-born (πρωτότοκος) son in Bethlehem, the Davidic ancestral home.[214] Luke emphasizes that she and Joseph were in Jerusalem's Temple to fulfil the Law's requirements.[215] Presenting Jesus in the Temple, they were fulfilling requirements that blended Exodus 13:11–16 and Numbers 18:8–20.[216] The former links the πρωτότοκος with the freeing of Israel from the house of slavery in Egypt, while Numbers associates πρωτότοκος with what is *holy*. Gabriel had already made that point to Mary – her son-to-be would be τὸ γεννώμενον ἅγιον.

Simeon typifies those in Israel characterized as righteous (δίκαιος), pious (εὐλαβὴς), and prompted by the Holy Spirit;[217] he was expectantly waiting for Israel's παράκλησιν. Given his canticle's wording Simeon's παράκλησιν probably echoes Isa. 40:1–2, signifying both consolation for past suffering continuing into his present, and strengthening encouragement for the People of God's hope-filled future. The Spirit that revealed to Simeon that he would live to see the Lord's Messiah, also led him into the Temple to encounter Jesus and his parents. Narratively, Luke had already rooted Jesus in scripture as the

---

[214] Luke 2:7 – ἔτεκεν τὸν υἱὸν αὐτῆς τὸν πρωτότοκον.

[215] Luke 2:22–24, covering both the parents' purification and the first-born's presentation.

[216] Note especially Num. 18:15.

[217] See WisdSol. 7:27 – Luke's three-fold reference to Simeon's Spirit-led life numbers this man among the prophets.

awaited Davidic Saviour, Messiah, Lord,[218] and this story of Jesus' presentation pre-echoes Luke's later conflict narrative that firmly links his two volumes.[219] In this child that he holds, Simeon recognizes the Lord's Messiah, God's salvation, the fulfilment of Isaianic hope.[220]

Luke here adds a second witness to this child's place in God's economy of salvation, this time a woman, the aged prophetess Anna. Committed to a life of prayer and fasting, to the service (of God), and constantly in the Temple, Anna thanked God and began to speak about (Jesus) to all who were waiting for the deliverance of Jerusalem.[221] At the mouth of two witnesses, Luke has confirmed Jesus' role in the coming story.

1. Message for Mary

Simeon, however, also has a less than consolatory message for Mary:

A οὗτος κεῖται – (a) εἰς – (b) εἰς – A* ὅπως ἂν (Luke 2:34).

Her child is destined (A οὗτος κεῖται) for (a) and (b) so that (ὅπως ἂν) A* may come about. That purpose[222] echoes the underlying piety of writings such as the Wisdom of Solomon.[223] We first examine the middle terms.

(a) Her child is destined for (εἰς) the falling and rising of many in Israel. Mary's canticle has already discerned that Gabriel's announcement implied that

---

[218] Luke 2:11,

[219] Luke 19:41-Acts 8:2. This conflict narrative essentially opens at Luke 19:45, where the Lord returns to cleanse this Temple, ending at Acts 7:55–56 where, in the Temple, Stephen's Spirit-filled affirmation of Jesus' exaltation by God reassures Israel's faithful of the faithfulness of God. See Doble, (2013).

[220] The leap from Isaiah's hope to the "suffering servant" is too far for safety; contra Pao and Schnabel (2007); readers already know that this child, seed of David, is the "Saviour who has been born for you" (Luke 2:11), Messiah, Lord. See Ch. 9.

[221] τοῖς προσδεχομένοις λύτρωσιν Ἰερουσαλήμ.

[222] ὅπως ἂν ἀποκαλυφθῶσιν ἐκ πολλῶν καρδιῶν διαλογισμοί.

[223] E.g., WisdSol. 1:1–11; 2:1–22; 5:4–13 on reasoning.

69

God has toppled the powerful from their seats and exalted the humble and meek.[224] In two later contexts Jesus' *logia* affirm that kind of reversal at the heart of God's kingdom.[225] In his vineyard parable, Jesus' saying about what God will do to the rapacious tenants carries that reversal to the heart of the matter – judgment may imply destruction of some and reallocation of the vineyard to others.[226] "Falling and rising" (πτῶσιν καὶ ἀνάστασιν) may well entail the reversal implied by the above paragraph, but Luke's narrative has proved to be resurrection-centred, and the strong possibility remains that Simeon's ἀνάστασιν resonates with all its harmonics; that possibility is strengthened by results from (b).

(b) Mary's child is destined as (εἰς) a sign (σημεῖον) that is opposed (ἀντιλεγόμενον). We need first to discriminate among Luke's uses of sign: very basically they may be understood as those in some sense offered by God,[227] and those demanded of God by humans.[228] Like the sign offered by an angel to shepherds,[229] this sign is signalled by the godly prophet Simeon to Mary; she will see that sign in her son's life and death. Since this child's destiny lies in the future, what has Luke's later narrative to say of Jesus as sign? That material clusters in two places, examined below, each emerging from pre-Lukan tradition

---

[224] Luke 1:50–54.

[225] Luke 14:11; 18:14.

[226] Luke 20:15b–16a.

[227] For example, the "signs and wonders" of Acts (e.g., 2:43; 4:30; 5:12,) that include the "signals of God" offered by Jesus' ministry in fulfilling his programmatic role as God's anointed Saviour (2:22).

[228] For example, those occasions that demand proof of God's agency or presence. For Luke the paradigm case is that of Jesus tested in the wilderness, whose response included his appeal to Deuteronomy's "Do not put the Lord your God to the test, as you tested him at Massah." (Deut. 6:16; Luke 4:12–13). Cf. Luke 11:16–20. Perhaps Luke's Herod should be included here (23:8–9; cf. 9:7–9). I have bracketed out requests for healing.

[229] Luke 2:12–16; see Doble (2000) for discussion of this sign's Solomonic resonances.

adapted to Luke's narrative purposes, and each thematically traceable from Simeon's words. The first is the sign of Jonah:

> "This generation is an evil generation; it asks for a sign, but no sign will be given to it except the sign of Jonah.[230] For just as Jonah became a sign to the people of Nineveh, so the Son of Man will be [a sign] to this generation." (Luke 11:29–30).

Luke's pre-text for this saying is his narrative unit associated with dispute about his healing activity [231] – a disputed sign. Drawing on tradition, and early into Jesus' journey to Jerusalem – to the Exodus he is to complete there – Luke highlights this σημεῖον ἀντιλεγόμενον. That the mute speak is not sign enough for some who accuse him of devilish exorcism; "Others, to test him, kept seeking from him a sign from heaven." That preceding narrative unit ends with a distinctive reference to Mary and Jesus,[232] and its *logion* "Blessed rather are those who hear the word of God and obey it!"[233] This "hearing-*logion*" introduces the sign of Jonah pericope.

Judgment and resurrection in relation to widely separated generations lie at the heart of this fragment of tradition. Its focus, however, is clearly the word "sign," and, ultimately, the Son of Man as sign. But that summary leaves a puzzle: why does tradition, and especially why does Luke, report that

---

[230] Cf. Matt. 12:38–42 D adapted; cf. 16:1–4 for "testing." The Dual tradition shares much, including the Ninevites repenting as a result of Jonah's proclamation; Matt. alone relates Jonah's ingestion and regurgitation by the huge fish to Jesus' resurrection. Luke's focus remains on Jesus' message and the conflict it generates.

[231] Luke 11:14–28.

[232] Following the Prologue's uses of her proper name, Jesus' mother has appeared in the narrative only at Luke 8:19–21, with a similar reference to οἱ τὸν λόγον τοῦ θεοῦ ἀκούοντες καὶ ποιοῦντες.

[233] Is this an echo from the temptation narrative (Luke 4:3), itself echoing Deut. 8:3 that is filled out by Matthew's version of the underlying tradition?

"something more than Solomon is here"? Why Solomon? This question will be unpacked in section 2.

Luke's setting alludes to Jesus' mother,[234] highlighting that those who hear and "guard" God's word are the really blessed. Notably Luke's previous allusion to Mary[235] is also a distinctive, again highlighting "hearing and doing God's word." Before that, his previous reference to Jesus' mother[236] is in the incident treated in Age note (c). There, pre-echoing his later conflict narrative, Luke reports Mary's conversation with her lost son Jesus and found him in the Temple καθεζόμενον ἐν μέσῳ τῶν διδασκάλων καὶ ἀκούοντα αὐτῶν καὶ ἐπερωτῶντα αὐτούς. In a concluding paragraph we crystallize the findings.

Luke's distinctive setting for this shared sign of Jonah tradition thus accents "hearing and keeping" God's word. And for those with ears to hear, this accent has powerful intertextual associations.[237] Further, Luke's setting for this "sign of Jonah" pericope evokes Simeon's word to Mary[238] that her son would be a disputed sign (σημεῖον ἀντιλεγόμενον) linked with Israel's destiny (πτῶσιν καὶ *ἀνάστασιν*). This narrative thread shapes Luke's appropriation of traditional material. But the sign of Jonah is complex: two elements – generation and judgment – carry significant parallelism in both examples of this tradition;[239] this parallelism needs to be explored.

> βασίλισσα νότου
> ἐγερθήσεται *ἐν τῇ κρίσει*
> *μετὰ* τῶν ἀνδρῶν *τῆς γενεᾶς ταύτης καὶ κατακρινεῖ* αὐτούς,

---

[234] Luke 11:27–28.

[235] Luke 8:19–21.

[236] Luke 2:46.

[237] See Ch. 7 on Stephen's Speech and its attention especially to Solomon's implied biography; see, e.g., 1 Kgs 9–11 et al.

[238] Luke 2:34–35.

[239] Cf. Matt. 12:38–42.

ὅτι ἦλθεν ἐκ τῶν περάτων τῆς γῆς ἀκοῦσαι τὴν
σοφίαν
Σολομῶνος,
     καὶ ἰδοὺ πλεῖον
Σολομῶνος ὧδε (Luke
11:31).

ἄνδρες Νινευῖται
 ἀναστήσονται *ἐν τῇ κρίσει*
  μετὰ τῆς γενεᾶς ταύτης καὶ κατακρινοῦσιν αὐτήν·
  ὅτι *μετενόησαν εἰς τὸ κήρυγμα* Ἰωνᾶ,
     καὶ ἰδοὺ πλεῖον Ἰωνᾶ
  ὧδε (Luke 11:32).

From the above extract, we see that two elements are parallel: both the Ninevites and Queen of Sheba are contrasted with "this generation." At the end time (ἐν τῇ κρίσει), both will rise (ἐγερθήσεται; ἀναστήσονται) with (the men of) "this generation" – those to whom Jesus was sent[240] – and condemn [them] it, for both *listened,* while one acted on that listening. Do we hear an echo of Simeon's πτῶσιν καὶ *ἀνάστασιν* that we discussed earlier?

Luke's Jonah sign is clear. Jonah forms Luke's pericope's *inclusio,* (11:29, 32), and Jonah is its intergenerational comparative element with the Son of Man. Each generation was offered its sign. For each "proclamation" (κήρυγμα) of God's word is the sign's key element. Notably, tradition knows that the Son of Man sign is "something more" (πλεῖον) than the Jonah sign.

This pericope is one among Luke's uses of tradition that give Luke-Acts its distinctive Son of Man trajectory. For example, his Zacchaeus story[241] crystallizes Luke's "Saviour" motif, announced earlier in the Prologue,[242]

---

[240] E.g., Luke 4:42–44; Acts 3:26; 10:34–43.

[241] Luke 19:1–10, especially its final Son of Man *logion.* Cf. Luke 15:1–32.

[242] Luke 2:11.

echoing Ezekiel's oracle of God's purposes,[243] and confirmed by Simeon's encounter with Jesus.[244] Above all, Stephen's vision (his last word to the Sanhedrin) is Luke's distinctive culmination of the Jerusalem conflict narrative, essentially focused on Jesus, who is both Son of Man and God's anointed. But this trajectory is rooted in Luke-Acts' "who is this?" puzzle that opens towards the end of the Galilee period,[245] disclosing Peter's perceptiveness[246] and Jesus' modifying of that "confession."[247] God's Messiah and Son of Man are interlocked concepts embodied in one person, Jesus, who, according to Luke's Prologue, is the Son of David who will at last fulfil the basic David-promise. In Chapter 3 I discuss that promise's ἀναστήσω dimensions that drive the reasoning of Luke 24 and the exegetical speeches in Acts. When Stephen witnessed to the Sanhedrin that he could see God's glory and Jesus standing at God's right hand, he did so in a form intended to evoke for them, Jesus' own judges, the words of Jesus' response to their questioning.[248] Stephen said: "I see the heavens opened and the Son of Man standing (ἑστῶτα) at God's right hand!" (Acts 7:56).

2. Why the Solomon comparison?

Both Luke and Matthew know and use the tradition that accords Solomon a neuter adjective (πλεῖον) that probably refers back to its distant, though focal, antecedent noun, σημεῖον. In Luke's narrative, is Solomon a sign by implication?

---

[243] Ezek. 34.

[244] Luke 2:29–32 where God's salvation reflects the angel's "Saviour" (2:11).

[245] Luke 9:7–27.

[246] Luke 9:20.

[247] Luke 9:21–27.

[248] Acts 7:56, cf. Luke 22:69; see Ch. 7.

From the Jesus-triptych forward we have been noting Luke's "Solomon" trajectory.[249] Both Jesus and Solomon are of the house of David; both are David's seed, though Jesus not through Solomon's line.[250] While Ninevites repented — that is, they heard and obeyed — the Queen heard Solomon's wisdom. Solomon's famed wisdom, however, did not entail his "guarding" God's word — recall this *logion*'s larger context[251] and its keynote, "Blessed rather are those who hear the word of God and obey it!" Solomon's folly proved decisive for Israel's story. He heard and spectacularly failed to act, to obey.

First-century hopes for a fulfilled David-promise imply Solomon's earlier failure.[252] The literary unit found in 1 Kgs 9–11 comprises a second theophany to Solomon; the Queen of Sheba's visit to him; the narrator's report of God's judgment of Solomon. Chapter 6A argues that 1 Kgs 9–11 underlies Luke's shaping of Stephen's speech. Later, ben Sira noted of him, "you profaned your seed";[253] but in the same cameo assessment ben Sira noted that God's promise to David remained:

> But the Lord did not abandon his mercy,
> and will not destroy [any of] his words;
> nor will he ever wipe out the family of his chosen,
> and destroy the seed of him who loved him.
> So he gave a remnant to Jacob,
> and to David a root from himself (Sirach 47:22).

---

[249] See Doble, (2000): Luke 2:12; Luke's apparently deliberate excision of Solomon from Jesus' genealogy (contra Matt. 1:6), and the probable significance of Solomon's ghostly presence in Stephen's speech combine to focus my mind on "house" in 2 Sam. 7:13, 16, 18–19, 25–26, especially 27, and the word's consequent bivalence in Stephen's speech and its intertextualities.

[250] Sirach 47:20 – ἔδωκας μῶμον ἐν τῇ δόξῃ σου καὶ *ἐβεβήλωσας τὸ σπέρμα σου ἐπαγαγεῖν ὀργὴν ἐπὶ τὰ τέκνα σου καὶ κατανυγῆναι ἐπὶ τῇ ἀφροσύνῃ σου.*

[251] Luke 11:27–36.

[252] See, e.g., Strauss (1995); Miura (2007).

[253] Sirach 47:20; cf. Luke's genealogy of Jesus from which Solomon is significantly absent.

75

From the outset, Luke has Jesus fulfilling God's long-unfulfilled promise to David, by implication filling the vacancy that Solomon's folly caused. Something greater than Solomon is here: a root from David himself, and raised up by God in more than one sense; one who died obedient to the death, the δίκαιος who at the judgment will stand, confronting his confounded persecutors. In Luke-Acts the Temple is standing; Jesus," the Son of Man's proclamation (κήρυγμα) that God is King demands of the Temple authorities a profound change of heart, mind, being and practice, a turning away from Mammon[254] to rediscover and reaffirm their serving God alone. Jesus *cleansed*, not threatened, God's house of prayer.[255] In this narrative, the conditional promise respecting the Temple remains (Isa. 55–66). The following sign is also related to the Temple and to the Son of Man.

> "As for these things that you see, the days will come when not one stone [of Jerusalem's Temple] will be left upon another; all will be thrown down." They asked him, "Teacher, when will this be, and *what will be the sign* that this is about to take place?" (Luke 21:6–27).

We discuss this long passage in Chapter 9, where false witnesses corrupt Jesus' word, framing a charge against Stephen that echoes Mark's and Matthew's accusations that Jesus said that he would destroy the Temple.[256]

The sign that Jesus offers his questioners is essentially that of the Son of Man's coming in a cloud with power and great glory, preceded, however, by the chaos generated by human disobedience. This eschatological timetable, like the passage discussed above, forms a part of Luke's distinctive Son of Man

---

[254] See Luke 16:13, an aphorism at the heart of the journey to Jerusalem to confront those rulers who refuse to give God his due, those among the rich who overlook the poor.

[255] Luke 19:45–48; see Ch. 7.

[256] Mark 14:53–64; Matt. 26:57–66.

trajectory, a trajectory that passes through the Sanhedrin's questioning before Jesus' condemnation[257] and, later, their hearing Stephen's witness that Jesus, Son of Man, was standing at God's right hand in God's glory.[258] Stephen's *apologia* hinges on "this house," Jerusalem's Temple, and on Solomon, but his final testimony to Jesus, the now exalted Son of Man, brings Luke's long conflict narrative to its decisive end; Jesus has completed his ἔξοδος in Jerusalem (Luke 9:31).

---

[257] Luke 22:69.

[258] Acts 7:55–56.

B. Age note (c). The boy and the Temple post-Passover

τί ὅτι ἐζητεῖτέ με; οὐκ ᾔδειτε [...] ὅτι ἐν τοῖς τοῦ πατρός μου δεῖ εἶναί με (Luke 2:49).

In Luke-Acts, these are Jesus' first words, and the final part of Luke's introducing Jesus. Consequently, they are probably of significance for the following twofold narrative. Arguably, they are pre-echoes of Luke's conflict narrative. Other pre-echoes are possibly present here too: the parents' day's journey from Jerusalem before returning; their three days' searching;[259] the question τί ὅτι ἐζητεῖτέ με;[260] are all linguistic links with Luke 24. I have argued elsewhere for a Solomon echo in Luke's Prologue.[261] Jesus' question, addressed to Mary to answer her question – "Why did you treat us in this way?"[262] – raises puzzling issues.

First, the interesting use of ᾔδειτε, a pluperfect of οἶδα, makes one wonder what Mary should already have known from her past. Second, the following clause reports that she should have known something of the necessity of Jesus' actions. In δεῖ εἶναί με, Luke's plan-of-God verb δεῖ makes its first Lukan appearance, revealing that Mary's son had to be ἐν τοῖς τοῦ πατρός μου. Third, that phrase's πατήρ has three possible antecedents, decision among which is of great interpretative significance:

> Joseph (e.g., 2:33; 2:48, 49);
>
> God (Luke 1:32, 35); or
>
> David (1:32, Δαυὶδ τοῦ πατρὸς αὐτοῦ).

---

[259] See Elliott, J K (1972).

[260] The similar pattern, "Why are you seeking?" / "remember" characterizes Luke's empty tomb scene: τί ζητεῖτε τὸν ζῶντα μετὰ τῶν νεκρῶν; [...] μνήσθητε ὡς ἐλάλησεν ὑμῖν ἔτι ὢν ἐν τῇ Γαλιλαίᾳ (Luke 24:5–6).

[261] See Doble (2000).

[262] τέκνον, τί ἐποίησας ἡμῖν οὕτως; ἰδοὺ ὁ πατήρ σου κἀγὼ ὀδυνώμενοι ἐζητοῦμέν σε.

Commentators tend to infer from Luke 1:32–35[263] that at 2:49 Jesus' filial relation with God is in view. I have argued that Luke's repeated κληθήσεται[264] should be taken seriously and seen as fulfilled by Jesus' anointing (3:22). This would accord with tradition's consistent reporting that Jesus was David's son.[265]

What Mary should have known was what Gabriel had revealed to her: that her son would be great, called the son of the Most High and that the Lord God would give him the throne of his father David; that he would reign over Jacob's house for ever.[266] That πατήρ is almost certainly the antecedent of the noun at 2:49. It would be banal to choose the alternative Joseph, who is himself of the house of David.[267]

The young man seated among the teachers in the Temple, asking questions and demonstrating understanding,[268] had to be involved in matters relating to his father David. If, this ἐν τοῖς τοῦ πατρός μου covers the affairs of and in David's house,[269] then it sets the scene for Luke-Acts' conflict narrative where the bivalence of David's house will be as much a Lukan David-promise's concern as its ἀναστήσω τὸ σπέρμα σου.[270]

C. Abraham in Luke-Acts

What God to Abraham revealed

---

[263] See, e.g., Green (1997), on Luke 10:21.

[264] Luke 1:32, 35; cf. 2 Sam. 7:14, ἐγὼ ἔσομαι αὐτῷ εἰς πατέρα, καὶ αὐτὸς ἔσται μοι εἰς υἱόν.

[265] E.g., Luke 18:38–39; 20:41–44; Rom. 1:3 τοῦ γενομένου ἐκ σπέρματος Δαυὶδ κατὰ σάρκα, see Peacocke, A., (2016).

[266] Luke 1:32–33.

[267] Luke 1:27; 2:4–7; 3:23–31.

[268] See WisdSol. 8:10.

[269] E.g., Luke 1:27, 69; 2:4.

[270] See Ch. 7.

He to the shepherds doth accord
to see fulfilled.
To shepherds, lo! Our gracious Lord
His purposes unfoldeth.
That blessing which in days of old
He to a shepherd first foretold
A shepherd first beholdeth.

(J S Bach *Christmas Oratorio,*

Pt II.14).[271]

Bach's librettist, possibly C F Henrici, was both a late tradent of Luke-Acts' reception history, and, through Bach's music, a powerful advocate of its valuing Abraham. So why, a friend enquired, had I ignored Abraham as a candidate for Luke's Jesus-triptych? That question is strengthened by two of Luke's canticles.[272] But I have not ignored Abraham[273] who is an unaccented Lukan theme integral to *Interpreter's* understanding of Luke-Acts' subtext. Luke's story is essentially about what the God of Abraham, Isaac and Jacob has done; he also presents Jesus as a son of Abraham, fulfilling one distinctive foundation promise in Israel's story, but subordinate to its focal promise to David.[274]

1. Canticles

Luke-Acts' argument is essentially about events in David's house, viewed from its distinctive perspective on the suffering and resurrection of God's Messiah. Promises to both Abraham and David speak of their "seed"; only that to David links "seed" with "ἀναστήσω." Two David-promises feature in Luke-Acts'

---

[271] (Sevenoaks, Kent: Novello; choir copy of 2008); Englished by Revd Dr J. Troutbeck.

[272] See, e.g., Green (1997), 52–55. Luke's "pervasive interest" in the Abrahamic material is beyond question; *Interpreter* is concerned with the focal *Problématique* of Luke's story amid its mass of detail.

[273] Abraham is named twenty-one times in Luke-Acts; in Acts 3 and 7.

[274] David has twenty-four Lukan references; those in Acts 2, 4, 7, 13 and 15.

annunciations,[275] each characterised by that ἀναστήσω. Two canticles reflecting on Jesus' birth interpret it within Abraham's continuing story. Luke's twice explicating an annunciation by a canticle enables him to root his Jesus-narrative in a Jewish context that looks towards God's wider blessing of the world's peoples.[276] In Chapter 2 we explored both annunciations, identifying 2 Sam. 7 and Ezek. 34 as base-texts for a promise of resurrection, neither of which refers to Abraham. The canticles are pre-drama explanation; the exegetical speeches in Acts[277] are *post-eventum* interpretation of Jesus' suffering and resurrection, attentive to his *logia*.

Both characters who received an angelic annunciation reflectively hymned God: Mary, in her *Magnificat*,[278] Zechariah in his *Benedictus*.[279] Each celebrated what God had proleptically accomplished as within God's foundation-purposes for Israel and promised to Abraham: Mary sings of God's bringing to mind his mercy as he helped Israel – by her son's agency;[280] Zechariah also speaks of God's mercy and bringing to mind his holy covenant, that mercy promised to the fathers.[281] Each of them celebrates a promised event within David's house.[282] Luke's genealogy,[283] Jesus' lineage by "seed,"

---

[275] See Gerber, D, (2008).

[276] Gen. 22:15; 26:4.

[277] *Interpreter,* Acts 4–7.

[278] Luke 1:46b, Μεγαλύνει ἡ ψυχή μου τὸν κύριον.

[279] Luke 1:68, Εὐλογητὸς κύριος ὁ θεὸς τοῦ Ἰσραήλ.

[280] Luke 1:55, καθὼς ἐλάλησεν πρὸς τοὺς πατέρας ἡμῶν, τῷ Ἀβραὰμ καὶ τῷ σπέρματι αὐτοῦ εἰς τὸν αἰῶνα. Cf. Gen. 22:15–18; 26:4.

[281] Luke 1:72–73, μνησθῆναι διαθήκης ἁγίας αὐτοῦ, ὅρκον ὃν ὤμοσεν πρὸς Ἀβραὰμ τὸν πατέρα ἡμῶν, τοῦ δοῦναι ἡμῖν.

[282] E.g., Luke 1:27, 69. Each Lukan canticle recalls God's "bringing to mind" his compassion (μνησθῆναι ἐλέους 1:54) or his covenant (ποιῆσαι ἔλεος μετὰ τῶν πατέρων ἡμῶν καὶ μνησθῆναι διαθήκης ἁγίας αὐτοῦ, 1:72; cf. Gen. 12:1–3; 15:1–21).

[283] Luke 3:23–38.

contrasts with that in Matthew, whose work begins with "Jesus the Messiah, the son of David, the son of Abraham." Luke's narrative almost takes that for granted, emphasizing, rather, Jesus' Davidic, non-Solomonic descent, ultimately from Adam as God's son.

2. Exegetical speeches

Chapter 3 focuses on *Interpreter*'s focal verses: there Jesus' disputed *logia* about the scriptures and Messiah's destined suffering and resurrection are related first to "Moses and all the prophets,"[284] and later to "the law of Moses, the prophets, and the psalms."[285] Chapter 1 has set out how exegetical speeches use these scriptural categories; Torah patently offered Luke both the promise to Abraham detailed in Genesis 22:15–18, reaffirmed in 26:4, and that to Moses of a prophet like himself (Deut 18:15–18).

Peter's key speech in Solomon's Portico[286] is framed by an Abraham *inclusio*,[287] arguing by means of *haruzin* that because Jesus had been raised, glorified, his Abrahamic descent entailed the retrospective fulfilment of the Genesis promise.

Similarly, Stephen's speech,[288] ostensibly a retelling of Israel's story, opens with the God of glory appearing to Abraham[289] and ends with a vision of Jesus, Abraham's seed, standing vindicated in the glory of God.[290] Within that

---

[284] Luke 24:27.

[285] Luke 24:44.

[286] Chapter 4.

[287] Acts 3:13, 25–26.

[288] See Ch. 7.

[289] Ὁ θεὸς τῆς δόξης ὤφθη τῷ πατρὶ ἡμῶν Ἀβραὰμ (Acts 7:2).

[290] Acts 7:55–56.

inclusio stands a narrative-midrash on Israel's exodus from oppression, foreseen in the dark side of Abraham's theophany.[291]

Again, Paul's sermon[292] at Antioch embraces fellow Jews[293] and God-fearers in a message of salvation that turns out to be the fulfilment of the David-promise in and through Jesus. From David's seed[294] came Israel's Saviour who fulfilled "for us" the promise made to "the fathers"; who was raised up in both senses of that word.[295] Given Paul's brotherly form of address to the Antioch congregants within the systematic argument of his exegetical speech, he, like Peter, probably understood this Jesus whom God raised up to be Abraham's seed. Abraham is integral to Luke-Acts, but not the focus of its narrative purposes. *Interpreter* has affirmed Luke's careful placing of his focal concern, events in David's house, within Israel's ongoing story, itself rooted in Father Abraham.

D. Summary

This Note is appended to Chapter 2 to avoid distracting from the significance of his triptych for the whole narrative, especially its proclamation of Jesus' principal descriptors – Saviour, Messiah, Lord. A single-issue monograph such as this focuses on what is germane to its case's three sub-issues, and its holistic method remains aware of Luke-Acts' narrative structuring portrayed by the analytical diagram. It is now clearer that Luke's introduction to Jesus points forward to Jesus' destiny in Jerusalem. We have seen above in two age notes how the Prologue alerts readers to Luke's focus on Jerusalem's Temple, where Jesus will later return to be among, and speak truth to its teachers, and its rulers.

---

[291] Acts 7:6–7, cf. Gen. 15:7–16.

[292] See Ch. 8.

[293] Acts 13:16b, 26, υἱοὶ γένους Ἀβραὰμ [...] ἡμῖν ὁ λόγος τῆς σωτηρίας ταύτης ἐξαπεστάλη

[294] Acts 13:23, τούτου ὁ θεὸς ἀπὸ τοῦ σπέρματος κατ' ἐπαγγελίαν ἤγαγεν τῷ Ἰσραὴλ σωτῆρα Ἰησοῦν.

[295] Acts 13:32–41.

It also prepares readers for themes and an abundance of descriptors about which we shall have much to say.

Our thesis is that Luke is the interpreter of Jesus's story, and consequently of Israel's scriptures; that this story is of an intra-faith conflict, so that to all concerned Abraham's foundational story is of the utmost significance. For this interpreter Luke, as for Jewish practice, event controls interpretation: Luke's event is Jesus' appearance on Israel's stage as David's seed; his Kingdom-focused "ministry" that conflicted with Jerusalem's murderously powerful elite, and God's raising him from the dead, glorifying him. Luke later develops an argument to prove that this seed of David is also that seed of Abraham by whom all earth's peoples will find blessing. (Acts 3:18–26; Gen. 22:18).

Chapter 3. Luke 24: Luke's hinge chapter

Since Schubert (1957) published his seminal paper, Luke 24 has been much discussed. Often, the discussion has focused on the relationship between Luke and Acts. For example, BNTS seminar papers by Gregory (2005a) and by Rowe (2007a), an article by Bockmuehl (2005), and essays by Dupont (1967; 1984) and Marshall (1993), exemplify Luke 24's role in establishing whether we speak of Luke-Acts or of Luke and Acts. Relationships between Luke 9 and Luke 24 are also a well-worked field.

Here the focus is on ways in which Luke's chapter illuminates *Interpreter*'s thesis – itself generated by this hinge chapter. A distinctively Lukan, unified narrative in three scenes, played out on the "third day,"[296] Luke's account is focused on and shaped by one event, Jesus' resurrection.[297] Readers move from the women's encounter with the Shining Ones, through the apostles' scepticism and failure to understand, before reaching this narrative's climax in encounters with the living one.[298] It is one encounter in Jerusalem – Jesus' commissioning his witness-hermeneuts – that makes this hinge chapter the ground on which Luke builds his second volume; ground that he would not have prepared had he not intended that building.

Bock (2012: 129–130, 408) helpfully discusses Luke 24 but misses two important factors: first, he underplays Luke's narrative that constitutes Jesus' followers as hermeneuts; then, by accenting Luke's reference to the Messiah's

---

[296] See Aletti (1989: 179).

[297] On "resurrection" see, e.g., Barton and Stanton (eds) (1994), Wright (2003), Wedderburn (1999), Catchpole (2000) and Dunn (2002).

[298] Acts 1:3, governing Luke's narrative. See Sleeman (2009).

suffering, he misses Luke's focus on Jesus' resurrection.[299] The site of Jesus' transition from Son of Man talk to problematic talk of the Messiah is where both examples of Luke's alleged oxymoron occur; Luke's context for *Interpreter*'s problem verses also contributes to its solution. This transition is, however, the core of Luke's implied narrative answer for Theophilus' implied question – were that sect's claims about Jesus truly grounded in Israel's scriptures? These problems and their solutions coexist in Luke 24.

The three chapters after this one, in Part II, present a detailed case for Peter's scriptural reasoning focused on this bivalent ἀναστήσω within the apostolic kerygma. That is why this chapter focuses on Luke's hinge narrative. Luke 24 is (A) About Jesus; (B) About Jesus' Resurrection; (C) About Israel's Scriptures as they interpret Jesus' story. Discussing evidence from its scenes, we trace the shape of Luke's argument by isolating these three key features – the "things fulfilled among us" (Luke 1:1; cf. Acts 13:32–37).

---

[299] In addition to Bock, Green (1997: 848–849); Johnson (1991: 152, 282, 395–396); Just (1993: 14–25); Pao and Schnabel (2007: 400–401) and Strauss (1995: 255–258) accent Messiah's suffering, and from whose accounts *Interpreter* dissents.

A. About Jesus

1. From Son of Man to Messiah

Luke's transition from Son of Man to Messiah is possible only because Theophilus brings with him memory from Luke's narrative of who this Jesus really is:[300] David's seed (2 Sam. 7:12–16), anointed as Son of God (Ps. 2:7),[301] who having suffered (Ps. 2:1–2),[302] has been uniquely raised from the dead.[303] Luke 24 focuses on this risen Jesus. Readers need to sustain this focus – how otherwise did Theophilus hear this unprecedented shift from Son of Man to Messiah?[304] What else would have convinced him that the Messiah must suffer and be raised?

Theophilus will have recognized in this transition Jesus' reversal of Peter's confession and its accompanying talk of the Son of Man (Luke 9:18–22). In his Prologue Luke had established his work's Davidic scriptural reference-frame, carefully distinguishing Jesus, who is God's Messiah,[305] from John, who emphatically denies that this is his role.[306] Readers with Luke's scriptural frame in mind knew the David-promises; and Luke rooted Jesus firmly in two such David oracles.[307]

---

[300] The focus of Luke 9.

[301] "Son of God" belongs to Luke's cluster of descriptors associated with the David-promise (see Luke 1:32, 35; 3:21–22; 4:40–41; Acts 9:19b–22; 13:32–33).

[302] See Ch. 6.

[303] Luke 24:5b, echoing Exod. 3:6 (Luke 20:37–38).

[304] So Green (1997: 827).

[305] Luke 2:10–11; cf. 9:20, then 24:26–27, 44–47 where Jesus *himself* sets his life-story in the context of scripture.

[306] Luke 3:15–17; cf. 1:76–79; Acts 13:23–25; 19:1–7.

[307] Discussed in section A.

The Shining Ones, announcing Jesus' resurrection (ἠγέρθη), reminded the women – and readers – of Jesus' talk about his now-fulfilled future.[308] Luke's ἀναστῆναι here reflects the David-promise (ἀναστήσω), echoes Luke's distinctive 18:31–34,[309] and looks forward to his overt statement of the *logion*'s fulfilment.[310] If this is not what Theophilus heard, then Luke's account remains deeply problematic; if it approximates to what he heard, then Luke's narrative becomes coherent. This case is more fully argued in section B.

2. According to which scriptures?

A second, much-discussed, issue associated with Luke's alleged oxymoron emerges from each of its occurrences.[311] On the road to Emmaus, the risen Jesus' initial response to the travellers' report of the women at the tomb (Luke 24:22–24) is to marvel at his companions' slowness to believe all that the prophets had written (24:25). Then, himself transferring Son of Man talk to that of Messiah, Jesus speaks of the necessity of the Messiah's suffering and entering into his glory.[312] Explaining this saying, Jesus turns to Moses and all

---

[308] Luke 24:7, τὸν υἱὸν τοῦ ἀνθρώπου ὅτι δεῖ παραδοθῆναι εἰς χεῖρας ἀνθρώπων ἁμαρτωλῶν καὶ σταυρωθῆναι [...] καὶ τῇ τρίτῃ ἡμέρᾳ ἀναστῆναι.

[309] Παραλαβὼν δὲ τοὺς δώδεκα εἶπεν πρὸς αὐτούς· ἰδοὺ ἀναβαίνομεν εἰς Ἰερουσαλήμ,

καὶ τελεσθήσεται πάντα τὰ γεγραμμένα διὰ τῶν προφητῶν τῷ υἱῷ τοῦ ἀνθρώπου·

παραδοθήσεται γὰρ τοῖς ἔθνεσιν καὶ ἐμπαιχθήσεται καὶ ὑβρισθήσεται καὶ ἐμπτυσθήσεται καὶ μαστιγώσαντες ἀποκτενοῦσιν αὐτόν, καὶ τῇ ἡμέρᾳ τῇ τρίτῃ ἀναστήσεται. καὶ αὐτοὶ οὐδὲν τούτων συνῆκαν καὶ ἦν τὸ ῥῆμα τοῦτο κεκρυμμένον ἀπ' αὐτῶν καὶ οὐκ ἐγίνωσκον τὰ λεγόμενα.

[310] This verb–shift is equally clear in Paul's Antioch sermon (see Ch. 8).

[311] E.g., Bock (2012: 186–187, 417–419), accents Messiah's suffering and death, locating their scriptural root in Isaiah 53, and finds Jesus' resurrection rooted in Ps. 15. Bovon (2006: 103–106, 135–136) offers a helpful survey to that date.

[312] Luke 24:26; οὐχὶ ταῦτα ἔδει παθεῖν τὸν χριστὸν καὶ εἰσελθεῖν εἰς τὴν δόξαν αὐτοῦ; I take this ταῦτα to refer to both παθεῖν and εἰσελθεῖν, not accenting the suffering; cf. Acts 26:22–23.

the prophets to interpret the things about himself.[313] Other than this broad sweep, Luke offers no referencing to scripture here.

Later, in the upper room, addressing his followers, the risen Jesus repeats that pattern: first, everything written about him (περὶ ἐμοῦ) in Moses, prophets and psalms had to be fulfilled, implying the necessity of the Messiah's suffering and being raised from the dead. Again, Luke offers no referencing to scripture here, other than the prophets.

Interpreter's case is that Luke's following verses (24:45–49) prepare Theophilus for what unfolds in Luke's second volume. Acts is Luke's account of Jesus' witnesses who argue from scripture that the Messiah is Jesus and that God raised him from the dead according to the scriptures. In six speeches that typify an activity that dominates his narrative, Luke reveals the core of what Jesus had taught his witnesses. Their minds have been opened to understand scripture (24:45); they are witnesses of these things (24:48); they are to be empowered for this task (24:49). They have become Jesus' scriptural hermeneuts. In Acts, the vagueness of 24:26 and 44 gives way to the precision of resurrection as his followers' hermeneutic key as they reason principally from God's David-promises.

3. Luke's transition

Notably, Luke has so written his distinctive resurrection narrative that readers must engage with Jesus' reversal of events in Luke 9. Peter's Messiah was refined by Jesus' Son of Man (Luke 9:18–22). The risen Jesus himself then transitions the Shining Ones' talk of this Son of Man into his renewed use of "Messiah."

---

[313] τὰ περὶ ἑαυτοῦ parallels the travellers' τὰ περὶ Ἰησοῦ τοῦ Ναζαρηνοῦ (24:19), expanded in the following verses (24:19b–24).

89

What evokes discernment in Luke-Acts' narrative is a reader's knowing and remembering both what God had promised and had done through this Jesus. Luke had introduced Jesus through a triptych's evoking two oracles – ἀναστήσω. In the opening verses of this hinge chapter, echoing the Prologue's angelic announcement of Jesus' birth, Luke offers an angelic announcement of Jesus' resurrection (ἠγέρθη/ἀναστῆναι).

Later, in Antioch's synagogue, Paul overtly unpacks the ἀναστήσω of both of these David-oracles, so that for the remainder of Luke-Acts no reader can be in doubt that in Jesus God had fulfilled the David-promises by anointing him with Holy Spirit and by raising him from the dead. Luke's scriptural argument is shaped by this *inclusio* where what the Prologue initially implied is almost explicitly spelt out in a narratively significant synagogue sermon by a major character arguing from God's bivalent ἀναστήσω.[314]

At his tomb, the women did not find the body of the Lord Jesus (Luke 24:3). On the road to Emmaus, "Jesus himself" (αὐτὸς) was present (Luke 24:15; cf. 36). On that road, the conversation evoked from the travellers a primitive kerygma, "the things about Jesus."[315] Responding, Jesus spelt out for them from scripture "the things about himself."[316] Again, Jesus "himself" (αὐτὸς) was present at his appearance to the assembled followers (Luke 24:36).

From the outset it is important to affirm Jesus' focal role because discussion of this chapter sometimes fails to recognize the force of Luke's narrative use of both Son of Man and Messiah as descriptors. Descriptors use symbolic language, derived from Israel's hope, to make sense of an otherwise inexplicable event. That event, however, adapts, without breaking both symbolic descriptors, to make sense of one person, Jesus.

Further, Luke's chapter is about the Jesus who is the focus of Luke's whole narrative for Theophilus and whose story is rooted in Luke's reference-

---

[314] See Ch. 8.

[315] Luke 24:19; τὰ περὶ Ἰησοῦ τοῦ Ναζαρηνοῦ.

[316] Luke 24:27; τὰ περὶ ἑαυτοῦ

90

frame.[317] For Luke, it is what happens to this person, his event, that is understood by reference to symbols, not the other way round. To make sense of what Luke is doing, *Interpreter* unpacks three scenes in Luke 24 as scenes about Jesus.

This unpacking begins from what Luke's alleged oxymoron's occurrences have in common: Messiah, suffering and resurrection. Notably, both of these Messiah sayings (Luke 24:26, 46) are attributed to Jesus himself. Formally, both sayings substantially parallel Jesus' more traditional *logion* earlier recalled from the Galilee period by the two Shining Ones at Jesus' empty tomb: "The Son of Man must (δεῖ) suffer and be raised (ἀναστῆναι)" (Luke 24:7); note that at both 24:7 and 24:46 Luke uses ἀναστῆναι for "to raise"; but Messiah and Son of Man are Luke's ways of talking about one specific person, Jesus.

In his Infancy Gospel Luke established the scriptural frame within which readers are to understand Jesus' story. Luke's concept of Messiah is governed by the manner of his introducing Jesus to readers, focused by God's promise – ἀναστήσω – and where Jesus is of David's seed.

B. About Jesus' resurrection

Luke narrates Jesus' resurrection through three key scenes.

1. At the tomb (Luke 23:55–24:12)

The characters in this scene are the women and two Shining Ones, later called "angels" (Luke 24:4, 23). Adapting Mark, Luke reports the core of the empty tomb tradition: the women came to Jesus' tomb very early in the morning on the first day of the week (Luke 24:21b; cf. 23:56), that is, "on the third day." They found no body. Distinctively, Luke has the Shining Ones interpret this event for

---

[317] See Ch. 2.

91

the women and his readers. Their interpretation has two layers: they first pose a question that evokes Jesus' discussion of resurrection in general terms (Luke 20:27–40); then, uniquely, they bid the women remember not a general, but this unique case. Each element is distinctive; each important to Luke's scriptural reasoning.

i. Question

"Why are you looking for the living [one] among the dead?"[318] The Shining Ones' question evokes a memory of Jesus' response to Sadducees' taunting about resurrection,[319] a scene drawn from the Jesus-tradition.[320] But in Luke-Acts, the Bush acquires a life of its own. Part of an active subtext shaping Luke's thought-world and narrative theology, it emerges in Luke's tomb-narrative (Luke 24:5); is taken up by the travellers to Emmaus (Luke 24:23); then appears briefly at Acts 1:3. Later, the Bush and tomb narratives govern both Peter's address explaining a lame man's healing by Jesus' name (Acts 3:13–26) and Stephen's response to a Sadducee-dominated Sanhedrin (Acts 7:1–56).[321] The Shining Ones' question is thus part of Luke's living tradition, as is their following injunction to remember.

ii. Remember

Their injunction is addressed to named women (Luke 24:10). Luke's narrative, however, is addressed to Theophilus; no subsequent reader can safely ignore this narrative signal, for what one remembers contributes to answering the

---

[318] τί ζητεῖτε τὸν ζῶντα μετὰ τῶν νεκρῶν; Luke 24:5, 23; cf. Acts 1:3; 3:13, 26; diff. Mk and Mt.

[319] "Now he is God not of the dead (νεκρῶν), but of the living (ζώντων); for to him they are all living" (Luke 20:34–38).

[320] Luke 20:27–33; cf. Mark 12:18–27; Matthew 22:23–33.

[321] See Ch. 7; cf. Doble (2013).

Shining Ones' opening question. Luke reports that the women remembered Jesus' words, but not whether they here connected Luke 9:21 with 24:26. Notably, Luke adapted his earlier ἐγερθῆναι replacing it here (24:7) with ἀναστῆναι.[322] This change of verb proves significant for Luke's Son of Man–Messiah transits in chapters 9 and 24.[323]

The women are bidden remember what Jesus said while he was still in Galilee, that is, before 9:51 in Luke's narrative.[324] By that bidding, Luke reshaped Mark's *logion* about Galilee (Mark 16:7), radically solving the problem of where Jesus' appearances occurred. For the present, we prescind from that wider discussion to focus on Luke's narrative.

Luke 9 focuses on who this is,[325] a theme paralleled in Jesus' trial scene in Jerusalem (Luke 22:66–71). Each of these narratives successively treats Messiah, a term refined then by Son of Man, and finally fixed by Son of God. Remembering Galilee involves readers' taking seriously Luke's reshaping of Markan tradition into Luke-Acts' integrated summary of who Jesus is before the long journey to Jerusalem begins. What the Shining Ones bade the women

---

[322] For ἐγερθῆναι see Luke 9:22. See also Ch. 8. At Acts 13:30 and 13:37, ἤγειρεν signifies resurrection-event; at 13:33 and 34, God's ἀναστήσω implies fulfilment. Luke has reserved ἀνίστημι for Paul's re-interpreting his base-text – confirming Luke's uses of ἀνίστημι in Luke 18:31–34 and 24.

[323] By the close of his journey narrative, at Luke 18:31–34, Luke had already transformed his Galilean passion predictions into what appears to be his preparation for the Shining Ones' word to the women. Both are about events in Jerusalem, about Jesus' ῥῆμα and about the Son of Man. The earlier τελεσθήσεται πάντα τὰ γεγραμμένα διὰ τῶν προφητῶν gives way at the tomb to δεῖ. It follows that the futures of Luke 18 are replaced by the Shining Ones as infinitives: παραδοθήσεται by παραδοθῆναι; ἀποκτενοῦσιν by σταυρωθῆναι; τῇ ἡμέρᾳ τῇ τρίτῃ ἀναστήσεται by τῇ τρίτῃ ἡμέρᾳ ἀναστῆναι. In each case Luke's "raise up" verb (ἀναστήσεται, ἀναστῆναι) alerts readers to the David-promise. The parallels between the two passages are careful Lukan writing.

[324] Reshaped at Luke 18:31–34 to a form that affects 24:5b.

[325] A key question for Theophilus also, and one central to the synagogue activity reported in Acts – the Messiah is Jesus through whom God fulfilled the promises to David.

93

recall is an adapted, post-event conflation of two Lukan forms of Markan sources:[326]

> λέγων τὸν υἱὸν τοῦ ἀνθρώπου ὅτι δεῖ παραδοθῆναι εἰς χεῖρας ἀνθρώπων [ἁμαρτωλῶν] καὶ σταυρωθῆναι καὶ τῇ τρίτῃ ἡμέρᾳ ἀναστῆναι (Luke 24:7).

Luke has conflated:

- 9:22 εἰπὼν ὅτι δεῖ τὸν υἱὸν τοῦ ἀνθρώπου πολλὰ παθεῖν καὶ ἀποδοκιμασθῆναι [...] καὶ ἀποκτανθῆναι καὶ τῇ τρίτῃ ἡμέρᾳ ἐγερθῆναι with his already radically shortened
- 9:44 ὁ γὰρ υἱὸς τοῦ ἀνθρώπου μέλλει παραδίδοσθαι εἰς χεῖρας ἀνθρώπων,[327]

though in his account of the Last Supper (Luke 22:3–5, 21–23, 47–48) his distinctive focus on Judas' "betrayal" of Jesus implies the remainder of this Markan Son of Man saying.

Luke's adaptation, in the setting of Jesus' empty tomb, strongly suggests that his whole narrative from 9:21 to 9:44 is in view, together with its associated, surrounding material. One cannot have Jesus' sharp introduction of teaching about the Son of Man without Peter's answer (Luke 9:18–21) to Jesus' direct question and its ambient *vox pop* (Luke 9:7–9) around "who is this?" For Luke, Jesus' Son of Man talk is his reconceptualizing of Peter's "You are God's Messiah."

---

[326] E.g., σταυρωθῆναι for ἀποκτανθῆναι, and ἀναστῆναι for ἐγερθῆναι; Ch. 9's specific ἀποδοκιμασθῆναι ἀπὸ τῶν πρεσβυτέρων καὶ ἀρχιερέων καὶ γραμματέων has given way to the Shining Ones' simple ἁμαρτωλῶν despite Luke's Herod narrative (Luke 23:10–12) with its apparent fulfilment of Jesus' word. Formally, Dunn (2003: 868) notes "the absence of any reference to Jesus as the Son of Man in the accounts of resurrection appearances" but the narrative integrity of Luke 24 implies that together the Shining Ones and Jesus himself move from Luke 9:21–22 to 24:26, from Son of Man (24:7) to Messiah.

[327] Diff. Mark 9:30–32.

Luke 9 differs substantially from its parallels in Mark and Matthew, in that it is both tightened and distinctively sequenced.[328] Luke's narrative highlights the apostles' role,[329] but we attend to the distinctively Lukan sequencing around the theme, "who is this?" (Luke 9:7–9; 18b–19; cf. 7:49; 8:25). In Luke 9, this question is answered three times over, then – significantly – replayed at Jesus' trial among differing characters.[330] This is a significant question for Luke. One constant, however, remains: Jesus' affirmation of Son of Man talk (Luke 9:21; cf. 22:69).

iii. Who is this?

First, Peter responds that Jesus is God's Messiah (9:20). A reader knows that Peter has discerned who Jesus "is," for through Luke's Infancy triptych (Luke 1:26–38; 2:1–7; 2:8–20), Simeon's song of thanksgiving (Luke 2:25–35), Luke's distinctive reports of Jesus' anointing (Luke 3:21–22), his choice of text at Nazareth,[331] and demons' recognition (Luke 4:40–41), Luke established in his Prologue who Jesus "is."

But how did Peter reach his conclusion? Many commentators recognize the close relation between Peter's recognition of Jesus and its preceding "feeding" narrative. The Elisha feeding is linked to the Lukan conceptually and para-lexically by the italicized verses in "Elisha said, 'Give it to the people and let them eat.' But his servant said, 'How can I set this before a hundred people?' So he repeated, 'Give it to the people and let them eat, for thus says the LORD, They shall eat and have some left.'" (2 Kgs 4:42–44).

---

[328] Luke's Markan "omissions" are extensive.

[329] Luke 9:1–6; 10–17; *23–27*; 51–56. We defer discussion of the disputed Son of Man *logion* [ὁ γὰρ υἱὸς τοῦ ἀνθρώπου οὐκ ἦλθεν ψυχὰς ἀνθρώπων ἀπολέσαι, ἀλλὰ σῶσαι] that forms an *inclusio* with 19:10; in Lukan narrative terms, this *logion* most probably should be read, clarifying 9:23–27.

[330] Cf. Luke 22:66–71, where the same three descriptors appear, but in changed circumstances.

[331] Luke 4:18a; "The Spirit of the Lord is upon me, because he has anointed me (ἔχρισέν με)."

Jesus' questioning of the disciples (Luke 9:18–19) ended with Peter's recognizing how much more (*qal wa-homer*) than a prophet Jesus was: he fed at least fifty times as many people with a quarter of the number of loaves; and the distributors were left with a basketful each. Only John and Luke add an assessment of who Jesus is to this sign's narrative: John's Οὗτός ἐστιν ἀληθῶς ὁ προφήτης ὁ ἐρχόμενος εἰς τὸν κόσμον (John 6:14) conceptually parallels Peter's Τὸν Χριστὸν τοῦ θεοῦ (Luke 9:20), and his answer launched the whole Messiah/Son of Man tension of Luke's narrative.[332]

Few,[333] however, note the probable Lukan subtextual link among the shepherds' birth announcement (2:8–20), tradition's report of a feeding in Galilee and Ezekiel's hope of a Davidic Messiah.[334] A Luke who chose an Ezekiel-based birth announcement cannot have failed to recognize how important feeding was to that prophet's David-oracle. However right Peter may have been, synoptic tradition reports that Jesus immediately refined discussion of that descriptor among his followers.

Second, by speaking of the Son of Man, Jesus reconceptualizes – he does not reject – Peter's answer (Luke 9:20–22, 44). Tradition reported the core of Jesus' *logion* to Peter. But, for Luke, who alone undoes Jesus' instruction in 9:21,[335] this saying further shapes his concept of "Messiah," for what is said of the Son of Man is true of Jesus, who had suffered and had been raised. At Luke 9:44 we encounter another Son of Man saying, this time about his betrayal into men's hands, a *logion* lacking talk of suffering and resurrection. While Luke

---

332 See North W. E. S. (2015: 88 esp. n.26; 123–124) for discussion of ὁ ἐρχόμενος.

333 Dunn (2003: 191), is among those who draw attention to the Ezekiel link; he does not, however, associate it with a subtext that includes Luke's Infancy narrative.

334 Ezek. 34:7–10; food is in focus, presumably in many senses, including bread; contrast 34:23 – καὶ ἀναστήσω ἐπ' αὐτοὺς ποιμένα ἕνα καὶ ποιμανεῖ αὐτούς, τὸν δοῦλόν μου Δαυιδ, καὶ ἔσται αὐτῶν ποιμήν), where, ποιμανεῖ probably has the sense of "graze" or "pasture," cf. Ps. 22:1–3.

335 See section B2.

abbreviated Mark 9:31–2, he transmuted Mark's 10:45 into his distinctive Ezekiel-shaped summary of Jesus' ministry – "the Son of Man came to seek and to save what was lost" (Luke 19:10). Luke reports that Jesus' refinement was lost upon his apostles who neither understood the saying nor were willing to ask Jesus about the betrayal-saying (cf. Luke 18:31–34). We return to Luke's account of the women at the tomb.

iv. Remember what?

Each reader brings unique narrative memory to Luke's empty tomb narrative, which probably recalls Jesus' betrayal by Judas, Peter's denial, Luke's distinctive passion narrative. This chapter's emphasizing the third day (Luke 23:56b, 24:21) probably stirs memory of tradition's τῇ τρίτῃ ἡμέρᾳ ἀναστῆναι.[336]

The Shining Ones' two affirmations are mutually interpretative – their τί ζητεῖτε τὸν ζῶντα μετὰ τῶν νεκρῶν is distinctively Lukan, recalling Jesus' own scriptural case for resurrection (Luke 20:38). Their question is answered by their own "remember" spelt out by Luke 9 summarized. "Remember Galilee" recalls Jesus' Son of Man talk, evoking more from Luke 9 and its discussion of who this is who can be the living from among the dead (cf. Ps. 88:49–50).

At Jesus' tomb Luke juxtaposes two narratives: Luke 9 with 24. Before the tomb-encounter, this Jesus had already suffered, been raised and entered into his glory, and Luke will exploit this to the full in Paul's Antioch sermon, but in the succeeding, closely-related story of a walk to Emmaus, the risen Jesus himself reinterprets his followers' account of those women at the tomb (Luke 24:25–27).[337]

---

[336] Note Luke's verb, a clue to his story's thrust.

[337] For Paul's Antioch sermon, see Ch. 8.

2. To Emmaus (Luke 24:13–35)

This much-discussed narrative unit has gathered a vast secondary literature around it.[338] Notably, this is Luke's first report of an encounter with the risen Jesus,[339] and its essence is that Jesus himself, by transmuting the Shining Ones' Son of Man summary, undoes his earlier prohibition on Messiah-talk.[340] Luke's "unparalleled move" (Green 1997: 848–849) constitutes Luke's first, decisive instance of his alleged oxymoron: "were not these things necessary, that the Messiah should suffer, then enter into his glory?"[341]

Luke's story has three characters, two of them named. Like its predecessor, this scene is set on the third day. Luke quickly establishes this scene's point as he brings Jesus into the narrative: "Jesus himself" (αὐτὸς Ἰησοῦς); the living from among the dead;[342] the Son of Man who, in Galilee had spoken of suffering and resurrection to uncomprehending followers;[343] the Jesus whose tomb women found to be empty. It is this Jesus who interprets events for two travellers to Emmaus.

Of these travellers, one can say little; one is named Kleopas. By "two of them" (δύο ἐξ αὐτῶν) Luke implies male disciples of Jesus from among those who treated the women's report as utter nonsense (λῆρος). Luke swiftly focuses on the travellers' conversation about "all these things that had happened" (περὶ πάντων τῶν συμβεβηκότων τούτων),[344] and their spelling out for their unrecognized companion what concerned them (Luke 24:19–24) – the things

---

[338] E.g., Dillon (1978); Fitzmyer (1978); Hays (2015); Just (1993). See also Read-Heimerdinger and Rius-Camps (2002).

[339] Deferring the question of Peter's meeting with Jesus (24:12, 34; cf. 1 Cor. 15:5; Jn 21:1–19).

[340] Luke 9:21.

[341] Luke 24:26; οὐχὶ ταῦτα ἔδει παθεῖν τὸν χριστὸν καὶ εἰσελθεῖν εἰς τὴν δόξαν αὐτοῦ;

[342] Luke 24:5, 23b; cf. 20:27–40; Ps. 88:49–50.

[343] Luke 24:7.

[344] Which in Jesus' hands (24:25–27) quickly becomes "the things fulfilled among us" (Luke 1:1–4).

concerning Jesus *Nazoraios*.[345] Most commentaries discuss the literary and theological processes of this first encounter and its assessment of who Jesus is. We, however, shall focus sharply on the structural centre of Luke's story, the travellers' account of the women's experience at the tomb:[346]

> Yet [ἀλλὰ καὶ], some women from among us astonished us. They had been at the tomb early [this] morning, and not having found his body, they came back saying that they had also seen a vision of angels who said that he was alive [οἳ λέγουσιν αὐτὸν ζῆν]. Some of those with us went to the tomb and found it just as the women said; but him they did not see (Luke 24:22–4).

Luke's irony is complete; their not-seeing typifies Jesus' followers. To interpret those events – τὰ περὶ Ἰησοῦ – Luke turns to the one whom none had "seen." Jesus interprets events in two ways: by transforming the Shining Ones' Son of Man saying (24:6–7) into a Messiah saying; then, by setting "the things about himself" (24:26b; τὰ περὶ ἑαυτοῦ) within the framework of Israel's scriptures. This verbal inversion is to be taken seriously.

i. Jesus and the transforming shift

Luke's scene makes Jesus both his first and authoritative interpreter of scripture, and his first proclaimer of this formula that underlies early Christian proclamation (see Rom. 1:1–6; 1 Cor. 15):[347]

> were not these things necessary,
> that the Messiah should suffer and enter into his glory? (Luke 24:26).

---

[345] τὰ περὶ Ἰησοῦ τοῦ Ναζαρηνοῦ/Ναζωραῖος, reading *v*/ Ναζωραίου. This contrast is a Lukanism; "Jesus *Nazoraios*" signals Jesus' publicly known ministry, followed by a contrasting proclamation of who he "really" is. Of fourteen appearances of *Nazoraios* in the NT, two are in Luke (18:37; 24:19 *v*/) and seven in Acts (2:22; 3:6; 4:10; 6:14; 22:8; 24:5; 26:9).

[346] Their report is this story's structural centre, for Luke's scene is a balanced inversion with Jesus' empty tomb central.

[347] The following scene (Luke 24:44–49) has Jesus equip his followers as hermeneuts in his cause.

99

For Luke, Jesus' suffering and resurrection, τὰ περὶ ἑαυτοῦ, illuminate scripture.[348] And, in Acts, exploring scripture's role in these "things about him" will characterize the apostles' Jerusalem ministry and dominate Paul's synagogue activity.[349]

In Luke-Acts, "the things about Jesus" began with two prophets – Samuel and Ezekiel. Remembering, important for women at the tomb, and for travellers to Emmaus, remains so for all Luke's readers. Luke has, of course, appealed to other prophets than these, but his David-matrix including his base-text is plainly his subtext here also. Emmaus's focal event is Jesus' empty tomb (Luke 24:22–24); Luke has now told this story twice. The women had fruitlessly reminded his followers what Jesus had said about the Son of Man's now-fulfilled destiny – that, after betrayal and suffering, on the third day he must be raised (ὅτι δεῖ [...] τῇ τρίτῃ ἡμέρᾳ ἀναστῆναι).

Apart from two narrative prompts (Luke 24:17b, 19), in this scene the unrecognized Jesus silently heard out the travellers. Then, for Luke, the first words of the risen Jesus apparently chide his companions for lack of understanding, for slowness to trust in what the prophets have said (24:25). Here, Luke's narrative turns from reported event, summarized by the travellers, to interpreted scripture, introduced by Jesus, is governed by the phrase, "the things about himself" (τὰ περὶ ἑαυτοῦ, 24:27b).

For these unperceiving travellers Luke's Jesus now speaks of the Messiah who, readers remember, had been announced by Luke's introductory

---

[348] Ch. 7 summarizes Luke's uses of scripture.

[349] That this phrase is Lukan shorthand for his understanding of what God has done in/through Jesus is confirmed by its summarizing presence in both a note about Apollos (Acts 18:25, ἐδίδασκεν ἀκριβῶς τὰ περὶ τοῦ Ἰησοῦ) and twice in Luke-Acts' closing scenes – 28:23 (πείθων τε αὐτοὺς περὶ τοῦ Ἰησοῦ) and 28:32 (διδάσκων τὰ περὶ τοῦ κυρίου Ἰησοῦ Χριστοῦ). Jesus interpreted (διερμήνευσεν), Paul persuaded (πείθων), and both Paul (διδάσκων) and Apollos taught (ἐδίδασκεν) the "Jesus-things."

triptych where Samuel's "I will raise up (ἀναστήσω) your seed" and Ezekiel's "I will raise up (ἀναστήσω)" together promised fulfilled hope. The promises' verb (ἀναστήσω), coheres with the Shining Ones' revised ἀναστῆναι (Luke 24:7; cf. 9:21–22), and presages Paul's scriptural reasoning for Antioch's congregants where the prophets' ἀναστήσω is heard metaleptically (Acts 13:16b–41).[350] Luke's carefully developed concept of Messiah; his narrative's David-matrix; his focus on Jesus' resurrection, together ensure that this risen Jesus' first words emerge not as foolishness, but validation for Theophilus of what Jesus' followers were saying of him. In this, Luke's scriptural case resembles Paul's, as he of the letters introduces his gospel to the church in Rome (Rom. 1:1–6).

ii. Interpreting the scriptures – what is written

Jesus interpreted (διερμήνευσεν) the travellers' report by appealing initially to prophets (Luke 24:25–27).[351] Earlier,[352] we noted Samuel and Ezekiel as probable candidates here, for their oracles' detail made possible how Luke introduced Jesus.[353] Now note Jesus' question:

> Were not these things [ταῦτα] necessary [ἔδει],
>
> that the Messiah [τὸν χριστὸν] should suffer and enter into his glory? (Luke 24:26).

Luke's verb (δεῖ) has been explored so often that it needs no comment here, save that it signals God's plan, typically revealed through scripture. This verb's subject, however, is the plural "these things" (ταῦτα), indicating that what follows is not solely suffering. These "necessary things" are that the Messiah should

---

[350] See Ch. 8.

[351] It is the event that Jesus interpreted: διερμήνευσεν αὐτοῖς [...] τὰ περὶ ἑαυτοῦ, beginning with Moses and ranging over "all the scriptures."

[352] Ch. 1 Ch. 2.

[353] Already confessed by Christian tradition, e.g., Rom. 1:1–6.

suffer and enter into his glory, the latter (Luke 24:7) a Lukan phrase paralleling but differing from the Shining Ones' Son of Man summary.[354] Two differences stand out: "be raised" gives way to Jesus' "enter into his glory," and Son of Man to "Messiah." Each of those descriptors speaks of one or more aspects of Jesus' experience, drawing from various scriptural reservoirs of hope. What, then, of these two changes?

First, "entering into his glory" reconfigures talk of Jesus' resurrection and exalted state (Acts 3:13–26).[355] This phrase distinguishes Luke 9:26, where Luke's Jesus speaks of the Son of Man's ultimate glory.[356] It reappears in Luke's retelling tradition's story of Jesus' Transfiguration, the proleptic vision of his glory.[357] This thread opens Peter's speech in Solomon's portico (Acts 3:13), before culminating in Stephen's vision of an opened heaven, of God's glory,[358] and of the Son of Man at God's right hand,[359] fulfilling Jesus' own word about the Son of Man's destiny.[360] For Luke, Jesus' resurrection entails his exaltation.[361]

---

[354] Sharing strong Johannine resonances.

[355] See Ch. 5.

[356] Luke's *logion* differs from Mark's in its additional "when he comes in his glory" (Mk 8:38).

[357] Of the synoptists, Luke alone has "they saw his glory" (Luke 9:32).

[358] Ch. 7; Stephen "saw the glory of God and Jesus standing at the right hand of God" (Acts 7:55–56). Paralleling Acts 3:19–21, on Luke's time-scale, Stephen's vision has Jesus ascended, exalted but yet to come in his glory (Luke 9:26).

[359] where Luke's Jesus-story began, as God's glory shone around shepherds who heard of their Saviour's birth (Luke 2:8–20).

[360] At 22:69, Luke adapted Markan tradition while retaining its *gezerah shewa'* – Son of Man with Ps. 109:1. See Ch. 7.

[361] In Peter's speech (Acts 3:13–26), a balanced inversion, Luke's initial verb, ἐδόξασεν (glorified), is balanced by his metaleptic ἀναστήσας (by raising up); his address is manifestly about Jesus' resurrection (Acs 4:1–4), and at its heart stands his statement of the time on God's eschatological timetable – 3:19–21. God raised Jesus from the dead to God's right hand; he is yet to come in glory (Luke 9:26).

102

Second, we noted above the significance of Luke's formal undoing here of Jesus' earlier ban – rooted in tradition – on talk of Messiah; a seemingly odd ban in view of Christian proclamation of Jesus as Messiah.[362] In this Emmaus scene, Luke has placed the alleged oxymoron on the lips of Jesus himself – who has suffered and been raised. We have been at pains to highlight that Luke conceptualized the word Messiah from his Prologue. In the context of his carefully conceptualized Messiah theme Luke's narrative tells of Jesus conceived and anointed, that is, "raised up" as Messiah; who said that the Son of Man must suffer and be raised; who has suffered, who has been raised.[363]

Luke's Jesus walked the Son of Man's path to its vindication (was raised from the dead), so Messiah-talk is now possible. That poses the question of where in scripture one might find talk of a Messiah to be raised from the dead. Luke's Prologue holds his hermeneutic key: it lies in God's metaleptic promise, ἀναστήσω. Nathan's and Ezekiel's oracles have been fulfilled in two senses. From here forward, Luke's narrative is concerned with explaining for Theophilus what *God* has done, interpreted in its scriptural context.

iii. Jesus the interpreter

The unrecognized, risen Jesus interpreted (διερμήνευσεν) events and opened (διήνοιγεν) the scriptures: he becomes Luke-Acts' source of how to place this event in scripture. The event itself is clarified by the risen Jesus' not dissenting from the travellers' summary report of the things about Jesus *Nazoraios* (τὰ περὶ Ἰησοῦ τοῦ Ναζωραίου), but rather interpreting the things about himself (τὰ περὶ ἑαυτοῦ) from Moses and the prophets. Luke's balance of τὰ περὶ Ἰησοῦ τοῦ Ναζωραίου and τὰ περὶ ἑαυτοῦ typifies his structural skills, offering one way of "hearing" his story-telling.

---

[362] Luke 9:21–22 (cf. Mark 8:31; Mt. 16:21).

[363] Agreeing with Rom. 1; 1 Cor.; and repeatedly in Luke-Acts.

What travellers reported of Jesus' life and death is simple: Jesus was a prophet mighty in deed and word, who, they had hoped, was the one to redeem Israel, but the chief priests and rulers handed him over (παρέδωκαν) to be condemned to death and crucified him (Luke 24:19b–21a; 62 words).[364] However, the travellers devoted most of their report about Jesus to that morning's puzzling happenings, rehearsing the previous scene's account of the women at the tomb (in the next 67 words):[365]

> Yes, and besides all this, it is now the third day since these things happened. Moreover, some women from among us astounded us. They were at the tomb early this morning, and when they did not find his body there, they came back and told us that they had really seen a vision of angels who said that he was alive. Some of those who were with us went to the tomb and found it just as the women had said; but him they did not see (Luke 24:21b–24).

We may reasonably infer that this represents Luke's narrative balance – with resurrection looming largest in his thinking. At this point modern interpreters must make a key decision: does Luke invite them to follow clues from Jesus' disciples' hopes of his being their Redeemer, or to follow Jesus' interpreting the things about himself? What fits Luke's *apologia* for Theophilus?[366]

If we take our cue from the balance within Luke's Emmaus narrative, then his immediate concern is to root Jesus' resurrection in scripture.[367] In one sense, he has already done this through fulfilled Son of Man *logia*. Now Luke

---

[364] Παρέδωκαν: reflecting the Lukan 9:44; 18:31–33; 22:4, 21, 48; 24:7; cf. Dan. 7:25.

[365] Luke has placed all the events of Luke 24 on the third day. It is possible that Christian concern with God's ἀναστήσω led interpreters of Jesus' story to Hosea 6:1–3, with its "on the third day we shall be raised up, and we shall live before him" (ἐν τῇ ἡμέρᾳ τῇ τρίτῃ ἀναστησόμεθα καὶ ζησόμεθα ἐνώπιον αὐτοῦ).

[366] This is the nub of my dissent from the account of Luke's echoing in Hays (2015; 2016).

[367] Luke's store is probably bigger than his condensed *apologia* for Theophilus. Once Christians had Luke's hermeneutic key, they could explore further. Ch. 7 discusses some of these issues.

does it for Jesus himself who, in the preceding verse, has crucially embraced the title, Messiah. We reflect on Luke's sentence:

> And beginning from Moses and all the prophets
> he interpreted for them in all the scriptures
> the things about himself. (Luke 24:27)

First, beginning from Moses – why begin here? Tradition reported that Jesus' own *apologia* for resurrection was rooted in the Bush (Exod. 3:6; Luke 20:27–39). Jesus' "God of the living" (Luke 20:37–38) opens a distinctive Lukan thread that continues in the Shining Ones' question to the women at the tomb: "why seek the living among the dead?" (Luke 24:5, 23). It then shapes Luke's initial presentation of Jesus in his second volume (Acts 1:3). The Bush controls Peter's speech at Acts 3:13,[368] and thereafter Deut. 18:18 (Acts 3:22; 7:37) roots the resurrection of Jesus the prophet in God's promise through Moses to Israel:

> I will raise up [ἀναστήσω] for them
> from among their brothers a prophet like you (Deut. 18:18).[369]

Both the Jesus-tradition, and its discovery that ἀναστήσω may be read bivalently, root Christian resurrection talk in "Moses," where Jesus began.

Second, Luke's phrase "all the prophets" is controlled by those with whom this evangelist began his story of Jesus – with Samuel, and with Ezekiel.[370] We need, however, to reaffirm that Luke introduces Jesus to readers by two David-promise (ἀναστήσω) oracles and concludes his scriptural reasoning through his sole example of Paul's synagogue preaching – where he finally spells out what he implied from his work's beginning (Acts 13:16–41). Between those poles

---

[368] See Ch. 5.

[369] προφήτην ἀναστήσω αὐτοῖς ἐκ τῶν ἀδελφῶν αὐτῶν ὥσπερ σὲ (cf. Deut. 34:10–12).

[370] Ch. 7 summarizes Luke's uses of prophets, including reflection on Isaiah's role.

stands Luke 24, confirmed by six examples of Jesus' followers' exegetical proclamation.

Third, through Jesus, Luke opens one of his significant themes in Acts – interpreting scripture: "he interpreted for them" (*διερμήνευσεν αὐτοῖς*) the things about himself (*τὰ περὶ ἑαυτοῦ*) in all the scriptures. In the following scene we shall see how Moses and the prophets are joined by "the psalms" (Luke 24:44–49). But first, at Emmaus, after recognizing their companion, two followers reflected: "were not our hearts burning within us as he [...] opened up the scriptures for us?" (*ὡς διήνοιγεν ἡμῖν*, Luke 24:32). Interpreting, opening scriptures hereafter becomes the core of Luke's work for Theophilus who learns where and how it is written that the Messiah must suffer and be raised from the dead.

3. Equipping and commissioning (Luke 24:36–49)

This final scene, now set in Jerusalem, among Jesus' gathered followers, continues Luke's account of the third day. The scene divides readily into three distinct parts:

(a) Jesus' appearance to his followers (24:36–43);[371]

(b) his siting key events in scripture (24:44–47);

(c) Jesus' commissioning his followers (24:48–49).

Luke offers links back to Emmaus (e.g., Luke 24:26) and forward to Acts. A brief note of Jesus' exaltation (Luke 24:50–53), located in Bethany, concludes Luke's first volume. This scene's characters are the silent apostles and their companions and Jesus, who is its sole speaker.[372] Around two-thirds of the words in 24:36–49 are attributed to Jesus.[373] Of these, just over one third belong

---

[371] Dunn (2003: 849) notes the common core of the gospels' diverse stories.

[372] Luke 24:36b, 38b–39, 41b, 44b, 46b–49.

[373] In NA[27] this text (Luke 24:36–49) contains 202 words, of which 128 (63.4%) are allotted to Jesus.

106

to his "appearance,"[374] a fifth occur in his commissioning his followers.[375] Significantly, Jesus' own "placing" his suffering and resurrection in scripture account for nearing one half of his speaking.[376] This placing illuminates one core issue – were Christian claims about Jesus truly grounded in Israel's scriptures?

Here we focus on (b) and (c) – *Interpreter's* central concern.[377] Particularly, we explore "He opened their minds" (Luke 24:45),[378] a key phrase in Luke's hinge between his first and second volumes. Here, for a second time, Jesus affirms that scripture knows of *a* Messiah who must suffer and be raised. We turn first to his setting events in scripture.

i. Luke 24:44–47

Here, we meet Luke's second clear affirmation in this chapter of the rootedness of Jesus' story in scripture (cf. Luke 24:27). This verse's constituent parts need to be unpacked:

> εἶπεν δὲ πρὸς αὐτούς· οὗτοι οἱ λόγοι μου οὓς ἐλάλησα πρὸς ὑμᾶς ἔτι ὢν σὺν ὑμῖν, ὅτι δεῖ πληρωθῆναι πάντα τὰ γεγραμμένα ἐν τῷ νόμῳ Μωϋσέως καὶ τοῖς προφήταις καὶ ψαλμοῖς περὶ ἐμοῦ (Luke 24:44).

First, οὗτοι οἱ λόγοι μου οὓς ἐλάλησα πρὸς ὑμᾶς ἔτι ὢν σὺν ὑμῖν (Luke 24:44a). Most commentators find this Greek construction obscure.[379] In their readings, Johnson (1991: 402) and Fitzmyer (1985: 1582) produce something like "this is what I meant when I spoke with you during my pre-resurrection ministry."[380]

---

[374] (a) Luke 24:36–43; of the 128 words allotted to Jesus, 46 (c. 36%) belong to (a).

[375] (c) Luke 24:48–49; 26 words, making c. 20% of Jesus' 128.

[376] (b) Luke 24:44–47; 56 words, or c. 44% of the total (128).

[377] See Ch. 1.

[378] Cf. Mann (2016).

[379] E.g., Evans (1990: 921). I remain unconvinced that Luke was recalling the opening of Deuteronomy.

[380] Marshall (1978: 904) offers "this is what I told you," declining to follow Creed's lead in linking this sentence directly with Jesus' crucifixion and resurrection, Creed (1950: 300).

Such contrast-in-continuity between Jesus' earthly and exalted states belongs to Acts.[381] It was probably already implied by the Shining Ones' "remember" at the tomb (Luke 24:6–7). This verse also has its περὶ ἐμοῦ,[382] paralleling the περὶ ἐαυτοῦ of Emmaus (Luke 24:27), and again in a final, strong position. This "me" is Jesus, the protagonist of Luke-Acts, whose περὶ ἐμοῦ then governs both of the following constructions:

(a) δεῖ πληρωθῆναι πάντα τὰ γεγραμμένα. The phrase "everything that is written" remains governed and newly illuminated by Jesus' story (περὶ ἐμοῦ) – the "things" highlighted here, especially resurrection, that have been fulfilled.[383] They had to be fulfilled, because God had promised David "I will raise up" (ἀναστήσω) your seed after you. In Paul's Antioch sermon, we shall see how a preacher reasoned his case for God's raising Jesus as the fulfilment of that basic promise to David.[384]

(b) ἐν τῷ νόμῳ Μωϋσέως καὶ τοῖς προφήταις καὶ ψαλμοῖς. This is not a general reference to scripture, but, as we shall see in Part II, an indicator of what Luke actually used in the Acts speeches discussed by Interpreter.

Second, and significantly, Luke notes that Jesus appointed and equipped the Apostles as hermeneuts (24:45–47). Again, we examine this segment's constituent parts:

> τότε διήνοιξεν αὐτῶν τὸν νοῦν τοῦ συνιέναι τὰς γραφάς· καὶ εἶπεν αὐτοῖς ὅτι οὕτως γέγραπται παθεῖν τὸν χριστὸν καὶ ἀναστῆναι ἐκ νεκρῶν τῇ τρίτῃ ἡμέρᾳ, καὶ κηρυχθῆναι ἐπὶ τῷ

---

[381] See Sleeman (2009).

[382] Cf. Luke 24:19, 27; Acts 18:24–28, where τὰ περὶ τοῦ Ἰησοῦ probably has a technical sense, similar to that in Luke's Emmaus story, contrasting strongly with Jesus' correcting περὶ ἐμοῦ at Luke 24:44.

[383] Cf. Luke 1:1–4, περὶ τῶν πεπληροφορημένων ἐν ἡμῖν πραγμάτων.

[384] Acts 13:32–33: ὅτι ταύτην ὁ θεὸς ἐκπεπλήρωκεν τοῖς τέκνοις [αὐτῶν] ἡμῖν ἀναστήσας Ἰησοῦν ὡς καὶ ἐν τῷ ψαλμῷ γέγραπται τῷ δευτέρῳ· See Ch. 8.

ὀνόματι αὐτοῦ μετάνοιαν εἰς ἄφεσιν ἁμαρτιῶν εἰς πάντα τὰ ἔθνη (Luke 24:45–47).[385]

(a) τότε διήνοιξεν αὐτῶν τὸν νοῦν τοῦ συνιέναι τὰς γραφάς. We recall opened eyes at Emmaus and travellers recalling burning hearts within (24:32).[386] This opening, notably of their minds, marks a decisive change from Jesus' followers' earlier failure to understand him;[387] meaning must be determined by Luke-Acts' context. Jesus himself now equips them for their public role as witnesses. Luke here roots a Christian interpretative tradition in Jesus himself. Reading backwards from Acts to this passage clarifies its meaning.

(b) καὶ εἶπεν αὐτοῖς ὅτι οὕτως γέγραπται. The earlier περὶ ἐμοῦ still governs this passage's sense: "it is written about me." This reading then gives the sense of οὕτως γέγραπται as "it is written (about me) as follows" (cf. 24:26),[388] modified by three aorist infinitives, again relating to "me":

- Messiah's suffering: παθεῖν τὸν χριστὸν (further unpacking περὶ ἐμοῦ);[389]

- Messiah's resurrection from the dead: καὶ ἀναστῆναι (that Luke uses whenever fulfilment of the David-oracle is in focus) ἐκ νεκρῶν; Luke's

---

[385] Following the punctuation of NA²⁷ and the internal logic of this passage, I associate ἀρξάμενοι ἀπὸ Ἰερουσαλὴμ with ὑμεῖς μάρτυρες τούτων. Luke offers a similar construction at 24:27.

[386] See Mann, J. L. (2016).

[387] Luke 2:50; 8:10 (adapts Isa. 6:9); 18:34 (cf. 9:45); 24:45; Acts 7:25; 28:26–27 (cf. Isa. 6:9–10).

[388] Acts 1:20; 7:42; 13:29, 33; 15:15; 23:5; 24:14.

[389] Luke initially introduced Jesus as Messiah (Luke 2:11); Peter recognized him as "God's Messiah" (Luke 9:20); in Acts, his followers proclaimed him to be Messiah (e.g., 2:36; 3:18–20; 5:42; 9:20–22; 18:5); Paul's letter to Rome makes this affirmation the heart of his gospel (Rom. 1:1–6); Luke's two-volume work ends (Acts 28:30–31) by echoing its opening.

conclusion to his first volume, firmly places its events on the third day, τῇ τρίτῃ ἡμέρᾳ;[390]

- In the Messiah's name, Jesus' witnesses are to proclaim "repentance" to all nations: κηρυχθῆναι […] *μετάνοιαν εἰς ἄφεσιν ἁμαρτιῶν εἰς πάντα τὰ ἔθνη*. Luke's passive κηρυχθῆναι becomes in Acts the activity of those whom he commissions as his representatives.

Because the first two points comprise *Interpreter's* focus, the third, of great moment in Luke's narrative theology, will remain marginal, though visible. Repentance can be proclaimed, because in and through Jesus, God has decisively acted, and Jesus equipped and commissioned his representatives for precisely such proclamation. Once more, Luke assures Theophilus that Jesus' *sheluchim* were both authorized and competent to root their proclamation in Israel's scriptures – scriptures towards which he had directed their now opened minds.

ii. Luke 24:48–49

ἀρξάμενοι ἀπὸ Ἰερουσαλὴμ ὑμεῖς μάρτυρες τούτων. καὶ [ἰδοὺ] ἐγὼ ἀποστέλλω τὴν ἐπαγγελίαν τοῦ πατρός μου ἐφ' ὑμᾶς· ὑμεῖς δὲ καθίσατε ἐν τῇ πόλει ἕως οὗ ἐνδύσησθε ἐξ ὕψους δύναμιν. (Luke 24:48–49).

What Jesus' apostles and companions then do in Luke's second volume sheds light on this section of the first: they witness to and for Jesus, and they interpret his story in the context of Israel's hopes.

Beginning from Jerusalem (ἀρξάμενοι ἀπὸ Ἰερουσαλὴμ) they witness,[391] especially to Jesus' resurrection, for Acts 1:21–22 governs the remainder of

---

[390] Jesus' word that the Messiah must suffer and be raised is affirmed by Peter (Acts 3:18–21) and by Paul (e.g., Acts 17:3; 26:19–23). In later chapters we explore separately followers' words about Jesus' suffering and resurrection.

[391] By following NA[27] here, we detach this phrase from "it is written."

110

Luke's text.[392] "Of these things" (τούτων) must also refer to the contents of "thus it is written (about me)."[393] Defending his activity for Jesus (Acts 26:19–23), Paul makes this proclamation of repentance his Luther moment: "I have taken my stand."[394] Moreover, he bases this proclamation on what Moses and the prophets have said: "that the Messiah must suffer, and that, by being the first to rise from the dead, he would proclaim light both to our people and to the Gentiles" (26:23). Their witnessing, however, also interprets scripture. Chapters 4–6 focus on this dimension of Acts, where in six major speeches, and one culmination,[395] Jesus' followers exemplify their scriptural reasoning.[396]

First, in a mirror structure, Peter (and John) have three scripture-argued speeches: at Pentecost (Acts 2:14b–36); in the Temple precincts (3:12b–26); and before the Sanhedrin (4:8–12). In these speeches, there is resonance from the Shining Ones' instruction to the women to remember Jesus' words; Jesus, who had himself spoken of suffering (provocatively in the vineyard parable) and of his entering into glory. In three speeches Peter now interprets Jesus' words in the light of Jesus' resurrection.[397]

Second, Jesus' references to scripture-genre in Luke 24:44–49 are exemplified by three culminations of scriptural reasoning. We here move from remembering to interpreting Jesus' words. For example, in the prayer of Jesus' assembled followers (Acts 4), Luke shows by *pesher* how David's Psalm (2:1–2) spoke prophetically of Messiah's suffering. Addressing the largely Sadducean Sanhedrin (Acts 7:2–8:3), Stephen extended Jesus' appeal to

---

[392] See also Acts 2:32; 3:15; 10:41; 13:30–31.

[393] See the earlier bullet points in section 3i.

[394] ἕστηκα (Acts 26:22).

[395] The revelatory end of a long Lukan thread where he discloses where and how "it is written that the Messiah must suffer." (Acts 4:24–28; Ps. 2:1–2).

[396] See also Ch. 7 for culminations in Stephen's speech and Ch. 8 for Paul's synagogue sermon.

[397] Acts 4 moves seamlessly in one narrative unit, from the mirror structure to the apostles' interpreting scripture independently.

Moses as scriptural authority for resurrection by a metalepsis of Deuteronomy 18:18 (with its ἀναστήσω).[398] Arguably, and most significantly, by his metalepsis of the ἀναστήσω of Luke's Prologue's base-text, drawn from prophets, Paul at Antioch argues in condensed detail what it means to read Nathan's oracle in the light of God's having first anointed Jesus, then raised him from the dead.[399] These exegetical matters lie in the following chapters; first we reflect on uses of Israel's scriptures in Luke 24.

C. About Israel's scriptures

Interpreter's primary focus is on two problematic passages (Luke 24:25–27; 24:44–47).[400] Their nature prompted our discussion of Luke's concept of Messiah (see Chapter 2) and of a Messiah who must suffer and be raised (sections A and B). Here, we reflect on Luke's use of scripture: he began this in Luke 1, ending it only in Acts 28, as he takes leave of his readers.

Jesus' resurrection is the basic, consistent statement of his witnesses – God raised Jesus from the dead.[401] This gave Luke his hermeneutic key to God's newly-illuminated "I will raise up" (ἀναστήσω).[402] *Interpreter's* initial hypothesis postulates God's David-promise as Luke's frame of reference, establishing a David-matrix that opens in his Infancy Gospel, reaching its culmination in Paul's Antioch sermon.

Christian attention to Jesus' words will surprise no one who has taken Dunn (2013a) seriously on an oral tradition leading to the emergence of written

---

[398] Ch. 7.

[399] Ch. 8.

[400] We carry forward to Ch. 8 this preliminary reflection on "according to the scriptures."

[401] E.g., Acts 3:15; 4:10; 5:30; 10:40; 13:30, 37, where ἐγείρω indicates the resurrection event; see below.

[402] Luke tends to use ἀνίστημι to indicate the resurrection event in the context of promise fulfilled; e.g., Acts 2:24, 32 re: Ps. 131; Acts 3:26; 13:33, 34 re: Luke's base-texts; Acts 3:22; 7:37 re: Deut. 18:15.

112

gospels.[403] The Shining Ones' "remember" alerts readers to this attentiveness (Luke 24:6–8). Jesus' words from Galilee appear here as different yet recognizably the same,[404] adapted in the light of key events, echoing Jesus' ending-of-journey saying at 18:31–34, obscure then to his followers, clearer now. Similarly, in a key scene, Jesus' "these are my words" (Luke 24:44) takes this process forward as he commissions his witnesses. That the Messiah must suffer and be raised from the dead is the burden of many of the Acts speeches and of summaries of disciples' activity. Chapters 4–6 explore the role of "twoness" in Luke's using Jesus' words. From Luke's narrative of the third day's events, readers learn that all talk of Messiah's suffering and resurrection is rooted in Jesus' final words and in Israel's scriptures.

In both the Emmaus and commissioning sections of this chapter Luke presents Jesus as interpreter of events (Luke 24:14, 18–19, 44): from the "things about Jesus" (τὰ περὶ Ἰησοῦ) to "the things about himself" (τὰ περὶ ἐαυτοῦ) Luke's Jesus himself makes sense of them by interpreting scripture (Luke 24:27, 44). Luke's way of establishing this authority also claims attention: it is Jesus' opening of eyes and of scriptures (Luke 24:32, 45) that leads into ways in which his followers then understand (Luke 24:45) and interpret scripture for others. Chapters 4–6 show how Jesus' followers actually unpack Jesus' "Moses, Prophets, and Psalms" (Luke 24:44) in their speeches.

From existing tradition Luke drew both Exod. 3:6 (the Bush) and Jesus' Son of Man sayings.[405] The Shining Ones developed both traditions: they speak of Jesus as the "living [from] among the dead,"[406] and of the implied fulfilment of his Son of Man *logia*. Luke has Jesus take up, and transfer to the Messiah's resurrection, traditional talk of the Son of Man's "glory" (Luke 24:26; cf. 9:26) –

---

[403] Cf. Kirk, A. (2018).

[404] Cf. Dunn ([1996] 2016: 4–5).

[405] Probably rooted in Daniel 7.

[406] Echoing Jesus' *logia* in his case for "resurrection" (Luke 20:27–38).

113

"that the Messiah should suffer these things and then enter into his glory." In that phrase, both resurrection and ascension are in focus. Thereafter, Peter's "glorified" includes this Messiah's being in heaven, waiting to be revealed at God's right time.[407] In such ways, Jesus' tradition is illuminated not only by the event of the resurrection, but by Luke's understanding of how Jesus interpreted it for his followers.

---

[407] Acts 3:19–21; cf. 2:32–36; Ps. 109:1.

D. Summary

This chapter has addressed two of *Interpreter*'s key problems: (a) the transition in Luke 24 from Jesus' Son of Man sayings to (b) his refining the concept of Messiah who must suffer and be raised from the dead/enter into his glory. Both the transition and the refinement were effected by Luke's chiastic uses of ἀνίστημι and τὴν δόξαν αὐτοῦ; the former recalls its bivalent use for resurrection inspired by God's promise to David; the latter appropriates the Son of Man's δόξα to clarify Jesus' resurrection as his exaltation.

Son of Man (24:7)   **Messiah** (24:26)

δόξα (9:26/24:26)   **ἀναστῆναι** (24:7, 46)

Luke's Son of Man and Messiah threads are narratively long: both are rooted in Luke 9 and Jesus' response to Peter; that chapter's Messiah had been conceptually formed by the Prologue and by Jesus' anointing. Jesus, the Davidic Messiah, cryptically embraced the Son of Man model and lived out his non-violent prophetic life that effected the Exodus of which Luke's Transfiguration scene spoke.[408] Luke's chiastic transition at Luke 24:26 made possible Jesus' preparation for his followers' kerygmatic activity in Jerusalem (24:44–49). That allegedly problematic Jesus-*logion* identifies "Moses, Prophets and the Psalms" as where it is written that the "Messiah is to suffer and to rise from the dead (ἀναστῆναι ἐκ νεκρῶν) on the third day."[409] From Luke's resurrection perspective, his Prologue's conceptualization of a Davidic

---

[408] See both the analytical diagram and Ch. 7.

[409] Itself an adaptation from Luke 9:22.

Messiah has been refined by his appropriating tradition's talk of Jesus' hesitancy to acknowledge *simpliciter* the descriptor "Messiah." Apostles commissioned and hermeneutically enabled need only the empowerment of the Spirit that commissioned Jesus to fulfil the task that he set them of witnessing. This hinge chapter completed, we turn to Part II on Peter's apostolic witness.

Part II. Peter and Exegesis

Simon, Simon, listen! Satan has demanded to sift all of you like wheat, but I have prayed for you that your own faith may not fail; and you, when once you have turned back, strengthen your brothers." And [Peter] said to him, "Lord, I am ready to go with you to prison and to death!" Jesus said, "I tell you, Peter, the cock will not crow this day, until you have denied three times that you know me" (Luke 22:31–34).[410]

Overview

Part II fleshes out Luke's narrative argument by focusing on two Jesus-*logia* (Luke 24:25–27; 44–49), identifying as Luke's purposes three strands from his systematic narrative written to reassure Theophilus.[411] Part II explores one strand in detail: Were Christian claims about Jesus truly grounded in Israel's scriptures?

Our thesis is that Luke retrospectively understood the bivalent ἀναστήσω of his triptych's David-promises in the light of Jesus' resurrection, governing where and how "it is written" that the Messiah must suffer and be raised from the dead.[412] Through six exegetical speeches by Jesus-followers,[413]

---

[410] *Σίμων Σίμων, ἰδοὺ ὁ Σατανᾶς ἐξῃτήσατο ὑμᾶς τοῦ σινιάσαι ὡς τὸν σῖτον· ἐγὼ δὲ ἐδεήθην περὶ σοῦ* ἵνα μὴ ἐκλίπῃ ἡ πίστις *σου·* καὶ σύ ποτε ἐπιστρέψας *στήρισον* τοὺς ἀδελφούς σου. ὁ δὲ εἶπεν αὐτῷ· Κύριε, μετὰ σοῦ ἕτοιμός εἰμι καὶ εἰς φυλακὴν καὶ εἰς θάνατον πορεύεσθαι. ὁ δὲ εἶπεν· Λέγω σοι, *Πέτρε,* οὐ φωνήσει σήμερον ἀλέκτωρ ἕως *τρίς με ἀπαρνήσῃ εἰδέναι.* (my italics).

[411] Ch. 1.

[412] Ch. 2.

[413] Speeches that exemplify identifiable scriptural reasoning to make their case. For Stephen's defence speech (Acts 6:13–8:3) and Paul's Antioch sermon (Acts 13:16–41) see Ch. 7 and Ch. 8. We shall take their confirmatory witness into account in Part III.

117

Luke exemplified that where and how. Uniquely, each speech looks back to Jesus' story retold in Luke, weaving many of its threads into one continuous narrative – Luke-Acts.

The three chapters in Part II are dominated by one figure, Peter,[414] whose mirroring of three Jesus-*logia* leads to the first of Luke's culminations – where it is written that the Messiah must suffer.[415] Peter's story in these chapters is defined by his changing relationship with Jerusalem's rulers (his "turning back") that enabled the corporate apostolic stance reported in Acts 5:12–42 (by Peter's strengthened brothers). In one sense Part II fulfils Jesus' headlined Peter-saying; in another it completes Peter's role in speaking truth to power, the central section of Luke-Acts' narrative shape.[416]

1. Peter in Luke-Acts

This study summarizes Luke's Peter thread that blends tradition and distinctiveness. The exchange at the head of this chapter links the Peter of the two volumes, an example of Luke's use of fulfilled Jesus-*logia*.

Among Jesus' earliest disciples (Luke 5:3–10), and the most frequently named, Peter was the first to recognize and acknowledge what was really happening in Jesus' activity and person – this man was God's Messiah (Luke 9:18–20). Peter figures large in Luke's distinctive Transfiguration narrative (Luke 9:28–36),[417] but his distinctive role (Luke 22:31–34, 54–62. Cf. 1 Cor. 15:5) in Luke's conflict-narrative (Luke 19:41 – Acts 8:3) demands our attention

---

[414] Please note: Luke frequently speaks of the duo Peter and John; as in his first volume all is confirmed by the testimony of *two* witnesses. To avoid repetitiveness we shall assume this and focus on Peter's principal role.

[415] The "culmination" of a thematic or narrative thread; here, Acts 4:23–28.

[416] See the analytical diagram.

[417] See Ch. 7.

here:[418] Peter is its focus;[419] Jesus' charge to him is clear – strengthen your brothers. The Peter who had three times denied that he knew his Lord, turned back in Acts 1–5 and strengthened his brothers.

The significance of this chapter's headline passage for *Interpreter*'s case can hardly be over-emphasized. Luke probably alludes to the tradition that this same Peter had been the first to encounter his raised Lord.[420] Peter then three times publicly "unpacked" Jesus-*logia* central to Luke-Acts' theological development, in the course of which he confronted the Sanhedrin that had condemned Jesus to death. Peter's trusting commitment (πίστις) had not abandoned him; Luke depicts Peter as the key follower whose hope was securely in Jacob's God (Ps. 145:5).

What follows owes much to wide discussion of this thread.[421] Here, however, I simply present my position: it would be odd indeed were Luke to allow Jesus' distinctive word to Peter at the Last Supper to remain hanging in the air (Luke 22:31–32).[422] Luke is interested in such fulfilment: for example, Jesus' gnomic word to the Sanhedrin (Luke 22:69) is "fulfilled" by Stephen's vision that precipitates a Christian diaspora.[423] Luke's Peter thread is not unique.

Tradition allots a significant role to Peter.[424] It particularly remembers that Peter also denied knowing Jesus (Luke 22:54–62). But when, in Lukan terms, did Peter "turn"? A clear thread runs from Luke 22:61 where, following his denial, Peter remembered. Luke left clues at 24:12 and 33–34, possibly

---

[418] See the analytical diagram.

[419] Simon, Peter, (Kephas); his twinning with John in no way detracts from Peter's central role in Acts 1–5.

[420] Luke 24:12, 33–35. Cf. 1 Cor. 15:3. Contra Stanford (2014: 194–195) who argues for the "Simon" Luke intends being Simon the Zealot; but see our headline quotation.

[421] E.g., Bockmuehl (2012: 153–163); Cullmann (1953).

[422] Diff. Mt. 16:13–20.

[423] Acts 7:55–8:3; Ch. 7.

[424] E.g., Luke 9; cf. 24:12, 33–35; 1 Cor. 15:3–9; Jn 21:15–23.

hinting that Jesus appeared first to Peter.[425] Peter plays a leading role in Acts, apparently "defining" the apostolate (Acts 1:21–22). In Acts 2–4, he three times publicly affirms his commitment to Jesus, ensuring that the Sanhedrin acknowledge that he had been "with Jesus," thereby transcending his denial (Luke 22:54–62). Invited by the Sanhedrin to resume his denial of Jesus (Acts 4:18), Peter's reply (vv. 19–20) probably constitutes the completion of his having "turned": his making his exemplary stand strengthens his brethren.

Interpreter's proposal that Peter's exegetical speeches engage with and unpack Jesus' own intertextual usage needs to be tracked through Luke's complex plaiting of many threads. In chapters 4 to 6, each scriptural reasoning section becomes a process of unpacking Jesus' *logion* by unthreading its narrative unit:[426]

    i. typically by identifying its speaker's "explaining" a remarkable event;

    ii. by then grounding that event in the reality of God's having raised and exalted Jesus;

    iii. by recalling the events that prompted Jesus' intertexts;

    iv. by setting these mirror-intertexts, now mutually illuminated, within Luke-Acts' Jerusalem-conflict narrative, a conflict shared by Jesus and his followers against their opponents (Luke 19:41 – Acts 8:3).

2. Rulers in Luke-Acts

"Rulers" is Luke's distinctive category-descriptor for Jerusalem's governing elite who conspired to secure Jesus' death. Arguably, this descriptor emerges from Ps. 145 in the pre-literary, exegetical period that preceded Luke's early drafts. Ps. 145 celebrates the polarity of God's unending kingship[427] and the transience

---

[425] Cf. 1 Cor. 15:3. Contra Stanford (2014: 194–195); – the "Simon" Luke intends is Simon the Zealot.

[426] See Ch. 8A.

[427] βασιλεύσει κύριος εἰς τὸν αἰῶνα, ὁ θεός σου, Σιων, εἰς γενεὰν καὶ γενεάν. (Ps. 145:10)

of earthly rulers.[428] Note that to question Peter and John, "their rulers gathered together,"[429] and Peter addressed them as "rulers of the People" (Acts 4:8). We shall see below how Luke prepares Theophilus to "hear" the meaning of the apostles' *pesher* on thw first two verses of Ps. 2:

παρέστησαν οἱ βασιλεῖς τῆς γῆς
καὶ οἱ ἄρχοντες συνήχθησαν ἐπὶ τὸ αὐτὸ
κατὰ τοῦ κυρίου καὶ κατὰ τοῦ χριστοῦ αὐτοῦ (Ps. 2:1–2).

Luke's use of "rulers" in Part II evokes one's curiosity. But this category appears earlier in Luke's narrative: at Luke 23:13–25 we encounter rulers distinctively complicit in hostility to Jesus; worse, at 23:35, "rulers" deride this dying man. Notably, in Luke-Acts' sole example of a synagogue sermon, Paul reports that it was Jerusalem's inhabitants and their rulers who engineered Jesus' death.[430] We shall return to this descriptor's significance, for it helps Luke set Jesus in the context of Israel's continuing story, particularly by means of a psalm.

3. Psalm 145

Chapter 6 offers us an insight into Peter's confronting his People's rulers: by his *pesher* on Jesus' vineyard parable's stone-saying,[431] Peter counter-charged these rulers with killing God's Messiah, Jesus. In the following scene,[432] by their *pesher* on Ps. 2:1–2, re-assembled Jesus-followers textually rooted how these rulers fulfilled scripture. Twice, by the light of Ps. 145, Luke continues his story of Jesus-followers' relations with rulers. This psalm evokes Luke's principal

---

[428] ἐξελεύσεται τὸ πνεῦμα αὐτοῦ, καὶ ἐπιστρέψει εἰς τὴν γῆν αὐτοῦ, ἐν ἐκείνῃ τῇ ἡμέρᾳ ἀπολοῦνται πάντες οἱ διαλογισμοὶ αὐτῶν. (Ps. 145:4).

[429] Acts 4:5; cf. Ps. 2:1–2, συναχθῆναι αὐτῶν τοὺς ἄρχοντας καὶ τοὺς πρεσβυτέρους καὶ τοὺς γραμματεῖς ἐν Ἰερουσαλήμ.

[430] Acts 13:27; see Ch. 8.

[431] Acts 4:8–12; cf. Luke 20:9–26; a Jesus-*logion* adapting Ps. 117:22.

[432] Acts 4:23–31; see Ch. 6.

descriptor of Jesus – Saviour. Luke pictured these scenes as the playing out of Ps. 145:3: "Do not put your trust in rulers, and in sons of men, in whom there is no salvation."[433]

This enriching psalm is present in both scenes as an adaptation (Acts 4:24), an echo (Acts 4:9, 12), and in its framing Luke's story of the early community by modelling their stance on an ideal Jewish figure – the righteous, described by Ps. 145 and by others like it. The righteous trust and hope in *HaShem,* Jacob's God.[434] In Chapter 6 we shall see that this psalm also shares elements with Pss. 2 and 117. In Part II Peter appears as *the* apostolic spokesman and hermeneut who uniquely re-interprets Jesus' story via his interpretation of Jesus-*logia* and of Israel's scriptures.

4. Mirroring in Luke-Acts

Each of Peter's speeches addresses a scriptural intertext traditionally ascribed first to Jesus himself, his use calling for answers or solutions. Each speech takes up an example of "twoness" in Luke-Acts – the twofold presence of intertexts in significant narrative settings – here linking Luke and Acts.[435] Peter's speeches mirror the order in which Jesus' appeals to scripture appear, his speeches spelling out for Theophilus what tradition had otherwise left in the air. Uniquely, Peter the hermeneut interprets each Jesus-intertext (a–c below) in the light both of Jesus' resurrection and of God's promise to David – "I will raise up (ἀναστήσω) your seed after you."

---

[433] μὴ πεποίθατε ἐπ' ἄρχοντας καὶ ἐφ' υἱοὺς ἀνθρώπων, οἷς οὐκ ἔστιν σωτηρία.

[434] Developed more fully in Ch. 6.

[435] See Doble (2004).

122

a) Citing Ps. 117:22/Acts 4:10–11,[436] Jesus responded to his hearers' "let it not be" (μὴ γένοιτο)[437] by posing a question at the end of his vineyard parable: "What, then, is this that is written?" Jesus' vineyard parable stands in the context of a dispute about his authority (Luke 20:1–8), echoing, while subverting, the parable in Isa. 5:1–7.[438] In synoptic tradition, Jesus' parable echoes Ps. 2:7–8 in that its "son" and "heir" already implied Messiah;[439] it portrays the son's' suffering and death, paralleling but distinct from Son of Man *logia*. Luke linked the authorities' reaction to Jesus' parable – that they perceived as told against them – with his distinctive redaction of "Caesar's coin" (Luke 20:20–26) that echoes the parable's implied "give God what is God's." Until Peter interprets "the Stone" in his encounter with the same authorities (Acts 4:5–22),[440] tradition leaves unanswered Jesus' question of what this saying means.

b) Exod. 3:1–6/Acts 3:13–26, "the Bush," appears in Jesus' dialogue with sceptics of resurrection-talk, Sadducees who later feature as members of the Sanhedrin.[441] Second Temple Judaisms shared no agreed understanding of or belief in Resurrection.[442] Jesus' reply to Sadducaean taunting is that God's new age will not be this life writ large. But the Bush as Torah teaching on the resurrection is fixed in synoptic tradition – "He is God not of the dead, but of the living."[443] For Jesus, God had signalled through Moses that the dead are raised (Luke 20:37–38). Recalling this word in the light of God's having raised Jesus

---

[436] Luke 20:9–26. See Ch. 6.

[437] Effectively, "un-Amen."

[438] Luke 20:9–26; diff. Mk 12:1–12; Mt. 21:33–46. Luke continues his narrative seamlessly to integrate the whole sequence.

[439] Luke 20:13–14; cf. Ps. 2:7–8 and Luke 3:21–22.

[440] See Ch. 6.

[441] Luke 20:27–40; Acts 3:13–4:4. See Ch. 5.

[442] See, e.g., Wright (2003: 85–206); cf. Tomson (2001).

[443] See Ch. 3; Luke 24:1–12, 23; Acts 1:3.

himself (ἀναστήσας ὁ θεὸς τὸν παῖδα αὐτοῦ) (Acts 3:26), Peter can retrospectively explore the Bush as pointing to the Messiah's resurrection.[444]

c) Ps. 109:1/Acts 2:34 (Luke 20:41–44) is the final Jesus-intertext in Luke's tight sequence, reworked from tradition's riddle for Scribes. Jesus asks: "David calls (the Messiah) Lord; how, then, (can he be) his son?" Notably, two of these three Jesus-intertexts hinge on the significance of the word "son," the vineyard parable (Luke 20:9–26) and this riddle (Luke 20:41–42). Readers know, while the narrative's Scribes do not, that Luke's concept of Messiah had been portrayed in his Prologue's Jesus-triptych. Shared with wider tradition, Jesus' riddle becomes the climax of Peter's first public venture into scriptural interpretation (Acts 2:34–36): "The LORD said to my Lord, Sit at my right hand."[445]

Differing from Mark's and Matthew's narratives, Luke tightened these Jesus-intertexts common to the Synoptic tradition into a sequence of Jesus' *logia* from his conflict with rulers.[446] Independent of his Son of Man sayings, Jesus' words were also about suffering and being raised. Through Peter's speeches Luke demonstrates how those *logia* were fulfilled. In Part II, we shall see the scriptural reasoning in these speeches as one step in Luke's assuring Theophilus that what Christians had to say about Jesus the Messiah is rooted as much in Israel's scriptures as in Jesus' teaching.[447] The speeches offer Theophilus – and all readers – insight into the world of post-resurrection, verbal and conceptual interpretation of Jesus' words, encouraging readers' confidence in the rootedness of Christian proclamation within Israel's story.

---

[444] Cf. Acts 3:18–4:4. See Ch. 5.

[445] See 1 Sam. 25:23–31 on OGT's using κύριος. Cf. Jesus' Son of Man *logion* at Luke 22:69 (Ch. 5), cf. Acts 7:55–56.

[446] Luke 20:9–26, 27–40, 41–44 / Mark 12:1–17, 18–27 [*al*] 35–37 / Matthew 21:33–46; [*al*] 22:15–22, 23–33 [*al*] 41–45, a distinctive Lukan narrative sequence.

[447] See Ch. 6.

Obviously, each speech is post-resurrection. Less obviously, resurrection is Peter's hermeneutic key in all three, perhaps most clearly so in his "big" speech in Acts 3, where an interrupting official party clearly identifies its concern about Peter's associating resurrection with Jesus (Acts 4:1–4). God's having raised Jesus is, however, Luke's key to the other speeches also. All three speeches are about salvation, echoing both Luke's Saviour focus announced in the Prologue, and Jesus' followers' commission to proclaim "repentance for the forgiveness of sins" (Luke 24:47). Each speech explains an event that happens only because God had raised Jesus from the dead, and exalted him.[448]

---

[448] E.g., Pentecost's outpouring of Spirit; a lame man's "salvation" (Acts 4:9).

Chapter 4. Mirror 1: Pentecost

The first of Peter's exegetical speeches (Acts 2:17–39) mirrors Jesus' story and Israel's scriptures, driving towards his public proclamation: "Therefore let the whole house of Israel know with assurance that God has made this Jesus whom you crucified both Lord and Messiah" (Acts 2:36).[449] Luke's Peter makes public what his Prologue made known to readers through its triptych: "Today, in David's city, a Saviour has been born for you who is Messiah, Lord."[450]

Luke's Jesus had instructed his followers to wait in Jerusalem for their empowerment by the Holy Spirit (Luke 24:49; Acts 1:6–8). Second Temple Judaisms knew of and were variously nourished by non-canonical books that led to a democratization of what had earlier been for a few. For Luke, Jesus is "essentially righteous" (Ὄντως [...] δίκαιος, Luke 23:47) and I have argued elsewhere that there is substantial evidence for the influence of Wis. 2–5 on Luke's portrayal of Jesus.[451] From Wisdom's reflection on σοφία Luke was able to understand "holy spirit" as God's invisible presence, living and active: "in every generation she passes into holy souls and makes them friends of God, and prophets."[452]

Empowered by God's Spirit (Acts 2:1–12), Peter is the named speaker of this speech explaining an event that was problematic for festal pilgrims. Peter's scriptural reasoning begins with his recalling a passage from Joel; this leads him to his accenting Jesus' resurrection-exaltation as the basis for his being Lord.[453]

---

[449] An emphatically placed ἀσφαλῶς; cf. Luke 1:4 and Ch. 1A1.

[450] Luke 2:11; see Ch. 2.

[451] Doble (1996); See also Ch. 7.

[452] Wis. 7:27 (see 7:22–8:1 for the relation of Spirit (πνεῦμα) with Wisdom (σοφία)).

[453] "Fulfilling" Joel's oracle (Acts 2:21; cf. 2:37–47).

Luke's Pentecost[454] narrative plays a significant role in his unfolding of Jesus' followers' obedience to their commission (Luke 24:44–49; Acts 1:4–5). Typically, Peter's scripture-reasoning explains puzzling events, doing so by means of a word of Jesus and appeal to God's David-promise. Peter makes sense of Pentecost's outpouring of Spirit for a crowd who ask what this event might mean (Acts 2:12). His "explanation," however, is arguably more about what God has done in and through Jesus than about the event Peter explains. Peter begins by rooting his response in a long, lightly-adapted, labelled Joel citation (Joel 2:28–32 (NETS); 3:1–5a (LXX)) that naturally invites exegesis.[455] Peter's interpretation, however, is retrospectively informed by Jesus' story. First, it is the "Jesus the Nazorean" his hearers had known (Acts 2:22) who, fulfilling Joel's vision, has "poured out this spirit" (Acts 2:32–3). Second, Jesus proves to be that "Lord" of whom both Joel and David spoke.[456] Peter reaches his conclusion by scriptural reasoning – "God has made this Jesus whom you crucified both Messiah and Lord" (Acts 2:36). Through his address's culmination (Acts 2:32–36), Peter resolved Jesus' riddling Ps. 109:1 for scribes about the Messiah, David's son, David's "Lord" and God's right hand (Luke 20:41–44). He did this via David-promises found in Pss. 131 and 15 that illuminate Jesus' enigmatic word about the Messiah. For Peter, Jesus the Nazorean is now the Risen One; notably, "raised up" (ἀνέστησεν) features twice in this speech (Acts 2:24, 32), echoing the presence of the David-promise.[457] These echoes from the ἀναστήσω of Luke's base-text, together with the David-promise at his

---

[454] Heb. "Weeks," reflecting its agrarian dating (Deut. 16:9–10) rather than its later developments.

[455] *Interpreter*'s references to Israel's scriptures are normally to Rahlfs' (1979) *Setuaginta*. Throughout this chapter, however, because many in discussion groups have used NETS, *A New English translation of the Septuagint*, a two-fold referencing has been used.

[456] Luke systematically uses Nazorean to contrast with a following disclosure of who Jesus really is.

[457] Acts 2:24, 32 – ἀνέστησεν; *Interpreter*'s core argument. Cf. Luke 24:5, 34.

speech's core (Acts 2:30), alert readers to that promise's active, though uncited, presence in Peter's speech.

To support his claim that, as a prophet, David spoke of the resurrection of the Messiah,[458] Peter argues that God raised up the Jesus whom Jerusalem killed (Acts 2:22–23). He re-interprets David's Ps. 15 (Acts 2:25b–28),[459] by adapting the psalm's core in the light of what God had done for Jesus, but not for David: "He was not abandoned to Hades, nor did his flesh experience corruption" (Ps. 15:10).[460]

Ps. 15 is not Luke's scriptural ground for resurrection;[461] it serves, rather, as an enriching device to enable understanding of the event of Jesus' resurrection in the context of Nathan's oracle. This psalm becomes an extension by David, a prophet (Acts 2:30), of the twofold promise made by God: first, to seat on his (David's) throne "the fruit of his loins," an echo from Ps. 131's celebration of the base David-promise.[462] Second, he had foreseen (Acts 2:31, προϊδὼν) his seed's resurrection, which event enabled him to explain the Spirit's outpouring at Pentecost in terms of God's raising Jesus from the dead and exalting him to God's right hand. Knowing that promise (εἰδὼς) enabled David to write as he did in Ps. 15.

---

[458] Acts 2:31; περὶ τῆς ἀναστάσεως τοῦ Χριστοῦ, echoing and supporting the twofold ἀνέστησεν we have noted.

[459] Apparently promising David freedom from Hades and life beyond it.

[460] Acts 2:29; ὅτι οὐκ ἐγκαταλείψεις τὴν ψυχήν μου εἰς ᾅδην οὐδὲ δώσεις τὸν ὅσιόν σου ἰδεῖν διαφθοράν. At Antioch Paul makes much of this verse's ὅσιος and διαφθοράν Luke's subtext ensures that Jesus' word from the cross excluded Ps. 22's ἵνα τί ἐγκατέλιπές με; Doble (1996).

[461] Dissenting from the nuanced discussion in Lindars (1961: 38–51).

[462] Ps. 131:11; ὤμοσεν κύριος τῷ Δαυιδ ἀλήθειαν καὶ οὐ μὴ ἀθετήσει αὐτήν Ἐκ καρποῦ τῆς κοιλίας σου θήσομαι ἐπὶ τὸν θρόνον σου.

A. Assurance for Theophilus

In his concluding proclamation (Acts 2:36) to the entire house of Israel,[463] Peter's emphatic ἀσφαλῶς (assuredly) probably reflects the ἀσφάλειαν (sureness) that Luke promised Theophilus:[464] Jesus-followers (including Paul) call Jesus Lord and proclaim him Messiah.[465] Peter's proclamation depends entirely on his affirming and arguing a scripture-based case for Jesus' resurrection, and Peter's hermeneutic key to understanding this Pentecost event proves to be Luke's implied base-text, God's David-promise, retrospectively interpreted by the light of Jesus' resurrection.

This narrative carries Peter's initial proclamation of Jesus-followers' normative claim: God has made Jesus the Nazorean (Acts 2:22) both Messiah and Lord (Acts 2:36). Implied by 2:31, here in Acts is Luke's first statement that "the Messiah is Jesus." This descriptor links with 2:36 as God's "marking out" by Jesus' anointing (Luke 3:21–22) and resurrection (Luke 24; Ch. 3) the fulfilling of God's promise to David.[466] Peter's proclamation is equally his first announcement that "Jesus is Lord," a phrase often identified as a pre-Pauline Christian confession: "if you confess with your lips that Jesus is Lord and believe in your heart that God raised him from the dead, you will be saved" (Rom. 10:9). Peter's speech offered Theophilus solid scriptural reasoning for setting firmly in Israel's history "the things about Jesus" (τὰ περὶ Ἰησοῦ) the Nazorean (τὸν Ναζωραῖον).

Theophilus had known from the anointing narrative that Jesus was the Messiah foretold by Gabriel's annunciation to Mary; he had heard from the angel's good news for the shepherds that Jesus was also Lord. The "lawless

---

[463] Addressing Theophilus's "How did we get to where we are – divided?"

[464] See Ch. 1; this root is found most often in Lukan settings.

[465] E.g., Rom. 1:1–6; Acts 28:30–31.

[466] Cf. Paul's τοῦ ὁρισθέντος υἱοῦ θεοῦ (Rom. 1:4).

129

men" (Acts 2:23, διὰ χειρὸς ἀνόμων) who crucified Jesus turn out later to be Jerusalem's rulers (Acts 7:51–53); Peter makes his hearers complicit with them – τοῦτον τὸν Ἰησοῦν ὃν ὑμεῖς ἐσταυρώσατε.[467]

Notably, Peter's proclamation is to "the whole house of Israel," to residents and festal pilgrims gathered for *Shavu'ot* (Acts 2:5–11). Luke-Acts concludes in a continuing debate within a Jewish context about these very things (Acts 28:17–31). In this continuity a reader sees one of Luke's purposes: he wrote to show Theophilus how we, the Jewish People, come to be divided as we are. This speech's scriptural reasoning roots the resurrection of the Messiah (Acts 2:31) and Christian confession of Jesus as Lord in Israel's scriptures. To the how of that reasoning we must now turn.

---

[467] See Ch. 7.

B. Peter's scriptural reasoning

Readers recognize in the ending of Peter's speech Luke's implied cross-reference to Jesus' riddle put to scribes (Luke 20:41–44). The conclusion of Peter's Pentecost speech proclaimed:

> Therefore let the entire house of Israel know with certainty that God has made him both Lord and Messiah, this Jesus whom you crucified (Acts 2:36),

assuring Theophilus that Jesus' riddle

> How can they say that the Messiah is David's son? [...] David thus calls him Lord; so how can he be his son? (Luke 20:44)

has been unlocked by God's both-and, in and through Jesus, whom Luke had introduced as David's son.[468]

That, however, is not the question Peter overtly addressed. The crowd's question was put by the event of the Spirit's outpouring – what they had seen and heard: "What can this mean?" First, recall Jesus' commissioning of his witnesses and hermeneuts:

> And see, I am sending upon you what my Father promised; so stay here in the city until you have been clothed with power from on high (Luke 24:49).

Peter's answer to the crowd's question of meaning is then embedded deep and late into in his speech:

> This Jesus God raised up, [...] Being therefore exalted at God's right hand, and having received from the Father the promise of

---

[468] Basic to Peter's case: "I will raise up your seed after you, who shall be from your gut" (ἀναστήσω τὸ σπέρμα σου μετὰ σέ, ὃς ἔσται ἐκ τῆς κοιλίας σου). Luke's Prologue affirms that is who Jesus is – genuinely a *Davidid.*

the Holy Spirit, he [Jesus] has poured out this that you both see and hear (Acts 2:33).

The crowd's question has been clearly answered: this outpouring from God's Spirit is possible because Jesus is raised up, exalted at God's right hand.[469] Further, Theophilus can recognize how Christian talk of the last days and of Holy Spirit illuminates Joel's prophecy.

But Peter can reach this answer about Pentecost only by having first demonstrated how that event to which Jesus-followers were witnesses, Jesus' resurrection, was itself meaningful "according to the scriptures," that is, graspable within his hearers' worldview. Peter's reasoning here comprises twin threads: (a) his resurrection reasoning; which is paralleled by (b) his reasoning that Jesus is Lord, and each illuminates the other.

Luke's resurrection reasoning is grounded in the event-ness of what God has done (Acts 2:24), before following a David route (Acts 2:25–34) firmly within Luke-Acts' reference-frame (2 Sam. 7:12) while events in David's house extend and enrich that frame. For example, it was impossible that death could keep its hold on Jesus because,[470] according to Ps. 15, God had made a further promise to David (Acts 25b–28).

> You will not abandon my life to Hades, nor will you give your
> holy one to see corruption;
> ὅτι οὐκ ἐγκαταλείψεις τὴν ψυχήν μου εἰς ᾅδην οὐδὲ δώσεις τὸν
> ὅσιόν σου ἰδεῖν διαφθοράν (Ps. 15:10).

---

[469] Acts 2:17, 18; Joel 2:28 (NETS); 3:1 (LXX) – ἐκχεῶ ἀπὸ τοῦ πνεύματός μου, cf. Wis. Sol. 7:24–28; cf. Ps. 138:7–10, ποῦ πορευθῶ ἀπὸ τοῦ πνεύματός σου.

[470] Echoing Ps. 17:5–6.

Peter affirms that David's psalm concerns Jesus (Acts 2:25a); it did not concern David as his mortality demonstrated (Acts 2:29). Peter, however, adapted Ps. 15 in the light of Jesus' resurrection:

> He was not abandoned to Hades, nor did his flesh experience corruption.
>
> οὔτε ἐγκατελείφθη εἰς ᾅδην οὔτε ἡ σὰρξ αὐτοῦ εἶδεν διαφθοράν (Acts 2:31).

His reasoning process from the psalmist's promise to Peter's highlighting its unexpected fulfilment involves two steps. First, Peter alludes to and recalls Ps. 131:11 that itself recalls Luke-Acts' reference-frame,[471] especially its base-text: David "knew that God had sworn with an oath to him that he would put of the fruit of his loins on his throne" (Acts 2:30).

Second, Peter re-reads Ps. 15:10 in the light of that basic promise: David was a prophet who foresaw the event of Messiah's resurrection (Acts 2:31; cf. Ps. 131:10, 17–18),[472] now retrospectively understood as "he was neither abandoned to Hades nor did his flesh see decay."

At the core of his rereading that promise in the light of Jesus' resurrection, Peter has read "fruit of his loins" from Ps. 131 as equivalent to "seed" in Luke's base-text; recognized that God's "holy one" David died,[473] but his "seed" lived on. He borrowed the psalmist's "flesh" (Ps. 15:9) from the preceding verse to confirm that David actually lived and wrote in the hope that this promise was true for his promised seed:

---

[471] Acts 2:30 – ὤμοσεν κύριος τῷ Δαυιδ ἀλήθειαν […] Ἐκ καρποῦ τῆς κοιλίας σου θήσομαι ἐπὶ τὸν θρόνον σου. Ps. 131:11.

[472] Peter's προϊδὼν (2:31) resumes the psalm's opening προορώμην in the light of his recalling Ps. 131:10–11. "For your servant David's sake do not turn away the face of your anointed one. The Lord swore to David a sure oath from which he will not turn back" followed by the text's allusion.

[473] David was very dead (2:29), cf. Acts 13:36–37; see Ch. 8.

Moreover, my flesh will encamp in hope

ἔτι δὲ καὶ ἡ σάρξ μου κατασκηνώσει ἐπ' ἐλπίδι (Ps. 15:9).

That move allowed Peter to realize that,[474] because of what God had made known to David, "the Lord" at David's right hand[475] might be his Lord at God's right hand.[476] David's fore-knowledge would account for his rejoicing (ἠγαλλιάσατο) and gladness (ηὐφράνθη) and the delights (τερπνότητες) of which his psalm speaks – though Peter's quotation omits. Crucially, *Interpreter* recognizes that when Luke cites, echoes, or alludes to scripture he occasionally expects a reader to supply what the author himself values in his subtext,[477] apparently omits, then sometimes takes up later in his narrative. Here Peter's quotation from Ps. 15:28a apparently omits τερπνότητες ἐν τῇ δεξιᾷ σου εἰς τέλος, an unvoiced but active source of Peter's conclusion at 2:32–33: that Jesus' resurrection should be understood as his exaltation to God's right hand – τῇ δεξιᾷ οὖν τοῦ θεοῦ ὑψωθείς – one more step along the road to Peter's resolving Jesus' riddle for Jerusalem's scribes.

Peter can, then, safely enrich Ps. 15:10 by its preceding clause – it was Jesus, David's seed, whom God had anointed,[478] who was not abandoned to Hades, whose flesh does not decay and whose resurrection retrospectively made sense of the David-promise affirmed in Ps. 15. David's living pathway is through his "seed," for the Jesus who has been raised up as David's promised

---

[474] In Gen. 14:7–24, later re-interpreted at Hebrews 7:1–10, there is a comparable argument to Peter's: "for [Levi] was still in the loins of [his] father (ἐν τῇ ὀσφύϊ τοῦ πατρὸς) when Melchizedek met him."

[475] Ps. 15:8; προωρώμην τὸν κύριον ἐνώπιόν μου διὰ παντός, ὅτι ἐκ δεξιῶν μού ἐστιν, ἵνα μὴ σαλευθῶ.

[476] Ps. 15:11; ἐγνώρισάς μοι ὁδοὺς ζωῆς, πληρώσεις με εὐφροσύνης μετὰ τοῦ προσώπου σου, τερπνότητες ἐν τῇ δεξιᾷ σου εἰς τέλος.

[477] *Aposiopesis* was, and remains, a valued rhetorical device.

[478] See Luke 3:21–22; Acts 4:27; 10:38; 13:32–33. For this thread see also Ch. 8.

seed is exalted at God's right hand.[479] David did not ascend into the heavens,[480] possibly echoing Ps. 138:7–10 and bearing its implied resonance between the "Spirit" of Acts 2:32–33 and that in Ps. 138:7.[481] David did, however say,

εἶπεν [ὁ] κύριος τῷ κυρίῳ μου· κάθου ἐκ δεξιῶν μου,
ἕως ἂν θῶ τοὺς ἐχθρούς σου ὑποπόδιον τῶν ποδῶν σου
(Ps. 109:1; Luke 20:41–44).

that Jesus riddled for Jerusalem's scribes and Peter has partially unpacked.

Peter's reasoning depends on the event of Messiah's resurrection (ἀνάστασις); alludes to Luke's base-texts' ἀναστήσω via the conditional form of God's promise to David found in Ps. 131:11–12,[482] and enriches that David-promise by clarifying that God also promised to David freedom from Hades and post-mortem corruption.

At this point we directly address evidence for the hypothesis on which this chapter works: that Peter, Jesus' hermeneut, interprets for Theophilus a traditional Jesus-intertext, and does so by reference to a David-promise and in relation to a puzzling event. Peter's Joel quotation announced that "everyone who calls on the name of *the Lord* will be *saved*" (Acts 2:21); Peter proclaimed to the house of Israel that God had made Jesus both Messiah *and* Lord (Acts 2:36);[483] tradition (cf. Mt. 22:41–46; Mk 12:35–37) reports that, for scribes, Jesus had riddled Ps. 109:1:

Then he said to them,

---

[479] Acts 2:32. Stephen's vision of Jesus standing at God's right hand, fulfilling Jesus' logion to the Sanhedrin (Luke 22:69) is the culmination of Luke-Acts' conflict narrative. See Ch. 7.

[480] Acts 2:34; οὐ γὰρ Δαυὶδ ἀνέβη εἰς τοὺς οὐρανούς.

[481] ποῦ πορευθῶ [David] ἀπὸ τοῦ πνεύματός σου καὶ ἀπὸ τοῦ προσώπου σου ποῦ φύγω; [8] ἐὰν ἀναβῶ εἰς τὸν οὐρανόν, σὺ εἶ ἐκεῖ, ἐὰν καταβῶ εἰς τὸν ᾅδην, πάρει.

[482] For Stephen's use of this psalm see Ch. 7.

[483] Joel 2:32a (NETS); 3:5a (LXX).

"How can they say that *the* Messiah is *David's son*?"
For David himself says in *the book of Psalms*,
"The *Lord* said to *my Lord*, Sit at my right hand,[484]
until I make your enemies your footstool."
David thus calls [the Messiah] *Lord*; so how can he be
[*David's*] *son*? (Luke 20:41–44).

The italicized words, a recognizable concept-cluster, disclose clearly both elements of primitive Christian proclamation, and the core of Peter's resolving Jesus' riddle. Peter's argument drives towards his citation of Jesus' saying (Acts 2:34–35). In Jesus God had fulfilled those promises to David highlighted by the Infancy Gospel's angelophanies that introduced Jesus, particularly heaven's announcement in Luke 2:11 – today, in David's city,[485] "a Saviour is born for you, Who is Messiah, Lord." Again, the core of Peter's argument is simple, as we saw in the previous section:

This Jesus, God raised up [ἀνέστησεν] – of which we are all witnesses.

Consequently, having been exalted [ὑψωθείς] by/to God's right hand,

And having received from the Father the promise of the Holy Spirit,

He [Jesus] has poured out this that you both see and hear (Acts 2:32–33).

---

[484] Κάθου ἐκ δεξιῶν μου, ἕως ἂν θῶ τοὺς ἐχθρούς σου ὑποπόδιον τῶν ποδῶν σου; this twice-cited *logion* must have priority for interpreting similar "right hand" exaltation passages; e.g., the ἐν τῇ δεξιᾷ σου of an unvoiced Ps. 15:11 will be (re-)heard locatively rather than instrumentally.

[485] Jesus' parents were in David's city because Joseph was of David's house (Luke 2:1–7).

136

Luke's Jesus-triptych had introduced Jesus as Saviour, Messiah and Lord (Luke 2:11). Jesus' own riddle exploits the bivalency of κύριος for both God and the exalted Jesus;[486] Jesus is that promised *Davidid* through whom God acted. Luke re-sets his citation from Joel in "the last days,"[487] and Luke's Pentecost-unit is essentially about his hearers' "being saved" in those days (cf. Acts 2:37–47). Theophilus learns that Luke's exalted Jesus is that same Son of Man who crystallized his work as having come to seek and to save what was lost.[488]

Given *Interpreter*'s stance that Luke reads scripture retrospectively while respecting that scripture's future-looking perspective, bivalent lexemes such as κύριος relating to Luke-Acts' reference-frame demand sensitivity to their both/and-ness: Joel foresaw God's acting to save a People. Luke now recognized how God had decisively acted in and through Jesus' story, and could re-read Joel's oracle in the light of that story-event. He also re-read this citation's unvoiced ending. Joel's key phrase that ends its Pentecost adaptation reads "Then everyone who calls on the name of the Lord shall be saved."[489] omitting the oracle's:

> for in Mount Zion and in Jerusalem there shall be one who escapes,
>
> as the Lord has said, and people who have good news proclaimed to them
>
> shall be those whom the Lord has called (Acts 2:21b).[490]

---

[486] Ps. 109:1. Users of Greek texts understood how to distinguish contextually between two senses of κύριος. See, e.g., 1 Sam. 25:26–31; note Acts 2:38–39, 47. See also Hurtado (2003: 179–182; 2014).

[487] Acts 2:17; καὶ ἔσται ἐν ταῖς ἐσχάταις ἡμέραις, adapting Joel 2:28 (NETS); 3:1 (LXX) – καὶ ἔσται μετὰ ταῦτα.

[488] Luke 19:10; Acts 7:55–56; cf. Luke 2:11.

[489] Acts 2:21(a), καὶ ἔσται πᾶς ὃς ἂν ἐπικαλέσηται τὸ ὄνομα κυρίου σωθήσεται,

[490] [καὶ ἔσται πᾶς, ὃς ἂν ἐπικαλέσηται τὸ ὄνομα κυρίου, σωθήσεται] ὅτι ἐν τῷ ὄρει Σιων καὶ ἐν Ιερουσαλημ ἔσται ἀνασῳζόμενος, καθότι εἶπεν κύριος, καὶ εὐαγγελιζόμενοι, οὓς κύριος προσκέκληται.

Notably, following his hearers' questioning response, "Brothers, what should we do?" Peter spells out clearly that they should "be saved from this crooked generation":[491] repent, be baptized in Jesus' name, for this newly democratized gift of the Spirit is for "whomever the Lord our God shall call."[492] Peter and his fellow apostles are in Jerusalem,[493] theirs is good news for their hearers, and those who welcomed their message are daily added to the number of "those being saved."[494] The lexical and thematic links between Peter's unvoiced ending of Joel's oracle and Luke's narrative of the address's consequences (Acts 2:37–47) indicate the *subtextual* presence of that ending: the promise of the gift of the Spirit;[495] being saved;[496] being called;[497] the Lord.[498]

C. Summary of Mirror 1

Joel 2:28–32a (NETS),[499] including its unvoiced conclusion, is the prophetic text on which Luke's Pentecost narrative initially reflects retrospectively and through midrash. Jesus' resurrection and exaltation form sufficient ground for Luke's re-reading of this scriptural subtext that gives meaning to both the outpouring from God's Spirit, and God's having made Jesus both Lord and Messiah – this Jesus "whom you crucified by the hands of those who live lawlessly."[500] Jesus' exaltation is also the ground of Luke's David-Jesus comparative biography,

---

[491] Acts 2:40b – σώθητε ἀπὸ τῆς γενεᾶς τῆς σκολιᾶς ταύτης. Contra NRSV's "save yourselves."

[492] Acts 2:39b – ὅσους ἂν προσκαλέσηται κύριος ὁ θεὸς ἡμῶν.

[493] Where Luke often locates them in Solomon's colonnade, on Mount Zion.

[494] Acts 2:47b – ὁ δὲ κύριος προσετίθει τοὺς σῳζομένους καθ' ἡμέραν ἐπὶ τὸ αὐτό.

[495] See reverse order, Acts 2:39, 33; 1:6–8; Luke 24:46–49.

[496] Reversed: Acts 2:47, 40, 21; Luke 2:11 and its thematic threads.

[497] Acts 2:39, but unvoiced at 2:21.

[498] Reversed: Acts 2:47, 39, 36, 34, 25, 21, 20; cf. Luke 2:11; 20:41–44.

[499] Joel 3:1–5a (LXX).

[500] Acts 2:23, διὰ χειρὸς ἀνόμων, cf. Stephen's charge against the Sanhedrin; Acts 7:51–53. See Ch. 7.

here focused on Ps. 15. His authorial perspective allows Luke to enrich his base-text's ἀναστήσω τὸ σπέρμα σου bivalently and by recognizable interpretative techniques found throughout Luke-Acts. In this speech we noted two unvoiced allusions, and lexical and thematic linkages, but Luke's controlling prophetic text is that found in David's Ps. 109:1, the first of three mirrorings of Jesus' own intertexts, the *logion* that enables interpretation to happen. Peter's speech thus exemplifies Interpreter's case.

Chapter 5. Mirror 2: Solomon's colonnade

A. Abraham and the Bush

To illustrate[501] the apostles' signs and wonders (Acts 2:43), Luke's narrative opens with the healing, in Jesus' name, of a lame man. His restoration to wholeness, or salvation (Acts 4:9), remains the "sign" that prompts both Peter's address to the People (Acts 3:12–26), and his following defence of that act before the Sanhedrin (Acts 4:5–22). This twofold narrative unit continues to 4:22; then Luke segues his narrative into its concluding scene (Acts 4:23–31).[502]

Moving from Jesus' argument for resurrection in general (Luke 20:27–38) to Jesus' own resurrection, Peter associates Torah with resurrection.[503] His argument builds on Peter's Pentecost speech; we assume that Theophilus remained engaged with Luke-Acts' narrative flow. We shall ask: (a) to which Jesus-*logia,* then (b) to what conclusion does this speech lead; and (c) what characterizes Peter's scriptural reasoning from (a) to (b)? In this process, his interpretative technique is stringing (*haruzin*).

1. Descriptors and Jesus

Again, Peter's address is to Israel (Acts 3:12b, 25–26), and, by implication, to Theophilus's probable question: how have we come to be where we now are?[504] Peter argues from Torah and Samuel (Acts 3:24) that by raising this Messiah Jesus from the dead and exalting him (Acts 3:19–21), God fulfilled both the

---

[501] Acts 3:13, 25–26; Luke 20:37–38; Exod. 3:1–12. Cf. Ch. 7.

[502] For Mirror 3 and the apostles' prayer, see Ch. 6.

[503] ὃν ὁ θεὸς ἤγειρεν ἐκ νεκρῶν; Acts 3:15b.

[504] See Acts 28 and *Interpreter*'s hypothesis respecting Luke's purposes.

ancient promise to Abraham (Acts 3:25–6),[505] and that to Moses of a prophet to come.[506] Luke now builds on Peter's proclaiming Jesus as both Messiah and Lord, rooting that proclamation in God's promises.

Luke's narrative remains focused on Jesus. The variety of descriptors in this speech has proved problematic for some commentators, but the heart of apostolic preaching is that the Messiah is Jesus. For example, "servant" (παῖς), forming an *inclusio* to this speech (Acts 3:13, 26), has prompted many scholars to have recourse to Isaianic talk of the suffering servant.[507] "Prophet" (Προφήτης), clearly implied of Jesus by 3:22–23, offers support to all who find Luke's controlling Christological category in that descriptor,[508] while "righteous one" (δίκαιον) prompts talk of the Psalms' suffering righteous one.[509] At 3:15, "the leader of life" (τὸν ἀρχηγὸν τῆς ζωῆς) probably encapsulates the Shining Ones' "living from among the dead,"[510] reflected in Paul's final *apologia* emphasizing that Jesus was the first to be raised from the dead (Acts 26:22–23). In this speech Peter's argument reaches its implied conclusion that this *Jesus* is also to be understood as that seed of Abraham,[511] by whom God will bless all of earth's families, beginning with Peter's hearers.

While they enrich Luke's Davidic reference-frame, elaborating descriptors do not replace it. Peter's focus, his frame of reference, remains in 3:17–21 where his scriptural reasoning is based: Jesus is the appointed and exalted Messiah of Peter's proclamation (Acts 3:20). Messiah is unquestionably the burden of apostolic preaching and the core of Christian confession. In this

---

[505] Cf. Luke 1:55 and its singular "seed."

[506] Acts 3:22–23; Deut. 18:15, implying 18:18; cf. Luke 20:27–38, indicating that in "Moses" the Bush story is found.

[507] Bock (2012); Pao and Schnabel (2007); Strauss (1995).

[508] Johnson (2013).

[509] Acts 3:14; a centurion (Luke 23:47) and Stephen (Acts 7:52; 22:14); on this term see Doble (1996).

[510] Cf. Heb. 2:10.

[511] Acts 3:25; σπέρμα; sing.

141

speech's reworking of Jesus' story, Peter's scriptural focus moves from the Prophets to Torah. In his ensuing encounter with the Sanhedrin his focus moves to the Psalms, recalling Luke's pattern for Peter's dialogue with Jesus' intertexts:

> These are my words that I spoke to you while I was still with you – that everything written about me in the Law of Moses, the Prophets, and the Psalms must be fulfilled (Luke 24:44).

2. To which Jesus-*logia* does this speech lead?

Peter's three speeches by mirroring engage with Jesus-intertexts and with Luke's sequencing of them. This speech addresses Jesus' handling of the Bush – modified by Jesus' resurrection. But does Peter open with an allusion to the Bush or not?[512]

> The God of Abraham, the God of Isaac, and the God of Jacob,
> the God of our fathers has glorified his servant Jesus (Acts 3:13).[513]

Interpreter concludes that this verse is a "paired resonance," linking Jesus' appeal to the Bush with Luke's distinctive and disputed Jesus-*logion* near Emmaus (Luke 24:25–26). We confirm that this is the case by addressing three basic issues:

i. the evidence linking this speech with Jesus' intertext;

ii. Luke's use of "glorified";

iii. establishing that Luke's narrative flow into its interruption scene (Acts 3:26–4:3)

determines the substance of the previous two sections.

---

[512] We here pre-empt this frequent seminar question.

[513] θεὸς Ἀβραὰμ καὶ [ὁ θεὸς] Ἰσαὰκ καὶ [ὁ θεὸς] Ἰακώβ, ὁ θεὸς τῶν πατέρων ἡμῶν, ἐδόξασεν τὸν παῖδα αὐτοῦ Ἰησοῦν.

i. The Bush

Moses himself showed the fact that the dead are raised, in the story about the Bush,[514] where he speaks of the Lord as the God of Abraham, the God of Isaac, and the God of Jacob. Now he is God not of the dead, but of the living; for to him all of them are alive.

Both Peter's and Jesus' discourses plainly address the question of resurrection,[515] and both concern Sadducees who move the narrative action. If Moses allowed Jesus to argue for resurrection as a concept, Peter allows Moses to throw further light on Jesus' unique resurrection as he, Peter, cites God's promise to raise up a Moses-like prophet.[516] Crucially, each passage sustains its own continuity with Jewish heritage by appealing to "our fathers' God" by the formulaic, "the God of Abraham, the God of Isaac, and the God of Jacob."

In Luke-Acts there are four instances of this grouping of patriarch's names: Luke 13:28; 20:37; Acts 3:13; 7:32. Luke 13:28, from Dual tradition, is about the Kingdom of God,[517] where these named patriarchs share in the Messianic banquet of the Age to Come.[518] Luke 20:37 stands in the Jesus-tradition about resurrection and Torah, and Luke takes up this specific focus on resurrection twice more, here and in Stephen's speech.[519] In Stephen's

---

[514] Luke 20:37–38; cf. Mark 12:18–27; Mt. 22:23–33.

[515] See Luke 20:27–33; cf. Acts 3:22, 26; 4:1–4.

[516] Acts 3:22; Deut. 18:15, 18; this ἀναστήσω is a key element in *Interpreter*'s case.

[517] See Borgman (2006: 203–214), who argues that this is the very heart of Luke's journey narrative, sharply focused on the Kingdom of God, in whose banquet imagery Abraham, Isaac and Jacob figure among the living participants.

[518] Luke 20:35–37, where the Age to come is linked with ἀνάστασις and the event of resurrection conveyed by ἐγείρω.

[519] Acts 7:32 see Doble (2013: 95–113); Ch. 7.

apologia for the Sanhedrin, Luke's characteristic twoness becomes a three-ness,[520] clearly indebted to Jesus' own handling of the concept of resurrection. Moreover, it is no accident that Stephen recalls "the God of glory" by rehearsing key encounters with "our fathers," Abraham, Isaac and Jacob (Acts 7:2–16).

Structurally, the Bush is central to the sequence whose Jesus-intertexts Luke shares with wider synoptic tradition.[521] The synoptists agree that Jesus responded to Sadducees; they reappear in Luke's crucial narrative intervention at Acts 4:1–4. Sadducees, common to earlier settings of the Bush, are part of Luke's thread to Stephen's speech where the Sanhedrin comprises a Sadducee core and where the Bush forms the speech's heart.[522]

The Bush also creates distinctive Lukan echoes: at the tomb, the Shining Ones ask why women seek "the living among the dead."[523] Luke's second volume quickly establishes that Jesus is the one who is living (Acts 1:3, ζῶντα μετὰ τὸ παθεῖν αὐτὸν). Sleeman (2009) makes a case for the living Lord's active presence in Luke's second volume, which illuminates Peter's case that this man walks because Jesus is still active.

Luke's subtext (Exod. 3) and narrative substructure cohere throughout his narrative,[524] from Luke 20, Jesus and the Bush, to Acts 26:22–23, where Paul maintains that Moses and the prophets agree that, after suffering, the Messiah is the first to rise from the dead. Thematic and lexical links, together with Luke's long narrative concern with Jesus' resurrection, strongly suggest that Peter's opening (3:13) alludes to the Bush. There remains, however, a verb to examine.

---

[520] Luke 20:37–38; Acts 3:13; 7:30–34.

[521] Luke 20:27–38; cf. Mk 12:18–27; Matthew 22:23–33.

[522] See Ch. 7.

[523] Luke 24:5–6, τὸν ζῶντα μετὰ τῶν νεκρῶν.

[524] Torah does support talk of resurrection.

ii. Glorified (Acts 3:13)

Stephen's martyrdom was guaranteed by his affirming to his accusers that he had a vision of Jesus in glory, standing at God's right hand.[525] And, in Solomon's colonnade, Peter announced to his hearers, astonished by a lame man's healing, that the God of Abraham, Isaac and Jacob had glorified his servant Jesus – whom they killed.

"Glorified" (ἐδόξασεν) and "raised up" (ἀναστήσας),[526] both predicated of Jesus as God's servant (παῖς), form an *inclusio* for Peter's speech. This pairing of "glorified" and "servant" has sent many commentators to Isaiah's "suffering servant" for the source of Peter's language. We return in Chapter 9 to Luke's use of παῖς. Here we focus on his using glorified following "The God of Abraham, Isaac and Jacob," and paralleled by his "God raised up his servant" (Acts 3:26). Rather than have recourse to Isaiah, we provisionally identify the "glorified" of Peter's speech as part of a thread beginning at Luke 9:26, culminating in Stephen's vision that closes Luke-Acts' conflict-narrative (Acts 7:55–56), with Jesus at the God of glory's right hand, a thread including *Interpreter's* focal Jesus-*logion,* Luke 24:25–26.

In Chapter 3 we examined Luke's distinctive transition from Son of Man to Messiah. The Shining Ones recalled Jesus' Son of Man talk in Galilee; the now-raised-from-the-dead Jesus himself opened the scriptures for two dispirited followers with:

> Were not these things necessary, that the Messiah should suffer and then enter into his glory?" Then beginning with Moses and all the prophets, he interpreted to them the things about himself in all the scriptures (Luke 24:26–27).

---

[525] See Ch. 7. Stephen's speech opens with "the God of Glory" (7:2) and ends with his vision of "the Glory of God and Jesus standing at God's right hand" (7:55); what began as a response to accusations about Jesus the Nazarene (6:14) ends with Stephen's affirming that this Jesus is the Son of Man at God's right hand in glory (7:56; cf. Luke 22:69).

[526] Acts 3:26, in a promise setting.

Luke's hinge chapter focused on Jesus who had lived the Son of Man's life, had suffered and had been raised. The same Jesus had been raised up as God's promised Davidic seed, anointed "my son," – God's Messiah – and raised from the dead. That transition from Son of Man to Messiah reports one event, resurrection; one person, Jesus; two descriptors, each evoking its respective scriptural foundations and role in Luke-Acts. What concerns us here is the Son of Man's – or the Son of God's – relation to glory.

That "the Messiah should suffer and then enter into his glory" is firmly rooted in Galilee:

- in Peter's recognizing Jesus as Messiah, followed by Jesus' corrective talk of the Son of Man who will come in his glory;[527]
- then in Luke's distinctive Transfiguration story where Peter and two others see, yet remain silent about, Jesus and his glory.[528]

Luke's hinge (see Chapter 3) reverses his Galilee reserve because in the light of Jesus' resurrection he reads "who do you say I am?" retrospectively;[529] Messiah may now be used; and we have learned from Peter's Pentecost speech that resurrection entails Messiah's being at God's right hand; Peter shortly re-affirms (cf. Acts 2:36) that Jesus is indeed his hearers' appointed Messiah

> who must remain in heaven until the time of universal restoration that God announced long ago through his holy prophets (Acts 3:20–21).

Luke-Acts' roots of "glorified" reach from tradition's Son of Man and from Ezekiel's prophetic message to Israel; they echo Luke's Infancy gospel, where the angelophany announcing Jesus' birth (Luke 2:8–20) surrounds shepherds

---

[527] Luke 9:26; ἐν τῇ δόξῃ αὐτοῦ is distinctively Lukan.

[528] Luke 9:32, 36, both Lukan distinctives.

[529] A question sharply focused by Luke 9.

with God's glory; they, like the angel chorus (Luke 2:13–14), later returned to their fields "ascribing glory to God for all that they had seen and heard."[530]

Peter's opening statement thus forms a paired resonance from two of Jesus' *logia*: from the Bush and from Luke 24:25–26 – with which *Interpreter* is focally engaged. Moreover, Peter actually begins with Moses and all the prophets to interpret the things about Jesus.

iii. Luke's narrative flow into Acts 4:1–4 and resurrection

Luke-Acts is narrative;[531] it flows. That is also true of Peter's speech where, in four brief movements, God's raising of Jesus transforms a reader's understanding of time,[532] of Jesus himself,[533] and of Israel's scriptures.

Peter's opening gambit (3:11–16) recalls the past: the lame man's healing, a "sign,"[534] was done in the glorified Jesus' name. His hearers had killed that same Jesus whom God raised from the dead (ὃν ὁ θεὸς ἤγειρεν ἐκ νεκρῶν),[535] Peter's first gloss on "glorified." In 3:17–21,[536] Peter calls for his

---

[530] καὶ ὑπέστρεψαν οἱ ποιμένες δοξάζοντες καὶ αἰνοῦντες τὸν θεὸν ἐπὶ πᾶσιν οἷς ἤκουσαν καὶ εἶδον καθὼς ἐλαλήθη πρὸς αὐτούς. On Luke's use of δοξάζω, see Doble (1996: 25–69).

[531] Luke 1:1; διήγησις.

[532] *Interpreter* prescinds from discussing Luke-Acts' salvation-calendar. Adapting Joel to ἐν ταῖς ἐσχάταις ἡμέραις (Acts 2:17); setting Peter's present in τὰς ἡμέρας ταύτας (3:24); highlighting the difference between καιροὶ ἀναψύξεως (3:19) and χρόνων ἀποκαταστάσεως, Luke's eschatological calendar builds on what he earlier adapted in Luke 17 and 21 and pictured in 13:24–30 – "these days" lie on the borders of the Ages.

[533] Pentecost revealed Jesus as both Lord and Messiah (Acts 2:36); in Solomon's Colonnade he is also the Moses-like Prophet (3:22) and that seed through whom God's promise to Abraham are fulfilled (3:25).

[534] See the Sanhedrin's confirmation; their σημεῖον (Acts 4:16) stands within a Lukan signs-and-wonders thread (Acts 2:19–5:12).

[535] Echoing Luke 22–24: Pilate, δίκαιος, etc. feature throughout the conflict narrative. See Ch. 6 where 4:24–28 is proposed as Luke-Acts' exposition of where it is written that "the Messiah must suffer."

[536] Cf. Acts 4:24–28; prophets knew that the Messiah would suffer.

hearers' repentance in response to that twofold event, so that their future might be a "time of refreshing" and that God might send their appointed Messiah, Jesus, who must be received by heaven until the "age of restoration."[537] I take this ἀποκατάστασις to refer to something like an eschatological new creation rather than to the restoration of an united Israel.[538] That time had been announced by the prophets (Acts 3:22–24). Peter names three: Moses, Samuel, Abraham. That time (Acts 3:25–26) was when, by Abraham's seed, all earth's nations would be blessed, and God's having raised up (ἀναστήσας) Jesus was the first stage in that time to bring about his hearers' repentance.

Luke's narrative development includes so-called interruptions that move his story along while leaving the speech's argument intact. For example, Jesus' rounded vineyard parable provoked the authorities to try to entrap him (Luke 20:19–20). Significantly, Luke has allotted Peter two exegetical speeches before another such interruption by the Temple authorities; each speech unpacks a Jesus-*logion*; each depends on and is driven by Jesus' resurrection-event. At Pentecost, Peter demonstrated how he was able to proclaim that God made Jesus both Lord and Messiah; in Solomon's Colonnade he further announced that by having raised up Jesus God fulfilled the promise to Abraham that "by your seed shall all earth's nations be blessed" (Acts 3:25–26).

Priests, guard commander and Sadducees put Peter and John into prison until the following day – whose events will be unpacked in Chapter 6. Their grounds for this arrest were twofold:

- Peter and John were teaching the People, and
- Jesus (ἐν τῷ Ἰησοῦ) was proclaiming that "the resurrection of the dead" (τὴν ἀνάστασιν τὴν ἐκ νεκρῶν) had happened (Acts 4:2).[539]

---

[537] Acts 3:31, cf. 2:35; Ps. 109:1 ἕως ἂν θῶ τοὺς ἐχθρούς σου ὑποπόδιον τῶν ποδῶν σου; "until […] time."

[538] On this see further Hoegen-Rohls (2002: 114 n.55 and bibliographical references).

[539] What is implied is enclosed in squared brackets; they were proclaiming an event (ἀναστήσας ὁ θεὸς τὸν παῖδα αὐτοῦ), not teaching an eschatological hope.

148

Luke's reference to the following day (Acts 4:5) indicates another narrative unit's beginning; his summarizing of the current day's effects was that Peter's message persuaded about five thousand men.[540] The narrator thus confirms that Peter's message depended on Jesus' resurrection, a key Lukan theme we have seen to be rooted in the tradition of the Bush, adapted by Jesus' enigmatic glory-*logion* near Emmaus, now extended by Peter's first exploration of this awesome sign.[541]

3. To what conclusion does Peter's speech lead?

> By raising up his servant for you first, God sent him, blessing you by turning each from your wicked ways (Acts 3:26).

This is the conclusion to which Peter's speech drives by developing his argument that opens with the Bush and ends with the Abrahamic covenant: Abraham forms its *inclusio*.[542] Abraham's God glorified (ἐδόξασεν) his παῖς Jesus. By raising up (ἀναστήσας) his παῖς, God fulfilled his covenant with Abraham; παῖς forms another *inclusio* paralleling "glorified" with "raised up." The resurrection event has changed Peter's perspective so that in Jesus' story he sees the beginnings of God's blessings of which that Abrahamic covenant spoke (cf. Gal. 3:6–14).

God is Peter's principal actor, raising, blessing, sending. Blessing is Peter's purpose-link between 3:25 ([ἐν-]εὐλογηθήσονται) and 26 (εὐλογοῦντα); such signs and wonders as the healing of the lame man are evidence that this blessing belongs to "these days." God's servant (παῖς) is that Jesus whom God had glorified (3:13); whose story is crystallized by 3:13b–16; rooted in scripture and in Peter's eschatological timescale of which prophets had spoken (Acts

---

[540] Acts 4:4; cf. 2:41, 47.

[541] See Luke's signs-and-wonders thread, exemplified in Jerusalem by the healing of one lame man.

[542] Contra Marshall (2007: 548–550), who twice affirms that this conclusion is unargued.

3:17–21). From among those prophets Peter names three to reach his conclusion that this focal παῖς, Jesus, is that seed (ἐν τῷ σπέρματί σου) whom God had promised to Abraham.

As ever, Luke's apparently vague references to "all the prophets" should be read in the light of what Luke-Acts actually does when arguing speeches. En route, Peter's resurrection language has been modified by events: glorified is that exalted state of being received by heaven until God's appointed time. The English "raised" obscures two Lukan uses: Peter's concluding ἀναστήσας usually points to a fulfilled and bivalent promise, here to the presence of God's implied ἀναστήσω at 3:22. Broadening the descriptors of the already appointed Messiah and moving firmly into Torah, Peter claims for Jesus a role as Abraham's seed.[543] Peter Oakes, discussing one of Paul's earlier letters, makes clear how this Genesis promise featured in one Jesus-follower's engagement with fellow Jews.[544]

There is much to be said for both Paul's and Luke's drawing on the kind of debating that characterized Christian witnessing from its origins. Even Dodd's proposed *Testimonia* is normally understood to refer to written collections, and *Interpreter* understands 4Q174 to be one such pre-Christian collection. But the *Testimonia* must have been collected on the basis of criteria and by experience – and may not Paul and Luke, both committed to the earliest known Christian credal affirmations, be numbered among those experienced practitioners of interpretation who generated such collections? Connecting Messiah with

---

[543] NRSV's "descendants" obscures Peter's plain argument that reasons from scripture's singular σπέρμα at whichever form of that promise is under discussion (Barrett (1994: 212–213)). Cf. Luke 3:34 where Jesus' genealogy establishes him as the son of Abraham, Isaac and Jacob.

[544] Oakes (2015: 119–120), helpfully discusses Paul's argument in relation to the Abrahamic blessing and problems facing Judaisms' interpretations of it.

Abraham's seed is written as deep into Luke's Prologue as it is into Galatians 3.[545] In Solomon's Colonnade Luke-Acts' Peter built on his own Moses case.[546]

B. Peter's scriptural reasoning: stringing (*haruzin*)

Peter's argument in Acts 3:22–4:4 is based solidly on Jesus' resurrection (ἀνάστασιν, 4:2): God glorified (ἐδόξασεν) him, raised him (ἤγειρεν, 3:15; ἀναστήσας, 3:26). Building on his Pentecost address,[547] Peter argues that God's promise to David (ἀναστήσω) is enriched by Torah because it is Jesus, David's seed, who was raised, while God also spoke of Abraham's seed (Acts 3:25). Orderly Luke (Luke 1:1–4) begins Peter's speech with "the God of Abraham" (Acts 3:13) and concludes that by raising Jesus from the dead the God of Abraham had sent Jesus to "turn" the hearers from their evil ways.[548] Peter's condensed argument is easily recognizable, shaped by its *inclusio* that reflects Jesus' commission "that repentance and forgiveness of sins is to be proclaimed in his name to all nations" (Luke 24:44–48).[549]

Peter twice calls for his hearers' repentance: first, so that

- their sins might be wiped out;
- God might send both "the times of refreshing" and
- "the Messiah already appointed for them" (τὸν προκεχειρισμένον ὑμῖν χριστὸν), namely Jesus, whom heaven had received until then.[550]

---

[545] See Ch. 2, appended note.

[546] Stephen will argue his from the house that Solomon built: Ch. 7.

[547] Acts 2:24–36; cf. 3:19–21.

[548] Acts 3:26, cf. 3:19.

[549] Acts 3:19, 26; an *inclusio* within an *inclusio* (3:13, 26).

[550] Cf. the time scale within Ps. 109:1 that forms the culmination of Peter's Pentecost speech: εἶπεν [ὁ] κύριος τῷ κυρίῳ μου· κάθου ἐκ δεξιῶν μου, ἕως ἂν θῶ τοὺς ἐχθρούς σου ὑποπόδιον τῶν ποδῶν σου. Peter's Christology here resembles that following Paul's report of traditional preaching (1 Cor. 15:20–28).

151

Peter's second, and implied, call for his hearers' repentance stands in his final word to them before he is interrupted:

> When God raised up (ἀναστήσας) his servant, he sent him first to you, to bless you by turning each of you from your wicked ways (Acts 3:26).

Readers know that this servant is Jesus (Acts 3:13); they know that this Jesus is the Messiah, David's seed, already in heaven, waiting (Acts 3:20–21). By now, readers recognize that when Luke has in mind a scriptural promise and needs a resurrection-verb he is most likely to choose the root of ἀναστήσας and to use it bivalently. How complex that David-promise becomes in Peter's hands emerges as his argument grows clearer. It is enough at present to grasp that Jesus emerged into Israel's history among Peter's hearers to secure their penitence and reform; they had been partners in killing Jesus, whom God had raised from the dead. They were now Jesus' first hearers of this fulfilled, covenanted blessing for all earth's families. How did Peter get there?

1. Peter's prophets sequence

The prophets sequence following Peter's first call for repentance, Moses (Acts 3:22), Samuel (3:24) and Abraham (3:25), is Luke's stringing the promises to Moses and to Abraham that he alludes to in this sequence, by means of the uncited third, his pervasive frame of reference that undergirds Luke-Acts God's promise to David. But how does this prophet-sequence function in Peter's argument?

Through all his prophets of old God had announced that there would be a time of restoration of all things (ἀποκατάστασις) (Acts 3:21); whether their announcing included Luke's timetable outlined in Acts 3:18–20 remains debatable. Luke illustrated his claim by naming three such prophets who, we must assume, spoke of "these days," days that include the healing of the lame man,[551] the event that gave rise to Peter's address, one example of the signs and wonders that distinguish "these days."[552] We turn to each of Peter's named prophets.

i. Moses

At Acts 3:22 Peter names Moses,[553] implying that he is a prophet. But how had Moses spoken of the coming of the Messiah (Acts 3:18, 20)? For Peter, the answer stands in a passage from Deuteronomy, "The Lord your God will raise up for you from your own brothers a prophet like me."[554] That, naturally, echoes the Deuteronomist's final assessment of Moses as a prophet (Deut. 34:10–12); it also, however, recalls Luke's prophet thread in relation to Jesus.[555]

While Johnson (2013: 145–161) undoubtedly focuses this important element within Luke's retelling Jesus' story, he has not taken into account both the pervasive presence of Luke's base-text and its enigmatic, fruitful ἀναστήσω. For what else does Peter's reference to Moses evoke but a reader's knowing that what Peter reports indirectly, Deuteronomy itself has God directly announce – προφήτην ἀναστήσω αὐτοῖς ἐκ τῶν ἀδελφῶν αὐτῶν ὥσπερ σὲ?[556]

The Moses whose Bush experience crystallized Jesus' argument for general resurrection has also reported God's promise, retrospectively identified, of specific resurrection – of that prophet who happens essentially to be David's seed, the appointed Messiah, currently in heaven until God's appointed time.

---

[551] Acts 3:2–12, 16; 4:7–10, 14, 16–17, 22. This lame man's healing remains the reason for the following two scenes' focal event. (See Ch. 7).

[552] Acts 2:19 (a Lukan gloss on Joel 3:3), 22, 43; 4:16, 22, 30, etc.

[553] Luke returns to Moses' story in Stephen's *apologia* (Ch. 7); there, as here, Deut. 18:15 (ἀναστήσει) implies 18:18 (ἀναστήσω) and the raised prophet as Jesus (Acts 7:51–53).

[554] Deut. 18:15; προφήτην ὑμῖν ἀναστήσει κύριος ὁ θεὸς ὑμῶν ἐκ τῶν ἀδελφῶν ὑμῶν ὡς ἐμέ.

[555] A thread discernible through e.g., Luke 4:24; 7:16, 39; 9:8, 19; 13:33–34; 24:19; Acts 3:22–23; 7:37, 52.

[556] Deut. 18:18; Acts 3:22 (Deut. 18:15).

ii. Samuel

Samuel here represents an unvoiced allusion. There are three references to Samuel in the New Testament. At Heb. 11:32 and at Acts 13:20,[557] his name stands in a promise context associated with "David."[558] At Acts 3:24, the name "Samuel" probably represents the prophet and the book that bore his name.[559] With that in mind, Peter's formula repays exploration: all the prophets spoke of and announced these days; at least, those who followed on from Samuel; particularly as many as spoke of these days.

In Peter's speech, the name Samuel stands between two clear allusions to prophetic promises, to Moses and to Abraham. Elsewhere in the New Testament, Samuel's name is associated with David and with promise. It is, consequently, probable that Luke, whose narrative's reference-frame is God's promise to David as it is carried in Samuel's book (see Chapter 2), intended by naming Samuel to evoke that same David-promise here also. That promise opened with God's ἀναστήσω; Peter's previous allusion (Acts 3:22–23) was to an ἀναστήσω in God's promise to Moses. Peter has joined Samuel with Moses and with Abraham in this list of named prophets,[560] and we postulate that Samuel's unvoiced allusion is to God's "I will raise up your seed after you": καὶ ἀναστήσω τὸ σπέρμα σου μετὰ σέ.[561]

Seminar groups rightly question whether "Samuel" represents an unvoiced allusion. Scholars accustomed to shaping arguments around a

---

[557] Heb. 11:32: "For time would fail me to tell of [...] of David and Samuel and the prophets" – Δαυίδ τε καὶ Σαμουὴλ καὶ τῶν προφητῶν. Notably, to speak of Jesus, Heb. 1:5 resorts to two David texts shared with Luke-Acts and 4Q174.

[558] For discussion of the Introduction to Paul's sermon and its reference to Samuel see Ch. 8.

[559] Samuel's Hebrew text was undivided.

[560] Named prophets are the heart of Luke-Acts' exegetical exemplars for Theophilus.

[561] 2 Sam. 7:12 with co-text.

hierarchy of quotation, allusion and echo tend to baulk at talk of an unvoiced allusion. If Nathan's oracle is so important to his narrative, why does Luke never cite it?

My response to this question lies in Luke's debt to Jewish exegetical traditions,[562] particularly to homiletic techniques entailing the non-citing of that text influential throughout the exposition of scripture.[563] Similarities between Peter's address in Solomon's Colonnade (Acts 3:12–4:4) and Paul's Antioch sermon (Acts 13:16b–41) initially led me to three modern writers:[564] Doeve (1954), Lövestam (1961), and Bowker (1967).[565] All three are concerned with Paul's sermon: Lövestam and Bowker substantially so; Doeve (1954: 172–75) as one of his case studies. All three discuss an underlying Hebrew, or Aramaic, form of the text for Paul's scriptural citations. Doeve specifically rejects the suggestion by Lake and Cadbury (1933b: 155 n.4) that the LXX must have been the source text for Paul's argument.[566] In varying ways, all three agree that Jewish, rabbinical exegetical traditions provide Luke's Paul with the structure of his argument.[567]

Significantly, all three agree that Paul's argument depends on his focus on God's promise to David through Nathan (2 Sam. 7:6–16). Following Doeve, Bowker (1967: 103) concludes that Nathan's oracle was Paul's *haftarah*, "tacitly employed throughout." Lövestam (1961: 7) is also indebted to Doeve, quoting

---

[562] So e.g., Bovon, (2006: 118).

[563] Maarten Menken sent me back to this fundamental question; this newer "answer" matches *Interpreter's* argument, developed from Lukan practice.

[564] See Ch. 8.

[565] I had referred to Bowker's article in Doble (1996).

[566] *Interpreter's* case, per contra, depends on Luke's using the verb ἀνίστημι bivalently; Luke's was a Greek Bible. See Marguerat (2002: 68n.11).

[567] Traditions with long-reaching roots into their past?

his conclusion that Nathan's oracle "forms the background of the speaker's entire argument so far."[568]

Bowker alone confronts my fundamental question – why is so significant an oracle never quoted? For his answer, thereafter pervading his short study, Bowker turned to Jacob Mann,[569] whose study of synagogue preaching techniques undergirds Bowker's work:

> During the course of *hazurin* [*sic*][570] the *haftarah* of the day may be quoted explicitly or more often it is implied in the homily throughout and simply alluded to. It is always in the background of the exposition, or, as Mann put it, it is always in the preacher's mind.[571] [...] The final text was usually taken from the seder reading of the day, though occasionally [...] from some other part of scripture; but even then it would point directly to the seder.[572]

So we have three advocates for Luke's basing his Antioch sermon on Nathan's uncited though pervasive oracle,[573] arriving independently at this conclusion, two of them, in varying measure, indebted to Doeve. Two argue for Luke's employing homiletic techniques where an uncited text pervades the preacher's

---

[568] Lövestam's Scriptural Index has forty-five entries relating to Nathan's oracle.

[569] Bowker refers extensively to Jacob Mann (1940), *The Bible as Read and Preached in the Old Synagogue,* giving no further bibliographic details for this 1940 work; a currently available edition is (1971) *The Bible as read and preached in the old synagogue: a study in the cycles of reading from* Torah *and Prophets, as well as from Psalms and in the structure of the Midrashic homilies,* New York: Ktav Publishing.

[570] *Haruzin* refers to the "stringing," as of pearls on a thread, of a sequence of scriptural quotations. this describes the sequence in Peter's speech.

[571] In a long footnote to Bowker's article (100, n.2), omitted here, is an italicized quotation from Mann: "The H[aftarah] was not used explicitly because it was tacitly employed throughout," precisely what Luke's narrative has led me independently to re-affirm.

[572] Bowker (1967: 100).

[573] Doeve (1954), Lövestam (1961) and Bowker (1967).

argument.[574] While my argument has emerged independently of these scholars – differing substantially in my affirming Luke's use of a Greek scriptural source – they offer sound reason for Luke's not citing so important a text during Paul's Antioch sermon.

By his opening Prologue – his overture to God's opera – Luke indicated two text-passages undergirding his two-volume narrative's understanding of Jesus' place in God's purposes. Witnessing to the sureness (ἀσφάλεια) of "the things fulfilled among us" (Luke 1:1–4), Luke drew on those two promises by:

- a birth announcement shaped by Ezekiel (Luke 2:8–20), and
- a pre-conception promise to Mary, his base-text that owes its language and thought to Samuel (Luke 1:26–38).

Thereafter, Luke need not cite what is now in a reader's mind. We see below how Peter's argument requires the presence of Nathan's oracle – Peter's speech's structure and substructure cohere, as they did in his Pentecost sermon and in Luke 24. Luke indicated his unvoiced allusion by his frame of reference.

iii. Abraham

Peter's opening words named Abraham;[575] completing his *inclusio,* Luke has placed Abraham in this sequence of prophets. "Prophet" naturally described Abraham among fellow Jews whom Peter was addressing, joint-heirs of the covenant (Acts 3:25). Crucially for Peter's argument, Abraham received God's covenant-promise: "and *by your seed* shall all earth's nations be blessed."[576]

---

[574] Bowker (1967) and Mann (1971).

[575] My debt to Nils Dahl's seminal essay in Keck and Martyn (1968: 139–158) is clear; my dissent from his case, obvious.

[576] καὶ ἐνευλογηθήσονται ἐν τῷ σπέρματί σου πάντα τὰ ἔθνη τῆς γῆς Acts 3:25; Gen. 22:18 et al.; cf. Sirach 44:19–21.

For Luke-Acts, Jesus is by descent a son of Abraham (Luke 3:34), and in its Prologue Mary rejoiced that God's David-promise to her implied God's promise to Abraham:[577]

> ἀντελάβετο Ἰσραὴλ *παιδὸς* αὐτοῦ,
> μνησθῆναι ἐλέους,
> καθὼς ἐλάλησεν πρὸς τοὺς πατέρας ἡμῶν,
> τῷ Ἀβραὰμ καὶ *τῷ σπέρματι αὐτοῦ* εἰς τὸν αἰῶνα (Luke 1:54–55).

Paralleling Mary's Magnificat, Zechariah's *Benedictus* (Luke 1:68–73) closely associated the appearance of a saviour (literally horn of salvation) in David's house with God's remembering his covenant-love and oath sworn to Abraham. Arguably, these canticles prefigure Peter's argument.[578]

From Luke's opening scenes, Theophilus and subsequent readers have been alerted to Luke's rich scriptural subtext, already pointing forward to the significance of this singular "seed" in Luke-Acts. Through his sequence of three prophets, Peter spells out for hearers, and Luke for Theophilus, how these things might be. For people who have searched their scriptures and followed Luke's narrative, who are accustomed to making conceptual and lexical connections often alien to later ages, Peter's stringing of three promises made a sound argument.

2. Stringing promises (*haruzin*)

First, line up God's promises that Luke cites or evokes:

> (a) προφήτην *ἀναστήσω* αὐτοῖς ἐκ τῶν ἀδελφῶν αὐτῶν ὥσπερ σὲ (Acts 3:22; Moses)
> (b) καὶ *ἀναστήσω τὸ σπέρμα σου* μετὰ σέ (Acts 3:24; Samuel, Luke's reference-frame)

---

[577] An example of Lukan "twoness," appearing twice in the Infancy Gospel.

[578] Cf. ἐλάλησεν διὰ στόματος τῶν ἁγίων ἀπ᾽ αἰῶνος προφητῶν αὐτοῦ. Luke 1:70; Acts 3:24–26.

(c) καὶ ἐν *τῷ σπέρματί σου* εὐλογηθήσονται πᾶσαι αἱ πατριαὶ τῆς γῆς (Acts 3:25; Abraham).

Then set them in Peter's substructural argument. His stringing consists in his middle term's (b) sharing its ἀναστήσω with (a), and its σπέρμα with (c); three promises become mutually illuminating. Crucially, Peter's middle term is Luke's base-text. Prophets have spoken of "these days" – days of the appointed Messiah but before the final restoration of all things, days when a lame man has been healed by trusting in Jesus' name – and to this point Luke-Acts' narrative has built on his base-text found in the prophet Samuel and on its fulfilment in God's anointing and resurrection of Jesus.

But Jesus' resurrection and Samuel's bivalent ἀναστήσω evoked the prophet Moses. Peter's opening had already recalled Moses at the Bush with its associated resurrection thread. It now recalled Moses, through whom God had promised another prophet like himself (a above), that is, from Abrahamic descent. Because God had raised Jesus from the dead then the retrospective bivalency of Deuteronomy's ἀναστήσω (Deut. 18:18) ensured that he, Jesus, was that prophet of whom Moses spoke and through whom God was addressing Israel.

"These days" of the Messiah in waiting before God's ἀποκατάστασις are days of signs and wonders, of God's fulfilling Israel's foundational promise (c above) because the Jesus who has been raised from the dead is also Abraham's seed (Luke 3:34).

Luke's Prologue continues to illuminate his ongoing narrative as Peter moves from the Bush and "the God of Abraham, Isaac and Jacob has glorified his servant Jesus" to Peter's conclusion that "by raising up his servant" Jesus, God has begun, first with Israel, to fulfil the Abrahamic promise of God's blessing all earth's families. And this is where Peter's speech is interrupted by

159

an official group, an interruption that leads seamlessly into his third Mirror speech – discussed in Chapter 6.

They have good cause to interrupt,[579] for this speech further threatens their authority in relation to Jesus. If this "raised-up" Jesus is being proclaimed as Torah's prophet like Moses, then its attached threat has implications for them:

> You must listen to whatever he tells you. And it will be that everyone who does not listen to that prophet will be utterly rooted out of the people (Acts 3:22–23).[580]

That listen (ἀκούω) will echo in Peter's response to the Sanhedrin's ordering him not to teach or act in Jesus' name when he appears before them.[581]

---

[579] Acts 4:1, Λαλούντων δὲ αὐτῶν πρὸς τὸν λαόν.

[580] Acts 3:22b–23; cf. Deut. 18:17–19, adapted in the light of Jesus' vineyard parable.

[581] Acts 4:19; cf. 5:29. (see Ch. 6).

C. Summary of Mirror 2

Building on his Pentecost narrative, Peter's speech in Solomon's Colonnade retrospectively reflects on Jesus and the Bush:[582] this Jesus God glorified, raised, exalted and sent to Peter's hearers. Peter's Jesus-descriptors encompass God's servant (παῖς), righteous (δίκαιος) and holy one (ἅγιος), Messiah (Χριστός) and, by implication, prophet (προφήτης). By a triple *inclusio*,[583] Peter framed his speech within Abraham's story and that of God's raising up his servant Jesus. It was by trust (τῇ πίστει) in that Jesus' name that one lame man became a walking sign that God's new age was dawning.

That framework encloses Peter's key statement of one fixed point in God's timescale and one conviction about Israel's prophets. The fixed point is that Jesus, God's appointed Messiah, is in waiting; Israel's prophets had spoken of "these days" that included the Messiah's suffering (Acts 3:18) and being raised.[584] From among Israel's prophets, Peter selected three and named them; their evoked words form the recognizable *haruzin* that enabled him to move from Moses' turning aside to the Bush,[585] where he encountered Abraham's God, to his (Peter's) conclusion that in the glorified and raised up Jesus Abraham's God had fulfilled the covenant promise. But Moses who turned aside at the Bush had also received a promise of a prophet like himself.

Peter extended the "Davidic" ἀναστήσω, found in the prophet Samuel into Torah's promise to Moses – and Sadducees were listening and pounced. They pounced because these apostles were proclaiming that the Jesus who affirmed that the resurrection from the dead was grounded in Moses' encounter

---

[582] Luke 20:37–38; cf. 24:5b. See Ch. 3.

[583] Abraham (Acts 3:13, 25), servant (3:13, 26), resurrection (3:13, glorified = 26, raised up).

[584] Acts 3:15, ὃν ὁ θεὸς ἤγειρεν ἐκ νεκρῶν, reasoned to its sequel, ἀναστήσας […] τὸν παῖδα αὐτοῦ, in 3:26.

[585] Alluded to at Acts 3:13.

with Abraham's God at the Bush had himself become living proof of that ἀνάστασις (Acts 4:2; cf. Luke 20:35–36).[586] Peter and John threatened Jerusalem's rulers' hegemony by proclaiming that Jesus was the sign that God's new age was dawning.

---

[586] Luke 20:37, ὅτι δὲ ἐγείρονται οἱ νεκροί, καὶ Μωϋσῆς ἐμήνυσεν ἐπὶ τῆς βάτου; cf. Acts 3:15, ὃν ὁ θεὸς ἤγειρεν ἐκ νεκρῶν.

Chapter 6. Mirror 3: Rulers and Culmination 1

This chapter continues the Temple-based events we began to explore in Chapter 5. Luke's long, continuous narrative sequence (Acts 4:5–31) covers less than forty-eight hours in the Jerusalem conflict; its focus is Jesus' resurrection (Acts 4:1–4); its event to be interpreted is the restoring to wholeness of a lame man, a sign present throughout Peter's final exegetical speech (Acts 3:1–16; 4:5–22). Three elements focus our concern in Peter's final speech.[587] First, facing Jerusalem's rulers, who condemned Jesus to death, Peter, reversing his earlier denial of Jesus, strengthens his brothers (see Luke 22:31–34). Second, while the rulers play a large role in Luke-Acts, here they share with Peter a crucial role in Luke's narrative that closes his "signs and wonders" sequence and heightens his conflict-account. Third, we explore how Luke's retelling of Jesus' story for Theophilus may be thought of as "fulfilling" Israel's scriptures.[588] These elements resolve into this chapter's main heads: A. Mirror 3 and Acts 4:12; B. On Luke's subtextual use of Ps. 145; C. Culmination 1.

---

[587] The culmination in a scriptural setting of a Lukan it-is-written thread concerning rulers – "you killed him" evokes David's Ps. 2. Two further culminations are identified in Stephen's speech (see Ch. 7) and Paul's Antioch sermon (see Ch. 8).

[588] Luke 1:1–4. Tradition's account of the conflict between Jesus and the rulers; Luke's systematic presentation of the conflict between Jesus' followers and the rulers; Luke's distinctive description of Jesus as δίκαιος (e.g., Luke 23:47; Acts 3:14; 7:51–53; 22:14), combined to convince me that Luke's subtext included not only psalms of the righteous one's conflict with the ungodly, but probably the Wisdom of Solomon also. See Doble (1996; 2013: 95–113); Ch. 7 below. Cf. Docherty (2009: 83–120).

A. Mirror 3 and Acts 4:12

Peter here interprets his third Jesus-intertext, one of three common to the synoptic tradition. At the simplest level, Peter's mirroring interprets while reversing tradition's Jesus-sequence. At another level, the players in Luke's two sequences are identical – Jerusalem's rulers and Jesus,[589] here represented by his Spirit-filled *shaliach,* Peter. The issues in each setting are identical: they focus on authority to act (in the Temple); on the psalmist's enigmatic stone-saying and, finally, on the fundamental issue of the Jerusalem authorities' relation to Israel's God.[590] Luke's Jesus was clear: Jerusalem had not known the things that belonged to her shalom (Luke 19:41–44); her rulers, reckless of God, were self-aggrandizing.

Luke's distinctive sequencing of tradition's siting of Jesus' intertexts creates one single unit (Luke 19:47–20:26) that reaches its climax in the questioners' having themselves to decide which really matters – God or Caesar. Luke mirrors that climax in Peter's initial appearance before Jerusalem's rulers.[591] Their challenging Peter's authority elicits his adaptation of the stone-saying,[592] and concludes with his giving the rulers a similar choice – you must choose for yourselves what is right (δίκαιόν); whether to obey God or you; we

---

[589] Luke presented elements of the Sanhedrin as Jesus' opponents in Jerusalem: scribes, principal priests and the "first among the People" (Luke 19:47); scribes and principal priests, (20:19–20; 22:1; cf. 22:1–5, 52 (where "elders" appear); some scribes, (20:41–47); Sadducees (20:27). At 22:66 Luke describes the Sanhedrin: συνήχθη τὸ πρεσβυτέριον τοῦ λαοῦ, principal priests and scribes, here implying that this eldership forms part of the συνέδριον. By 23:13, before Pilate, Jesus' accusers have become the principal priests, rulers (ἄρχοντας) and "the People"; at 23:35, the rulers mock Jesus.

[590] Note Luke's distinctive, scathing sequence about scribes who figure so large in his narrative (20:45–21:6).

[591] Recall that in Luke's duo Peter is the spokesman while John, his corroborating witness, remains a silent partner (Luke 10:1); narratively, Luke's focus is on the fulfilling of Jesus' Peter-*logion* (Luke 22:31–35).

[592] Ps. 117:22; Luke 20:17; Acts 4:11.

have chosen. The ensuing scene among "their own" confirms Peter's and his brothers' choice (Acts 4:23–31).

The focus of Mirror 3 is first on Peter's mirroring of Jesus' Stone-*logion*. It is, however, obliquely used, indirectly accusing the rulers while Peter answers their opening question – "by what name did you do this?" (Acts 4:7, 12b). The stone-saying has its special place in Christian tradition: sited at the conclusion of Jesus' vineyard parable, it presents a probing question for the crowds, authorities and Luke's readers.

1. The vineyard parable in Luke-Acts

This parable's role in Luke-Acts throws clearer light on Peter's interpretation of the Stone-*logion*. Notably, Luke re-built tradition's parable into his distinctive narrative sequence that contributes to readers' grasp of the rulers' role in Jesus' death (Luke 20:1–21:6). Following a hostile challenge to Jesus' authority for acting and teaching in the Temple, Jesus told his parable to the crowd (Luke 19:47–20:8; 20:9–18). From his narrative's outset Luke's readers have known what constituted Jesus' authority: the Infancy Gospel, followed by Luke's distinctive account of Jesus' anointing and the sequence that led to his being recognized by demons as "Son of God, the Messiah" (Luke 4:41), all affirmed that his authority was from God. Jerusalem's rulers,[593] who failed to discern, or refused to acknowledge, John the Baptist's source of authority, could hardly be expected to acknowledge that of Jesus (Luke 20:1–8). Official dislike of him was already deep – they kept looking for a way to kill him (Luke 19:45–48).[594]

---

[593] With Tannehill (1990), who reads οἱ πρῶτοι τοῦ λαοῦ as synonymous with rulers.

[594] Luke's ἐζήτουν αὐτὸν ἀπολέσαι rephrases Mark's ἐζήτουν πῶς αὐτὸν ἀπολέσωσιν (Mk 11:19). Possibly, Markan tradition et al. sent Luke to Ps. 36:32 – κατανοεῖ ὁ ἁμαρτωλὸς τὸν δίκαιον καὶ ζητεῖ τοῦ θανατῶσαι αὐτόν, thence to a psalm that influenced his passion story, – ἐν τῷ ἐπισυναχθῆναι αὐτοὺς ἅμα ἐπ᾽ ἐμὲ τοῦ λαβεῖν τὴν ψυχήν μου ἐβουλεύσαντο (Ps. 30:14).

i. Davidic, not Isaianic

The New Testament's vineyard parable[595] speaks of an owner, tenants and the owner's "son and heir." Isaianic echoes, clearer in Mark and Matthew, are minimized by Luke who has thoroughly reworked this parable.[596] None of Jesus' hearers could mistake either its referents or his parable's threat. Here, its tenants, not the vineyard, are Luke's focus; the scribes and principal priests realized that Jesus had directed the parable to them (Luke 20:19). Together, within Luke's reference-frame, "son" and "heir" can evoke only Ps. 2:7–9 and a Davidic reading of Luke's text.[597] Luke's narrative of Jesus' anointing probably appropriated David's experience – "You are my son; today I have begotten you."[598] That psalm's following verse speaks of this Son's "inheritance" (κληρονομία), the word used also by the vineyard's tenants (Luke 20:14). Jesus' parable posed his question – whose is this vineyard and whose is its fruit (καρπός)?

ii. Luke's sequencing

Luke's distinctive sequencing of Jesus' final week in Jerusalem brought more closely together than in Mark and Matthew the twin traditions of parable and Caesar's coin: Luke did this via his theme of the rulers' plotting:

> When the scribes and principal priests realized that he had told this parable them-wards [πρὸς αὐτοὺς], they wanted to lay hands on him at that very hour, but they feared the people. So they kept him under surveillance [παρατηρήσαντες] and sent agents who pretended to be righteous [δικαίους], in order to

---

[595] Cf. Isa. 5:1–7.

[596] So also Elliott (2001: 1318), who recognizes similarities between Luke's and Thomas's versions of this parable (*Logion* 65). Thomas's Stone-*logion* (66), however, functions differently from that in Luke.

[597] Luke's qualifier τὸν ἀγαπητόν, lacking in Mark or Matthew.

[598] Luke 3:21–22; Ps. 2:7; see Doble (2013: 95–113).

trap him by what he said, so as to hand him over [παραδοῦναι] to the jurisdiction and authority of the governor (Luke 20:19–20).[599]

Luke's transition from parable to Caesar's coin differs significantly from Mark's or Matthew's: Pharisees disappeared earlier from his narrative,[600] and while he is interested in Herod's household,[601] Luke makes no reference to Herodians. In Jerusalem, Jesus' opponents are firmly scribes, principal priests and "elders," the people whom Peter confronts in Acts. Their motive is manifest – "to hand over" Jesus to Gentile authority.[602]

In this transition, Luke's language is of interest, especially his using the unusual verb παρατηρέω.[603] Further, why were their agents "play-acting" (ὑποκρινομένους) the part of the "righteous" (δικαίους)? Given Luke's assessment of Jesus as righteous (δίκαιος),[604] and his rooting Jesus' story in Israel's scriptures, one naturally seeks places where this verb and noun work together. Luke proposed to narrate for Theophilus "things fulfilled among us"; his appeal to psalms is his drawing on David's, Israel's and his community's experience of God.[605] Luke's distinctive portrayal of Jesus' death has a centurion characterize him as genuinely righteous.[606] This distinctiveness owes much to the psalms' accounts of David's suffering, particularly that portrayed in

---

[599] Some English translations (and UBS5) place a heading between vv 19 and 20, obscuring Luke's construction.

[600] At Luke 19:39.

[601] See, e.g., Stanford (2014: 49–76, 303–304).

[602] παραδοῦναι, cf. Luke 9:44, 18:32.

[603] Also Luke 6:7; 14:1; 20:20 and Acts 9:24; see, e.g., Susanna 12, 15, 16, for this verb's hostile sense.

[604] See Doble (1996; 2013); cf. *Interpreter*'s discussion of Stephen's speech.

[605] See, e.g., Doble (2004) and examples in *Interpreter*'s earlier chapters of Luke's using enriching psalms. Ch. 7 synthesizes these findings.

[606] ὄντως [...] δίκαιος (Luke 23:47); Peter (Acts 3:14), Stephen (7:52–53) and Paul, reporting Ananias, (22:15) for this Jesus descriptor; Luke is interested in those whose character is δίκαιος.

Ps. 30 where both Jesus' last word and the centurion's judgment on what he had seen and heard find their source.[607] Ps. 36 thoroughly explores the life of a "righteous one" in the presence of hostile "ungodly."[608] So, given Luke's ways of using scripture, it is unsurprising that the language of persecution drawn from another psalm of a suffering righteous one illuminates Luke's story of Jesus' walk towards death:

παρατηρήσεται ὁ ἁμαρτωλὸς τὸν δίκαιον
καὶ βρύξει ἐπ' αὐτὸν τοὺς ὀδόντας αὐτοῦ (Ps. 36:12).

Further, at the empty tomb the Shining Ones identified those to whom Jesus was handed over as "sinful men";[609] might not their description also have emerged from a scriptural subtext that apparently shaped Luke's thought and language about Jesus? If so, we have a full house from Ps. 36:12, for the sinful man (ὁ ἁμαρτωλὸς) seeking to put the righteous to death (Ps. 36:32), keeps him under surveillance. Luke's depiction of Jesus' opponents looks very like the psalmists' understanding of David's life and of others like him – "righteous ones" among God's People suffering at the hands of the ungodly.[610]

"Twoness" has a special place in Luke-Acts, and the stone-saying encapsulates its conflict narrative: Peter engages with the Sanhedrin as had Jesus before him.

---

[607] Luke 23:46, (Ps. 30:6); 23:47, (Ps. 30:19); Doble (1996: 70–160).

[608] Luke's distinctive shaping of the vineyard parable's setting prepares readers for the later scenes of Jesus trials and death, evoking what wisdom psalms see as the age-old conflict between the righteous (who suffer) and the ungodly (who transiently flourish). The righteous' characteristic is their commitment to God and to God's People as a community of righteousness and justice.

[609] Luke 24:7, ἀνθρώπων ἁμαρτωλῶν.

[610] One characteristic of psalms of the righteous is that they contrast the righteous (*tsaddiq*) and the wicked (*rasha'*). Both Pss. 30 (influential in Luke's account of Jesus' death) and 36 (that influenced Luke-Acts' conflict-narrative (Luke 19:41-Acts 8:3)) present this contrast as a vigorous hostility towards the righteous by the wicked. The portrait of the δίκαιος in Wis. 2–5 has probably been strongly influenced by wisdom psalms. See, e.g., Perry, T. A. ([2008] 2014: 109–121).

iii. The stone-saying (Acts 4:11)

Peter's response to the rulers' question (Acts 4:7) assumes that they refer to the lame man's healing. Throughout this scene, the man remains the visible, undeniable sign of Jesus' continuing activity.[611] Here, definitively answering the rulers' question, echoing that put to Jesus at his trial (Luke 22:67), Peter replies that this lame man was saved by Jesus' name (Acts 4:10), Jesus Messiah, the Nazorean – the dual phrase used by Peter at the man's healing (3:6).

Peter reminds them, this Jesus is he "whom you crucified" (ὃν ὑμεῖς ἐσταυρώσατε, Acts 4:10a), evoking for them, and readers, this Sanhedrin's having engineered Jesus' death. Despite their actions, Peter continues, Jesus was the one "whom God raised from the dead" (ὃν ὁ θεὸς ἤγειρεν ἐκ νεκρῶν, 4:10b), the very proclamation that had provoked the officials who imprisoned Peter and John. "It is by this [name] that this [man] is healthy, present before you."[612] "This" name, however, entails two scriptural descriptors: the Stone and the Saviour.[613]

a. Stone descriptor (Acts 4:10–11)

Peter's adapted intertext makes yet tighter links with earlier events by evoking Jesus' question posed at the end of his vineyard parable – what does this mean? Luke's readers will make the connection that Peter the interpreter clearly intends: this Jesus is ὁ λίθος, ὁ ἐξουθενηθεὶς ὑφ' ὑμῶν τῶν οἰκοδόμων, ὁ γενόμενος εἰς κεφαλὴν γωνίας (Acts 4:11). The differences between Peter's "citation" and the intertext's earlier settings in Luke-Acts and in Psalms are best

---

[611] Acts 4:7, 9, 10, 14, 22.

[612] My rendering clarifies Luke's pronouns.

[613] Cf. Taylor, V. (1953).

understood as *pesher*, adaptation to the source-text's new situation: λίθον, ὃν ἀπεδοκίμασαν οἱ οἰκοδομοῦντες, οὗτος ἐγενήθη εἰς κεφαλὴν γωνίας.[614]

Peter does here what his brethren do with Ps. 2 in the following scene – recognize Jesus' story in scripture. Key differences between his adapted and source-text versions are threefold. First, Peter identifies the *logion*'s "builders" as "you" (ὑφ' ὑμῶν), resuming his earlier "whom you crucified." Second, Peter's adaptation changes the verb describing what the builders did: the psalm's ἀπεδοκίμασαν becomes Peter's ἐξουθενηθεὶς. While I cannot know Luke's reasoning here, familiarity with his subtext and narrative threading suggest that two lexical possibilities may be working together.

(a) In his account of the authorities' plotting to hand Jesus over to Roman justice, Luke offered a vivid and distinctive scene, with this story's principals gathered in one setting:

> [Herod] questioned him with many words, but Jesus gave him no answer. The chief priests and the scribes made their stand, vehemently accusing him. Then, after Herod with his soldiers had treated him with contempt [ἐξουθενήσας] and mocked [ἐμπαίξας] him, he put an elegant robe on [Jesus], and sent him back to Pilate (Luke 23:9–11).

Herod, chief priests, scribes (corporately described as rulers) and Pilate will reappear in the prayer-scene following Peter's release (Acts 4:25–28).

(b) We also know that Luke told the story of Jesus' death in language drawn from psalms describing the righteous one's sufferings at the hands of the impious, especially Ps. 30 that sourced Jesus' last word and a centurion's assessment of the man whose death he witnessed.[615] That psalm's righteous

---

[614] Ps. 117:22; Luke 20:17.

[615] ἄλαλα γενηθήτω τὰ χείλη τὰ δόλια τὰ λαλοῦντα κατὰ τοῦ δικαίου ἀνομίαν ἐν ὑπερηφανίᾳ καὶ ἐξουδενώσει. Cf. Luke 23:46; (Ps. 30:6); Luke 23:47; (Ps. 30:19).

man was conscious of the trap his opponents had hidden for him; of the contempt (ἐξουδένωσις) in which their pride held him.[616]

Luke who systematically planned his fulfilment narrative for Theophilus by rewriting Jesus' story within the language and thought-forms of Israel's scriptures was he whose scriptural-subtext was his matrix, not additional illustration. Whatever was happening, Peter's *pesher* on the stone-saying employed a verb whose presence suggests long lexical-narrative roots.

The third difference explains itself: addressing rulers and interpreting this saying so as to answer Jesus' question about it – what does this mean? (Luke 20:17)[617] – Peter makes Jesus the subject of the whole: nominatives transform his adaptation. This Jesus has figuratively become the capstone, ὁ γενόμενος εἰς κεφαλὴν γωνίας.[618] Peter's insistence that death has not held the one they crucified, that God had raised him from the dead (ὃν ὁ θεὸς ἤγειρεν ἐκ νεκρῶν), carries his *pesher* into Peter's present where the Jesus appointed as Israel's Messiah is in heaven, but whose presence as Saviour among his followers is evidenced by the lame man's presence in the Sanhedrin (Acts 3:19–21; 4:16).

---

[616] Ps. 30:5, 19; readers recall that these rulers had "thumbed their noses" (ἐξεμυκτήριζον δὲ καὶ οἱ ἄρχοντες) at the dying Jesus, echoing Ps. 21:8.

[617] τί οὖν ἐστιν τὸ γεγραμμένον τοῦτο; diff. both οὐδὲ τὴν γραφὴν ταύτην ἀνέγνωτε· (Mk 12:10) and οὐδέποτε ἀνέγνωτε ἐν ταῖς γραφαῖς; (Mt. 21:42) Luke's form invites a response.

[618] Whether capstone or cornerstone makes no difference to this passage's thrust: Jesus' standing is transformed from rejection to exaltation.

b. Saviour (Acts 4:12)

Peter here alludes to one of Luke's principal three Jesus-descriptors.[619] In this much-discussed verse, he returns to Jesus' "name" by which the lame man was "saved," reaffirming the words' linkage:[620]

> There is *salvation* in no one else, for there is no other name under heaven given among men by which we must be save*d* (Acts 4:12).

Still addressing rulers, "You [...] crucified" him, Peter's accusation recalls Luke's distinctive scene of Jesus' crucifixion where, he says, these rulers mocked Jesus: "he saved others; he cannot save himself" (Luke 23:35). Their mockery itself focuses Luke's salvation thread that began in his Prologue (Luke 2:11) – "a Saviour, who is Messiah, Lord" – and culminates in Paul's Antioch speech (Acts 13:23) – "from [David's] seed, as promised, God brought a Saviour to Israel, Jesus."[621] Along this thread are accounts of Jesus' saving activity and purpose; healings in his name; and kerygmatic affirmations (e.g., Acts 5:31). Peter's reply, shaped by the dual *inclusio* formed by "save" and "name" (Acts 4:7–9, 12), implicitly identifies Jesus as the Saviour (Acts 4:10, 12), contrasting the rulers with Jesus. Section B demonstrates why Ps. 145 is a key element in Luke's scriptural-subtext, warning that rulers cannot save; Jesus manifestly does.[622]

Luke's much discussed verse (Acts 4:12) belongs firmly in the context of his depiction of:

---

[619] Luke 2:11 – Saviour, Messiah, Lord.

[620] Acts 4:7, 10; on Jesus' "Name" see Marguerat (2007: 145–146). Marguerat has not however made a link with Luke's Prologue where the introductory triptych has disclosed Jesus principal descriptors – Saviour, who is Messiah, Lord (Luke 2:11).

[621] See Ch. 8.

[622] Ps. 145:3; Acts 4:9, 12; see Section B.

172

- Peter's "turning" and fulfilling Jesus' word to him in the Upper Room (Luke 22:31–34);
- Jesus-followers' opening encounter with the rulers responsible for Jesus' crucifixion and for the scattering of the Jerusalem church;
- Peter's mirroring of Jesus' question about the stone-saying (Ps. 117:22);
- His strengthened brothers' resultant, and prayerful, *pesher* on Ps. 2:1–2, to which we turn in section C.

These scenes centre on two psalms, 117 and 2, both strongly associated with David; both scenes are undergirded, probably shaped by Ps. 145, a psalm focused on "two ways."[623] Both scenes evoke Luke's distinctive portrayal of Jesus' suffering and death; we recalled that portrayal's recourse to two "Davidic" psalms of the suffering righteous one, Pss. 30 and 36 that characterized plotting against the δίκαιος. The scenes are richly evocative of scripture and closely interlinked.

Notably, in 4:12, Luke has firmly fixed his contrasting of Jesus the now-exalted Saviour with Jerusalem's rulers, the not-to-be-trusted, plotting sinners. Peter has answered their question (4:7). Their response to Peter confirms both their character and his "turn."

2. Peter and the rulers

i. Peter turned (Acts 4:13)

Here, rulers assess Peter (and John); note Luke's four verbs:
- they observed, or noted (θεωρέω) the apostles' "boldness" (παρρησία);
- they realized, or comprehended (καταλαμβάνω) that these were unschooled amateurs;

---

[623] Ps. 145:8 (κύριος ἀγαπᾷ δικαίους) – 9 (καὶ ὁδὸν ἁμαρτωλῶν ἀφανιεῖ); cf. Prov. 4:14–18.

- they were amazed (θαυμάζω).

- they recognized (ἐπιγινώσκω) that the apostles "had been with Jesus" (ὅτι σὺν τῷ Ἰησοῦ ἦσαν).

That phrase undoes Luke's distinctive narrative of Peter's denying that he was with Jesus (Luke 22:54–62): first, a girl said, "this man was with him" (οὗτος σὺν αὐτῷ ἦν); next, a man, "you also were with him" (καὶ σὺ ἐξ αὐτῶν εἶ); a third, "this man was certainly with him" (ἐπ᾽ ἀληθείας καὶ οὗτος μετ᾽ αὐτοῦ ἦν) (Luke 22:56–59). Peter's denials that he was "with Jesus" include, "I don't know him" (οὐκ οἶδα αὐτόν).[624] Per contra, before the Sanhedrin he spoke courageously as Jesus' *shaliach* and hermeneut. Peter had turned. Now, he was ready to go to prison for Jesus (Luke 22:34).

ii. The rulers

Still interpreting this one sign,[625] Luke contrasts rulers with "the People" who "glorify God" for what happened;[626] throughout Luke's account, these rulers make no reference to God. Plotting against and threatening the righteous was a serious matter: rulers planned to suppress what God had done, threatening the apostles and forbidding them to speak in Jesus' name (Acts 4:13–18). By contrast, Peter and John responded that the Sanhedrin must judge for themselves (κρίνατε) what was δίκαιόν, right or appropriate.[627] The apostles put the question of God firmly at this dialogue's heart: "in God's presence" (ἐνώπιον τοῦ θεοῦ); "to listen to (obey) you rather than to God" (ὑμῶν ἀκούειν μᾶλλον ἢ τοῦ θεοῦ); "as for us (γὰρ ἡμεῖς), we are unable to not speak (μὴ λαλεῖν) about things we have seen and heard" – while the Sanhedrin can. Earlier, we noted

---

[624] Luke 22:34, λέγω σοι, Πέτρε, οὐ φωνήσει σήμερον ἀλέκτωρ ἕως τρίς με ἀπαρνήσῃ εἰδέναι.

[625] Cf. 4:29–30; 5:12–16; on "glorifying God" see Doble (1996: 25–69).

[626] Acts 3:1–4:23; cf. 4:30.

[627] Acts 4:19–20; this has overtones here – their behaviour fits the "way of the righteous" (Ps. 145:5–9).

their reply's rootedness in Ps. 145.[628] Peter has boldly confronted the rulers whom he accused of killing Messiah Jesus – his "turning" is complete. He has, however, more to say of Jesus' name, appealing to the psalm that takes up his earlier transition from healing to saving – Ps. 145.

---

[628] See Part II, Overview, Ps. 145. Scaer (2005) uncovers possible sources for Luke's Passion – "possible" focuses his problem, for Luke insisted that Jesus' suffering and death fulfilled the scriptures. Scaer makes much of Acts 4:19 as words reminiscent of Socrates (pp. 65, 68, 78, 124), but they echo Pss. 117:8–9 and 145:3–6, arguably Luke's subtext in his narrative. Similarly, while Socrates was famously a δίκαιος, so was the psalmist whose words Luke attributed to the dying Jesus (Luke 23:46–7; cf. Ps. 30:6, 19). Scaer, excluding Luke's scriptural subtext, may not properly claim that Luke "formed and fashioned his passion narrative in order to present Jesus as noble and therefore praiseworthy according to well-known standards of the Graeco-Roman world." Pss. 2, 30, 36, 117 and 145 tell a different culture's story.

B. Luke's subtextual use of Ps. 145

Peter's reply, shaped by the dual *inclusio* (Acts 4:7–9, 12) formed by "save" and "name," implicitly identifies Jesus as the Saviour (Acts 4:10, 12), contrasting the rulers with Jesus. This section demonstrates why Ps. 145[629] is a key element in Luke's scriptural subtext: it warned that rulers cannot save; Jesus visibly does.[630] Further, this Jesus whom these rulers crucified had been declared righteous by a centurion; this descriptor early passed into Christian proclamation.[631] Ps. 145:5–9 contrasts the way of the "righteous" with the self-defeating way of "sinners," implying that Jerusalem's not-to-be-trusted rulers were among such sinners.

We noted above that at Jesus' empty tomb Shining Ones spoke of his being betrayed into the hands of sinful men (Luke 24:7); Luke's subtext has shaped both the Shining Ones' recall and his reporting of Peter's response to the rulers. We also noted how the rulers' plotting Jesus' death probably echoed the language and thought of Ps. 36, and how Ps. 30 suggests the source of Luke's distinctive last word of Jesus and a centurion's description of him – righteous (δίκαιος).

The case for Ps. 145 in these two scenes is cumulative. If, as is probable, both Luke and Theophilus were people for whom psalms were a devotional and theological resource – shaping Luke's worldview – then the synergy of three factors confirms the influence of Ps. 145 in Luke's subtext.[632]

---

[629] For Ps. 145 see also Acts 14:15; 17:24; Rev. 5:13; 10:6.

[630] Ps. 145:3; Acts 4:9, 12, 16.

[631] E.g., Luke 23:47; Acts 3:14; 7:52; 22:14.

[632] Why, otherwise, might Luke use them so much? See Doble (2004).

1. Ps. 145:3–4

Luke's focus in 4:8–12 is on a combination of "rulers" and "salvation," and in Ps. 145 both words belong together.[633] Luke's duplication of "rulers" (Acts 4:5, 8) and his describing this healing as "being saved" (σέσωται, Acts 4:9),[634] alerts readers to his implied contrasting of rulers with Jesus – who alone is "Saviour."[635] The σωτηρία of 4:12, emphasized by its following δεῖ σωθῆναι ἡμᾶς, occupies a curious construction – it is οὐκ ἔστιν ἐν ἄλλῳ οὐδενί, matching the psalmist's οἷς οὐκ ἔστιν σωτηρία of rulers.

2. Ps. 145:5–6

Luke depicts "their own" to whom Peter and John report their Sanhedrin experience as among "the blessed" (μακάριος) (Ps. 145:5), those whose "helper" is Jacob's God and whose hope is God – an adaptation from Ps. 145:6 This psalmist characterized God as – τὸν ποιήσαντα τὸν οὐρανὸν καὶ τὴν γῆν, τὴν θάλασσαν καὶ πάντα τὰ ἐν αὐτοῖς (Ps. 145:6a). In prayer, the group addresses God as "Sovereign Lord" (δέσποτα), ὁ ποιήσας τὸν οὐρανὸν καὶ τὴν γῆν [καὶ] τὴν θάλασσαν καὶ πάντα τὰ ἐν αὐτοῖς (Acts 4:24) an adaptation of Ps. 145:6. Apart from their added καὶ and a change from third to first person in addressing God, those at prayer, echoing this psalmist, plainly commit themselves to Jacob's God.

---

[633] Ps. 145:6 re-appears at Acts 14:15 associated with Paul's healing a lame man.

[634] Rulers first appeared in Acts at 3:17, where, with Jerusalem's inhabitants, they acted in ignorance when handing over and killing Jesus.

[635] καὶ οὐκ ἔστιν ἐν ἄλλῳ οὐδενὶ ἡ σωτηρία, οὐδὲ γὰρ ὄνομά ἐστιν ἕτερον ὑπὸ τὸν οὐρανὸν τὸ δεδομένον ἐν ἀνθρώποις ἐν ᾧ δεῖ σωθῆναι ἡμᾶς (4:12; 5:31, cf. Luke 2:11; 19:10). See Luke 23:35 where Luke's distinctive variation on tradition's portrayal of Jesus' crucifixion combines rulers (vice principal priests and scribes) mocking (ἐξεμυκτήριζον) Jesus: ἄλλους ἔσωσεν, σωσάτω ἑαυτόν, εἰ οὗτός ἐστιν ὁ χριστὸς τοῦ θεοῦ ὁ ἐκλεκτός. Luke's salvation and ruler threads continue into Acts.

3. Ps. 145:10

The group's prayer is that despite the Sanhedrin's threats (Acts 4:29), God will give them the bold, confident speech (παρρησία) characterizing Peter's reply to his interrogators.[636] Like Peter and John, this group has made its choice for God's "holy servant Jesus" (Acts 4:27, 30), against these rulers: "The LORD will reign (βασιλεύσει) forever, your God, Sion, for generation upon generation" (Ps. 145:10). Their praying contrasts with the Sanhedrin's contriving to suppress the sign of the lame man's healing (Acts 4:15–18). In a concluding scene to this "renewal" section, Gamaliel warns that their stance may be described as "warring against God," for the Sanhedrin, enraged (διεπρίοντο), wanted to kill the apostles (Acts 5:33–39). Enraged (Acts 7:54, διεπρίοντο),[637] later they did kill Stephen.

Ps. 145 is influential throughout Luke's transitional scene. Adapted at 4:24,[638] this psalm's verbal echoes account for the joint appearance of "rulers" and "save" in 4:5–12. But Luke's subtext offers more than quotation and allusion; by drawing on the psalms' underlying theological stance it models his portrayal of both the rulers and Jesus-followers. Ps. 145 shares the standpoint of Ps. 1: "the LORD loves the righteous [...] but the way of sinners he brings to ruin."[639] Both Luke and the psalmist contrast rulers with the righteous; Luke-Acts' conflict narrative reaches its climactic ending as Stephen confronts the Sanhedrin.[640]

---

[636] cf. Acts 4:13, 19–20.

[637] See Ch. 7.

[638] Cf. the allusion to Ps. 145 (Acts 14:15); subtextually secure.

[639] Cf. Ps. 145:8–9.

[640] Luke-Acts' conflict narrative polarizes the Jesus movement and Jerusalem's rulers, emphatically not its Temple. See Ch. 7.

4. Ps. 145: modelling Jesus-followers

Acts' narrative recounting witness in Jerusalem falls into three parts, each ending in confrontation between Jesus-followers and the Sanhedrin.[641] This reflects larger Lukan structures, including Luke's emerging portrayal of Peter. Luke's subtextual use of Ps. 145 becomes clearer in that scene (Acts 5:17–42) where the whole apostolic band adopts Peter's and John's stance before the Sanhedrin, a scene retrospectively illuminating the apostles' prayer (Acts 4:23–31).

Consider Ps. 145:3 – μὴ πεποίθατε ἐπ' ἄρχοντας καὶ ἐφ' υἱοὺς ἀνθρώπων, οἷς οὐκ ἔστιν σωτηρία. Then note the apostles" πειθαρχεῖν δεῖ θεῷ μᾶλλον ἢ ἀνθρώποις (5:29). Their stance shares a verb-root (πείθω/πειθαρχέω) and two nouns (ἄρχων, ἄνθρωπος) with the psalmist's comparable eight words: trust in God (πείθω) entails obeying (πειθαρχέω) God rather than rulers. Their δεῖ demands our word "entails"; because it is "our fathers' God" who has acted, the inclusivity of that phrase makes this intra-communal conflict's root clearer: God raised up Jesus, in two senses. This Sanhedrin, however, took Jesus violently and killed him – the vineyard owner's "son and heir."[642] A reader carefully following Luke's unfolding tale would grasp clearly how this Sanhedrin had "fulfilled" Ps. 2.

Additionally, confirming their stance, the apostles corporately emphasize that God gives his holy spirit to those who obey him:[643] readers recall the narrator's conclusion to the apostles' prayer.[644] Luke reports that before replying to the Sanhedrin Peter was filled with the Holy Spirit,[645] and that before

---

[641] Peter and John (2:1–4:22); the apostles (4:23–5:42); Stephen (6:1–8:3). These confrontation scenes depict mounting tension.

[642] Ps. 2:7–8, soon to be joined by vv. 2:1–2 (section C below).

[643] Acts 5:32, τοῖς πειθαρχοῦσιν αὐτῷ; cf. Wis. 7:27–28.

[644] Acts 4:31; cf. 5:32, reflecting wider Christian tradition: see Mt. 10–20 (16–23); John 14:26.

[645] Acts 4:8, πλησθεὶς πνεύματος ἁγίου.

179

speaking God's word with a boldness like Peter's, the apostles were all filled with the Holy Spirit.[646] By contrast, this emphasis on "spirit" recalls one reason why Jesus-followers do not trust rulers:

> When his spirit (πνεῦμα) departs, then he returns to his earth; on that very day all their plans perish (Ps. 145:4).[647]

Per contra, it was the exalted Jesus who poured out God's gift of the Spirit on his followers. Those for whom psalms celebrated Israel's stance before God would recognize in Psalm 145's words their foundational perspective in Psalm 1:

> οὐχ οὕτως οἱ ἀσεβεῖς, οὐχ οὕτως,
> ἀλλ' ἢ ὡς ὁ χνοῦς, ὃν ἐκριπτεῖ ὁ ἄνεμος ἀπὸ προσώπου τῆς γῆς.
> διὰ τοῦτο οὐκ ἀναστήσονται ἀσεβεῖς ἐν κρίσει
> οὐδὲ ἁμαρτωλοὶ ἐν βουλῇ δικαίων,
> ὅτι γινώσκει κύριος ὁδὸν δικαίων,
> καὶ ὁδὸς ἀσεβῶν ἀπολεῖται (Ps. 1:4–6).

Earlier, replying to the Sanhedrin's instruction that they desist from witnessing in Jesus' name (Acts 4:18), Peter and John imply that they must listen to God rather than "to you": εἰ δίκαιόν ἐστιν ἐνώπιον τοῦ θεοῦ ὑμῶν ἀκούειν μᾶλλον ἢ τοῦ θεοῦ, κρίνατε.[648] Note how their "you" (implied in κρίνατε) echoes the "you" addressed to the rulers earlier in the encounter, with all that it implies: you crucified Jesus, you are the builders spoken of by the psalmist (4:10–12); now you must judge for yourselves. Jesus' witnesses are unable to not-speak about what they have seen and heard. Peter has emphatically "turned." In its context of rulers and "save," his stance (4:19) looks much more like an implied version

---

[646] Acts 4:31, καὶ ἐπλήσθησαν ἅπαντες τοῦ ἁγίου πνεύματος.

[647] ἐξελεύσεται τὸ πνεῦμα αὐτοῦ, καὶ ἐπιστρέψει εἰς τὴν γῆν αὐτοῦ, ἐν ἐκείνῃ τῇ ἡμέρᾳ ἀπολοῦνται πάντες οἱ διαλογισμοὶ αὐτῶν.

[648] Listen implies "obey" as in Luke 9:35; Acts 3:20–23 (both echoing Deut. 18:15 LXX).

of the whole apostolic group's consequent "we must obey God rather than men," crystallizing the stance proposed by Ps. 145.

This first encounter between Jesus-followers and the Sanhedrin focuses Luke's implied polarity between rulers and God, (Acts 4:19–20) more explicitly in both succeeding clashes.[649] Assuring Theophilus that Christian claims about Jesus were indeed rooted in scripture, Luke-Acts presents Jesus as the Psalms' archetypal Righteous One (δίκαιος); it also contrasts Jesus' followers with hostile, plotting rulers who closely resemble the psalmists' "ungodly."[650]

5. Summary

In Ps. 145 Luke had a psalm that paralleled the Godward stance of Jesus and his followers. A psalm of the righteous (δίκαιος), it character-sketched the truly blessed (μακάριος);[651] by excluding rulers and "the sons of men," from such a role, it focused Jesus' core role as Saviour. Luke's portrayal of those same rulers as the builders of the stone-saying (Ps. 117:22), connects them with both Jesus' vineyard parable and his distinctive presentation of rulers in Luke's passion narrative.[652] Per contra, Peter and the apostles consistently witness, both publicly and to the Sanhedrin, that Jesus is the Messiah and Saviour.[653] There are verbal, conceptual and interpretative indications that Ps. 145 is inter-textually influential in Luke's presentation of this encounter and of relations between rulers and Jesus-followers. Luke's subtext is also his work's presupposition. With Luke's subtext in mind, as we resume Luke's narrative

---

[649] Acts 5:29–32; 7:51–53. Stephen's vision (7:54–60) evokes the triumph of the "righteous" Jesus (Acts 7:52) and his persecutors' character (Wis. 5:1–8); see Ch. 7, Ch. 9; cf. Doble (2013: 95–113).

[650] Cf. Wis. 1:16–2:20.

[651] See, e.g., Kraus (1986: 154–162).

[652] A trigger for Luke-Acts' conflict-narrative.

[653] Acts 4:10, 12, 26–28; 5:42.

sequence readers cannot miss his portrayal of Jerusalem's rulers in the ensuing scene.

C. Culmination 1

1. Structural transition

Having threatened the apostles, the rulers released Peter and John (4:21, προσαπειλησάμενοι ἀπέλυσαν αὐτούς), who moved (4:23, ἀπολυθέντες) from the gathered Sanhedrin to a gathering of "their own" (τοὺς ἰδίους).[654] Their report to this gathering by a "turned" Peter prompted his "strengthened" brothers' corporate prayer that affirmed their commitment to God "who made the sky and the earth, the sea, and all that is in them" (Ps. 145:6a). Thus opens the second stage in these Jesus-followers' witness in Jerusalem that ends in a heightened state of tension between them and the Sanhedrin (Acts 5:17–42).

Importantly for *Interpreter*'s case, readers learn from these Jesus-followers' praying where they identified that "it is written" that "the Messiah must suffer." Luke here exemplifies another fulfilled Jesus-word to his followers (Luke 24:44–46): their *pesher* on Ps. 2:1–2 is the culmination of Luke's implied scriptural argument in Peter's appeal to the stone-saying. These scenes share one subtextual structure.

i. Subtextual structuring

Luke gives about two-thirds of this narrative (Acts 4:5–31) to the Sanhedrin setting and its remainder to the apostles' prayer. That prayer's opening (4:24) adapts Ps. 145:6, portraying the truly "blessed" person's "help," Jacob's God. Section B offered detailed reflection on that psalm's role in Luke's modelling of his characters' roles in this drama. Rulers are unworthy objects of life's ultimate commitment; such devotion is for God alone (Ps. 145:3–4, 5–9). Israel knows that there are two "ways": the Lord loves the righteous, but he will destroy the sinners' way. These Jesus-followers pray, while rulers threaten and are

---

[654] See Tannehill (1990: 59–79); Stanford (2014: 109–151).

responsible for the death of God's anointed, Jesus (Acts 4:26–28). By their praying, "their own" align themselves with Peter's and John's stance, strengthened to defy the Sanhedrin's ban and to speak God's message boldly (Acts 4:29–31).[655]

ii. "It is written" – in Pss. 2:1–2 and 117:22

Sovereign Lord, who made the heaven and the earth, the sea, and everything in them, it is you who said by the Holy Spirit through our father David, your servant:
> Why did the Gentiles rage,
> and the peoples imagine vain things?
> The kings of the earth took their stand,
> and the rulers have gathered together
> against the Lord and against his Messiah (Acts 4:24b–26).

A key issue in the sequential scenes is the Sanhedrin's ban on speaking in Jesus' name (Acts 4:18, 29–30; 5:27–29). That continues into a second confrontation with these rulers and sustains the apostles' affirmation of the Sanhedrin's blood-guilt concerning Jesus (Acts 5:17–42). Their guilt was plainly asserted by Peter, who echoed Jesus' own vineyard parable's tale of murderous tenants (Acts 4:10; Luke 20:15a): these rulers inhabited the "builders'" role from the psalmist's proverbial saying; they were, indeed, murderous tenants of a vineyard.

The followers' prayer commits them to fidelity to Jesus. Like David, Jesus is God's servant (παῖς); like David, he was God's anointed (ὃν ἔχρισας) (Acts 4:23–30). This last phrase evokes Luke's distinctive account of God's anointing Jesus, establishing the probability that that brief scene's *bat qol* announced, "You are my son; today I have begotten you" (Luke 3:22; Ps. 2:7).[656]

---

[655] See B4.

[656] See Doble (2014: 175–199).

That is the heart of the matter: in Psalm 2 God's servant David confronted Gentiles, kings and rulers assembled against God and against his Anointed (Messiah). Likewise, David's promised seed, God's anointed servant Jesus had confronted Jerusalem's gathered rulers and their associates "in this city," Jerusalem.[657] The outcome of Jesus' story was different from David's – Jesus' story had been "previously marked out" (προώρισεν), a way of suffering and being raised from the dead.   Following Peter's report, Luke's readers now recognize where "it is written that the Messiah must suffer" as his "own" uncover it to be in Ps. 2:1–2.

One of *Interpreter*'s goals is to reflect on Luke's uses of scripture: here, he moves by *pesher* from Jesus' parable to David's psalm. Essentially, Jesus' vineyard parable was about a rejected and murdered "son" and "heir" – words echoing David's Ps. 2:7–8 that reported God's decree, "You are my son," evoking the apostles' quoted words, Ps. 2:1–2 (Acts 4:25–26). For Luke Messiah and Son of God share semantic space.[658] Peter was clear: Jesus whom the rulers crucified was God's Messiah (Acts 4:10). Reflection on tradition, event and on Jesus' words underlies this early Christian interpretation of scripture.

iii. Ps. 145 is Luke's middle term between two Lukan citations

Gathered apostles identified in Ps. 2:1–2 a quotation (Acts 4:25b–26) that was both illuminated by Jesus' story and rooted his story in Israel's story. Traditionally ascribed to David, Psalm 2 probably led early Christians to reflect on the role of rulers in Jesus' story. Equally probably, Luke understood the parallel conviction in the co-text of one of his key Jesus-intertexts, Psalm 117. Certainly, through Peter, Luke had interpreted the stone-saying (Ps. 117:22)

---

[657] Acts 4:25–27; cf. Luke 9:31; 13:31–35.
[658] Ch. 2.

that capped Jesus' vineyard parable. This psalm played a significant role in both Jewish and Christian traditions,[659] and earlier in the psalm, last of the full Hallel sequence (Pss. 112–117), Luke would have found:

> The Lord is a helper [βοηθός] to me;
> I will not fear what man can do to me.
> The Lord is a helper [βοηθός] to me;
> I shall look in triumph on my enemies.
> It is better to trust [πεποιθέναι] in the Lord
> than to trust [πεποιθέναι] in a man.
> It is better to hope [ἐλπίζειν] in the Lord
> than to hope [ἐλπίζειν] in rulers [ἄρχοντας] (Ps. 117:6–9).

Ps. 2 depicts rulers assembled against God's Messiah (Ps. 2:1–2) "whom you anointed" (Acts 4:27b; Ps. 2:7). Ps. 117 carries the stone-saying illuminating Jesus' parable about the vineyard owner and his son and heir (Luke 20:13–14). Add Ps. 145 to this mix and we see how their shared vocabulary and conceptual stance enrich Luke's understanding of rulers in Jesus' story:

Rulers –	Pss. 2, 117 and 145;
Trust –	Pss. 117 and 145;
Helper –	Pss. 117 and 145;
Save –	Ps. 145 adds Luke's contrast between rulers and Jesus.

One further feature of Luke's narrative calls for comment: confronting the Sanhedrin, Peter and John stand firm (Acts 4:13–21). Ultimately, confronting a now-hostile Sanhedrin, the newly-strengthened apostles together echo Peter's stand – "We must obey God rather than men" (Acts 4:19–20; cf. 5:29). Ps. 145 throws further light on the apostles' common stance. Peter has strengthened his brethren. Luke has interpreted Jesus' story by cradling it in Israel's scriptures.

---

[659] See Miura (2007).

186

iv. How "it is written" – Luke's pesher on Ps. 2:1–2

> The kings of the earth took their stand,
>   and the rulers [ἄρχοντες] have gathered together
> [συνήχθησαν]
>   against the Lord and against his Anointed [τοῦ χριστοῦ αὐτοῦ]
> (Acts 4:25–26).

Luke starts from a quotation of Ps. 2:1–2.[660] We noted in Chapter 1 that this extract appears also in the *pesher* found in 4Q174, paired there with what we have argued to be a Lukan base-text.[661] Luke attributes this psalm to God, speaking via the Holy Spirit through David, "your servant" (παῖς). Named, David remains sharply in focus. This is no accident, for Luke-Acts' reference-frame is Davidic: its events unfold "in the house of David your servant."[662] We shall return to Luke's use of παῖς in Chapter 9 for a reader's interpretation of this whole scene rests on one's hearing of this word's echoes. There follows an apostolic *pesher* (Acts 4:27–28) shaping Jesus' story on the template of the quotation. Their *pesher* naturally evokes earlier scenes in Luke's narrative flow;[663] three verbal hooks guide readers: gathered; peoples; anointed.

a. Συνηχθήσαν – Rulers

"Gathered together" evokes not only the preceding scene,[664] but Luke's distinctive account of Jesus' suffering and condemnation to death at the hands of Pilate, Herod and the Peoples of Israel, including their principal priests and

---

[660] Acts 4:25–26, agreeing with Old Greek Text, which coheres with Masoretic Text.

[661] See Ch. 2 on the Prologue's triptych.

[662] Luke 1:69: ἐν οἴκῳ Δαυὶδ παιδὸς αὐτοῦ. Cf. Luke 1:27; 2:4.

[663] "Remember what he said to you."

[664] This verb, opening the sentence, emphasizes the conspiring of those present.

rulers, typically assembling.[665] Further, these rulers' mockery of the dying Jesus (Luke 23:35) comprised their deriding his "saving" and being "anointed." Luke's ruler thread is to be taken seriously: they ganged up on this intruder into their fiefdom.

b. Peoples

The "peoples" (λαοὶ) of Ps. 2:1 (Acts 4:25) become this pesher's "peoples of Israel" (λαοῖς Ἰσραήλ). Again, Luke has evoked scenes of Jesus' condemnation and death (e.g., Luke 23:13, 35 and, possibly, 49). The People and Gentiles (Ps. 2:1) gathered together against God and God's hoped-for, anointed one (Ps. 2:2) presents a shocking picture of communal infidelity – but this is an evil generation.[666]

c. Anointed

The psalm's "anointed" (χριστός) becomes a significant link between their quotation and Jesus-followers' pesher on it: Jesus, "whom you anointed" (ὃν ἔχρισας), makes him God's χριστός. "Whom you anointed," echoing Ps. 2:7's "You are my son," and Ps. 2:1–2 (hostile rulers gathered against God's anointed), belong together in this scene. But as we saw earlier, Jesus' vineyard parable that tells of an owner and his son and heir, itself evokes Ps. 2:

> He said to me, "You are my son";
> today I have begotten you.
> Ask of me, and I will make the nations your heritage
> [κληρονομία],
> and the ends of the earth your possession (Ps. 2:7–8).

---

[665] Acts 4:5; Luke 23:1–25, esp. 23:13 – Pilate συγκαλεσάμενος τοὺς ἀρχιερεῖς καὶ τοὺς ἄρχοντας καὶ τὸν λαὸν.

[666] E.g., Luke 9:41; 11:29–32; Acts 2:40.

And from the Prologue's attention to Jesus as God's fulfilment of Nathan's oracle to David (Luke 1:26–35; 2 Sam. 7:12–14) we learn that the yet-to-be born Jesus "will be called 'son of God.'"[667] Further, we need to consider the threefold presence of παῖς in this scene.

2. παῖς – of David and of Jesus (Acts 4:25, 27, 30)

> it is you who said by the Holy Spirit through our father David, your servant
>
> ὁ τοῦ πατρὸς ἡμῶν διὰ πνεύματος ἁγίου στόματος Δαυὶδ παιδός σου εἰπών (Acts 4:25).

So far, the burden of this prayer has been to transfer David's story[668] from "his" psalm to Jesus.[669] Consequently, the descriptor παῖς, "servant," may properly be seen as Jesus' continuing in David's agency for God. We briefly summarize why this is so.

Luke's Prologue emphatically places Jesus in David's "house," born of David's seed; there, David is God's servant (παῖς) (Luke 1:69); in popular usage also, David is God's servant.[670] Luke introduced David's "seed," Jesus, as the one to fulfil God's promises to David: we identified two oracular "panels" each carrying God's promise in the form "I will raise up" (ἀναστήσω);[671] Luke's distinctive account of God's anointing Jesus probably cited "David's" Ps. 2:7 verbatim, a feature that controls Jesus' Isaiah quotation at Nazareth.[672]

---

[667] Luke 1:35, cf. 32.

[668] See Ch. 7C5.

[669] Luke has done this also in his account of Jesus' death.

[670] E.g., Ps. 17 title; Isa. 37:35.

[671] See Ch. 2.

[672] Luke 3:21–22; Luke 4:18 – "the Spirit of the Lord is upon me, because he has anointed me." Scripture explains event. See Ch. 7; cf. Doble (2014).

For Luke, God's unique act in raising Jesus from the dead threw new light on the ἀναστήσω of God's promises to David, including that in Ezekiel 34:23 where David's agency is clear. The verb's implied, active presence in Luke 24 explained Jesus' transformation of Son of Man sayings into sayings about the Messiah;[673] ἀναστήσω becomes a clearer presence in Peter's Pentecost speech and makes sense of his speech in Solomon's Portico.[674] At Antioch Paul offers his own midrash on the ἀναστήσω in God's promise to David.[675]

Luke's base-text is the David-promise; his scriptural matrix is Davidic. In the followers' prayer David's psalm became the template for Jesus' story. There has been no hint of an Isaianic subtext in Peter's Pentecost speech, his address in Solomon's Portico, or his defence before the Sanhedrin.

These speeches in Acts do not carry Luke's whole material intent. But *Interpreter*'s focus is on Luke-Acts' distinctive account of followers' witnessing to Jesus' using scripture in the service of his enigmatic, and disputed, "it is written" that the Messiah must suffer and be raised from the dead (Luke 24:44–46), an often-repeated claim in Acts. We have taken seriously the hinge nature of Luke 24, groundwork for Luke's orderly assurance for Theophilus including:

- Jesus said "these are my words";
- what is "written about me" in "Moses, prophets and psalms" "must be fulfilled";
- he opened their minds to understand the scriptures that spoke of the Messiah's suffering and resurrection;
- then commissioned his companions as his witnesses (Luke 24:44–48).

In chapters 4 to 6 we have been exploring *one* witness's interpretative witness in Jerusalem as Peter attended to tradition's reports of Jesus' own intertextual

---

[673] See Ch. 3.

[674] See Ch. 4 and Ch. 5.

[675] See Ch. 8.

190

activity – "my words," strengthened Jesus-followers as their interpreting scripture builds on and extends Jesus' own uses. In that long thread, it is consistently David's story that is fulfilled. To "see" Isaiah's Servant in Peter's παῖς used of Jesus (Acts 4:27), divorces this descriptor from its Lukan *pesher*,[676] and from Luke's David-matrix.

---

[676] Contra e.g., Mallen (2008). See Ch. 7C5 below.

D. Summary

Chapter 6 concludes Part II, ending Luke's sequence of signs and wonders:[677] Jesus' gift of the Holy Spirit forms its *inclusio*;[678] a lame man's healing by Jesus' name is a long exemplary sign within it.[679] This chapter also completes Peter's post-resurrection mirroring of Jesus' *logia*, fulfilling Jesus' word specifically to Peter (Luke 22:31–32). It exemplifies Jesus' words to his gathered followers in Jerusalem that commissioned them all as his witnesses (Luke 24:44–49) to *Interpreter's Problématique*: "it is written" that the Messiah must suffer (Ps. 2:1–2) and be raised from the dead.

Chapter 6 has focused on a single narrative sequence (Acts 4:5–31), continuing that in the previous chapter (Acts 3:1–4:4). This present sequence comprises Peter's third mirroring and the apostles' scriptural culmination of Luke's long thread on suffering. Peter's *pesher* on Jesus' Stone-*logion* (Mirror 3) and his lexical play on "salvation" (4:12) constitute a single reply to the ruler's questioning. Notably, Luke highlights Peter and John's "articulate boldness," especially their refusal to obey the rulers' ban on their teaching in Jesus' name (Acts 4:19).

Lexical play on "salvation" together with Luke-Acts' central conflict between the righteous and the rulers led to our uncovering Ps. 145's unifying subtextuality that links Peter's mirroring with the apostolic culmination, including its synergy with Pss. 2 and 117. The role of Ps. 145 in Jesus' story sheds light on Luke's narrative perspective and leads readers into the first of Luke's three culminations, where the re-gathered apostles give thanks in prayer.

---

[677] See Acts 2:43; 4:30; 5:12.

[678] Acts 2:1–4 – 5:32; cf. Luke 24:49; Acts 1:4–5.

[679] Acts 4:14–20, 22, 30.

These strengthened brothers complete Luke's theme of Peter "turned" and clarify how Luke's conflict-narrative polarizes Jerusalem's rulers and the Jesus movement; its rulers, not its Temple, are Luke's focus in Jerusalem.[680]

---

[680] See Ch. 9, where I have justified this claim.

Part III. Two Witnesses

Chapter 7. Stephen's Speech

Stephen's is the longest exegetical speech in Luke-Acts, dense with scriptural allusions and echoes, but few quotations. This much-debated speech is integral to Luke's narrative's development, purposes, and discernible plan. At a twofold structural shift in Luke's narrative,[681] Stephen presents a definitive account of what divides Jerusalem's rulers and their associates from Jerusalem's infant Church as both read Israel's scriptures:[682] what divides them is the David-promise, Luke's "things fulfilled among us."

Proto-martyr Stephen is the first of those "ministers of the word" to whose "passing on of tradition" Luke's narrative is indebted.[683] For any discussion of Luke-Acts' integrity, Stephen's speech remains a problematic narrative unit that has generated an immense scholarly literature.[684] Particularly, Stephen's stance towards Jerusalem's Temple tends to provoke one of that literature's most vigorous discussions.

In this chapter I offer my argument for the integrity of this unit to that of Luke-Acts' whole *apologia,* replying to what is essentially a scholarly problem

---

[681] (a) From Jerusalem to a wider mission; see Acts 1:8. (b) Widened persecution (Acts 8:1b), following Gamaliel's earlier intervention (Acts 5:33–42).

[682] This speech continues Luke's dialogical interpretation of those scriptures. See Alexander, P.S. (2015) on the complexities of such interpretation.

[683] Luke 1:1–4.

[684] For further details see Doble, P. (2013: 96, n. 9).

(set out in section A). While Stephen's witness is indeed a narrative unit, signalled by its two boundary summaries and two Christological paradigms, in *Interpreter* I firmly position this unit in Luke-Acts' architecture.[685] Section B sets out the evidence for that integrity. It identifies Luke's Jerusalem conflict narrative as the appropriate immediate context for Stephen's speech,[686] indicates its structural-transitional function, and demonstrates the unit's thematic dependence on the covenant-infidelity of Luke's tenants in the vineyard.[687] That conflict was between Jerusalem's rulers and Jesus and his followers. Luke's polemical focus is plainly on the Sanhedrin, rather than on the building they control; his speech's *volta* is his counter-charge based on his probable *aposiopesis*.[688] Section C then locates that conflict in those rulers' charges against Jesus by re-locating them, as Luke did, in the charges laid against Stephen.[689] Focused sharply on his accusers' "this place" and "Moses' traditions," Stephen's reply addresses three sub-foci: Jesus, Solomon and Torah. Section D identifies Stephen's speech as his narrative midrash on Israel's ongoing Exodus-story, highlighting God's promises to Abraham, Moses and David, and the contrasting covenant-fidelity of two of David's sons.

Section E traces Stephen's scriptural reasoning that accuses his hearers, Jerusalem's priestly elite, of sharing in Solomon's idolatrous faithlessness (and that of his ilk), and of their murdering God's anointed, Jesus – the glorified Son of Man now standing in proleptic judgement at God's right hand.[690] Thus another Jesus-*logion* is fulfilled.[691] A key element in his reasoning

---

[685] Markers – Acts 6:7 and 8:3; Paradigms – Jesus *Nazoraios* (Acts 6:14) & Jesus standing at God's right hand (Acts 7:55–56) as the glorified Son of Man (cf. Luke 22:69); see the analytical diagram.

[686] Luke 19:41 – Acts 8:3.

[687] Luke 20:1–26 is a single unit.

[688] Acts 7:51–53; cf. Isa. 66:2b.

[689] Acts 6:13–14.

[690] Acts 7:55–56, cf. Wis. 4:20—5:1.

[691] Luke 22:69, a Lukan distinctive.

is Luke's handling of the bivalence of "house" in his subtext, climaxing in Isaiah 66:1–2, especially Stephen's *aposiopesis*.[692] Section F concludes that Stephen's speech is his pro-Temple, anti-idolatrous witness to the raised and glorified Son of Man before whom he, Stephen, stands as he dies as a faithful disciple.[693] Luke's readers are left in no doubt that Jerusalem's rulers will come to their judgement wondering at the paradox of Jesus," this righteous one's, salvation.

---

[692] Acts 7:48–50.

[693] Luke 21:36 within its context (20:45–21:36).

A. A Scholarly Problem?

1. Scarcely Christian?

That this speech "fits its context poorly" is among the kinder scholarly comments on Stephen's *apologia*.[694] Dunn continues, "the denunciation of the Temple in 7:48 runs quite counter to Luke's otherwise consistently positive appraisal of the Temple."[695] Others find that it lacks reference to key Lukan concerns such as resurrection and repentance, and even urge that the bulk of the speech is scarcely Christian.[696] The literature on Stephen's speech is immense. To present *Interpreter*'s case clearly and positively, this chapter rarely engages with individual writers; a note of the many who, in varying ways, have most influenced its case has been placed in the bibliography.

2. Purposes

Focally, this speech is about Jesus, both overtly[697] and by implication.[698] The gathered rulers are murderers and betrayers of the δίκαιος[699] their brother, the prophet like Moses.[700] At the speech's climax one finds David's house and Jerusalem's rulers in relation to it[701] – this divides "your" fathers from "our"

---

[694] So Dunn, J.D.G., (2009), 265.

[695] Ibid., 267. Dunn's footnote 109 lists his evidence for this positive appraisal. His sole reference in this volume to the immensely important Luke 19:46 appears at 83n117, without comment on Jesus' composite quotation (Isa. 56:7a, c; Jer. 7:11) that justified his cleansing the Temple (19:45–48) before teaching there daily, to the provocation of principal priests and scribes.

[696] See, e.g., Foakes Jackson, F.J., (1930) "Stephen's Speech in Acts," JBL 49, 283–86. He pondered whether the speech's excision would affect Luke's narrative.

[697] Acts 6:14; 7:55.

[698] Acts 7:52.

[699] Acts 7:52; a distinctive thread running from Luke 23:47.

[700] Acts 7:52; a prophet thread running through 7:37; 3:22; Luke 24:19, cf. 13:31–35; 4:24.

[701] 7:44–53.

fathers. Stephen's speech is not an anti-Temple tract. In Luke-Acts, Jesus and his apostles relate positively to the institution, but are in conflict with its custodian-priesthood. Commentators tend to build too much on the force of its χειροποίητος,[702] and too little on the shape of Stephen's argument within Luke-Acts, matters dealt with below.

Stephen's speech actually fits well with Luke's purposes, his *apologia* for Theophilus – why are we, the Jewish People, further divided?[703] In the Stephen-unit, Jesus' opponents' problems with him and his followers are stated;[704] a High Priest asks, "Are these things so?" and Stephen-Luke[705] spells out how and why the bivalence of the word "house" matters,[706] and how the Christian sect relates to Moses – and to its opponents. The discussion below of Luke-Acts' long conflict narrative[707] reveals how central to Luke-Acts this particular sectarian division really is, and how important Stephen's speech is in itemizing its reasoning.

---

[702] Acts 7:48. Stephen's χειροποίητον probably picks up the Markan version of false witnesses accusations at Jesus' trial (Mark 14:55–58), or oral tradition of that false accusation.

[703] If Anderson were right, and Luke's dedicatee really a former High Priest, then Stephen's speech to a Sadducee-dominated Sanhedrin would become even more important within Luke's account of "things fulfilled among us."

[704] See Section C.

[705] "Stephen-Luke" represents a character's presentation reported in a narrator's words.

[706] "House" is basic to the David-promise in 2 Sam. 7, bivalently as lineage and as structure.

[707] Luke 19:41-Acts 8:3, around 40% of Luke-Acts' narrative. See sections 3&4.

3. *Interpreter's* focus

Stephen's speech substantially contributes to *Interpreter's* focal issue – was Luke mistaken?[708] Previous chapters have demonstrated how the ἀναστήσω[709] underlying Luke's reading of the David-promise informed his scriptural reasoning, especially the transformation in Luke 24 from Jesus' talk of the Son of Man into that of the Messiah. In Stephen's speech, set in the Temple precincts, Luke's reference-frame extends its scope beyond the ἀναστήσω implied by 7:37, important as that is, to include the house that figures large in the David-promise base-text.[710] Luke's conflict narrative highlights the Jerusalem Temple's deeply unpopular, because suspect, hierarchy and its defective service (λατρεία) of God, recalling Solomon's choice of privilege without responsibility. Luke's David-promise conjoins the Temple as God's authentic focus for serving God with a godly David-descendant as its ruler-guarantor.

4. Commemoration and tradition

This chapter crystallizes an interpreter's problem: Luke's readers knew and recalled a complex of traditions about Moses, David and Solomon – their thought-worlds. They might readily have recalled those traditions in ways that later readers currently need to infer from Luke's text. From Luke-Acts we learn

---

[708] At Luke 24:26, 46.

[709] Stephen, recapitulating Acts 3:22–26, notes Deuteronomy's reported ἀναστήσω-promise, of a Moses-like prophet (7:37). Arguably, the δίκαιος of 7:52 evokes the Sanhedrin's treatment of Jesus, and Stephen's reference to "prophets" includes that as a Jesus-descriptor (e.g., Luke 13:31–35).

[710] 2 Sam. 7:1–29; note both the frequency of "house" and its bivalence. Both 4Q174 and Amos 9:11 (cf. Acts 15:16–17) carry a sense of such bivalence; Amos's two-fold ἀναστήσω is paralleled by its twofold ἀνοικοδομήσω. Luke-Acts explored the word's underlying tensions, especially in Stephen's crucial reference to Solomon (7:47) followed by Isaiah's focal question (7:49b), "What kind of house will you build for me, says the Lord?"

of long debates around scripture. Concerning the charge that Jesus sought to change the customs handed down by Moses, we may properly infer that Stephen re-reads Israel's story in the light of Israel's persistent rebelliousness, much as scripture had often done (e.g., Ps. 105) – though for Stephen the rebellious were mostly "our fathers." To rebut the charge that Jesus sought to destroy "this place" we may also infer that Stephen's process, cueing or prompting, evokes from Moses a story – of worship, of the appointed place of worship, of defection from worship, and the question of what kind of house is appropriate for serving God. But above all, we may infer that Moses' story brings to mind God's gracious, generous love for a People that should have elicited their willing obedience: grace precedes Torah.[711]

Stephen's Exodus story, however, leads to David's house, to David's two sons, and to the unspoken condition that binds Jesus, Temple, David-promise, "your fathers" and Solomon into one whole, where Isaiah's question – What kind of house will you build for me? – focuses this speech's mass of scriptural detail. Essentially, Stephen's is a Lukan exegetical speech about the David-promise, and about David's two sons.

---

[711] Cf. Jer. 7:22–26 where grace should have evoked gratitude; but they stiffened their necks (cf. Acts 7:51).

B. Stephen's speech within Luke-Acts

Far from fitting its context poorly, Stephen's speech is structurally, programmatically and thematically integral to Luke-Acts.

1. Lukan narrative structure

Structurally, Stephen's speech is about Jesus, Luke-Acts' focal character; he is named twice, with fundamentally differing descriptors. First, he is identified as Jesus *Nazoraios*,[712] and the speech is occasioned by charges against him via Stephen's public witnessing. Finally, he is revealed as Jesus, the glorified Son of Man[713] standing at God's right hand. But he is also implied by two previously-deployed descriptors: Righteous One (δίκαιος) and Prophet.[714]

Many critics identify a problem in what they find to be a long gap between Stephen's initial Jesus *Nazoraios* and his return to the betraying and murdering of the δίκαιος. When, however, we recall Luke's narrative development, it becomes clear from Peter's scriptural reasoning in his speech in Solomon's Portico that this Jesus is that seed of Abraham whose mission was to secure first his Jerusalem hearers' repentance.[715] Moreover, his having been raised from the dead revealed that this Jesus was the Moses-like prophet rejected by his brothers.[716] Stephen's retelling of God's gracious acts from Abraham to David was also implied in Luke-Acts' Prologue. Acts 7:2–45 may seem overlong to modern readers, but it exemplifies Luke's earlier hymning of Jesus' mission in Luke 1:69–75. Within Luke's long time-frame, two distinctive

---

[712] Acts 6:14.

[713] Acts 7:55–56; one vision, twice narrated.

[714] Acts 7:52; see the discussion in Ch. 4.

[715] See Ch. 4.

[716] The resurrection event retrospectively illumined the earlier text.

*inclusio*s bind Stephen's speech thematically into Luke's earlier narrative – Son of Man and Glory.

i. The Son of Man

The first and clearest *inclusio* is that formed by two Son of Man sayings, Luke 22:69 and Acts 7:55–56. Each is a *logion* addressed to Jerusalem's Sanhedrin; their shared setting significantly encloses much of Luke's conflict narrative.[717] The earlier saying belongs to Jesus' initial interrogation. Luke's distinctive account of that event, differing from that shared by Mark and Matthew, also differs from Stephen's vision that effectively reports the fulfilment of Jesus' saying:

(a) ἀπὸ τοῦ νῦν δὲ / ἔσται / ὁ υἱὸς τοῦ ἀνθρώπου / καθήμενος / ἐκ δεξιῶν / τῆς δυνάμεως / τοῦ θεοῦ. (Luke 22:69)

(b) ἰδοὺ / θεωρῶ / τοὺς οὐρανοὺς διηνοιγμένους καὶ / τὸν υἱὸν τοῦ ἀνθρώπου / ἐκ δεξιῶν / ἑστῶτα / τοῦ θεοῦ. (Acts 7:56)

These widely-separated *logia* share a common core: the Son of Man is at God's right hand (ὁ υἱὸς τοῦ ἀνθρώπου [...] ἐκ δεξιῶν [...] τοῦ θεοῦ). All three synoptists report a Jesus-saying commonly thought to be his own *gezerah shewa'* linking Ps. 109 with Son of Man in mutual interpretation.[718] We note two kinds of difference: that between Luke and the other synoptists, and that between the Lukan Jesus' saying and Stephen's.

First, where Mark and Matthew read ὄψεσθε, Luke has ἔσται. This variant entails Luke's use of the nominative for Son of Man, an adaptation rather than substantial difference. Luke qualifies tradition's τῆς δυνάμεως with τοῦ θεοῦ (unequivocally, God exalted Jesus). So, because Stephen – not yet the Sanhedrin – sees the vision of the exalted Jesus, ἔσται is Luke's affirmation of

---

[717] See 2c below.

[718] See Doble, P., (2013).

202

what will be the case – the Son of Man at God's right hand – and Luke's form lacks ἐρχόμενον μετὰ τῶν νεφελῶν τοῦ οὐρανοῦ. Acts 1:9–11, his target narrative development, makes the same point: Jesus' followers will see his return as they saw his departure.[719] Throughout his Jerusalem narrative Luke has sequenced and adapted his uses of tradition in ways that prepare for his extended narrative.

Second, while Stephen shares Jesus' core saying (ὁ υἱὸς τοῦ ἀνθρώπου [...] ἐκ δεξιῶν [...] τοῦ θεοῦ) their differences are essentially:

- that Jesus' ἔσται is replaced by Stephen's θεωρῶ;
- that Jesus' allusion to the καθήμενος of Ps. 109 is replaced by Stephen's ἑστῶτα.

Each variant results from its distinctive perspective:

- for Jesus, the Son of Man's suffering and vindication lie in the future;
- for Stephen, they belong to the past – and, for him, Jesus' word has been fulfilled.

For Luke, Jesus' death at the hands of Jerusalem's rulers was symbolized by the centurion's Jesus-descriptor δίκαιος.[720] Echoing that scene, Stephen accused those rulers of having betrayed and murdered the δίκαιος. We established earlier that this descriptor probably evokes the model crystallized by Wis. 2–5, where, at the judgment, the Righteous One's opponents, dread-filled, are astonished to find him standing (ὄντως), boldly confronting them.[721] Jesus' followers are witnesses to two facts of which they are sure: ὄντως ὁ ἄνθρωπος οὗτος δίκαιος ἦν (Luke 23:47) and ὄντως ἠγέρθη ὁ κύριος (Luke 24:34).

---

[719] Is Acts 1:6–11 an echo of the ἔξοδος to be completed in Jerusalem (Luke 9:31)?

[720] Luke 23:47.

[721] Wis. 5:1–2; see also Doble, P., (1996).

Visioning that existential reality, ὄντως, Stephen, echoing his Lord, could both pray for his opponents' forgiveness and commend his own spirit to his Lord.[722] We see below how Stephen's vision probably presents a *proleptic* judgment scene: not yet, but the eschatological timetable is inexorably unfolding.[723] His vision possibly parallels Peter's call in Solomon's Portico for his hearers' repentance. They had rejected the δίκαιος, preferring to have a murderer released to them.[724]

ii. Glory

The word "glory"[725] shapes a second Lukan *inclusio*. At one level it encloses Stephen's speech: the God of glory appeared to Father Abraham (Acts 7:2); towards the end, Stephen saw the glory of God (7:55). At another level, "glory" belongs to Luke's retelling of Jesus' story through a number of descriptors. We return to Stephen's vision: "[he] gazed into heaven and saw the glory of God and Jesus standing at the right hand of God."[726] However, what he publicly witnessed to was "the Son of Man standing at the right hand of God" in glory.[727] That theme opened far back in Luke's narrative, where the Son of Man, destined to suffer at the hands of elders, principal priests and scribes[728] had another destiny:

> Those who are ashamed of me and of my words, of them the Son of Man will be ashamed when he comes in his glory and the glory of the Father (Luke 9:26).[729]

---

[722] Acts 7:59–60; cf. Luke 23:46.

[723] See Doble, P., (2013); cf. Ch. 4.

[724] Acts 3:14, 19–22.

[725] See Ramsey, A.M, (1949); see also Ch. 4.

[726] Acts 7:55.

[727] Acts 7:56.

[728] Luke 9:22; cf. Mark 8:31; Matt. 16:21.

[729] Here differing from Mark and Matthew by an αὐτοῦ that opens a Lukan thread.

Following that saying, Luke's distinctive Transfiguration narrative has three figures in glory discussing the Exodus that Jesus was about to complete in Jerusalem, and three apostles seeing [Jesus'] glory.[730] This pericope culminates in the *bat qol,* "This is my chosen Son; listen to him," an αὐτοῦ ἀκούετε that echoes the αὐτοῦ ἀκούσεσθε of Moses' word to Israel about God's promise to raise up a prophet like himself, together with its threatened eradication from the People of any who do not listen.[731] But links between Luke's Transfiguration narrative and Stephen's vision belong to another place.[732]

Further, we saw in Chapter 3 how Luke's scriptural reasoning transformed this fulfilled Son of Man saying[733] into Luke-Acts' post-resurrection principal Jesus-descriptor: "Were not these things necessary, that the Messiah should suffer then enter into his glory?"[734] The event of Jesus' resurrection fulfilled tradition's Son of Man talk while illuminating the ἀναστήσω of Luke's base-text.[735] Hence Peter, at Solomon's Portico,[736] could announce to wondering onlookers that "the God of our fathers has glorified his servant Jesus"[737] Stephen's vision of Jesus at God's right hand in glory is the culmination of Luke's "things fulfilled among us" relating to his Jesus, Son of Man, thread.[738]

---

[730] Luke 9:31–32. Cf. John 1:14; here is another instance of the traditions shared by Luke and John.

[731] Deut. 18:15–19, that includes an ἀναστήσω-promise (18:18); cf. Ch. 4.

[732] Its ἔξοδον (Luke 9:31) anticipates Stephen's affirmation of God's gracious dealing with Israel.

[733] Luke 24:6–7.

[734] Luke 24:26.

[735] 2 Sam. 7:12 et al.

[736] See Ch. 4. Peter's reasoning makes much of Deuteronomy's prophet-promise, προφήτην ἀναστήσω αὐτοῖς ἐκ τῶν ἀδελφῶν αὐτῶν (Deut. 18:15, 18), as does Stephen's *apologia* (Acts 7:37, cf. 7:52).

[737] Acts 3:13.

[738] Ch. 2.

iii. Jesus Nazoraios

Stephen's speech opened in the Sanhedrin following a complaint against his talk of Jesus Nazoraios.739 That descriptor, however, is a Lukan narrative device that begins with what may be publicly known and said about Jesus before moving hearers to an enriched understanding of who Jesus "really" is.740 The High Priest asked, "Are these things so?" Stephen's primary answer is that God has glorified this Jesus,741 who is now, as he had told them at his interrogation,742 at God's right hand. The Son of Man suffered at the hands of principal priests and scribes; he was murdered by them – God raised him from the dead, and he had entered into his glory.743 But Stephen has more to say about other aspects of the initial complaint against him:744 that "more" is his process of enriching their Nazoraios.

2. A transitional narrative

Stephen's speech raises the curtain on Paul's role in Luke's *apologia* for Theophilus, closing, then moving beyond the Jerusalem phase.745 Scholars frequently note the role of summaries in Luke-Acts; whether summaries conclude or introduce a narrative-section remains a moot point; we simply note

---

739 Acts 6:13–14.

740 *Nazoraios* occurs thirteen times in the NT, one is in Luke (18:37; (possibly also *vl* at 24:19)), and seven in Acts (2:22; 3:6; 4:10; 6:14; 22:8; 24:5; 26:9); in Luke-Acts they all link with an enriching statement about Jesus.

741 Acts 7:55; cf. 3:14 where, again, it is the δίκαιος who is betrayed and killed (cf. 7:52).

742 Luke 22:69.

743 Acts 7:55–56. Cf. Dodd, C.H., (1952), 32–34 on Ps. 8 and the Son of Man's glory (Luke 24:26).

744 See section 3.

745 A Lukan structural plan (Acts 1:8; Luke 24:47b–9).

that they bracket Stephen's.[746] Closing a sequence in which Peter and his fellow disciples had engaged with Jerusalem's rulers in an increasingly tense conflict,[747] Luke summarized their activity:

> And every day in the temple and at home they did not cease to teach and proclaim Jesus as the Messiah.   Now in those days, when the disciples were multiplying in number (Acts 5:42–6:1).

Having briefly introduced Stephen as someone filled with faith and the Spirit, one of a group authorized by the apostles for a specific task, Luke continued summarizing:

> The word of God continued to spread; the number of the disciples multiplied greatly in Jerusalem, and a great many of the priests became obedient to the faith (Acts 6:7).

Following that summary, Luke's concern is with Stephen whose story he summarized:

> That day[748] a severe persecution began against the church in Jerusalem, and all except the apostles were scattered throughout the countryside of Judea and Samaria. Devout men buried Stephen and made loud lamentation over him. But Saul was ravaging the church by entering house after house; dragging off both men and women, he committed them to prison (Acts 8:1b–3).

Between these summaries Luke offers readers an account of how his earlier geographical marker – "and you will be my witnesses in Jerusalem, in all Judea and Samaria, and to the ends of the earth" (Acts 1:8) – moved from its first stage (Jerusalem) to its second (Judaea and Samaria). His story's Jerusalem witness ends; Saul makes his first, brief appearance; the Gentile mission is about to

---

[746] There is much to be said for the both-and of these summaries: they both conclude one section while introducing the following.

[747] See Ch. 4 and Ch. 5.

[748] The day Stephen died (ἐν ἐκείνῃ τῇ ἡμέρᾳ); see also 11:19; 22:20.

open. The narrative between these summaries is a significant narrative development, effectively, the culmination of Luke-Acts' Jerusalem conflict narrative.

3. Stephen's conflict thread

Stephen's story precipitates a change of locality and of narrative mood. A death such as Stephen's has been in view since the early stages of the Journey to Jerusalem,[749] then sharply focused by the narrative following Jesus' Temple-*logion,* a trigger for Stephen's speech.[750]

i. Stephen

Luke presents Stephen as one approved by the whole community of Jerusalem disciples[751] and authorized by the apostles.[752] Stephen embodies the culmination of Luke's even longer conflict discourse that reaches back through his Son of Man thread to Luke 9:20–27: Stephen is characterized as one Jesus-follower embodying Jesus' words about discipleship: the language describing him draws on that used in two discipleship contexts.

---

[749] Luke 12:8–12; note its references to Son of Man and Holy Spirit, both of which feature strongly in Stephen's story. This address to disciples on the way takes up the opening exchange of Luke's Son of Man thread (Luke 9:20–27); while Messiah remains an individual concept, Son of Man symbolizes the saints of the Most High (Dan 7:13–14, 27). See also Acts 5:27–33.

'.

[751] τὸ πλῆθος τῶν μαθητῶν (Acts 6:3); παντὸς τοῦ πλήθους (6:5).

[752] Acts 6:6.

208

ii. Luke 21:6–36

"Jesus *Nazoraios* will destroy this place" is one charge that initiates Stephen's speech. Its source,[753] however, is Jesus' saying – "not one stone upon another" – that opens Luke's sequencing of an apocalyptic discourse with its distinctive Lukan ending that envisions faithful disciples ultimately "standing before the Son of Man."[754] This discourse offers an eschatological timetable from the End[755] to the coming of the Son of Man.[756] Stephen's vision is of a medial state on this eschatological timetable – the Son of Man is exalted in glory, still "to come."[757] Within Luke's long discourse stands a discipleship passage (21:12–18) echoing an earlier warning to disciples, and Luke's description of Stephen reflects its italicized elements:

> they will arrest you and persecute you; *they will hand you over to synagogues and prisons,*[758] *and you will be brought before kings and governors because of my name*[759] [...] *I will give you words and a wisdom that none of your opponents will be able to withstand or contradict* [ἀντιστῆναι ἢ ἀντειπεῖν].[760] [...] *they will put some of you to death. You will be hated by all because of my name* (Acts 7:57–60).[761]

---

[753] Luke 21:6; cf. 1 Kgs 9:1–9. Cf. Jesus' lament over Jerusalem (Luke 19:41–44) which focused on its destruction, sharing ἀφίημι and λίθος ἐπὶ λίθῳ with Luke 21:6; resulting from the city's failure to recognise what belongs to *shalom*, and discern the time of God's visitation – a both/and.

[754] Luke 21:36.

[755] 21:7–11.

[756] Luke 21:25–28.

[757] Acts 7:55–56; cf. 3:17–26.

[758] Acts 6:12.

[759] Acts 6:13–14.

[760] Acts 6:10.

[761] Cf. Acts 28:22.

iii. Luke 12:4–12

This earlier address to disciples on their way to Jerusalem amplifies the opening exchange of Luke's Son of Man thread, cited below;[762] significantly, while Messiah remains an individual concept, Son of Man symbolizes the saints of the Most High.[763]

> everyone who publicly acknowledges allegiance to me, the Son of Man also will acknowledge before the angels of God; but whoever denies me before others will be denied before the angels of God. And everyone who speaks a word against the Son of Man will be forgiven; but whoever blasphemes against the Holy Spirit will not be forgiven. When they bring you before the synagogues, the rulers, and the authorities, do not worry about how you are to defend yourselves or what you are to say; for the Holy Spirit will teach you at that very hour what you ought to say (Luke 12:8–10).

Both Jesus' discipleship warning (Luke 12) and the eschatological persecution passage (Luke 21) use language about discipleship that plainly characterizes Stephen as the kind of disciple who may be put to death:[764] he is Spirit-filled,[765] while, by contrast, the Sanhedrin resist the Holy Spirit;[766] his synagogue opponents cannot resist the wisdom with which he speaks;[767] he is possessed of wisdom.[768] Peter and the apostles had earlier been brought before the Sanhedrin; they had been imprisoned.[769] They continued to speak for Jesus,

---

[762] Luke 9:20–27; there are a few earlier instances of this descriptor.

[763] Dan 7:13–14, 27.

[764] Luke 12:8–12; 21:16.

[765] Acts 6:3, 5, 10, 55; cf. Luke 12:10, 12. Contra Dunn, J.D.G., (1996), 83, who infers from Acts only that this use of "wisdom" implies a Hellenist source; cf. also Luke 2:52; 7:35; and Luke's distinctive uses of δίκαιος as a Jesus-descriptor.

[766] Acts 7:51.

[767] Acts 6:10; Luke 21:15.

[768] Acts 6:3, 10; Luke 21:15.

[769] Acts 4:1–4; 5:17–23; cf. Luke 21:12.

and narrowly evaded death in the conflict.[770] Stephen, however, is the first follower whose death Luke reports as the result of his faithful witnessing. He is the last in the chain of Jesus-followers who in Jerusalem bear witness before its rulers and fulfil Jesus' *logia* about those who follow the Son of Man.

Readers leave Stephen as he proleptically fulfils the aim of discipleship: having taken up his cross,[771] he is standing before the Son of Man,[772] his "Lord Jesus." Stephen's conflict stands within a much bigger conflict narrative.

4. Conflict in Jerusalem

Jerusalem has long been Luke's narrative focus. Recall Luke's Prologue, where two scenes place Jesus' introduction firmly in Jerusalem's Temple: the Presentation (2:22–38) and the young Jesus' Temple post-Passover (2:41– 52).[773] Implied by Luke's first Son of Man passion prediction,[774] the city is further highlighted by Luke's distinctive Transfiguration narrative, where tradition's Moses and Elijah[775] here speak with Jesus concerning the Exodus[776] that he is about to fulfil in Jerusalem.[777] Shortly thereafter, the pregnant words of Luke 9:51 announce Jesus' goal: "When the days were completed for his ascension,

---

[770] Acts 5:27–42.

[771] Luke 9:21–27.

[772] Luke 21:36. Whether there is a link between the angels of Luke 12:8 and Stephen's angel-like face (Acts 6:15) is a moot point best left to others.

[773] See Ch. 2, appended note.

[774] Luke 9:22 / Mark 8:31 / Matt. 16:21b; elders, principal priests and scribes suggest a Jerusalem rather than Galilee setting.

[775] Cf. Mark 9:4; Matt. 17:3.

[776] οἳ ὀφθέντες ἐν δόξῃ ἔλεγον τὴν ἔξοδον αὐτοῦ, ἣν ἤμελλεν πληροῦν ἐν Ἰερουσαλήμ, where ἔξοδος probably carries a multi-layered, figurative sense: Jesus' leaving the stage (cf. Acts 13:24); perhaps his death; very probably, given its Moses/transfiguration/mountain setting, an evocation of Israel's freedom from its oppressors (cf. Heb. 11:22). An ear attuned to Luke's harmonics may hear all three senses at once.

[777] Luke 9:30–31, οἳ ὀφθέντες ἐν δόξῃ ἔλεγον τὴν ἔξοδον αὐτοῦ, ἣν ἤμελλεν πληροῦν ἐν Ἰερουσαλήμ.

211

he set his face to go to Jerusalem."[778] With tradition, Luke conceived it as the city that killed prophets,[779] an assessment taken up by his third passion prediction.[780] Within the city, its Temple has been in sharp focus, both as the setting for much of the action, and as one element in the trigger for the conflict.

i. The conflict's trigger

Together, Jesus' "cleansing" of the Temple[781] and his consequent vineyard parable[782] should be seen as the trigger for this Jerusalem-centred conflict. Each pericope is deeply rooted in tradition's telling of Jesus' story, but Luke-Acts' sequencing of tradition has produced its coherent, distinctive account. Further, each unit of that trigger is rooted in scriptural tradition, and in such a way as to throw this conflict's emphasis on the Temple's authorities, not on the Temple itself; on the tenants, not on the vineyard. That distinction becomes crucially important for reading Stephen's speech. However, *Interpreter* focuses on Luke's continuous narrative, not on his redacting of tradition; that was a task I undertook for earlier projects.

ii. Cleansing the Temple

The cleansing is the eviction of "sellers" (πωλοῦντας) from the Temple for which Jesus' explanation is:

> It is written, "My house shall be a house of prayer";[783]

---

[778] Luke's long journey narrative has been much explored; its significance probably depends on the ἔξοδος that Jesus was about to complete in Jerusalem (Luke 9:31).

[779] Luke 13:34–35, cf. Matt. 23:37–39.

[780] Luke 18:32–34; cf. Mark 10:32–34; Matt. 20:17–19. Notably, Luke has summarized tradition in a way that emphasizes Jesus' death at Gentile hands.

[781] Luke 19:45–48, cf. Mark 11:11, 15–19; diff. Matt. 21:10–17; Jn 2:13 -22.

[782] Luke 20:9–26.

[783] See Isa. 56:7c; see below for a brief discussion of Isa. 55–66 in Luke-Acts.

but you have made it a den of robbers (Luke 19:46).[784]

This composite quotation probably came to Luke through tradition. The uses he made of its first element, Isa. 55–66,[785] are clear enough, and we shall continue to draw on these uses as part of Luke-Acts' subtext.[786] In addition to its plain implication of "robbery" through trading in the Temple courts,[787] the Jeremiah element's context will play a significant further part in *Interpreter*'s argument, for Luke-Acts highlights rulers' greed and self-aggrandizement, especially in the conflict narrative. The Temple, however, remains the prime locus for Jesus' teaching,[788] generating the rulers'[789] desire to kill him. Luke identifies Jesus' key opponents as primarily the principal priests and scribes.[790] It was they who demanded to know Jesus' authority for what he was doing, and they who, fearing "the people," prevaricated over his response.[791] And, without Lukan pause,[792] it is to "the people" that Jesus addressed his vineyard parable.[793]

---

[784] See Jer. 7:11, though the whole chapter is of interest in this context.

[785] While now commonly understood as part of a single Isaiah, these chapters appear to have a "restoration" setting on which Luke has drawn; *Interpreter* continues to argue that their uses are governed by Luke-Acts' Davidic reference-frame.

[786] Luke's distinctive account of Jesus' Nazareth sermon drew on Isa. 61 (see Ch. 2); Stephen's speech has drawn on Isa. 66:1–2a (*infra*); Paul's reasoning at Pisidian Antioch engages with Isa. 55:3 (see Ch. 8); in each case, the co-text is implied.

[787] Probably the Court of the Gentiles, as Jesus entered the Temple – hence Luke's evoking Isaiah's "house of prayer for all peoples" (Isa. 57:6).

[788] Luke 19:47a; 20:1; 21:5, 37; 22:53; cf. 24:53.

[789] On Luke's use of "rulers" see Ch. 5 and below.

[790] Luke 9:22; 19:47; 20:1, 19; 22:2, 4, 52, 54, 66; 23:4, 10, 13, 23 *vl*; and into Acts.

[791] Luke 20:1–8

[792] Unlike Matt. (Huck 204).

[793] See Ch. 4 and Ch. 5.

iii. Jesus' vineyard parable

The principal priests and scribes realized that this parable[794] had been directed against them; it was they who then, seeking to entrap Jesus, "monitored him and sent spies who pretended to be righteous."[795] "Giving to God what belongs to God" crystallizes both Jesus' parable and its "coin" sequel. This phrase flows from Jesus' proclaiming God's Kingship: the vineyard's murderous tenants, principal priests and scribes, were arrogating to themselves what was properly God's.[796]

Jesus' scathing critique of the scribes[797] characterizes them as greedy. Luke reports that some Pharisees who ridiculed Jesus' teaching were "money-lovers" (φιλάργυροι), mere pretenders to righteousness who misconceived what God valued.[798] Luke's form of the beatitudes that bring hope to the poor, the hungry and the mourners is matched by his lament for the rich and sated.[799] His was a world of debtors, and of those who longed for bread enough for each day. With cumulative force,

- Luke's statement "You cannot serve God and Mammon";[800]
- the setting of his "Saviour" announcement within Ezekiel's oracle of judgment on Israel's cupidinous, self-regarding shepherd-rulers;[801]

---

[794] Echoing, while adapted from, Isa. 5:1–7.

[795] Cf. Ps. 36:12.

[796] Luke 20:19–20.

[797] Luke 20:45–21:4, whose widow recalls the little Lukan parable at 18:1–8 – the unrighteous judge who has no fear of God and no respect for people doesn't want to be bothered with the little people.

[798] "You are those who in the sight of others enrol yourselves among the righteous; but God knows your hearts; for what is prized by men is an abomination in God's sight." (Luke 16:14–15)

[799] Luke 6:20–26.

[800] Luke 16:13c; the entire chapter throws light on the indifference of the rich to the needs of the poor.

[801] Luke 2:11; cf. Ezek. 34:2–24.

- his implied recollection of Solomon's amassing wealth at the expense of forced labour while simultaneously turning away from serving God;[802] all speak of Jesus' task of bringing good news to the poor and setting free the oppressed.[803]

Giving God what belongs to God is directed primarily to Jerusalem's elite gathered around a priesthood whose reputation for greed, self-indulgence, heartless exercise of power and suspect legitimacy[804] energized an unpopularity that made them "fear the people." In an era of unrest and internecine conflict it is unsurprising that the people listened attentively to Jesus.[805] The long Jerusalem conflict was fuelled by Jesus cleansing the Temple – "my house"[806] – that raised questions of authority and issued in the vineyard parable and its sequel. Jesus' message challenged Jerusalem's rulers, not its Temple. Stephen did likewise. Given that Stephen's speech is structurally, programmatically and thematically integral to Luke-Acts, what of a common view that it does not answer the charges made against Stephen?

---

[802] Acts 7:47 taken up by 7:49b; cf. 1 Kgs 9:15–28; 10:14–29; cf. 11:1–13. This is one memory of the Solomon who built a house for the Lord, the focus of Stephen's speech. Cf. Ps. 131; Wis. 9:7–18.

[803] Luke 4:18–19; cf. Isa. 61:1–2a, adapted.

[804] The Sadducees owed their position to Herod; their allegiance was to Rome; their link with the David-promise tenuous. *Psalms of Solomon* throw light on this period's wealth, distrust and conflict; Charlesworth, J.H. (1983), Vol II, 639–670; Flavius Josephus, *Antiquities,* XIX.6-XX; see Sanders, E.P., (1993), 1–43; Wright, N.T., (1992).

[805] Luke 19:45–48.

[806] Isa. 56:7, Luke 19:46, and 1 Kgs 6–11 lead to Acts 7:47.

C. The charges against Stephen (Acts 6:13–14)

Stephen's speech is primarily about Jesus: replying to the High Priest's "are these things so?" his vision witnesses to the Son of Man,[807] affirming that Jesus' response to his judges had been fulfilled:

> Look, I see the heavens opened and the Son of Man standing at the right hand of God! (Acts 7:55–56).[808]

The charges alleged against Stephen are basically against Jesus. In his reply, Stephen-Luke develops the narrative-theological link between his understanding of Jesus' Temple-*logion* that triggered the eschatological discourse and the false witnesses' charges against Jesus and Stephen.[809] Their charges are: that Jesus will destroy "this place," and that he will change the customs that Moses "handed on to us."[810]

Like a piece of music, Luke-Acts' narrative moves horizontally from its Prologue to an end fading into silence in Rome. Music's horizontal progress has its melodic line and rhythm, but music's sound flows from "the vertical pressure of the horizontal discourse,"[811] where harmonies and chording that intersect with the horizontal, constantly create tensions and resolutions. Similarly, in literary terms we may think of a narrative's vertical resonances, its evocations, and its subtext. Musicians interpret a score's horizontal and vertical axes simultaneously, seeking to reproduce the sound that its composer probably had in mind. *Neutestamentler* listen to a text whose subtext, as in all literature, emerges only when its visual clues are married with their perceived cultural contexts. The Jerusalem conflict's horizontal is relatively easy to follow – and is

---

[807] Acts 7:56, cf. Luke 12:4–12.

[808] Cf. Luke 22:69.

[809] Luke 20:1–8; Acts 6:13–14.

[810] Acts 6:13–14; cf. Mark 14:55–58.

[811] I have borrowed this image, and its cited words, from Barenboim, D., and Said, E., (2004), 148.

often read as a denunciation of Jerusalem's Temple. The conflict's vertical axes are lightly indicated – prompting questions of how to interpret their significance.

That the charges alleged against Stephen are essentially those against Jesus is easily seen. How those charges' scriptural subtexts should be heard is a debatable, sometimes ignored, vertical pressure. One of *Interpreter's* principal objectives is to identify Luke's uses of scripture.[812] While Stephen's speech poses distinctive challenges, it emerges from that quest as a key stage in his David-reference-frame for telling Jesus' story as narrative, and readers who have followed Luke to this point remember that:

- Jesus' Temple-saying was different from what false witnesses alleged;
- witnessing to the fact of Jesus' resurrection entails witnessing to God's fulfilled promises (ἀναστήσω);[813]
- including God's fulfilled promise to Moses – "I will raise up for them a prophet like you from among their own brothers" (ἀναστήσω);[814]
- responding to sceptical Sadducees, Jesus found in the Bush, scriptural warrant for affirming that the God of Abraham, of Isaac and of Jacob is God not of the dead but of the living.[815]

Luke-Acts offers its distinctive substructure. Below, we listen for scriptural resonances in the charges alleged against Stephen-Jesus – and ἀναστήσω is loudly heard as Stephen corrects their Jesus *Nazoraios*.[816] Stephen does not denounce the Temple.

---

[812] See sections D & E; cf. Ch. 8.

[813] 2 Sam. 7:12; Ezek. 34:23; see Ch. 2.

[814] Deut. 18:18; see Ch. 4.

[815] Luke 20:27–40; notably, this passage is narratively linked with Jesus' riddling Ps. 109:1 for the scribes, posing a problem linking exaltation, Messiahship, Davidic sonship, and Lordship.

[816] See section B1iii.

1. Jesus will destroy this place

False witnesses claim to have heard Stephen say that, "this Jesus *Nazoraios* will destroy this place." Their claim echoes non-Lukan accounts of Jesus' preliminary questioning.[817] At his "parallel," substantially shorter account of Jesus' questioning,[818] Luke makes no reference to this charge against Jesus. He has, however, brought "their" false witnesses[819] to the same Sanhedrin to make their more focused charge against Jesus and to allow Stephen to speak for Jerusalem's Jesus-followers.[820]

Readers of Luke's narrative already know, however, that his Jesus said no such thing, nor, indeed, expressed any desire that the Temple be dispensed with. Tradition does know of a Temple-*logion*, and Luke's version is similar to its synoptic parallels. There Jesus had indeed spoken of the Temple's impending destruction:

> As for these things that you see, the days will come when not one stone will be left upon another; all will be thrown down (Luke 21:6).[821]

That saying not only introduces Luke's apocalyptic-eschatological discourse that unpacks those "coming days," but also echoes prophetic sayings[822] about the Temple that offer important clues to hearing Stephen's speech. We recall that Jesus' cleansing of the Temple carried his appeal to a compound scriptural quotation.[823] Luke's version differs in two respects from that in Mark and

---

[817] Mark 14:55–58; cf. Matt. 26:60–61; Jn 2:19.

[818] Luke 22:66–71; cf. Mark 14:55–64; Matthew 26:57–65.

[819] Acts 6:13; cf. Matt. 26:60; Mark 14:55–56.

[820] We reserve Mark's χειροποίητον for discussion of Stephen's scriptural reasoning (Acts 7:48).

[821] Cf. Mark 14:55–64; Matthew 26:57–65.

[822] E.g., the co-texts of the compound quotation at the cleansing of the Temple (Luke 19:46): Jer. 7:11–15, 22–26; Isa. 56:7c; cf. 1 Kgs 8:27–53 also witness to the Temple's essence as a house of prayer: 8:30, 33, 35–36, 38–39, 41–51;

[823] See section B4ii.

Matthew: his version lacks "it will be called (κληθήσεται)" and "for all peoples" (πᾶσιν τοῖς ἔθνεσιν). These differences make Luke's version more immediate to Jesus' present situation: it is "my house of prayer" that you have turned into "a robbers' den." Here, Jesus' appeal to adapted scriptural tradition evokes two prophetic co-texts whose resonances were very probably heard.

First, while the Jeremiah element highlighted trading in the Temple precincts as robbery, its context[824] points to an earlier Temple's destruction at God's hands, recalling the grounds for its destruction: Shiloh was "my place" where I made my name dwell at first. Jeremiah's warning, addressed to a threatened Israel that did not listen to God was:

> therefore I will do to the house that is called by my name, in which you trust, and to the place that I gave to you and to your fathers, just what I did to Shiloh (Jer. 7:14).

Notably, Jeremiah's oracle grounded this threat in his recalling of God's gracious act in bringing their fathers out of Egypt.[825] That act, preceding Sinai's later covenant, called for obedience to God. Israel's appropriate response to this unearned act of loving-kindness to Abraham's children should have been gratitude, but

> From the day that your fathers came out of the land of Egypt until this day, I have persistently sent all my servants the prophets to them, day after day; yet they did not listen[826] to me, or pay attention, but they stiffened their necks. They did worse than their fathers did (Jer. 7: 25–26).[827]

---

[824] Jer. 7.

[825] Jer. 7:22–26; see section D.

[826] The Sanhedrin, hearing Stephen's witness to the glorified Son of Man (Acts 7:57), closed their ears to him (συνέσχον τὰ ὦτα αὐτῶν); we shall return to this.

[827] Stephen's peroration (Acts 7:51–52) accords well with Jeremiah's references to fathers, prophets and stiff necks, and to ears that refuse to listen; both Jeremiah and Stephen root their judgments in Israel's Exodus story.

Second, Isaiah's element in the conflict's trigger envisioned a restored Temple as a house of prayer in a restored Jerusalem. Earlier, we noted the influence of Isa. 55–66 on Luke-Acts.[828] Isaiah 66:22–23 further amplified the role of a restored Jerusalem and of its Temple. Note the themes in Isaiah 56: my holy mountain; my covenant; hold fast my covenant; "for my house shall be called a house of prayer for all peoples."[829] Interpreters of Stephen's speech must above all recall that one crucial quotation from Isa. 55–66 reads: "What kind of house will you build for me?"[830]

Further, the trigger's compound quotation carries Temple-resonances that can hardly fail to point readers to another prayer of the Temple's consecration: Solomon's prayer[831] stresses his Temple's grounding in God's gracious act. It is not God's dwelling place;[832] it is where God's Name is;[833] it is a house of prayer.[834] It is the place where this wayward people may turn repentantly and pray because

> you have separated them for yourself from among all the peoples of the earth, to be your heritage, just as you promised through Moses, your servant, when you brought our fathers out of the land of Egypt, O Lord God (1 Kgs 8:53).

Once more, Solomon's Temple and Israel's liberation from Egypt are linked; this time Moses is included. There are good grounds for holding that Luke's pre-

---

[828] See section B4.

[829] Isa. 56:4–7; cf. Luke 19:46.

[830] ποῖον οἶκον οἰκοδομήσετέ μοι; ἢ ποῖος τόπος τῆς καταπαύσεώς μου; (Isaiah 66:1–2a); cf. Ps. 131:14; 94:7–11 (on which see Docherty, S, (2009), 181–198). Common "Exodus" elements in Hebrews and Stephen's speech have long exercised me: hard-heartedness and faithlessness here link Ps. 94 with Isaiah's ἢ τίς τόπος τῆς καταπαύσεώς μου; and with Stephen. See section E.

[831] 1 Kgs 8:27–53.

[832] 1 Kgs 8:27, 29, 44.

[833] 1 Kgs 8:26, 44, 49. Cf. Jer. 7:14.

[834] 1 Kgs 8:30, 33, 35–36, 38–39, 41–51; cf. Isa. 56:7.

draft subtext included Isa. 55–66; it is less sure that his subtext included Jer. 7. Both elements, however, indicate a clear prophetic, Deuteronomic attitude to that house as an appointed focus for serving God – where serving is a semantic basket that includes both worship and covenant faithfulness that responds obediently to "I will be your God and you shall be my People."[835] For Luke, that house is God's conditional gift.

2. Jesus will transform the traditions received from Moses

Scholars tend to note the length of Stephen's Moses section; they also tend to note the vehemence of his counter-charge:

> Stiff-necked, uncircumcised in heart and ears,[836] you are forever opposing the Holy Spirit, just as your fathers used to do [You are those] who received the law as ordained by angels, and yet you have not obeyed it (Acts 7:51, 53).

Here, Stephen more vigorously charges Jerusalem's rulers with what Jesus implied by his act of cleansing the Temple, then clarified by his adaptation of Isaiah's vineyard parable.[837] Rulers had arrogated for themselves what was properly God's – and this was a sensitive area for unpopular rulers![838] God had sent Moses to bring Israel into freedom; Stephen itemized "our fathers'" deafness to God's call.[839] If the issue is Jesus' alleged threat to Moses' traditions, then what traditions are at stake?

---

[835] Cf. Exod. 6:7; Lev 26:12; Jer. 11:4, 30:22; Ezek. 36:8–11.

[836] See Deut. 10:12–22, esp. v16.

[837] Section B4iii.

[838] See, e.g., PssSol. 1, 2, 8, 17. Luke's attention to Jesus as the Righteous One and his depiction of the rulers' plotting Jesus' death point to a subtext that includes something like Wis. 2–5. Both Wis. and PssSol. emerge from the post-Maccabean upheavals: both view rulers as opposing God's righteous people.

[839] See Jer. 7:22–26.

It is almost impossible to locate Jesus on a sectarian map of his time. His emphasizing piety and righteousness[840] puts him on a scale between Pharisees and Qumran. Tomson speaks for what seems to fit the evidence best: "Jesus was not at home anywhere, except perhaps in the proximity of the 'nonconformistic companionship' of pious individuals."[841] Moessner, however, works on the principle that "one conceptual canopy of Israel's past and the role and fate of her prophets within that history covered all [that period's] literature."[842] And Luke thinks of Jesus as a Prophet, especially as the raised-up Prophet like Moses. It is arguable that for someone such as Jesus to challenge Jerusalem's elite's authority looked very like his threatening the fabric of Mosaic tradition, the orderly transmission of Torah in one People however divided by sects.

Participants in Luke's account of the Jerusalem conflict, especially the Stephen unit's dramatis personae, often appear in sectarian guise. But Stephen and a diverse Sanhedrin shared a common Judaism underlying sectarian divisions.[843] Jewish life typically comprised ritual and calendar; synagogue and Temple; home[844] and assembly; hearing and reflecting on Torah. Morning and evening at home, then in the weekly liturgy, their shared custom was to pray[845] – at the heart of which was *Shema'*, Moses words sequenced from Torah.[846] Moses' five books of instruction underlay common Judaism's shared practice.

Crystallized Torah, shorter even than the *Shema'*, focused Jewish minds on piety towards God and righteousness towards humans. Stephen's

---

[840] E.g., Luke 10:25–28; 18:18–23.

[841] Tomson, P.J., (2001), 159.

[842] Moessner, D., (2016), 243, drawing on Steck (1967), whose four tenets match what also emerges from close study of Stephen's speech.

[843] See, e.g., Sanders, E.P., (1992), 190–240; Tomson, P.J., (2001), 70–110; Wright, N.T., (1992), 215–243.

[844] E.g., *mezuzot,* and *tefillin, kashrut* and daily prayer.

[845] Note Luke's attention to Jesus at prayer; cf. Acts 4:24–30.

[846] Deut. 6:4–9; 11:13–21; Nu 15:37–41.

vehement counter-charge, cited above, evokes one saying of Moses from one Torah-summary:[847]

(a) καὶ περιτεμεῖσθε τὴν σκληροκαρδίαν ὑμῶν
(b) καὶ τὸν τράχηλον ὑμῶν οὐ σκληρυνεῖτε ἔτι (Deut. 10:12–22).

Stephen adapted Deuteronomy's summary for his judges:

(b) Σκληροτράχηλοι καὶ
(a) ἀπερίτμητοι καρδίαις [καὶ τοῖς ὠσίν] (Acts 7:51)
they had not listened.[848]

3. Jesus, Solomon, Torah

Luke, and Luke's Jesus-followers, read their scriptures retrospectively, post-event. The Deuteronomist's Moses was already doing this in the aphorism cited above. The Jesus-dual-tradition was doing this in its account of their Lord's testing in the wilderness,[849] where Jesus' citations from Deuteronomy evoke their co-texts.[850] In them, remembering leads to obedience and well-being; forgetting leads to disobedience that entails destruction. The Jesus who was anointed "My son"[851] was the Jesus whom Luke's narrative recounts as resolutely obedient throughout his re-experiencing of Israel's foundational experience – the Exodus through the wilderness.[852] From his wilderness onward, this obedient son of David stands in stark contrast to Solomon, that disobedient son of David, whose story entailed destruction. Stephen's complaint against Jerusalem's rulers is that they are Solomon's offspring, for Solomon's

---

[847] Cf. Marshall, I.H., (2007), 539, who identifies Jer. 4:4 as the source for hardened hearts (περιτέμεσθε τὴν σκληροκαρδίαν ὑμῶν) and Jer. 6:10 for uncircumcised ears (ἰδοὺ ἀπερίτμητα τὰ ὦτα αὐτῶν, καὶ οὐ δύνανται ἀκούειν). Deuteronomy is Torah, Jeremiah is not.

[848] Ἄκουε, Ισραηλ (Deut. 5:1); Ἄνδρες ἀδελφοὶ καὶ πατέρες, ἀκούσατε (Acts 7:2b)

[849] Luke 4:1–12; Matt. 4:1–11.

[850] Deut. 6:10–25; 8:1–20.

[851] Luke 3:21–22; cf. 9:34–6.

[852] Cf. Luke 9:31; cf. Acts 7:17–45.

name provokes his speech's *volta*: thereafter, "our fathers" become "your fathers."[853]

Echoing the *Shema'*, Stephen's speech opens "Listen." His charge against Jerusalem's rulers was that like their fathers they did not listen (ἀπερίτμητοι [...] τοῖς ὠσίν), and they shortly proved him right: they held their ears closed (συνέσχον τὰ ὦτα αὐτῶν), then killed another who spoke out as Jesus had done. Significant figures in Torah's handing-on, these rulers did not guard it.[854] That was also scripture's complaint against Solomon, David's son.[855]

---

[853] Acts 7:47–51 is the crucial passage to unpack.

[854] ἐλάβετε τὸν νόμον [...] καὶ οὐκ ἐφυλάξατε (Acts 7:53).

[855] Sirach 47:12–20; 1 Kgs 11:1–13.

D. David's two sons

1. Solomon in Israel's memory: Temple or house?

Solomon is the elephant in Luke-Acts' room. Luke retold Jesus' story to reassure Theophilus of the sure-foundedness (ἀσφάλεια) of what he had been taught about the "things fulfilled among us."[856] His reference-frame for retelling Jesus' story was the David-promise;[857] he built on God's having raised up Jesus in two senses to fulfil that promise, for Luke-Acts read Nathan's oracle retrospectively.[858] That oracle emerged, however, with semantic unclarity about its word "house"[859] that also made David's son(s) the builder of a "house for my name"; and Israel's history identified that builder as Solomon: "He shall build a house for my name, and I will establish the throne of his kingdom forever."[860]

Stephen cryptically noted: "But it was Solomon who built a house for him."[861] Simply that; for that son's dynasty had ended disastrously, and nothing needed to be said about what everybody knew and selectively mentioned – Solomon's "turning aside."[862] Nevertheless, God's forever remained.[863] Stephen exploits both senses of house in Nathan's oracle, its ambivalence made explicit by his citing Isaiah's "what kind of house will you build for me?" That sentence's

---

[856] Luke 1:1–4.

[857] See Ch. 2.

[858] 2 Sam. 7:12.

[859] 2 Sam. 7:1–29.

[860] 2 Sam. 7:13.

[861] Acts 7:47.

[862] 1 Kgs 9:6, 8b–9.

[863] 2 Sam. 7: 13 -καὶ ἀνορθώσω τὸν θρόνον αὐτοῦ ἕως εἰς τὸν αἰῶνα. See Sirach 47:22; cf. 1 Kgs 11:11–13 and his disobedient kingly succession until the Exile.

omitted clause invites readers to evoke its co-text.[864] For Luke's protagonist, Jesus, is also emphatically of David's house; that is the first thing readers learn of him.[865] Of his kingdom there is to be no end, and his rule over Jacob's house is to be unending.[866] Stephen's single reference to Solomon reminds readers that David's blood line includes two sons whose kingdoms are in Lukan focus.

Reflection on the Temple-charge against Stephen revealed how the resonances from Jesus' cleansing of the Temple and Solomon's consecration prayer both pointed to the Temple's conditionality and to its founding on the basis of God's gracious act in bringing Israel out of Egypt. Similarly, in relation to the accusation that Jesus would change Moses' traditions, Stephen's counter-charge is that his judges, the Sanhedrin who betrayed and murdered Jesus, are they who have not obeyed Torah.[867] Jesus had not said that he would destroy this place, but that days would come when not one stone would be left upon another.[868] Stephen's hermeneutic key arguably lies in his using the name Solomon.[869] Why should this be?

Another question first confronts an interpreter: what scripture-hoard can reasonably[870] be expected of Luke's earliest readers/hearers?[871] Theirs was an age of internal unrest, conflict, dissent,[872] its writings marked by polarization of

---

[864] Acts 7:49b, citing Isa. 66:1–2a, part of the restoration subtext we earlier identified. Cf. 1 Kgs 6:11–14. But Isa. 66:2b–3, an *aposiopesis*, clarifies the personal as well as a structural sense of "house" – καὶ ἐπὶ τίνα ἐπιβλέψω ἀλλ' ἢ ἐπὶ τὸν ταπεινὸν καὶ ἡσύχιον καὶ τρέμοντα τοὺς λόγους μου; See Doble (2000).

[865] Luke 1:27.

[866] Luke 1:33.

[867] Acts 7:51–53.

[868] Luke 21:6.

[869] Acts 7:47; in Luke-Acts Jesus and his followers are Torah-observant.

[870] Here, "reasonably" points to what *Interpreter* has already unearthed from Luke's narrative; see Ch. 10.

[871] Most of the essays in McLay, R.T., (ed), (2015), *FS* for Robert Hayward, contribute to an understanding of how this question may be asked and answered.

[872] Either shortly before the Jewish War, around 65–66 CE, or pondering its effects (post 70 CE); we keep open questions of dating Luke-Acts.

the righteous and wicked, the godly and ungodly. Qumran's influence reached beyond its desert location. The Psalms of Solomon were the hymns of dissenters hopeful for God's fulfilment of the David-promise; the Wisdom of Solomon offered advice, warning, and exemplars for rulers concerning righteousness; Sirach's summary neatly encapsulated the heart of Solomon's story[873] – he was the wise,[874] over-rich, and, finally, lamentably ungodly son of David. Notably, their ostentatious riches and indifference to godly justice lie at the root of much complaining about post-Hasmonean rulers.[875] In a context where, according to Luke 4–7, people argued long and hard over scripture, especially in this Temple-context, we may assume a substantial knowledge of Israel's scriptures relating to David's house. Because Luke's *apologia* for Theophilus claims to be about the fulfilment of Israel's scriptures – especially those David-related – that assumption may be judged appropriate.

So how much of Solomon's story may one assume that Luke's earliest readers knew? And in what ways might such awareness affect their hearing of Stephen's speech? Luke clearly expects his readers to recall, and in reading to share his subtext. Towards the climax of Stephen's speech, Amos 5:25–27a and Isa. 66:1–2a are present as adaptation and quotation, and there is very probably an allusion to Ps. 131 with its conditional promise to David. Between Nathan's oracle and that psalmist, however, lies a prophetic view of history encapsulated by Deuteronomy.[876] Then, between Stephen's references to Amos and to Isaiah stands his pregnant reference to Solomon: "but it was Solomon who built a house for him."[877] A quotation from Isaiah introduces Stephen's *volta*. His direct, accusatory addressing the Sanhedrin sharply

---

[873] Sirach 47:12–22.

[874] Cf. 1 Kgs 3:3–14 for Solomon's first theophany and his prayer for wisdom (3:9).

[875] See Sanders, E.P., (1992); Wright, N.T., (1992).

[876] See section E1a for this psalm's links with Isa. 66.

[877] Acts 7:47.

distinguishes "your" fathers from his implied "our" fathers. Their spiritual, if not genetic, ancestry is from Solomon and his ilk. Luke's genealogy of Jesus omits Solomon,[878] offering another paternal route for David's promised seed.[879]

Crucially, why does Stephen reason from house rather than Temple[880] throughout this speech, leading to its focal "But it was Solomon who built a house for him"? His use of "house" (οἶκος) arguably derives not from some ill-digested source, but from Luke-Acts' narrative focus on David's house, and the role of Nathan's bivalent οἶκος in Luke's pervasive David-subtext.

Once one hears the chords and discords from Luke's brief references and allusions, their vertical pressures on horizontal narratives become irresistible – perhaps most significantly when hearing Isaiah 66:1–2a as an incipit citation retrospectively "explaining" Stephen's cryptic Acts 7:47.[881] Moreover, both false charges against Jesus-Stephen – concerning "this place"

---

[878] Luke 3:31; diff. Matt. 1:6. Both evangelists make clear that Jesus is a *Davidid*, and that this sonship undergirds their use of Messiah as a principal descriptor for him.

[879] See Sirach 47:20, 22 (σπέρμα); the basic David-promise is clearly alluded to in 47:11 and echoed in 47:22 ("a root out of himself"); but Sirach's two references to "seed" (σπέρμα) make it almost certain that, for Luke, Samuel's καὶ ἀναστήσω τὸ σπέρμα σου μετὰ σέ, ὃς ἔσται ἐκ τῆς κοιλίας σου, καὶ ἑτοιμάσω τὴν βασιλείαν αὐτοῦ (2 Sam. 7:12) entailed genetic descent for Jesus that bypassed the corrupted Solomon See Ch. 1 and Ch. 8.

[880] Luke's narrative readily uses "Temple" (ἱερόν) elsewhere, especially in his conflict narrative (including Paul's conflict with Jerusalem's authorities): the Prologue's introducing Jesus prefigures that conflict (see Ch. 2, appended note). Apart from Luke 4:9 and 18:10, ἱερόν next appears as Jesus enters Jerusalem and triggers the conflict narrative (Luke 19:45) that arguably ends with his followers' diaspora from Jerusalem (Acts 8:3). [Cf. Luke 2:27, 37, 46; 19:45, 47; 20:1; 21:5, 37, 38; 22:53; 24:53; Acts 2:46; 3:1, 2, 3, 10; 4:1; 5:20, 21, 24, 25, 42].

[881] "But it was Solomon who built a house for him."

and "Moses" – coinhere in Solomon's theophany,[882] a divine response to Solomon's dedicatory prayer.[883]

Solomon's second theophany remained a foundation narrative for Herod's rebuilding the Second Temple, reaffirming the link between this house of prayer and David's house, while emphatically confirming that link's being conditional on covenant-fidelity. Jesus' Temple-*logion* echoes that theophany's warning.[884] Bundled together in Solomon's theophany are lexical and thematic features that also characterise Stephen's speech. For example: this house that [Solomon] built; God, who brought their fathers out of Egypt; if, expressing the conditionality of God's twofold David-promise; turning aside from God to serve foreign gods. Stephen's speech arguably reflects and is probably shaped by Solomon's uncited second theophany.

2. A Lukan narrative midrash

By reflecting on the main elements in Solomon's theophany Stephen demonstrated for the High Priest and the Sanhedrin why these things are not so;[885] though uncited, as in a homily his focal text becomes obvious. This theophany coheres with the standpoint of Ps. 131 to which Stephen alludes,[886] and with that of Jeremiah 7 that undergirds Jesus' cleansing of the Temple. Underlying Luke's David-theology and strongly implied by Stephen's speech is a foundational strand of early Christian reasoning – that God, who "tore the

---

[882] 1 Kgs 9:1–9; see its parallel, 2 Chron 7:11–22.

[883] Cf. 1Kgs 6:11–14 (house); 8:1–11 (Ark); 22–53 (Dedicatory prayer); cf. 9:8b–9 that resembles Deut. 29:24–28; cf. Jer. 7.

[884] 1 Kgs 9:6–9; Luke 21:6.

[885] Acts 7:1. See Docherty, S., (2014), 13; the second paragraph reports and stimulates continuing questions about scripture "using" scripture.

[886] Act 7:45b.

kingdom" from Solomon,[887] had anointed[888] and uniquely raised up Jesus, thereby rebuilding David's fallen house.[889]

Jesus' *logion,* "not one stone will be left upon another," parallels the devastation implied by Kingdom's "I will throw from my sight the house that I have consecrated for my name" and its awe-inspiring consequences. This fundamental conditionality in Solomon's story pervades Luke's subtext. His awareness of 1 Kgs 9:1–9 arguably shapes Stephen's whole story of grace from Abraham to Jesus, using Moses as Stephen's accusers' chosen focus for its telling. It is that shaping of the content of Stephen's speech to which we turn.

i. The shape of Stephen's speech

Stephen's[890] Exodus-centred[891] story of Israel and Luke's canticles introducing Jesus are both rooted in Abraham's story. For Stephen, Israel's story begins:

(a) with God's promise to Abraham[892] about fearless worship in freedom. That promise (Acts 7:7) entailed

(b) Moses' story as the fulfilling of that promise;[893] the further promise to Moses of a prophet in his mould[894] was illuminated by Jesus' story as it ended with his completed Exodus.[895]

---

[887] 1 Kgs 11:9–13.

[888] Luke 3:21–22; Acts 4:27b; 10:38.

[889] *E.g.,* Acts 15:15–18; cf. Amos 9:11

[890] Bracketed capitals below refer to the following Table's headings (3).

[891] For Deuteronomy, Jeremiah, and 1 Kings, God's freeing this People from bondage in Egypt is the very core of their being and the reason for their grateful obedience to Torah. Stephen's speech presents the culmination of the *Exodus* that Jesus was *to complete* (πληροῦν) in Jerusalem. (Luke 9:31).

[892] See the *Magnificat* (Luke 1:54–55); *Benedictus* (1:69–75).

[893] Acts 7:17.

[894] Acts 7:37.

[895] Cf. Peter's *haruzin* at Acts 3:18–26.

(c) Luke's Jesus fulfilled God's promise to David.[896] The distinctive, Jesus-focused conclusion to Stephen's speech, which

(d) is of Jesus, exalted to God's right hand, standing (Wis. 5:1) in proleptic judgment on the Sanhedrin who condemned him.[897] Various descriptors embed him in Luke-Acts as the one whose resurrection fulfilled Israel's hopes in God's promises to:

- David of a seed who would reign, and a house that would endure, forever;
- Moses of a prophet such as he;
- Abraham of a freed, worshipping inheritance, through a seed by whom all earth's families might be blessed.[898]

For Stephen, the issue dividing Sanhedrin and Jesus' followers is not the Temple as an institution, but its custodians' covenant-disloyalty, and their leavening role in Israel's life.

ii. The content of Stephen's speech

That previous sentence becomes clearer from the Table outlining Stephen's speech.[899] Its content reflects both Solomon's consecratory prayer for his house

---

[896] See Ch. 2; cf. Acts 7:45b; Ps. 131 and the base David-promise, (2 Sam. 7).

[897] Luke-Stephen has melded Ps. 109:1 with Wis. 5:1 (Acts 7:55–56). Luke-Acts' one protagonist, Jesus, bears many descriptors including Son of Man and δίκαιος. Luke's retrospective reading of scripture through a resurrection lens enabled him to make transitions, e.g., from Son of Man to Messiah (see Ch. 3). Stephen's vision of a now glorified, once murdered Jesus (Acts 7:51–55) allowed him to hold together in his mind the (distinctively Lukan) rejected δίκαιος, recalled at Acts 7:52 (Luke 23:47) and tradition's Son of Man-*logion* distinctively remembered by Luke (Luke 22:69) then fulfilled at Acts 7:55–56. Luke's resurrection-glory-exaltation perspective allowed him to segue between the vindications of the Son of Man and of Wisdom's δίκαιος. Thus the psalmist's and Jesus' pre-resurrection καθήμενος (Luke 22:69) emerged as Stephen's and Wisdom's post-glorification-vindication ἑστῶτα (Acts 7:55–56).

[898] See Acts 3:12b–26.

[899] See section 3.

231

and its following theophany. *Interpreter*'s narrative route to this point has indicated this conclusion:[900] Stephen's *apologia* is essentially his counter-charge on the two issues dividing Jesus' followers from the Sanhedrin who had received the Law, but had not kept it (οὐκ ἐφυλάξατε). Solomon's *Benedictus*[901] following his prayer of consecration of the house, tightly links God's promises through Moses with the Exodus from Egypt with God's giving rest (κατάπαυσις)[902] to his People with commitment to God's Torah – walking in his statutes, keeping (φυλάσσειν) God's commands.

David's contrasting sons distinguish Stephen's "your fathers" from his implied "our fathers." Solomon had defiled (David's) seed and brought down wrath on his children.[903] God, however, true to his oath,[904] had given Jacob a remnant, and "to David a root out of himself."[905] Stephen's speech is focally about Jesus, David's obedient son,[906] whose story binds together the quotations, allusions and subtext that dominate the speech's closing phases from 7:39 to 7:53.

Having anointed Jesus, David's seed, God raised him from the dead, thereby fulfilling Moses' announcement of God's promise (ἀναστήσω) of a prophet like Moses. Peter had earlier prepared readers for this move by his *haruzin*[907] during an address in Solomon's Colonnade.[908] Jesus also lived out the destiny of both Daniel's Son of Man and Wisdom's Righteous One. Luke had earlier prepared readers for Stephen's δίκαιος by a centurion's distinctive

---

[900] See sections B4, C and D1,

[901] 1 Kgs 8:56–61.

[902] This Solomonic "rest" links Stephen's allusion to Ps. 131 with his appeal to Isa. 66:1–2a; see section C1. We return to this linkage below.

[903] Sirach 47:20.

[904] E.g., Ps. 88:29–38.

[905] Sirach 47:22c.

[906] See Luke 4:1–13.

[907] A form of scriptural reasoning by linkages among a sequence of texts.

[908] Acts 3:13–26; see Ch. 4.

word on Jesus' death.[909] Stephen's bivalent word "house," like Luke's ἀναστήσω, reinterprets Nathan's oracle and David's prayer.[910] Isaiah's question – "What kind of a house will you build for me?" – re-focuses that bivalence, and Isaiah's "restoration" co-text[911] accents Israel's mixed response to God's gracious acts.

iii. Why narrative midrash?

Stephen's speech argues his case by retracing the story of Israel's Exodus and Sinai covenant. In dialogue with Deuteronomy, his perspective is its conditionality of both Temple and Davidic house;[912] his retelling unfolds from Abraham to Jesus. Were this a book, it might be called rewritten scripture.[913] However, its being extended narrative within Luke-Acts suggests this alternative descriptor for scriptural interpretation: the enrichment of Torah through a new event (Jesus) and prophetic insight into that event (Solomon's theophany) may usefully be called narrative midrash.[914]

---

[909] Luke 23:47; used also by Peter in his address in Solomon's colonnade, (Acts 3:14).

[910] 2 Sam. 7:1–29.

[911] Isa. 66:1–6, and probably beyond. See Doble, P., (2000).

[912] Stephen's faithful Ἰησοῦς completed his Exodus (cf. Luke 9:31; Acts 7:55–56); whether readers are to hear resonances from Deut. 34:9 – Josh. 1:10 remains an interesting question.

[913] Alexander, P.S., (1988).

[914] Adelman, R., (2014).

3. A narrative midrash on Solomon

A. 2–16 **How we came to be in Egypt**

Abraham, oracle (Gen. 15 with Exod. 3:12);

Isaac and Jacob; Joseph.

Note density (2–16) of "Egypt," of "Jacob" (= Israel).

B. 17–40 **Moses as God's agent**

17–29 Promise to Abraham fulfilled. Moses born, nurtured,

encounters his brothers

30–34 **The Bush**

God of Abraham, Isaac and Jacob

commissions Moses, "go [...] Egypt"

35–40. This [Moses] (οὖτος/ ὃς sevenfold),

Israel's response to, assessment of Moses,

where **Deut 18:15** (18) is central and making

its second appearance [cf. Acts 3:22–3].

C. 41–50[915] Ἐν ἐξόδῳ Ισραηλ ἐξ Αἰγύπτου[916] (cf. 1 Kgs 9:9)

a question of whom to worship

41–44 two tents

---

[915] The division is marked by "in those days" (7:41).

[916] Ps. 113:1; cf. Ps. 114.

	45–50	two houses
D.	**51–60**	**Stephen's peroration**
	51–54	counter-charge, leading to
	55–56	his vision of the Son of Man, then
	57–60	his death as Jesus' disciple, witness-martyr

(Luke 9,12, 21).[917]

---

[917] Adapted from Doble, P., (2013).

E. Stephen's scriptural reasoning

That table reveals the speech's Exodus shape and its "worship-in-service" emphasis. Its shape emerged from earlier sections of this chapter that set Stephen's speech in the context of Luke-Acts;[918] re-examined the charges made against Jesus-Stephen;[919] and focused on Stephen's implied contrasting of David's two sons.[920] Stephen's reasoning initially appears complex because it is the product of three narrative-vectors:[921]

- Luke-Acts' scriptural substructure within its Davidic reference-frame;
- the work's unfolding narrative nature;
- the rootedness in both the above of false charges against Stephen.

Stephen is clearly an interpreter within an existing tradition. Earlier, we explored Peter's role as Luke-Acts' principal retrospective interpreter of Jesus-*logia* and of scripture, and his using recognizable techniques to explicate recent events.[922] Similarly, Stephen's response to the High Priest's question is his retelling of scripture from a disciple's perspective; his focal Jesus-*logion* mirrors Luke 22:69, itself adapted to its role here.[923] Readers have already learnt that *Nazoraios* is inadequate,[924] for Luke's Jesus is the goal of God's dealings with Israel, God's Messiah, their Lord. Unlike Solomon, this Messiah is David's Torah-faithful son.[925]

---

[918] Section B.

[919] Section C.

[920] Section D.

[921] Section A.

[922] See chs 4–6; cf. Doble, P., (2006; 2013).

[923] At Acts 7:55–56.

[924] Section B1iii.

[925] See Luke 4:1–13.

1. Sinai, seed and house

Stephen-Luke's rewriting of scripture emerges as part of Luke-Acts' Davidic substructure.[926] As Paul's good news for Antioch clarified the bivalent ἀναστήσω dimension of the David-promise, so Stephen's speech placed David's bivalent οἶκος in Israel's ongoing story. In a densely condensed 7:45b–50, he implicitly contrasted David's two sons, Solomon and Jesus.[927]

David's story completed Moses' story that occupied most of Stephen's speech,[928] stories linked by Sinai's Ark of the Covenant, a linkage focused by Stephen's allusion to Ps. 131 and its own lexical, and thematic links with both Amos 5:25–6[929] and with Isa. 66.[930] That psalm evokes both 2 Sam. 6–7 and Solomon's theophany. Solomon's story appeared to be the fulfilment of God's promises to David – readers know what happened: Sinai's Ark of the Covenant was safely lodged in its house in Zion; the wise son turned fool. Moses' story had flowed from Abraham's story, for it was foretold by Abraham's dark vision,[931] then reactivated at the Bush[932] where God commissioned Moses as his agent for delivering Israel from Egypt. As Moses' story fulfilled God's promise to Abraham, David's fulfilled both, but through Jesus,[933] not Solomon – who ignored his theophany's "if."

---

[926] So Rom. 1:1–6; cf. 4Q174; Luke worked a well-tilled field.

[927] A thread from Luke 1:27 to Acts 15:16–17, where Amos's twin verbs echo 2 Sam. 7:13, and a play on οἶκος/σκηνή, echoes 2 Sam. 7:2. (For Amos 5 see section D).

[928] Caiv.

[929] Acts 7:42b–43.

[930] Acts 7:49–50,

[931] Acts 7:7b, καὶ μετὰ ταῦτα ἐξελεύσονται καὶ λατρεύσουσίν μοι ἐν τῷ τόπῳ τούτῳ. Cf. 6:13–14, Ἰησοῦς ὁ Ναζωραῖος οὗτος καταλύσει τὸν τόπον τοῦτον. Cf. Exod. 3:12.

[932] Acts 7:30–34.

[933] Cf. Acts 3:18–26.

i. The memory of "if"

Israel's shared memory of Solomon's theophany underlies and shapes Stephen's speech.[934] Additionally, cultic-memories within Ps. 131 emerge from the gravitational pull of this brief evocative allusion. For *Interpreter*, the phrase "according to the scriptures" is a portmanteau for passages evoked by incipit scriptural triggers, together with associated contemporary interpretative practices. Neither of Luke-Acts' basic ἀναστήσω-texts is ever quoted, nor is Solomon's theophany, yet in a narrative such as Luke's it would be bizarre to excise Israel's scriptural traditions from an attempt to grasp the essence of a conflict-narrative focused on those very issues – Moses' traditions and Solomon's Temple-founding in the context of Jesus' story. In Luke-Acts both Psalm 131:11–12[935] and 1 Kings 9:6–9,[936] witness to the covenant-conditional nature of the David-promise.

Stephen's Weltanschauung was the arena within which this action unfolded to its crucial *volta,* distinguishing the narrative's two conflicting groups. Throughout ages "our fathers" had respectfully ignored or rejected Moses' traditions shared by Jesus-followers with all Israel's faithful children; the assembly that Stephen addressed represented the powerful elite that "turned aside" from covenant fidelity[937] to worship Mammon – "Stiff-necked, uncircumcised in heart and ears, just like your fathers [whose outstanding exemplar was Solomon] you are always resisting the Holy Spirit."[938] That same Spirit, however, anointed and commissioned Jesus; tested and confirmed his

---

[934] Section Ci.

[935] ἐὰν φυλάξωνται οἱ υἱοί σου τὴν διαθήκην μου.

[936] ἐὰν δὲ ἀποστραφέντες ἀποστραφῆτε ὑμεῖς καὶ τὰ τέκνα ὑμῶν ἀπ᾽ ἐμοῦ καὶ μὴ φυλάξητε τὰς ἐντολάς μου καὶ τὰ προστάγματά μου, ἃ ἔδωκεν Μωυσῆς ἐνώπιον ὑμῶν.

[937] 1 Kgs 9:6–9.

[938] Acts 7:51; cf. Deut. 10:12–22.

fidelity to Torah; raised him up in both senses of ἀναστήσω.[939] His story evoked models of the righteous one (δίκαιος)[940] and the prophet like Moses (προφήτης).[941] As he had told his judges, he became the glorified, vindicated Son of Man[942] – so Messiah[943] and Lord. Central to Stephen's reasoning is this psalmist's evoking a ritual-memory of the David-promise's conditional nature: the unquoted, clearly present Ps. 131 is the linchpin of Stephen's reasoning process.

ii. Ps. 131 and its concept-fields

By evoking this psalm,Stephen focuses his Ark of the Lord theme that opened with his quotation from Amos 5:25–27.[944] In its tent, the Ark was with "our fathers" from Moses[945] until David's time – though it was Solomon who settled that Ark into its building.[946]

If his allusion to Ps. 131 was Stephen's evocation of Israel's national saga, complete with ritual and cultural mental furniture, then strictly literary-critical methods fail an interpreter. For Luke, memory-dynamics and scribal practices nourished the living Jesus-tradition turning Luke's *apologia* into the artefact we call Luke-Acts.[947] Ritual and cultural mental furniture include concept-fields

---

[939] Cf. Rom. 1:4.

[940] Acts 7:52; cf. Luke 23:47; Acts 3:14; 22:14

[941] Acts 7:52; cf. Luke 4:18–24; 24:19; Acts 3:20–23; 7:37.

[942] Luke 22:69; Acts 7:55–56.

[943] See Ch. 3. Luke's story is of the man Jesus; descriptors enrich his story by evoking scriptural models that root him in Israel's story. The Lukan Jesus' shift from Son of Man to Messiah is a hinge in Luke-Acts.

[944] Acts 7:42b–43.

[945] Acts 7:44.

[946] David figures large in Ps. 131: vss 1 (remember David), 10 (for David's sake), 11 (the Lord's oath to David), 17 (a horn for David).

[947] See Kirk, A., (2018), 114–137; cf. Larry Hurtado's blog, (https://wp.me/pYZXr-2eL), accessed 23 November 2018.

where words have a semantic penumbra, and thoughts evoke varying responses to single lexical units. Ps. 131 carries more concept-fields than those noted below, concepts central to Stephen's reasoning:

- the Ark[948] was Israel's portable witness to its covenant with God, and to Moses' agency at Sinai; this Ark of the Covenant prompted David to seek
- a house[949] for this Ark, a resting-place for its portable tent (σκηνὴ) of meeting with God,[950] then to Solomon's Temple, a building contingent on
- the David-promise,[951] modified by
- Solomon's theophany,[952] a house-focused, post-Solomonic, Deuteronomic reflection on the David-promise, and on the covenant's moral universe,[953] implied in
- the service of God[954] who brought "our fathers out of the house of slavery"; to whom obeisance leads to service (λατρεύειν) of *HaShem* whom Moses encountered, who led the house of Israel out of Egypt into a promised land. The alternative is renewed slavery (δουλεύειν) to gods made with human hands, for example, the Mammon symbolizing Jesus' radical critique of Jerusalem's rulers and others.

The semantic-conceptual interconnectedness of Stephen's reasoning around this allusion to Ps. 131, bracketed by two inter-related, adapted quotations

---

[948] Ps. 131:3–8; Exod. 25:9–22. (Throughout this list italics suggest a word's concept-field).

[949] Ps. 131:13–18; 2 Sam. 7:1–29; 1 Kgs 8:1–53; 9:1–9.

[950] Portable sacred space, recalling Sinai.

[951] Ps. 131:11–12; 2 Sam. 7:12–29; Ezek 34:20–31.

[952] 1 Kgs 9:1–9; 11:9–13; cf. Sirach 47:12–22.

[953] Torah, crystallized as the common good and neighbourliness; see Brueggemann (2017).

[954] Exod. 20:1–17; Deut. 5:6–21; cf. Deut. 10:12–22.

requires that interpreters familiarize ourselves with the scriptural background, text and hermeneutic conventions most likely to have been available to Luke-Stephen in that narrative setting.

For example, this psalmist's σκήνωμα may be translated "dwelling";[955] by extension, the tent (σκηνὴ) of Acts[956] echoes Luke's base-text where it is clearly a dwelling-place; ἀνάπαυσις suggests a locus of relief from travail,[957] while κατάπαυσις suggests a corresponding state of being, a Shabbat.[958] Κατοικέω, and its substantive κατοικία, echo Luke's base-text,[959] shadowing its richly bivalent οἶκος exploited by Stephen.[960] If Acts 7:46 is excluded, there are four undisputed instances of οἶκος in this speech. Two carry the sense of "household";[961] and Amos 5:25–27 addresses Israel-Jacob's children (our fathers);[962] two carry the bivalent dwelling/kinship sense that makes for Stephen's dynamic and this section's David-focus.[963]

Stephen's focal issue is: who really changed Moses' traditions; who really threatens the Temple?[964] He counter-charged his hearers – Temple functionaries[965] identified throughout Luke-Acts' conflict narrative as conspirators against Jesus – as guilty. Solomon's theophany[966] following the

---

[955] Ps. 131:5; Acts 7:46.

[956] Acts 7:43, 44–5; cf. 2 Sam. 7:2, 6; lacking in Ps. 131.

[957] Ps. 131:8.

[958] Ps. 131:14; cf. Isa. 66:1.

[959] Ps. 131:13–14; 2 Sam. 7:2, 5, 6; cf. 1 Kgs 8:12–13 (53a LXX).

[960] E.g., ποῖον οἶκον οἰκοδομήσετέ μοι; Isa. 66:1–2; Acts 7:49b.

[961] Acts 7:10, 20.

[962] Acts 7:42.

[963] Acts 7:47, 49; cf. Cai; 1 Kgs 8:12–13; Isa. 66:1b.

[964] Cf. Acts 6:13–14

[965] Luke 9:20–22 opens Luke's thread.

[966] Reading from a version like LXX, where Moses set God's commands and statutes before Israel (Acts 7:38; 1 Kgs 9:6).

Temple's consecration reveals the essential interrelatedness of those two charges:

- that of abandoning Israel's covenant-God and his agent Moses, and
- effectively becoming enslaved to an alien god.

Luke's conflict-narrative identified this alien deity as Mammon, named during Jesus' Exodus-journey to Jerusalem.[967] Stephen's apologia is narrative midrash on Acts 7:47 as it evokes Solomon's theophany; argued from Stephen's disciple-perspective to rebut false charges against Jesus and himself.

2. Reasoning in the shadow of Solomon's theophany (1 Kgs 9:1–9)

In Stephen's scriptural substructure, Psalm 131 and Solomon's theophany[968] testify that God's consecrated house is conditional on David's seed's faithful covenant-keeping. Consequently, Jesus' alleged threatening of the Temple and interrupting Moses' *paradosis* are interdependent charges. Stephen's reasoning from the Sinai covenant (Acts 7:38–47) to his counter-charge (7:48–53) draws on "our fathers'" persistent rebelliousness to crystallize his themes of Moses, house and Law.

i. Inclusio – Acts 7:38–53

Stephen's peroration[969] is the culmination of Luke-Acts' conflict narrative, and his *volta* its core. "Your fathers" implies "not our fathers"; Stephen identified "you" (7:51) with the rebellious assembly at Sinai who abandoned *HaShem* in favour of their handmade calf-god (7:39–40). In Luke-Acts twin tracks lead to this defining *volta*.

---

[967] See Ch. 8C; Luke 16:1–15, 19–31.

[968] See section C3.

[969] Acts 7:51–53.

Retrospectively, readers look back through Jesus' trial focused on his authority and identity; its triggers in Jerusalem, challenging the Temple authorities; Jesus' journeying with his followers to Jerusalem; his focusing their learning on God's Kingdom and its life-outcomes; Luke's characterizing of Jesus' Davidic anointing as fulfilling Isaiah's vision of a spirit-filled prophet proclaiming the Lord's "favourable year,"[970] and of his multiple, now-fulfilled Son of Man sayings.[971] Stephen's hearers murdered Jesus (7:52); they were murderers "who received (ἐλάβετε) the Law" yet had "not guarded (ἐφυλάξατε) it." Jesus strongly implied that these rulers had turned aside to serve Mammon.[972]

A second track relates the *inclusio* formed by 7:38 and 53 to the witnesses' charges against Jesus-Stephen[973] that focused on Israel's chain of tradition.[974] It began with Moses who received (ἐδέξατο) these living words "to give to us." It ends, again, with "you" who at their end of the chain received (ἐλάβετε) Torah but did not guard (οὐκ ἐφυλάξατε) or keep it. Φυλάσσω – the word's semantic range is wide but it parallels the conditional "if you do not guard" of Solomon's theophany in relation to Moses at Sinai.[975] Φυλάσσω is the verb used in Deuteronomy's crystallization[976] of Torah that probably gave Stephen his excoriating description of his hearers: "stiff-necked, uncircumcised in heart and ears, you."[977] To guard or keep Torah, the Deuteronomist's Moses bade Israel "circumcise your hard-heartedness, and no longer harden your neck." This *inclusio* forms the heart of Stephen's counter-charge.

---

[970] Luke 4:19; cf. Deut. 15:1–18; Lev 25:1–55.

[971] Especially Luke 9:20–22; 18:31–34; 22:66–71>Acts 7:55–56.

[972] See sections B4 and C.

[973] Acts 6:13–14 – the false witnesses' accusation.

[974] Deut. 6:4–9 et al.

[975] ἐὰν […] μὴ φυλάξητε (1 Kgs 9:6).

[976] Deut. 10:12–22.

[977] Acts 7:51; cf. Deut. 10:16.

ii. Six reasoning steps

Six steps trace Stephen's reasoning within that *inclusio*. Each step reports the results of *Interpreter's* process of engagement with Luke-Acts. Stephen's narrative-midrash had necessarily[978] focused on Moses whose story reached its climax at Sinai.

a. Moses (Acts 7:38–44)

Stephen's characterizing "our fathers" as those who took up alien gods and worshipped them,[979] abandoning *HaShem* who led them out of Egypt, opens the culmination of his speech's central section.[980] As for the prophet Moses, his brothers "pushed [him] aside."[981] Preparing for his *volta's* division, Stephen reaffirmed Peter's identifying Jesus as the promised prophet like Moses.[982] By evoking Israel's foundation story, frankly acknowledging their being a rebellious People[983] who at Sinai itself made for themselves an idol to worship, Stephen kept in clear view the post-Solomonic conditional bond between Israel's *locus* of worship and the covenant between *HaShem* and this People, led from servitude in Egypt, a bond evoked by Ps. 131[984] and by memory of Solomon's second theophany. Because this People's primal apostasy broke their covenant

---

[978] Acts 6:13–14.

[979] See sections C and D.

[980] On Moses; 7:17–44.

[981] Acts 7:23–28 (ἀπωθέομαι), 35–39 (ἀπωθέομαι), 40b.

[982] Acts 7:37, 52; Deut. 18:18 (ἀναστήσω). For Jesus as prophet, see, e.g., Luke 4:24; 13:31–35; 24:17–20; Acts 3:22–23.

[983] Cf. Exod. 32 – Num. 14; Deut. 1–4 (preceding the *Shema'*), 9–10 (remembering rebellion and crystallizing *Shema'*).

[984] See section E1ii.

with *HaShem,* God handed them over to servitude to astral deities, "as it was written in the book of the prophets," and Amos is summoned as witness.

b. Amos 5:25–27 (Acts 7:42–44)

"Was it to me that you brought sacrifices?" Amos (5:25–27) demanded of "our fathers" who had "made a calf, offered a sacrifice to the idol, and revelled in the works of their hands" His question was not his querying sacrificial worship, but about the house of Israel's commitment to *HaShem* during the wilderness period. "Our fathers" did indeed bring sacrifices, but to alien deities. Worse, they allegedly corrupted covenantal provisions by taking along with them Moloch's tent (σκηνή).[985] Their alien deities were idols that "our fathers" hand-made to worship – radically rejecting *HaShem*'s basic command.[986]

Luke-Stephen adapted the prophet's message for his present: for his hearers Amos's post-Solomon threat of exile named "beyond Damascus"; recalling Isaiah's more recent experience of exile, Stephen[987] warned his hearers of exile "beyond Babylon." Heir to existing interpretative traditions,[988] Luke adapted Amos to his contextual needs; for a later, crucial moment James adapted Amos 9:11–12.[989] Stephen's adaptation probably evoked the whole lamentation of Amos 5, paralleling his hearers with their long-dead Judaean fathers. Amos 5:16–22 is an oracle against a house of Israel that sought neither the Lord nor the good.[990] Dodd taught generations to think in terms of narrative

---

[985] Cf. 1 Kgs 11:5–10.

[986] Deut. 5:6–10; 10:20–22.

[987] Solomon's theophany is present.

[988] Eg., 4Q174 is *Midrash* rather than *Florilegium.*

[989] Acts 15:16–17.

[990] Amos 5:6–9, 14–15.

wholes and common clusters:[991] the LXX of Amos 5:21–24 carries its distinctive perspective on judgment.

> Remove from me the noise of your odes, and I will not listen to your accompanied psalm. Then [at the Day of the Lord][992] judgment will roll down like water, and righteousness like an impassable flood (Amos 5:23–24).

The reason for that threatening judgment lay in Israel's inhabiting the moral universe of alien gods (Amos 5:7–13), rejecting the justly-living, mercy-filled, neighbour-loving moral universe decreed by *HaShem*.[993] This threat is the immediate co-text for Stephen's adaptation, introducing Amos's question to Israel's house – now addressing Stephen's generation.

c. The Ark (Acts 7:44–48) and Ps. 131

At Acts 7:44[994] Stephen returned briefly to his opening at 7:38 – the authentic symbols of Israel's covenant with God were also with "our fathers" through to Solomon's time. That tent, originating through Moses' encountering *HaShem,* enclosed the Ark bearing its stone witnesses to their covenant. David's role, basic to Luke-Acts, here becomes focal in Stephen's speech. Cultic-memory of the Ark's transition from a portable "holy place" (a tent) to its settled site on Zion (a house) underlies and amplifies Stephen's brief evocation. Essentially,[995] the key to Stephen's speech is in 7:47–48: Σολομὼν δὲ οἰκοδόμησεν αὐτῷ οἶκον.

---

[991] Dodd, C.H., (1952), 61–110; the debate over parts and wholes continues vigorously. Luke, however, in common with 4Q174, developed focal passages concerning the house of David, including Amos 9:11. His appeal to Amos 5 suggests his awareness of the prophet's message that expects resonances in hearers' minds.

[992] Amos 5:18–20.

[993] Here visible in Amos 5:14–15; later crystallized by Deut. 10:17–22.

[994] See section D1; contra Pervo, R.I., (2009), 191–192.

[995] Section Cai.

ἀλλ' οὐχ ὁ ὕψιστος ἐν χειροποιήτοις κατοικεῖ. Solomon knew that well;[996] Stephen and his hearers also knew it; some commentators seem not to know that it was known. Isaiah's adapted quotation is commentary on Solomon's prayer, asking of exiles returning to Jerusalem, "What kind of house will you build for me?" Like Amos, Isaiah posed his focused question.

d. Isa. 66:1–2a (Acts 7:49–50)

καθὼς ὁ προφήτης λέγει: The word "house" tightly links Isaiah's words with Solomon's evoked story, not solely with Acts 7:48. Here, Isaiah's sense-unit in 65:17–66:1–16, 22–23, envisions God's new, post-Exilic creation, where on the holy mountain worship happens. Stephen adapted[997] this Isaianic foundation-vision, of a Temple built[998] to replace Solomon's house that the Babylonians destroyed. Isaiah's affirmation is here a question – οὐχὶ ἡ χείρ μου ἐποίησεν ταῦτα πάντα; – and by transferring its λέγει κύριος more sharply to focus ποῖον οἶκον οἰκοδομήσετέ μοι, Stephen formed an inverted *inclusio* of Acts 7:47 with 7:48. Σολομῶν δὲ οἰκοδόμησεν αὐτῷ οἶκον [...]

ποῖον οἶκον οἰκοδομήσετέ μοι, λέγει κύριος (Acts 7:47–48).

Luke-Acts' Isaianic substructure, however, includes Isa. 55:3 affirming that God's proffered, conditional, everlasting covenant remains.[999] Luke's bivalent "house of David" matrix began in his Prologue that introduced Jesus as the seed for David's renewed house. Weltanschauung, cultural and ritual memory, and Luke's evoking narrative wholes co-operate to thrust Stephen's argument towards his *volta*. Stephen spoke of house rather than place or Temple, though readers understand that his accusers focused on Jesus' Temple-*logion*.

---

[996] 1 Kgs 8:27.

[997] Acts 7:50.

[998] The Ark, its covenantal symbol, was missing.

[999] Acts 13:34; cf. Isa. 55:1–9; 65:1–16.

Aposiopesis – rhetorical purpose rather than emotional inability to continue – links Acts 7:50 with 7:51. Some find Stephen's abrupt ending of this "quotation" preceding his direct challenge to his hearers problematic; *Interpreter* reads this as a rhetorical leap filled by hearers' recalling how Isa. 66:2b–5 encapsulates the "two ways" – of the lawless,[1000] and of those who quake at God's word.

> πάντα γὰρ ταῦτα ἐποίησεν ἡ χείρ μου, καὶ ἔστιν ἐμὰ πάντα ταῦτα, λέγει κύριος, *καὶ ἐπὶ τίνα ἐπιβλέψω ἀλλ' ἢ ἐπὶ τὸν ταπεινὸν καὶ ἡσύχιον καὶ τρέμοντα τοὺς λόγους μου;* ὁ δὲ ἄνομος ὁ θύων μοι μόσχον ὡς ὁ ἀποκτέννων κύνα (Isa. 66:2b, 5; 65:15b–16).

The italicized words, uncited by Stephen, are part of Isaiah's restoration polarity focused on *my holy mountain,* the *locus* of a freed Israel's service of God. The words are about people, not a building. Isaiah's contrast between "the lawless" (ὁ ἄνομος) and the one who is humble, peaceable, who takes God's word seriously, is sharpened by the continuing list that echoes both Solomon's impossibly extravagant celebration of the house's dedication, and the question posed earlier by Stephen's quotation from Amos: for whom, and to what end are these sacrificial offerings brought? Isaiah's repeated questioning expects the kind of answer that Luke-Acts also expects. Peter has already associated this Sanhedrin with "the lawless,"[1001] and that is sharpened by Stephen's conclusive answer to the High Priest: "You are those who received the law as ordained by angels, and yet you have not kept it."[1002]

Stephen's peroration replaces Isaiah's omitted words by his *pesher* on that unvoiced allusion – "you are those." His charge is against those whom both Jesus and his followers in Jerusalem held to be failing in their loyalty to God. They had not listened to this prophet and righteous one whom God had raised

---

[1000] Isa. 66:3–4; 65:2–7, 11–15a.

[1001] Acts 2:23.

[1002] Acts 7:53.

up, whom they had murdered, and whom readers know to be both Lord and Messiah. Stephen's speech is not against the house that God conditionally sanctified for Solomon; his scriptural reasoning demonstrates that Stephen is concerned with the service (λατρεία) of Israel's God.

Two ways have marked Luke's conflict-narrative; for example his distinctive δίκαιος and tradition's Son of Man models describe Jesus. Scriptural reasoning, even when implied, enabled Stephen to refute by reversing the charges against Jesus and himself.

e. "You" (7:51–54)

"You" [1003] are Stephen's hearers, the Sanhedrin, the "rulers"[1004] whom Peter, alluding to priestly roles in the ongoing rebuilding of Herod's refashioned Second Temple,[1005] had characterized as "you, the builders."[1006] Luke-Acts portrayed Jerusalem's principal priests and scribes as Jesus' chief opponents. A mixed body, this Sanhedrin was dominated by Sadducees. Notably, Luke's description of their reaction to Stephen's peroration resonates with the "two ways" of Ps. 36,[1007] ways of the righteous and ungodly: being enraged and grinding their teeth at the righteous[1008] certainly follows Stephen's accusing them of murdering the Righteous One, the promised prophet like the rejected Moses. The stiff-necked, uncircumcised in heart and ears of Acts 7:51[1009] were those who, inhabiting the moral world of an alien god, had forsaken HaShem

---

[1003] See section B.

[1004] Pss 145 (Acts 4:10–12, 24) and 2 (4:25–27) contribute to Peter's subtextual reasoning.

[1005] Acts 6:13–14, "this holy place."

[1006] Acts 4:10–11, mirroring Ps. 117:22 in Jesus' vineyard parable.

[1007] The psalm's παρατηρέω characterized Jesus' opponents following his vineyard parable (Luke 20:19–20).

[1008] Ps. 36:8, 11–12.

[1009] Deut. 10:16.

249

their God, who, through Moses, led their fathers out of the land of Egypt. In reality they had taken up serving an alien god, Mammon.[1010] The vision that Stephen added to this toxic atmosphere precipitated his stoning.

f. Stephen's vision (7:55–56)

Stephen's vision[1011] is first narrated, then reported. First, the Spirit-filled Stephen had affirmed that Jesus *Nazoraios*[1012] was that same person now standing at God's right hand in God's glory.[1013] Second, Stephen evoked for his hearers the response[1014] Jesus gave to his inquisitors at their questioning before handing him over to Pilate:[1015] "I see the heavens opened, and the Son of Man standing at God's right hand!" For brevity, we note only that this first paradigmatic martyrdom was this conflict-narrative's culmination, and precipitated a diaspora from Jerusalem that opened a programmatic change in Acts.[1016]

Luke's Son of Man *inclusio*[1017] is his rhetorical-structural device binding Luke-Acts' conflict-narrative into its unity distinguished by fulfilled Jesus-*logia*. Jesus' Son of Man *logion* may indeed be his own *gezerah shewa'*, melding Messiah[1018] with Son of Man,[1019] a move paralleled by Luke 24. But Luke-Acts is rich in Jesus-descriptors, and Stephen had just affirmed that his hearers had

---

[1010] Section Civ.

[1011] See Doble, P., (1985, 1996, 2000, 2013).

[1012] Acts 6:14–7:1.

[1013] The resonance is with an adapted Ps. 109:1 mirroring Luke 20:41–44; "glory" completes an *inclusio* with Acts 7:2b, one God.

[1014] Adapted at Luke 22:69 to prepare for its link with Stephen's vision.

[1015] Luke 22:66–23:2.

[1016] Acts 8:1. cf. 1:8.

[1017] Luke 22:69 / Acts 7:55–56.

[1018] Ps. 109:1.

[1019] Luke 9:21–27.

murdered Jesus the δίκαιος,[1020] a descriptor that probably prompted Stephen's twice-affirmed adaptation from "sitting"[1021] to "standing" (ἑστῶτα).[1022]

For Luke-Acts, Wisdom 2–5 crystallized the contrasting ways of the righteous and the ungodly; many psalms celebrated the same division. However, Wisdom 4:16–5:2 portrays a judgment scene, reversing roles: at God's judgment, the righteous one stands. Via Stephen's vision Luke completed his conflict-narrative with this proleptic judgment scene modelled by his source – ironically, the Wisdom of Solomon.

[1020] Acts 7:52.

[1021] Luke 22:69.

[1022] Acts 7:55–56.

F. Summary

By thoroughly Jewish scriptural reasoning,[1023] Stephen retrospectively read Israel's story through the lens of Jesus' story, a story that ended in God's vindicating his anointed, thereby fulfilling the scriptures – ἀναστήσω, "I will raise up."[1024] Luke-Acts' key to Stephen's speech is its scriptural substructure and its perspective on "things fulfilled among us." That substructure's matrix is the David-promise, entailing his family's complex history that had left a source of hope.[1025] Luke-Acts' case is that through Jesus' story God fulfilled Israel's hope; that he is David's seed who restored David's house.[1026] Stephen's speech embodies that case by contrasting David's two sons, using the criterion of covenant-fidelity with *HaShem*. The Torah-faithful Jesus' *logia* about Temple and Son of Man were both "fulfilled." Stephen's was a pro-Temple, anti-idolatry refutation of false charges against Jesus and himself. His vision and his martyrdom define why and how Jesus and his followers fleshed out the scriptural descriptors to this point. The Jerusalem conflict ended; Paul's story had begun. Further, Stephen's speech confirms that in the matter of *Interpreter*'s focal verses, Luke was not mistaken.

[1023] See Dodd, C.H. (1952), 27.

[1024] See sections A and Ci.

[1025] E.g., Sirach 47:12–22.

[1026] See Acts 15:16–17.

Chapter 8. Interpreting Paul's Sermon

The Jerusalem conflict culminated in Stephen's *apologia*; Paul's condensed sermon (Acts 13:16–41), the last of Luke-Acts' six exegetical speeches, is his *kerygma* for the conflicts that will gather around his unfolding story that ends in Rome. Not having journeyed from Galilee to Jerusalem with Jesus, Paul, like Stephen, features among Luke's "ministers of the word" (ὑπηρέται τοῦ λόγου) rather than the eyewitnesses (αὐτόπται) of the Jerusalem conflict.[1027] For Theophilus Luke presented Paul as a genuine witness to Jesus,[1028] different from, but continuous with, the work of the Twelve.[1029] The sole example in Luke-Acts of Paul's synagogue preaching, and the culmination of Luke's resurrection-thread, this sermon demonstrates how Paul/Luke reasoned from scripture that "it is written" that the Messiah must rise from the dead.

The analytical diagram offers a good starting point, for only after Luke-Acts' shape became clear could I begin to discern its author's probable purposes in writing his apologia for Theophilus, among which I asked whether this Paul a genuine representative of the Jesus movement.[1030] Paul makes his appearance only at the very end of the central conflict-narrative,[1031] where he is introduced as the vigorous opponent of Jesus and his Way.[1032] Luke's threefold affirmation of Jesus' illumination and commissioning of Paul,[1033] together with

---

[1027] Acts13:30–33b; cf. Luke 1:1–4.

[1028] Hence the narrative's threefold affirmation of Paul's calling; Acts 9:1–19; 22:3–16; 26:4–18; cf.1 Cor. 15:3–11.

[1029] See Ch. 1:1.

[1030] See Ch. 1.

[1031] Acts 7:58; 8:1, 3.

[1032] Acts 22:19–20; 26:9–11.

[1033] Acts 9:1–22; 22:6–21; 26:12–20.

the latter's commendation by Barnabas,[1034] bolster the central fact that this baptized Paul became a scripture-reasoning advocate for the Kingdom of God and "the things about Jesus."[1035] Luke presents Paul primarily as a tradent-interpreter engaged in vigorous debate with fellow Jews.

The central figure of the second half of Acts and the solitary witness at its conclusion, Paul is the second of Luke's "ministers of the word."[1036] For Pisidian Antioch's synagogue congregants Paul is the Expositor of the "work" that God has newly done,[1037] and the culminating Exegete of Luke's base-text established by his triptych – Nathan's previously uncited David-promise.[1038] Readers past and present have waited since the Prologue for Lukan confirmation that our hypothesis relating to ἀνίστημι is valid, and that Luke's two contested Jesus-*logia* say what he intended. The culmination of Luke's resurrection thread, event controlling interpretation, Paul's exegesis exemplifies how witnesses argued their case that "it is written that the Messiah must rise from the dead."

Paul's sermon falls into three parts: exposition of message of salvation (13:16–31); exegesis of that message as the fulfilment of the David-promise (13:32–39); warning to the congregants to hear the prophets' warning adapted from Hab. 1:5.[1039]

Crystallizing Israel's story, Paul introduced Jesus as the Saviour to whom John the Baptist had pointed, the fulfilment of the promise to David.[1040] Ps. 106:17–22 subtextually enriches this message of salvation. When a lost and lawless Israel cried out to God, he saved (ἔσωσεν) them; "he sent out his word

---

[1034] Acts 9:26–31; Luke's summary at 9:27–31 ends the section introduced by 8:1–4.
[1035] Τὰ περὶ Ἰησοῦ – Luke 24:17–24; Acts 9:22, 27; 28:23.
[1036] Luke 1:2.
[1037] Acts 13:41; cf. Hab. 1:5.
[1038] 2 Sam. 7:12; Luke 1:26–35; see section 2A.
[1039] Acts 13:40–41.
[1040] Acts 13:17–25; cf. Luke 2:8–12.

and healed [ἰάσατο] them"; "rescued them from their corruption(s)" (διαφθορῶν).[1041] Exposition of message of salvation (Acts 13:16–31): To us this message about the Saviour has been sent.[1042]

Structurally, this exposition is marked by its double *inclusio*: within a crystallization of Israel's story, Jesus is named only twice. First, as the Saviour whom God brought to Israel, but whom Jerusalem and its rulers, failing to grasp the prophets who had written of him, rejected and killed.[1043] Second, as the one whom God raised from the dead, thereby fulfilling the promise God made to the hearers' fathers.[1044]

Then, linked with Jesus' naming, Luke's Paul offers Antioch's congregants his "baptismal" *inclusio*: John the Baptist's "one coming after me" recalls for readers Luke's clear-cut division in Israel's story;[1045] Paul's "good news" bivalently links God's "raising up Jesus' with Ps. 2:7, that is with Luke's account of Jesus' anointing.[1046]

Lexically, Paul's "good news" both reflects and validates his practice of distinguishing the event of Jesus' resurrection by using ἐγείρω, while deploying ἀνίστημι when accenting that event as the fulfilment of the David-promise (Acts 13:30, 33).

Distinguishing the Galilean witnesses from his own ministry Paul segues from his exposition of the Message to his exegesis of it as the fulfilment of the David-promise.[1047] That exegesis is explored in section B3, here noting only that its repeated διαφθορά continues the opening of Paul's exposition[1048] – "to us the message of this salvation has been sent."[1049]

[1041] Ps. 106:19–20.
[1042] Acts 13:26; echoing Ps. 106:20; cf. Acts 13:23, Saviour.
[1043] Acts 13:27–29.
[1044] Acts 13:23; 13:32.
[1045] Acts 13:24–25; cf. Luke 16:16.
[1046] Acts 13:32–33; Luke 3:21–22. (Luke's scene emphasizes Jesus' anointing with Holy Spirit as he prayed.)
[1047] Acts 13:31–32; 32–39.
[1048] Acts 13:34–37, cf. Ps. 106:22.
[1049] Acts 13:26; cf. Ps. 106:20 – ἀπέστειλεν τὸν λόγον αὐτοῦ.

Paul's warning to the congregants to hear the prophets' warning, adapted from Hab. 1:5, concludes his sermon.[1050] Paul and Barnabas's appointed "work" was their witnessing to the message of God's "incredible work" – Jesus' life and resurrection.[1051] Jerusalem had not listened; Paul now "unpacked" (ἐκδιηγῆται) it for Antioch; his hearers needed to choose.[1052]

This sermon stands within a clearly defined work narrative unit:[1053] the work to which the Holy Spirit summoned Barnabas and Saul, their proclaiming of God's new work and its implications for Israel. That new work was God's anointing Jesus as Messiah and raising him from the dead[1054] when Jerusalem had rejected and crucified him. That twofold event, fulfilling God's ἀναστήσω, implied that Jesus' summoning Israel to repent was to be taken seriously – through him God was calling Israel to respond by reforming itself around Torah. Paul's hermeneutic key, like Luke's, was Jesus' resurrection – God's scarce-believable work of Hab. 1:5,[1055] here set in the context of the work the Spirit gave to Paul and Barnabas,[1056] both elements part of God's activity in Israel.

Confirming *Interpreter*'s stance, the bivalency of ἀναστήσω in God's fulfilled promises[1057] was central to Paul's good news for Antioch's synagogue; this "new work" had enabled his earliest insight – that Jesus is Son of God,[1058] and that consequently he is the Messiah, as scripture proves.[1059] The very heart

---

[1050] Acts13:40–41.

[1051] Acts 13:1–3 / 14:26–27.

[1052] Acts 13:42–43.

[1053] Acts 13:2–14:26; cf. 15:38. See the refrain of Ps. 106.

[1054] See section B3ii.

[1055] Acts 13:41; cf. Rom. 1:1–7; 10:9–13.

[1056] Acts 13:2; 14:26.

[1057] Acts 13:23 (implied by κατ᾽ ἐπαγγελίαν), 33 (ἐκπεπλήρωκεν); cf. Luke 1:1 (πεπληροφορημένων); Rom. 1:1–6. See Whitsett (2000).

[1058] Echoing Ps. 2:7.

[1059] Acts 9:20b, 22.

of Paul's sermon is his affirmation that ὃν δὲ ὁ θεὸς ἤγειρεν, οὐκ εἶδεν διαφθοράν[1060] – from this, Paul's fulfilment-gospel flows.

Interpreter's focal purpose is to explore the narrative coherence of Luke-Acts in the light of Luke's being right and his critics mistaken. However, scholarship's history of dividing the Paul of Acts from the Paul of the undisputed letters made it impossible to ignore this "extraneous" issue when dealing with this sermon's conclusion and final warning.[1061] Its conclusion is thoroughly Lukan, and not un-Pauline; its appeal to Habakkuk to warn Antioch's congregants is subtextually shared with other writers, including Paul (to the Galatians and Romans), the writer to the Hebrews and 1QpHab. Recent developments in Pauline studies strongly suggest that the Paul of this condensed sermon's conclusion and warning (Acts 13:38–41) is not unlike the Paul of his undisputed letters, which are a different genre.

[1060] Acts 13:37.

[1061] Acts 13:38–41.

A. Paul in Luke's narrative

Paul dominates about one half of Acts (13–28).[1062] Before that, he shares with Peter a twin track from Stephen's martyrdom[1063] until he emerges as the principal speaker at Antioch (13:16a). Thenceforward, Luke's Paul-narrative falls into two parts, divided by his arraignment. From chapters 13 to 20 readers encounter Paul witnessing to synagogues, proclaiming the word, travelling extensively and establishing churches. In 22–28, Paul's story is of his witnessing to rulers and authorities, confined for long periods. His final journey is related at length. Luke's account ends enigmatically with Paul in Rome proclaiming God's kingdom and teaching "the things about the Lord Jesus Messiah";[1064] in Rome, but in chains for "the hope of Israel."[1065] Rome's Jewish elders knew nothing against Paul, heard much against "this sect," and wished to learn more. For them, from dawn to dusk on an appointed day, Paul witnessed to God's Kingdom, persuading them about Jesus, doing both from Torah and prophets.[1066] At this long day's end, a divided group of elders left. For those who did not hear,[1067] Paul recalled Isaiah's words – as in Antioch's synagogue he warned his hearers by recalling Habakkuk. Luke's ending is not Paul "writing off the Jews"; he resembles the Jewish Paul of Romans 9–11.

1. Paul, synagogues and scripture

Acts 28 crystallizes Paul's proclamation, revealing little of his presentation's content. But narrative readers understand the Paul portrayed throughout Acts,

---

[1062] See the analytical diagram.

[1063] Acts 7:54–8:3.

[1064] Acts 28:31.

[1065] Acts 28:17b–20; on "Israel's Hope," see Wright, N.T. (1992: 280–338).

[1066] Acts 28:23.

[1067] Echoing the Jesus-tradition; cf. Luke 8:10.

including his condensed sermon at Antioch, and the wider narrative within which it stands. That sermon both reflects tradition about Paul and coheres with Luke's narrative theology.

Paul has six speeches in Acts.[1068] Four of them are: an address to Athenian philosophers;[1069] a farewell charge to Ephesian elders; self-defence before a mob; a hearing before Festus and Agrippa. These four[1070] are framed by two of Paul reasoning with fellow Jews:[1071] briefly, in Rome; more substantially, in Antioch's synagogue, arguably exemplifying Paul's characteristic activity. Paul's synagogue activity runs from Damascus to Ephesus.[1072] Before Paul's arrest,[1073] the nature of his synagogue activity[1074] is characteristically debate around scripture, focused on Jesus. Paul may be "the apostle to the Gentiles," but for Theophilus his story is firmly rooted among fellow Jews.

Paul's principal *apologia* offers a retrospective organizing principle for his story.[1075] There, he roots his work in God's promise, Israel's hope,[1076] tightly linked with the resurrection of the dead.[1077] His task is witnessing,[1078] in accord with Moses and prophets, to the Messiah who must suffer, be the first to rise from the dead, and proclaim light to "our people" and to the Gentiles.[1079] Paul's

---

[1068] Diff. Borgman (2006).

[1069] Acts 17:22b–31; focused sharply on Jesus and the resurrection (e.g., 17:29–34).

[1070] Acts 17:22–31; 20:18b–35; 22:1–21; 26:2–29.

[1071] Acts 28:17b–20; 13:15–41.

[1072] Acts 9:20–22; 19:1–10; see also, 17:1–9, 10–14; 18:1–6, 7-ll; 19:1–10. cf. 18:19–21.

[1073] Acts 21:17–28:31

[1074] Acts 13:1–20:36–38.

[1075] Acts 26:2–23; see Marguerat (2015) *ad loc.*

[1076] Acts 26:6–8; cf. 28:20.

[1077] As at Antioch; cf. Rom. 1:1–6.

[1078] Acts 26:16–23.

[1079] Cf. Simeon (Luke 2:28–32), echoed at Acts 13:47. For Messiah, see Wright (1992: 319–320). On Paul's witnessing, see Acts 20:24; cf. Luke 24:44–49.

apologia, summarizing his activity and message, reminds readers of narrative they have traversed – including God's work unpacked for Antioch's synagogue; his task illuminates *Interpreter*'s topic.[1080]

2. Paul's scriptural reasoning

Luke's final portrayal of Paul summarizes in one and a half verses a debate stretching from dawn to dusk.[1081] A lector needs three and a half minutes to read Paul's Antioch sermon, a brevity ill-matching that preacher's form. If he briskly reads Romans as a sermon in absentia, the same lector needs fifty-five minutes. If Luke's account of Paul's Antioch sermon represents the pure milk of Paul's gospel, then it is condensed milk.

Beneath Luke's narrative lies vigorous dialogue focused on scripture, issuing in successive partings of the ways.[1082] Acts' evidence indicates that debate centred on whether Jesus was the Messiah; whether the Messiah would suffer and rise from the dead; Paul's witnessing is essentially to the Messiah's being Jesus.[1083] We saw in Paul's final *apologia* how both suffering and resurrection characterized the Messiah of whom the prophets and Moses spoke.[1084] In Luke-Acts, twenty-first century readers enter a culture where verbal and conceptual "association" counts for much, and interpretation exploits the richness of language in scriptural texts.[1085]

[1080] Acts 13:44, 46; cf. Luke 24:26–27, 44–46.

[1081] Acts 28:23–25a.

[1082] E.g., 13:44–51 (pre-James); 18:5–6; 19:8–10; 28:25–28.

[1083] Acts 9:20–22; 17:2–3; 18:5; 24:24; 28:31.

[1084] Acts 26:2–29; cf. Luke 24:26–27, 44–46.

[1085] Acts offers various descriptors of such scriptural engagement's character in a synagogue setting: διαλέγομαι – Acts 17:2, 17; 18:4, 19b; 19:8; πείθω – Acts 13:43, 17:4; 18:4, 19:8; ἀνακρίνω – Acts 17:11; διανοίγω – Acts 17:3; cf. Luke 24:32; συμβιβάζω – Acts 9:22. Surprisingly, διερμηνεύω only Luke 24:27; here, at Antioch, ἐκδιηγέομαι (Acts 13:41) is Paul's "unpacking," making known by clear explanation.

260

Readers take leave of Paul, not among "the brethren" who welcomed him to Rome,[1086] but among the city's Jewish leaders, still vigorously arguing (ἐξετίθετο διαμαρτυρόμενος; πείθων), from Torah and prophets. Luke understands Paul's Gentile mission, but he reports more of Paul's activity among Jewish groups, about which Paul's Antioch sermon is our sole detailed source of information, a Paul true to early Jesus-tradition and the scriptural roots of Christian talk of Jesus' resurrection.

3. Antioch: a synagogue sermon

Paul's synagogue activity[1087] had begun in Damascus following his vision.[1088] Readers meet it again in Salamis, at the opening of the circular journey that Luke characterized as God's work.[1089] At Antioch, Luke highlights Paul the Jew among Jews. Those assembled are "brothers," descendants of "our fathers,"[1090] or God-fearers.[1091] Following the reading, the synagogue's presidents invite Paul and Barnabas to bring a word of consolation.[1092] Dense with scriptural citation, allusion and echo, Paul's address unfolds like a synagogue sermon;[1093] its forms of argument are thoroughly Jewish,[1094] unlikely to impress a classicist.

[1086] Acts 28:14b–15 – and to whom he had written such a careful introductory letter.

[1087] A sermon, not a rhetorician's speech. See, e.g., Bowker (1967: 1); Doeve (1954); Lövestam (1961); Mann, J. (1971); cf. Marshall (2007: 520–521).

[1088] "Synagogue" without qualifier; occasionally "of the Jews" (e.g., Acts 13:5) suggests a synagogue whose majority comprises Judaeans among the diaspora. In Antioch, Paul's scriptural reasoning is from a Greek version of Israel's scriptures, common among the diaspora.

[1089] Acts 9:19–22; 13:5; 13:2; 14:26–27; God's "work," echoing Ps. 106:20–22, also describes the content of Paul's sermon (13:41, Hab. 1:5).

[1090] Acts 13:15, 17, 26, cf. 32.

[1091] Note "'you first'" (13:46) before Gentiles; cf. 3:26.

[1092] Acts 13:15b; cf. Luke 2:25–32.

[1093] Bowker (1967); Doeve (1954).

[1094] See Ch. 1.2 and Ch. 2.3.

Luke is explicitly unpacking for Theophilus how "we got to where we are" – a divided community.[1095]

In this synagogue Paul exemplifies exposition rather than debate or the report of Acts 28.[1096] His exposition is of 2 Sam. 7.[1097] Because he pairs Ps. 2 with 2 Sam. 7 in Paul's sermon, I deduce that with Hebrews and with 4Q174, Luke is engaging with existing interpretative tradition. Readers know that Antioch's David-promise implies God's Kingdom, God's Rule exercised through David's son; this Kingdom is revealed in the "things about Jesus."[1098] Like Acts 28, Antioch offers its *inclusio* with Luke's introductory triptych.

Paul's hermeneutic key is an event – "God raised him from the dead."[1099] Through his midrash Paul "clearly explained"[1100] the Hope of Israel. His sermon demonstrates how Paul's preaching was rooted in Luke's systematic narrative of "the things fulfilled among us,"[1101] focusing on God's fulfilling both the promises to David[1102] – ἀναστήσω – and the hopes of John the Baptist.

Acts implies communities that knew their scriptures and could detect semantic echoes and cross-fertilizations; people living by scriptural interpretation of a kind from which current scholarship often dissents. But to "hear" Paul in Antioch's synagogue readers need to make that cultural leap. We noted earlier a possible, distant relationship between Luke-Acts and 4Q174 –

[1095] See, e.g., Acts 13:44–48.

[1096] Distinguishing Paul's sermon from the narrative of the following week's events (Acts 13:44–52).

[1097] See Bock (2012); Doeve (1954); Lövestam (1961); Marshall (2007); Morgan-Wynne (2014); Strauss (1995).

[1098] Alexander, L. C. (2005: 217).

[1099] See Wright, N.T. (2003: 277–374). Paul's own affirmations must be taken seriously: see Rom. 1:1–6; 10:5–13; 1 Cor. 15. The Paul of Antioch is very like the Paul of Rom. 9–11.

[1100] Acts 13:41 ἐκδιηγέομαι.

[1101] Luke 1:1–4; Acts 13:33.

[1102] Acts 13:23, 32–36.

indebtedness to an interpretative tradition concerning God's David-promises. Luke's distinctive contribution to Israel's interpretative tradition is that he re-reads shared scriptures from the perspective that, uniquely, God raised Jesus from the dead – ἀναστήσω.

4. Paul's sermon's role in Luke-Acts

At Acts 13 Luke's narrative is nearing James's scriptural culmination of Jesus' story – God's rebuilding David's fallen tent.[1103] Luke introduced Jesus to readers as David's promised seed. In the apostles' prayer (Acts 4:24–28), he recognized that this Messiah had to suffer (Ps. 2:1–2). At Antioch, he demonstrated how God's David-promise, Luke's base-text, retrospectively figures Messiah's resurrection; the scriptural spine of Qumran's exegesis remains, but Jesus' story reshapes its body. To this end, Luke summons help from other psalms, other prophets.

How might Luke-Acts' early auditors have heard Paul's sermon for Antioch's congregation? While we do not know what the lections were for that setting, we can explore what Luke has used. Brooke's case for incipit phrases illuminates Paul's sermon's condensed presentation.[1104] Condensation requires a reader's being alert to those scriptural sense-units within which any "reference" is found,[1105] for Paul's sermon evokes a broad, interlocking range of scriptures. This is not a sermon with added illustration, but a web of scriptures re-interpreted in the light of God's work – raising up Jesus from the dead. In that light, event determining interpretation, we turn to re-read Paul's sermon that falls readily into five parts:

[1103] Acts 15:15–17; Amos 9. Marguerat (2007: 21) rightly treats 13:1–15:35 as a major stage in Luke's scheme.

[1104] See Dupont (1979: 151–152).

[1105] So both Dodd (1952) and Hays (2015).

1. Introduction (Acts 16b–25) that culminates in the arrival of Jesus the Saviour.

2. Message of Salvation (26–31), outlining that Saviour's story, summarizes Paul's statement of events.[1106]

3. God's work, (32–37), locating Jesus' story in scripture (22–25), shows how this event is good news.[1107]

4. Conclusion (38–39) and

5. Warning (40–41) both issue from Paul's condensed argument; they are not add-ons – in fact, Paul's Habakkuk quotation is implied by 13:26, paralleling that from Isaiah 28:24–28.

[1106] Luke is alleged to have been mistaken in affirming that scripture knew of a suffering Messiah whom God would raise up. See Doble (2006: 267–83).

1107 Reflecting Paul's εὐαγγελιζόμεθα.

B. Paul's sermon

1. Introduction (Acts 13:15b–25)

Paul begins by surveying Israel's history.[1108] Mark Strauss[1109] clarified links between this survey and that in Nathan's oracle. More recently, John Morgan-Wynne has painstakingly confirmed Paul's survey as Luke's digest of that oracle.[1110] Paul's survey reaches its climax in the arrival of Jesus on Israel's stage. David's promised seed[1111], Jesus is identified as Israel's Saviour, and the "coming one" of John the Baptist's oracular word. This introductory section is the stuff of Luke's Prologue and distinctive account of Jesus' anointing.

The prime position of "Saviour" in this résumé significantly anticipates Paul's "message of salvation." Luke's distinctive theme of salvation, first announced to shepherds,[1112] reached an earlier climax in his transformed Son of Man *logion*: the Son of Man came to seek and to save what was lost.[1113] But Luke's theme of salvation links also with his distinctive handling of John the Baptist's ministry: Luke adapted tradition's contextualizing John to include Isaiah's announcement of God's salvation to all flesh.[1114] At Antioch, Paul's

---

[1108] See the discussion in Ch. 7: Jesus-followers understand themselves as those standing within and continuing Israel's story.

[1109] Strauss (1995: 154–155); see Vesco (2012: 465–466). If 13:15b–22 crystallizes 2 Sam. 7, we need not exhaustively explore its other scriptural echoes.

[1110] Morgan-Wynne (2014: 73–91, 217–223).

[1111] 13:23, 32–33.

[1112] Luke 2:8–20.

[1113] Luke 19:10; Contrast Mark 10:45; Mt. 20:28.

[1114] Luke 3:6 / Isa. 40:5; contrast Mark 1:1–8; Matt. 3:1–12.

reference to John's previous activity,[1115] recalling his promising a "coming one,"[1116] leaves unvoiced a reader's recalling of Isaiah 40.[1117]

So, allusions to and echoes from Luke's Infancy Gospel[1118] combine at Antioch with Paul's evocation of John the Baptist, whose "coming one" had already been identified by Simeon, who was waiting for Israel's παράκλησις and saw salvation:

> for my eyes have seen your salvation [σωτήριόν],
> which you have prepared in the presence of all peoples,
> a light for revelation to the Gentiles
> and for glory to your people Israel (Luke 2:30–32).

Simeon anticipates Luke's later (Luke 3:4–6), distinctively extended opening from Isaiah 40:3–5, καὶ ὄψεται πᾶσα σὰρξ τὸ σωτήριον τοῦ θεοῦ.[1119]

i. Who can reign forever? (Ps. 88:49–50)

How might readers have heard Paul's incipit "I have found David" (εὗρον Δαυὶδ), echoing Ps. 88:20?[1120] Israel sang her theology; Ps. 88 is its great celebration of God's David-promise. Paul's allusion probably hints at this psalmist's problem with God's promise: "Where now is your loving-kindness?" (τὰ ἐλέη σου,

---

[1115] Acts 13:24–25

[1116] Cf. Acts 19:4.

[1117] προκηρύξαντος Ἰωάννου πρὸ προσώπου τῆς εἰσόδου, where εἰσόδου suggests Jesus' entry on to history's stage, reflecting Luke 3:21–22, and προκηρύξαντος crystallizes Luke's emphatic conclusion (3:19–20) to John's activity before Jesus' anointing.

[1118] Itself an announcement of God's fulfilling the promise of both 2 Sam. 7 and Ezek. 34.

[1119] Omitting Isa. 40:5a, καὶ ὀφθήσεται ἡ δόξα κυρίου. That happened at the Saviour's birth (Luke 2:8–20).

[1120] Acts 13:22b.

hesed).[1121] How might any of David's descendants rule forever?[1122] Mortality remains their certainty. Gabriel's announcement to Mary embraced God's promise – David's seed would rule on David's throne forever[1123] – but who might rule forever? Recalling David's mortality,[1124] the remainder of Paul's sermon – note its fourfold "decay" (διαφθορά) – suggests that this psalmist's taunting question exercised Israel's thought-world, that of Luke, of Paul, and Antioch's congregants. Paul spelled out his answer;[1125] for that, he first evoked another psalm.

In his sermon's introduction, Paul crystallized for Antioch what Luke's introduction portrayed for Theophilus. Luke's narrative Christology indicates that Jesus, primarily David's seed, Ezekiel's Saviour, and Simeon's salvation, fills the role of John's coming one who now enables "all flesh to see the salvation of our God."[1126] Once more, Luke's many descriptors tell this one person's story. For Luke, God's David-promises are primary, the source of his theme of salvation.

[1121] ποῦ εἰσιν τὰ ἐλέη σου τὰ ἀρχαῖα, κύριε, ἃ ὤμοσας τῷ Δαυιδ ἐν τῇ ἀληθείᾳ σου; (Ps. 88:49–50). Ps. 88 appears to underlie Mary's canticle also (Luke 1:46–56). Both celebrating (88:2–5) and questioning (88:50–52) God's loving-kindness (ἔλεος), this psalm echoes 2 Sam. 7:15–16 by linking God's David-promise with ἔλεος (2 Sam. 7:15). Mary's response celebrates God's remembering, his ἔλεος in his fulfilling the promise (Luke 1:50, 54). In her canticle there is also a clutch of words from Ps. 88:8–11, especially her talk of God as ὁ δυνατός. Ps. 88 belongs to Luke's subtext.

[1122] τίς ἐστιν ἄνθρωπος, ὃς ζήσεται καὶ οὐκ ὄψεται θάνατον, ῥύσεται τὴν ψυχὴν αὐτοῦ ἐκ χειρὸς ᾅδου; (ibid.).

[1123] Luke 1:33.

[1124] Acts 13:36; cf. 2:29; cf. 2:29–32.

[1125] In their canticles – human responses to heaven's announcements of God's initiative in and through Jesus – both Mary and Zechariah recognized that God had remembered his ἔλεος, (e.g., Luke 1:54, 72). Readers bring insider knowledge that in Jesus "God had raised up a horn of salvation for them in the house of his servant David" (Luke 1:69; cf. Ps. 88:25).

[1126] See Luke 3:6; cf. Isa. 40:5b.

2. Message of salvation (Acts 13:26)

Acts 13:26 refocuses listeners' attention first, by its renewed address – "brothers, sons of Abraham's stock, and the God-fearers among us"; then by its emphatic "to us (ἡμῖν) this word of salvation has been sent," soon to be contrasted with Jerusalem's initial rejection of that word (13:27).[1127] Intratextual and intertextual resonances in Paul's Introduction prepared readers for this section: God has brought to Israel a Saviour; Paul brings to Antioch a message of salvation, good news about God's David-promises.

Commentators regularly note that Paul's "to us the message of this salvation has been sent" (13:26) alludes to Ps. 106; some, that this allusion appeared earlier, in the Cornelius episode (Acts 10:36–43). It coexists there, as here, with a John the Baptist reference. Multiple usage of a scripture reference, especially in narratively significant settings, suggests that the passage forms part of Luke's pre-draft subtext.[1128] But why might Ps. 106 feature in Paul's sermon?[1129] Probably an incipit phrase, Acts 13:26 evokes a theological framework (106:16–22) within which Paul's distinctive argument develops.

Ps. 106 illustrates God's saving acts (ἔργα, θαυμάσια), indicating appropriate human responses to them, characteristically recognizing God's loving-kindnesses (ἐλέη) in God's works.[1130] The psalm's repeated response-refrains vary around:

> Let them acknowledge the Lord for his mercies [τὰ ἐλέη αὐτοῦ]

[1127] Acts 13:26; because it works with the narrative in NA[28] *Interpreter* prescinds from discussion of the *vl.* On internal grounds I prefer the second pers. direct address, ὑμῖν, cf. 13:40–41.

[1128] Cornelius and Antioch's congregants hear summaries of "the word." See Marguerat (2007: 26–27). See especially Stanton (1974: 70–78), to whose reflections on the role of Ps. 106 in Acts 10, and on scriptural exegesis, I owe much.

[1129] On Ps. 106, see Marshall (1980: 579).

[1130] Notably, in this, Ps. 106 parallels Ps. 88's celebration (before questioning) of God's ἐλέη.

and for his wonderful works [θαυμάσια] to the sons of men (Ps. 106:21).

Ps. 106:16–22 is a section whose action and language map onto those in Paul's sermon: paralleling the synagogue's presidents, the troubled "cried out" to God,[1131] who saved them.[1132] God saved them by rescuing them from their corruptions (διαφθορῶν), paralleled by Paul's four references to "decay" (διαφθορά).[1133] "They" laid Jesus in a tomb (13:29; cf. Ps. 106 18b), beyond death's portals. Then, Paul's doubling of "work" in his adaptation of Habakkuk at 13:41 echoes fundamental "wisdom" questions about God's works (e.g., Ps. 106:22) and Israel's response.[1134] The psalm's conclusion questions whether "they will understand God's loving-kindness" (τὰ ἐλέη τοῦ κυρίου).

Did Theophilus, Antioch's congregants, and Luke's auditors hear these echoes from Paul's incipit phrase? Given this psalm's multiple usage, and the conceptual and verbal links between Ps. 106:16–22 and Paul's sermon, we may infer that Luke expected that they would. That is why Ps. 106 cryptically appears here in the first place; Paul's is, we recall, a condensed sermon argued from the scriptures for those who searched the scriptures.

i. God's new work

Following his announcement that "to us this message of salvation has been sent" (13:26), Paul summarizes Christian tradition about Jesus' suffering and resurrection. Though innocent, Jesus suffered according to the scriptures;[1135] entombed, God raised him from the dead, according to the scriptures,[1136] God's

---

[1131] See Ford (2007: 14–51).

[1132] Ps. 106:19b – καὶ ἐκ τῶν ἀναγκῶν αὐτῶν ἔσωσεν αὐτούς.

[1133] Acts 13:34b, 35b, 36 37; cf. Ps. 106:20.

[1134] 106:22 – καὶ θυσάτωσαν θυσίαν αἰνέσεως καὶ ἐξαγγειλάτωσαν τὰ ἔργα αὐτοῦ ἐν ἀγαλλιάσει.

[1135] Acts 13:27–29; cf. 1 Cor. 15:3.

[1136] Acts 13:29–30; Cf. 1 Cor. 15:4; Rom. 1:1–4; Luke 24:25–27, 44–48.

work, attested by those who travelled with him from Galilee to Jerusalem.[1137] This central part of Paul's sermon coheres both with what he elsewhere affirms to have come to him from early tradition[1138] and with Luke's alleged oxymoron at Luke 24:26, 44–7.[1139] Paul's central section is basic, traditional proclamation of the Jesus-message, essentially, what God has done: "God raised [Jesus] from the dead" (ὁ δὲ θεὸς ἤγειρεν αὐτὸν ἐκ νεκρῶν); God brought (ἤγαγεν) Jesus, David's seed, to Israel as Saviour;[1140] God sent to Antioch this "word of salvation"[1141] – answering Israel's cry of distress expressed both in the presidents' request for "a word of consolation," and implied by the echo from Ps. 88:21, 49. Luke-Acts is essentially God-talk (θεός- λόγος). Paul affirms that Jesus' companions witnessed to God's having raised him[1142] – but where in Israel's scriptures does one find God's promise to raise Messiah from the dead?

3. God's work "according to the Scriptures" (Acts 13:32–37)

In Acts 13:27–29 Paul associated Jesus' rejection and death with unspecified scripture. In 13:32–37 he demonstrates how God's work of raising Jesus from the dead fulfils the congregants' hopes, and which passages of scripture lead to his conclusion. These verses crystallize his midrash on Luke's base-text (2

[1137] Acts 13:31, cf. 1 Cor. 15:5–6; Luke 24:34–48.

[1138] 1 Cor. 15:1–11.

[1139] See Doble (2006). It would be hard to overestimate the importance of Luke's use of tradition; see Wright, N.T. (2003: 277–374) on the impact of Jesus' resurrection on Paul's modelling of Jewish thought about resurrection.

[1140] Acts 13:30; 13:23.

[1141] Acts 13:26; the ἐξαπεστάλη of 13:26 is a reverential periphrasis for "God sent." This message was "the work" that God had sent Paul and Barnabas to do (Acts 13:1–3; 14:26–28), to announce God's amazing "work" as did Habakkuk (1:5, θαυμάσατε θαυμάσια, ἔργον ἐγὼ ἐργάζομαι) and the psalmist, (Ps. 106:21, τὰ θαυμάσια αὐτοῦ), cf. 8, 15, 31; cf. 43.

[1142] Acts 13:30–31.

Sam. 7:12), especially its "mortality" problem.[1143] In six verses of condensed scriptural reasoning, Luke's base-text discloses its "meaning" through four layers of interpretation: (a) Jesus' anointing; (b) his resurrection; (c) his rescue from decay, and (d) his "answering" a psalmist's long-standing problems with God's promise.

First, however, we establish that this base-text is present in Paul's sermon. Luke's base-text, Nathan's oracle, reports God's promise to David:

> And it shall be [when] your days are fulfilled and you sleep [κοιμηθήσῃ] with your fathers, that I will raise up your seed [ἀναστήσω τὸ σπέρμα σου] after you who shall be from your belly, and I will ready his kingdom [...] and I will restore his throne forever [ἕως εἰς τὸν αἰῶνα] (2 Sam. 7:12–13).

While Luke never cites this text, Paul's sermon clearly alludes to it.[1144] Three features confirm this allusion. First, throughout Paul's sermon David is a major character (13:22–23, 34, 36). Second, Paul identifies David's promised seed (13:23) as Jesus. Third, Paul announces the good news entailed by God's fulfilling his promise in Jesus.[1145] Paul thus links together his sermon's Introduction, culminating in God's having brought Jesus to Israel as Saviour, and his scriptural demonstration that Jesus' story is "good news."[1146]

Distinctive lexical features then confirm Paul's allusion to his base-text. Paul twice alludes to the key verb of God's promise to David, "I will raise up" (ἀναστήσω).[1147] Further, Nathan's oracle euphemistically refers to David's

---

[1143] Cf. Ps. 88:49–52.

[1144] See Vesco (2012: 465).

[1145] Acts 13:32–33; promise (13:23, 32); fulfil (13:33, ἐκπληρόω; 13:27, πληρόω; 13:29, τελέω); cf. Luke 1:1, πληροφορέω.

[1146] Acts 13:23; 13:32–33, Καὶ ἡμεῖς ὑμᾶς εὐαγγελιζόμεθα τὴν πρὸς τοὺς πατέρας ἐπαγγελίαν γενομένην, ὅτι ταύτην ὁ θεὸς ἐκπεπλήρωκεν τοῖς τέκνοις [αὐτῶν] ἡμῖν.

[1147] 13:33–34, ἀναστήσας, ἀνέστησεν.

death as "sleeping with his fathers": καὶ κοιμηθήσῃ μετὰ τῶν πατέρων σου.[1148] Paul does the same: "For David, after he had served God's purpose in his own generation, fell asleep (ἐκοιμήθη), was laid beside his fathers (τοὺς πατέρας αὐτοῦ), and saw corruption"[1149] Lexically and conceptually, Luke's base-text underlies Paul's unpacking of his "good news."[1150]

That "good news" is God's having fulfilled this promise to David, first by anointing Jesus,[1151] then by raising him from the dead;[1152] fulfilment is Paul's focus here.[1153] In Paul's appropriated base-text, God's promise is "I will raise up" (ἀναστήσω).[1154] Paul finds in this verb two significations, exploiting each in successive verses;[1155] Acts 13:33 is this sermon's interpretative crux.

i. Anointing Jesus

> And we are announcing good news [εὐαγγελιζόμεθα] for you about the promise [ἐπαγγελίαν) made to the Fathers, that God has fulfilled [ἐκπεπλήρωκεν] this for us, their children by raising up [ἀναστήσας] Jesus just as it is written in the second psalm:[1156] "You are my son, today I have begotten you" (Acts 13:32–33).

[1148] 2 Sam. 7:12.

[1149] Acts 13:36.

[1150] Acts 13:32–37; note εὐαγγελιζόμεθα; apostles witness to Jesus' resurrection, Paul interprets that event.

[1151] Acts 13:33; here I simply present my case, currently a minority position. See, e.g., Morgan-Wynne (2014) for a recent alternative view and survey of the majority case.

[1152] Acts 13:30, 34–37.

[1153] Echoing Luke 1:1–4.

[1154] Cf. Rom. 1:1–4.

[1155] A form of metalepsis; see Hays (2015).

[1156] With NA[28]; the psalm's numbering makes no difference to arguing from its text.

This ἀναστήσας is the first of Paul's two understandings of his base-text's ἀναστήσω.[1157] Plainly, 13:33 is Paul's resumption of his Introduction's "from this man's seed, as promised God has brought [ἤγαγεν] to Israel a Saviour, Jesus." There, reflecting Luke 3:1–22, and wider tradition,[1158] Paul brought Jesus on to history's stage, following John's exit.[1159] Now, at Acts 13:33, he overtly recalls Luke's scene of Jesus' anointing, hinted at by the sermon's Introduction.[1160]

From his prologue onward, Luke distanced John from Jesus while preserving a tradition of their association. Luke strengthens this distancing by his drama's adapted formal opening.[1161] There God's anointing Jesus with Holy Spirit follows John's imprisonment, firmly separated from Jesus' baptism. That Luke understands Jesus' experience as God's anointing him emerges both in the apostles' thanksgiving-prayer and in Peter's gospel for Cornelius.[1162] It almost certainly underlies Luke's distinctive report of Jesus' Nazareth sermon where the event of Jesus' anointing governs one's reading of his citation from Isaiah:

> The Spirit of the Lord is upon me,
> because he has anointed me (Luke 4:18).

[1157] Acts 13:32–33; cf. Ps. 2:7 (cf. Luke 3:21–22). Note how Paul associates Ps. 2:7 with the David-promise of 2 Sam. 7, an association established by 4Q174, and found in Rom. 1:2–4, and Heb. 1:5.

[1158] Cf. Mark 1:9–11; Matthew 3:13–17; John 1:29–34.

[1159] With Barrett (1994: 645). Note how τῆς εἰσόδου αὐτοῦ (13:24) that parallels ἤγαγεν (13:23), and Luke's reference (Luke 9:31) to Jesus' departure as his ἔξοδος, hint at his "dramatic" language in relation to narrative characters. On "bringing Jesus on to history's stage" see also e.g., Rese, M. (1969); Bruce (1952); Marshall (2007); contra Lövestam (1961); Haenchen (1971); Conzelmann (1987); Fitzmyer (1998); Jervell, J. (1998); Pervo (2009).

[1160] Luke 3:21–22; see Doble (2014).

[1161] Luke 3:1–22.

[1162] Acts 4:27–28; 10:37–38; "that message spread throughout Judea, beginning in Galilee after the baptism that John announced: how God anointed Jesus of Nazareth with the Holy Spirit and with power."

Luke has accented this event as God's anointing Jesus with the Holy Spirit.[1163]

But what did Jesus hear?[1164] Evangelists agree that God's word to Jesus affirmed that he was "Son."[1165] Luke's readers expected this, for Gabriel's word to Mary was that her son "will be called" Son of God.[1166] This clearly alludes to Luke's base-text, and David's promised seed: "I will be a father to him, and he a son to me."[1167] Ps. 88 celebrated this relationship:

> I have found my servant David [εὗρον Δαυὶδ];[1168]
> with my holy oil I have anointed him [...]
> He shall call me, "My Father"
> I will make him the firstborn [πρωτότοκος],[1169]
> the highest of the kings of the earth (Ps. 88:21, 26, 28).

David's own psalm also celebrated his appointment by God in comparable language:

> I will tell of the decree of the Lord:
> He said to me, "You are my son;
> today I have begotten you" (Ps. 2:7; cf. Acts 4:25–28).

This is precisely what Paul recalls at Antioch, and there are good grounds for holding that in Luke's *Ausgangstext* this also appeared at Luke 3:21–22. I have argued this case elsewhere,[1170] but here summarize external and internal reasons for re-assessing the NA^{28} text at Luke 3:21–22.

[1163] Arguing contra e.g., Bock (1987; 2012); Jipp (2010: 255–274); Vesco (2012); Weren (1989). See Marshall (2007: 584–585) for a helpful discussion.

[1164] This crux confronts all commentators on Paul's sermon: does "today I have begotten you" imply that Jesus' resurrection was the moment of his becoming Son of God, that is Messiah?

[1165] Mark 1:11; Matthew 3:17; John 1:34.

[1166] Luke 1:35, cf. 1:32; note the future κληθήσεται in both verses.

[1167] 2 Sam. 7:14.

[1168] Recall how at the echo of Ps. 88 at Acts 13:22 implied David as Son.

[1169] See Luke 2:1–7.

[1170] See Doble (2014).

Regarding external evidence, Ehrman's case for the orthodox corruption of scripture at this point is well presented.[1171] He argues that together D05 and early non-canonical evidence point to Luke's use of Ps. 2:7. Major fourth-century witnesses, anxious about adoptionism, adapted Luke's baptismal narrative to Mark and Matthew's versions. By then, Luke's first volume was categorized as "gospel" so separated from his second. To Ehrman's external evidence we should probably add that of Heb. 1:5–9 (cf. Heb. 5:6) where 2 Sam. 7:14 and Psalm 2:7 are tightly linked with Jesus as anointed Son.[1172]

Regarding internal evidence, a stronger version than Ehrman's better supports his case. Luke characteristically takes up and re-interprets in Acts material from his first volume. We saw Luke's distinctive mirroring of three of Jesus' conflict-sayings in Peter's speeches.[1173] Luke adapted Jesus' *gezerah shewa'* at his interrogation before Stephen's witnessing to its fulfilment.[1174] Paul's Introduction to his sermon evoked and paralleled Luke's distinctive Infancy Gospel and reworked opening of Jesus' ministry.[1175] Further, Luke tends to parallel Jesus' life with David's.[1176] Luke earlier turned to David's Ps. 2 as his scriptural focus for Messiah's suffering (Acts 4:25–28), echoing 4Q174, where 2 Sam. 7, Ps. 2 and Amos 9 synergize to explain events in its writer's own time. Given Luke's overall David-focus, it is probable that, in this narrative, God appointed David's promised seed by that same formula with which he had appointed David. This literary characteristic suggests that at Acts 13:32–33, Paul's associating Jesus' anointing with Ps. 2:7 was what D05 "rightly" reads at Luke 3:21–22.

[1171] Ehrman (1993).

[1172] See Ellingworth (1993: 108–116); Brooke (1998); cf. 4Q174.

[1173] Luke 20:1–44; Acts 2:1–4:22, citing Ps. 109:1; Exod. 3:6; Ps. 117:22.

[1174] Luke 22:69; Acts 7:55–56; Ch. 7; cf. Doble (2014).

[1175] Luke 1:1–3:22.

[1176] See Doble (2004).

Consequently, at Antioch the psalm's "this day" most probably refers to Jesus' "anointing."[1177] This is where Paul's good news began – in the ministry of the anointed Saviour who forgave sins.[1178] Jesus was among Israel as Messiah before he was rejected and killed.[1179] Crucially for *Interpreter*'s case, Luke's earlier narrative allots to apostles assembled in Jerusalem the clearest understanding of that same psalm that Jerusalem's rulers had gathered together with others against God's Messiah, his anointed Son:

> παρέστησαν οἱ βασιλεῖς τῆς γῆς
> καὶ οἱ ἄρχοντες συνήχθησαν ἐπὶ τὸ αὐτὸ
> κατὰ τοῦ κυρίου καὶ κατὰ τοῦ χριστοῦ αὐτοῦ (Ps. 2:2; Acts 4:26).

Decisively, in Acts 4:27 apostles identify first that son, τὸν ἅγιον παῖδά σου Ἰησοῦν ὃν ἔχρισας; then those assembled against him as principals in the process against Jesus that secured his crucifixion: Herod, Pontius Pilate, Jerusalem and her rulers crucified God's anointed Messiah. Jesus' whole ministry was integral to his story retold by Luke. Jerusalem should have understood, for they read the scriptures weekly.[1180] In anointing Jesus, God had fulfilled the plainest sense of Nathan's oracle. Further, uniquely, God had raised Jesus from the dead (13:30, 34).[1181]

ii. Raising Jesus from the dead

> But that he raised him up [ἀνέστησεν αὐτὸν]
> from the dead [ἐκ νεκρῶν]
> no longer waiting to return to decay [εἰς διαφθοράν] (Acts 13:34).

[1177] Not to resurrection; contra Bock (1987); Jipp, (2010). Cf. Whitsett (2000).

[1178] Expressed succinctly by Gerber (2008: 262). Cf. Luke 2:10; Acts 13:32 (εὐαγγελίζω).

[1179] Cf. Acts 2:22–24, 36b.

[1180] Acts 13:27; cf. vss. 15, 40.

[1181] On this uniqueness, see Wright, N.T. (2003).

With this ἀνέστησεν Paul returns to his base-text's ἀναστήσω, this time with two qualifiers.[1182] His resumption indicates both a change in the verb's signification, and sharpened focus on the place of resurrection in Paul's argument.

First, ἀνέστησεν αὐτὸν ἐκ νεκρῶν is a variant on Paul's earlier ὁ δὲ θεὸς ἤγειρεν αὐτὸν ἐκ νεκρῶν (Acts 13:30), both statements about Jesus. In Paul's sermon, ἐκ νεκρῶν features twice (13:30, 34), yet his ἀναστήσας of 13:33 carries no modifier – because it refers to the "David-promise" (13:23, 32) rather than "the resurrection from the dead" (13:30, 34).[1183] At 13:34 ὅτι δὲ confirms that Paul resumes his announcement, this time replacing ἤγειρεν with ἀνέστησεν. While at 13:30 and 13:37, ἤγειρεν signifies resurrection-event, at 13:34, ἀνέστησεν[1184] implies fulfilment of God's promise, ἀναστήσω. Luke has reserved ἀνίστημι for Paul's re-interpreting his base-text.

Second, Paul then modifies ἐκ νεκρῶν by μηκέτι μέλλοντα ὑποστρέφειν εἰς διαφθοράν. The fourfold presence of "decay" (διαφθορά) in Acts 13:34–37, noted earlier in Ps. 106:20, suggests that Paul's modifier serves two purposes. It directly addresses human mortality that had frustrated the forever of God's promises,[1185] the problem confronted in Ps. 88 (cf. Acts 13:22):

> Who is the man who shall live [ζήσεται], and not see death,
> Who shall rescue [ῥύσεται] his life from Hades' hand? (Ps. 88:49).

Indirectly, Paul's attention to διαφθορά adds further scriptural witness to God's plan to raise David's seed from the dead. Paul's rhetoric will not depend solely on his twofold interpretation of Nathan's oracle, for God had reaffirmed the

---

[1182] Cf. Acts 13:30, 34; Rom. 1:4; 10:9–10; 1 Cor. 15.

[1183] Morgan-Wynne (2014: 117–124) makes a textually and logically insecure case.

[1184] As in Nathan's oracle, the referent of "promise" in Acts 13:23, 32.

[1185] Note the threefold affirmation in 2 Sam. 7:12–16 of the David-promise's perpetuity.

same promise through two further linked promises to David, again contrasting Jesus' story with David's – David decayed; Jesus will not.

Paul reinterprets these linked promises within the framework given by Ps. 106:20 of his message of salvation: "He sent out his word and healed them, and rescued [ἐρρύσατο] them from their corruptions [διαφθορῶν]." He uses interpretative techniques practised at Qumran, in the letter to the Hebrews, and in other Christian canonical writings, but does so on the grounds of the decisive event of God's raising Jesus from death and corruption (Acts 13:30, 37).[1186]

iii. Rescuing Jesus from corruption

Directly addressing the problem posed by human mortality, Paul's two linked, unmarked passages are:

> [God] has spoken thus, "I will give you the sacred, trustworthy things of David" [τὰ ὅσια Δαυὶδ τὰ πιστά, Isa. 55:3]. Because he also says in a different [place] "You will not give your holy one to see decay" [ἰδεῖν διαφθοράν, Ps. 15:10] (Acts 13:34–35).

The introduction to both citations is oral (λέγω); for the synagogue, scripture *speaks* to its hearers as more than historical record. First, God spoke (εἴρηκεν) in Isaiah's oracle where David is foregrounded:

> listen to me and your soul will live in good things.
> I will make with you an everlasting covenant,
> the sacred things of David that are sure [τὰ ὅσια Δαυὶδ τὰ πιστά] (Isa. 55:3–13).

Isa. 55 reads like a stand-alone oracle whose final verses embody Israel's hope of return from Exile. At Antioch, Paul's adapted incipit phrase evokes this "everlasting covenant" embracing God's promises to David. Like Ezekiel, Isaiah

---

[1186] Contra Soards (1994: 86–87): the logic of each speech differs substantially, and midrash entails a both/and rather than Soards' either/or. Paul's argument from Ps. 15:10 explores its διαφθορά element; Peter's argument, facilitated by Ps. 131, notes that through David's seed, Jesus, both elements are fulfilled.

reworks for exiles God's David-promise. In Paul's sermon τὰ ὅσια [...] τὰ πιστά echoes both Nathan's oracle and Ps. 88's celebratory reformulation of that promise, oath, or covenant.[1187] While Isaiah's reworking, unlike Ezekiel's or Amos's, makes no appeal to Paul's base-text's ἀναστήσω, Paul has here recruited Isaiah to his argument via one link word, ὅσια.

Second, superficially in Ps. 15:10 the psalmist David speaks, but Luke understands David to be the prophet through whom God speaks (λέγει).[1188] Focused on David, named as its author earlier in Luke's subtext (Acts 2:25–31), Paul's adapted phrase highlights David's confidence that God will rescue the mortal David, τὸν ὅσιόν σου, from Hades' clutches and consequent decay.[1189] Gezerah shewa' links these passages.

Among the synagogue's interpretative techniques, gezerah shewa' features often in Luke-Acts. One word common to two passages allows each to interpret the other – an equal decision. Here, OGT Isaiah's τὰ ὅσια [...] τὰ πιστά shares a common root, ὅσιος, with David's τὸν ὅσιόν σου.[1190] Consequently, God's promise of an eternal Davidic covenant (Isa. 55:3b) is newly illuminated by what God also speaks through David the prophet-psalmist.

Peter earlier explored Jesus' resurrection and David's seemingly impossible hope.[1191] Knowing that God had sworn with an oath to put the fruit of his loins on his throne,[1192] David spoke of Messiah's resurrection:

> he was neither abandoned to Hades [εἰς ᾅδην]
> nor did his flesh see decay [εἶδεν διαφθοράν] (Acts 2:31).

[1187] Variously described, that covenant-promise remains "God's *word*" (Isa. 55:11); its πιστά recalls the πιστωθήσεται of Nathan's oracle (2 Sam. 7:16) and πίστωσον of David's following prayer (7:25); cf. Ps. 88:29, 38.

[1188] So Acts 4:25–26 cf. 2:25, 30.

[1189] ὅτι οὐκ ἐγκαταλείψεις τὴν ψυχήν μου εἰς ᾅδην οὐδὲ δώσεις τὸν ὅσιόν σου ἰδεῖν διαφθοράν.

[1190] Old Greek Text, various Greek versions or revisions possibly available to Luke.

[1191] Acts 2:30–32.

[1192] Ps. 131:11–12.

Before Paul's sermon, David's Ps. 15:10 was part of Luke's subtextual foundation for Messiah's resurrection, though not his principal scriptural ground. Paul here mutually interprets Ps. 15 and Isaiah's reworking of Nathan's oracle, Luke's base-text. Further, if a Greek-speaking synagogue was sensitive to the OGT's underlying Hebrew text, then Paul's *gezerah shewa'* obliquely recalls the David-promise's essential association with God's covenant-love.[1193] Paul's focus then becomes also God's covenant-love (ἔλεος), and he answers both of Ps. 88's probing questions.[1194]

iv. Answering the psalmist's two questions

Acts 13:22, εὗρον Δαυὶδ, indicated that Paul had in mind Ps. 88, that asked its probing question:

> Who is the man who shall live [ζήσεται] and not see death,
> Who shall rescue [ῥύσεται] his life from Hades' hand? (Ps. 88:49).

Then, Acts13:37 "but the one whom God raised up did not see decay [διαφθοράν]" confirms that Jesus is that man who lives,[1195] though Christian tradition affirms that Jesus did die.[1196] He is that man whom God rescued from Hades – so from decay.[1197] Subtextually, Ps. 88's ῥύσεται [...] ἐκ χειρὸς ᾅδου links verbally and conceptually with Ps. 106's ἐρρύσατο αὐτοὺς ἐκ τῶν

[1193] 2 Sam. 7:15 – τὸ δὲ ἔλεός μου οὐκ ἀποστήσω ἀπ' αὐτοῦ, καθὼς ἀπέστησα ἀφ' ὧν ἀπέστησα ἐκ προσώπου μου (cf. Ps. 88:2–5, 28–29, 47–52). Notably, the following verse's πιστωθήσεται offers the probable source of Isaiah's τὰ πιστά. See Marshall (2007: 586).

[1194] Implied by Ps. 88:49–50.

[1195] Cf. Luke 24:5 (τὸν ζῶντα), 23 (αὐτὸν ζῆν); Acts 1:3 (ἑαυτὸν ζῶντα).

[1196] Cf. οὔτε ἡ σὰρξ αὐτοῦ εἶδεν διαφθοράν (Acts 2:31).

[1197] See Luke's resurrection narrative (Luke 24:1–12) and its distinctive τί ζητεῖτε τὸν ζῶντα μετὰ τῶν νεκρῶν;

διαφθορῶν αὐτῶν. Thus, Acts 13:37 becomes Paul's decisive reinterpretation of 13:30 as God's fulfilment of the David-promises – ὁ δὲ θεὸς ἤγειρεν αὐτὸν ἐκ νεκρῶν – God's remembered loving-kindness[1198] resolving Israel's "mortality" problem. Paul's summary verse forms an *inclusio* with 13:30. Between them, his midrash on ἀναστήσω has demonstrated how Jesus' resurrection fulfilled God's David-promises in both their plainest and most unexpected senses.

4. Paul's conclusion

> γνωστὸν οὖν ἔστω ὑμῖν, ἄνδρες ἀδελφοί, ὅτι
> διὰ τούτου ὑμῖν ἄφεσις ἁμαρτιῶν καταγγέλλεται,
> [καὶ] ἀπὸ πάντων ὧν οὐκ ἠδυνήθητε ἐν νόμῳ Μωϋσέως δικαιωθῆναι
> ἐν τούτῳ πᾶς ὁ πιστεύων δικαιοῦται. (Acts 13:38–9).

Paul's proclamation[1199] to his brothers is his argument's consequence from its preceding sentence:

> for David, after he had served God's purpose in his own generation, slept, was laid with his fathers, and saw corruption; but [Jesus] whom God raised up [ὃν δὲ ὁ θεὸς ἤγειρεν] saw no corruption (Acts 13:36).

The thrust of this chapter has been that the core *inclusio* of Paul's sermon is that God has raised up (ἤγειρεν) Jesus from the dead (Acts 13:30 to 37), an event that fulfilled God's promises[1200] to Jesus' ancestor David (ἀναστήσω), rooting Jesus' resurrection in the same promise that issued in his anointing. Jesus' story parallels David's story, while transcending David's undisputed

---

[1198] Cf. Luke 1:50, 54; Ps. 88:50.

[1199] γνωστὸν οὖν [...] καταγγέλλεται.

[1200] E.g., 2 Sam. 7; Ps. 15; cf. Isa. 55.

mortality. God's raising up Jesus transformed Paul's world-view.[1201] Consequently, exegetes have three, not two, sequenced pronouns to consider (see section 3iv above):

- ὃν δὲ ὁ θεὸς ἤγειρεν (Acts 13:37) governs both
- διὰ τούτου (13:38) forgiveness of sins is being proclaimed (καταγγέλλεται) to you; and
- ἐν τούτῳ (13:39) everyone who lives by faith is "counted righteous" (δικαιοῦται).

Between these clear statements stands a problematic, infinitive-governed phrase – [καὶ] ἀπὸ πάντων ὧν οὐκ ἠδυνήθητε ἐν νόμῳ Μωϋσέως δικαιωθῆναι.

i. γνωστὸν οὖν ἔστω ὑμῖν, ἄνδρες ἀδελφοί, ὅτι

Paul and Barnabas had been greeted as ἄνδρες ἀδελφοί (Acts 13:15a). They, in turn, first address the congregants as ἄνδρες Ἰσραηλῖται καὶ οἱ φοβούμενοι τὸν θεόν (13:16b), later as ἄνδρες ἀδελφοί (13:26, 38), one community of faith. Asked for a word of encouragement (λόγος παρακλήσεως, 13:15b), Paul responded with his word of salvation (ὁ λόγος τῆς σωτηρίας ταύτης, 13:26) that includes his scriptural argument (13:30–37) leading to his conclusion and warning.

Paul's formulaic γνωστὸν [...] ἔστω[1202] emphasizes the significance for his brothers of what is to be known; its οὖν signals the consequential nature of that known. That is twofold: it relates to the forgiveness of sins, and to two

---

[1201] God's new work, his raising up Jesus in fulfilment of the David-promises, was for Paul as for the earlier Jesus-followers the transformation of Judaism: Jesus' ministry, rejection and crucifixion, his resurrection have decisively placarded what God requires of his covenant-People. The first Luke-Acts' readers learn of Paul's transformed mind is that Jesus is the Son of God, proving from scripture that Jesus is the Messiah (Acts 9:20–22; cf. Acts 5:42, etc.), two terms for the one reality (See Ch. 2).

[1202] Γνωστός is distinctively Lukan, with 80% of NT uses; γνωστὸν [...] ἔστω is a formula unique to Acts (2:14; 4:10; 13:38; 28:28).

passive forms of the verb δικαιόω. These consequences are the substantive element in God's "work" that features in Paul's final warning to Antioch (13:40–41), although Luke has already broadened God's "work" to include Jesus' followers' activity in his name[1203] – he is essentially ὃν δὲ ὁ θεὸς ἤγειρεν (13:37).

ii. διὰ τούτου ὑμῖν ἄφεσις ἁμαρτιῶν καταγγέλλεται

The passive form of καταγγέλλω is probably Luke's reverential periphrasis for God's announcing the "forgiveness of sins." That announcement was διὰ τούτου – "by means of this man" – Jesus, whose whole life, not simply his death and resurrection, was God's agency among Israel. We saw this clearly in Peter's address to a crowd astonished by a lame man's walking: [1204] "When God raised up [ἀναστήσας] his servant, he sent him first to you, to bless you by turning each of you from your wicked ways" (Acts 3:26);[1205] there, Jesus is the Messiah already designated for Israel.[1206] Peter can call for his hearers to repent "so that their sins might be wiped out" (3:19).[1207]

Paul's introduction to his sermon focused the matter. God brought Jesus to Israel as Saviour (13:23), and readers bring a thread running from Luke 2:11 – heaven's announcement of the birth of a Saviour – to Luke's distinctive "for the Son of Man has come to seek and to save the lost" (Luke 19:10). Luke's theme of salvation is rooted in Ezek. 34,[1208] distinctive of Jesus' activity and parodied in the crucifixion scene.[1209]

[1203] Acts 13:2; 14:26.

[1204] See Ch. 4.

[1205] ἐν τῷ ἀποστρέφειν ἕκαστον ἀπὸ τῶν πονηριῶν ὑμῶν. Cf. Moses' agency (Exod. 3:4–12).

[1206] τὸν προκεχειρισμένον ὑμῖν χριστὸν Ἰησοῦν.

[1207] εἰς τὸ ἐξαλειφθῆναι ὑμῶν τὰς ἁμαρτίας.

[1208] See Ch. 2.

[1209] E.g., Luke 5:20–26; 7:36–50; 23:35, 39.

Paul's introduction, however, linked Jesus' arrival on Israel's stage with John's exit from it. The elements of that note are John's baptizing, his summoning people to repent, and the question of his identity. Those three verses[1210] summarize Luke's longer version at Luke 3:1–22 where John's activity was contextualized by reference to Isa. 40; there, John's voice proclaimed a baptism of repentance for the forgiveness of sins. Luke, while echoing tradition, distinctively includes one Isaianic phrase that appears in no other gospel version – "and all flesh shall see God's salvation."[1211] Isaiah probably understood this to be the widest recognition of what God has done for Israel; Luke's Paul probably interprets it as illuminating the widening of this community of God's people by an influx of Gentiles. For Luke as for Isaiah, forgiveness of sins and salvation belong together in one concept – Exile from God is over, and the initiative is God's.

Paul's message of salvation coheres with Luke's theological scheme:[1212] Jesus' commission to his witnesses[1213] integrated their newly-acquired hermeneutic skills with scriptures that spoke of a suffering and raised Messiah, and with proclamation in his name of repentance and forgiveness of sins.[1214] At Pentecost, then later for Cornelius, Peter exemplified Jesus'

[1210] Acts 13:23–25.

[1211] At the same time, Luke has omitted "Then shall the glory of the Lord be revealed"; John made plain for his readers how that word was fulfilled (Jn. 1:14); Luke simply bathed in glory the whole of his proclamation panel (Luke 2:8–14).

[1212] Announced in the Prologue, where Zechariah celebrates God's new work (Luke 1:68–79) – first, reflecting on the Jesus-story (1:69–75), and echoing Ps. 88:20–26, he blessed God for raising up "a horn of salvation in David's house"; then foretelling John's prophetic role (1:76–79), and echoing tradition's associating Isa. 40 with John, saw him giving knowledge of salvation to Israel through the forgiveness of their sins. Cf. Acts 13:22–26; Luke 16:16.

[1213] Luke 24:44–49; Acts 13:31.

[1214] Epitomized by Luke's summary at Acts 5:29–32.

284

commission.[1215] Before Agrippa Paul recounts his own commission: "to open [Gentiles'] eyes so that they may turn from darkness to light and from the power of Satan to God, so that they may receive forgiveness of sins and a place among those who are sanctified by faith in me."[1216] At Antioch readers encounter Paul engaged in this activity for fellow Jews first.[1217]

iii. [καὶ] ἀπὸ πάντων ὧν οὐκ ἠδυνήθητε ἐν νόμῳ Μωϋσέως δικαιωθῆναι

What has Moses' law to do with its verb δῐκαιόω, linked with the succeeding δικαιοῦται? For Jesus-followers Torah matters supremely: it was the focus of the Jerusalem conflict-narrative in Luke-Acts;[1218] it had been refocused through Jesus' transformative interpretation of crystallized Torah.[1219] He was ὄντως [...] δίκαιος:[1220] tradition's temptation narrative[1221] spelled out his trusting commitment to the God of Abraham, Isaac and Jacob; his inaugural sermon at Nazareth announced his Messianic programme for God's new work, probably calling for a Jubilee.

The priority of *HaShem* and of neighbour in Israel's ongoing story was being reaffirmed. Luke's narrative of the journey to Jerusalem tells of both a

---

[1215] Acts 2:37–39; 10:42–44; cf. Luke 24:46–48: "Thus it is written, that the Messiah is to suffer and to rise from the dead on the third day, and that repentance and forgiveness of sins is to be proclaimed in his name to all nations [...] you are witnesses of these things."

[1216] Acts 26:15b–18.

[1217] Within his clear kerygmatic-confessional framework (Rom. 1:1–7; 10:5–13), Paul's undisputed writing implies the concept of forgiveness, e.g., Rom. 4:2–13 (echoing Ps. 31); 6:4–14 (baptismal context); 8:1–17 (echoing the disciples' prayer?); Rom. 12:1–13:8 (echoing Jesus' focus on God-centred Torah obedience).

[1218] See Ch. 7.

[1219] Luke 10:25–28; 18:19–22.

[1220] Luke 23:47; cf. Acts 3:14; 7:52; 22:14. See also δίκαιος-δικαιόω below.

[1221] Luke 4:1–12, embodying Deut. 6–9.

scribe and a rich young ruler who found such commitment hard.[1222] Likewise, the parable of the pauper Lazarus at the gates of his rich fellow Jew emphasized the Law's role in living justly,[1223] in loving one's neighbour as oneself, sharing what God had given.

Scribe or rich young aristocrat; Dives with Lazarus; Jesus' conflict with Jerusalem's elite, all point to the seductions of riches or power or difference that had led astray so many in Israel.[1224] Remaining Jews in a renewed Judaism, Jesus-followers were committed to following God's Messiah, Jesus δίκαιος, in his way of living out Torah. Arguably, Luke-Paul's δικαιόω then points to being reckoned among the δίκαιοι.

iv. ἐν τούτῳ πᾶς ὁ πιστεύων δικαιοῦται

Paul's argument from Acts 13:30 to 13:41 – his final word to Antioch's congregation – is his dialogue between event and scripture. This is particularly true of 13:39 that probably echoes a David-psalm,[1225] firmly tying off a distinctive Lukan thread (δίκαιος-δικαιόω) and bonding it with trusting[1226] the Messiah. We discuss both concepts – trusting and righteousness; their uses are certainly Lukan and not, as many hold, un-Pauline.

[1222] Luke 10:25–37; 18:18–30.

[1223] Luke 16:19–31; esp. 27–31.

[1224] See, e.g., Luke 4:5–8.

[1225] Ps. 142:2 (ὅτι οὐ δικαιωθήσεται ἐνώπιόν σου πᾶς ζῶν); cf. Oakes, (2015), 80–91, discussing Gal. 2:15–16 – εἰδότες [δὲ] ὅτι οὐ δικαιοῦται ἄνθρωπος ἐξ ἔργων νόμου ἐὰν μὴ διὰ πίστεως Ἰησοῦ Χριστοῦ.

[1226] See πίστις/ πιστεύω below.

5. Paul's warning (Acts 13:40–41)

Paul's "message of salvation" maps. on to his use of Ps. 106:22. The presidents' "cry"[1227] led to God's sending his word to save them.[1228] At death's portal, Jesus was rescued from decay;[1229] that θαυμάσιον[1230] should have evoked hearers' acknowledging God's θαυμάσια, ἐλέη, and proclaiming his works.[1231] Paul, finally, offers congregants a word of warning that links directly with his conclusion. Again, through a prophet, God speaks:

> Look, you scoffers!
> Be astonished [θαυμάσατε], then vanish,
> for in your days I am doing a work [ἔργον],
> a work that you will never put your trust in [πιστεύσητε],
> even if someone spells it out [ἐκδιηγῆται] for you[1232] (Hab.
> 1:5).

The verb πιστεύσητε (Acts 13:39) here is undoubtedly within an adaptation of Hab. 1:4. At Acts 13:39, πᾶς ὁ πιστεύων is followed immediately by δικαιοῦται, evoking both Hab. 2:4–5 and Ps. 143:2. We remarked earlier that Luke shared his interest in Habakkuk with Qumran,[1233] the author of Hebrews,[1234] and with Paul.[1235] This shared use of common multiple citations or adaptations goes beyond the 4Q174 where *Interpreter* began, and in a *pesher* on his adaptation Luke's Paul punches home his conclusion: "So watch out that what has been spoken by the prophets doesn't come upon you" (Acts 13:40).

[1227] Acts 13:15b; Ps. 106:19.

[1228] Acts 13:26; Ps. 106:19–20.

[1229] Acts 13:37; Ps. 15:10; Ps. 106:20.

[1230] Ps. 106:21.

[1231] τὰ ἔργα αὐτοῦ, Ps. 106:21–22; cf. Ps. 88:49–50.

[1232] This is precisely what Paul has just done.

[1233] 1QpHab; as he did 2 Sam. 7; Amos and Ps. 2. We're looking at different groups' interpretations of their common scriptural pool.

[1234] Heb. 10:37–39.

[1235] Rom. 1:17; Gal. 2:15–16.

In their days Antioch's congregants had heard Torah and prophets, as had Jerusalem and her rulers.[1236] Paul had spelt out God's work – God raised Jesus from death and decay[1237] – before demonstrating how God's work fulfilled Israel's hope.[1238] Responding, some of his hearers would commit their trust to God's work, others refuse.[1239] The psalmist – and Paul – recognized that God's saving and loving acts do not necessarily result in understanding and change of ways.[1240]

[1236] Acts 13:15a, 27.

[1237] Acts 13:30–31, 37.

[1238] On Hab. 1:5, see Marshall (2007: 526–527).

[1239] Acts 13:44–52.

[1240] Ps. 106:43. Cf. Acts 28:24–28.

C. The roots Δίκ- and Πίστ- in Luke-Acts

1. Δίκαιος-δικαιόω

This Lukan thread began with John's destiny to prepare a People for the Lord,[1241] turning "the disobedient to the wisdom of the righteous."[1242] Luke's "righteous" are a distinctive people: they included John's parents, Simeon, Joseph from Arimathea and Cornelius.[1243] Some, like the Sanhedrin's agents, pretended to be δίκαιος, others arrogantly assumed that they were.[1244] Luke knows of a resurrection of the righteous and of the unrighteous.[1245] Luke's Jesus is his model δίκαιος,[1246] whose task was to summon "sinners" rather than the righteous to repent.[1247]

Zechariah's "the wisdom of the righteous" prepared readers for wisdom's children.[1248] Luke has discussed John's and Jesus' missions; both were widely rejected, but through them Wisdom was shown to be "just."[1249] Luke had reported Jesus' tribute to John and the popular response that acknowledged God's being δίκαιος.[1250] Luke's righteous seem to be those who acknowledge God to be δίκαιος; who confront ungodly authority, yet who live by

---

[1241] See Wright, N.T. (2013).

[1242] Luke 1:17; cf. 7:35.

[1243] Luke 1:6; 2:25; 23:50; Acts 10:22.

[1244] Luke 20:20; 18:19.

[1245] Luke 14:14; Acts 24:15.

[1246] Luke 23:47; Acts 3:14; 7:55; 22:14.

[1247] Luke 5:32; 15:7; cf. Rom. 12:1–2 for Paul's probable understanding of μετάνοια as transformed life with a new perspective.

[1248] Luke 7:35.

[1249] See Wis. 7:22–8:2; like God's "word" or "spirit," wisdom was one way of speaking of God's agency in creation and human affairs.

[1250] Luke 7:28–29; ἐδικαίωσαν τὸν θεόν.

God's wisdom mediated through Torah's essence, not its scribal interpretation.[1251] They are portrayed by psalms of the righteous, and by the Wisdom of Solomon. In Luke-Acts, this word's context is characteristically human beings' relationship with God and with one another, focused by the persisting post-Deuteronomic question – "What does the Lord require of you?"[1252]

If that be so, then δικαιόω probably operates in the same relational way, signalling someone's having been acknowledged or reckoned as δίκαιος.[1253] This seems to be confirmed by Jesus' riposte to Pharisees who derided his key *logion* that none can serve both God and Mammon.[1254]

Luke 16:1–31 comprises two parables about rich men, one in relation to his steward, the other relating to a rich man's ignoring a pauper.[1255] These parables enclose, first, sayings of Jesus that essentially explore δίκ-[1256] and πιστ-[1257] roots before concluding with his key God and Mammon saying. Second, that *logion* provoked listening, money-loving Pharisees to deride him.[1258] Jesus responded that they actually (mis)represented themselves as δίκαιοι because their values were not God's values.[1259] Then, the much-discussed Luke 16:16–17 both follow Jesus' riposte and introduce his Lazarus parable; they tightly bind entry into God's Kingdom with the eternity of *HaShem*'s covenantal Torah: the powerful rich, like the tenants in Jesus'

[1251] Luke 10:25–28; 18:9–14, 18–26.

[1252] E.g., Deut. 10:12–22.

[1253] See Luke 7:28–29; Oakes (2015: 85) arrived at a similar conclusion via his helpful discussion of δικαιόω pass. in LXX; cf. Wright, N.T. (2015: 90–91).

[1254] Luke 16:13–15; cf. Mt. 6:24. See Ch. 7E on idolatry.

[1255] Luke 16:1–9, 19–31.

[1256] Luke 16:8, 9, 10, 11.

[1257] Luke 16:10, 11.

[1258] ἐκμυκτηρίζω, conveying a sense of contemptuous laughter; see also the rulers' derision (Luke 23:35).

[1259] ὑμεῖς ἐστε οἱ δικαιοῦντες ἑαυτοὺς ἐνώπιον τῶν ἀνθρώπων, (16:15; cf. 18:9–14).

vineyard parable, seek to seize control of what is properly God's gift.[1260] Arguably, Luke 16:18 belongs with 16:16 – tradition reports that John had rebuked Herod for his marriage arrangements;[1261] Pharisees are often present in Herod contexts; is this *logion* an example of the violence of the powerful rich who ignore Torah for their own ends?[1262]

i. Luke-Acts' δίκαιος and Paul

That thematic summary suggests that Acts 13:39 marks the conclusion of Luke's δίκαιος theme by Jesus, "everyone who lives by faith is counted righteous" (ἐν τούτῳ πᾶς ὁ πιστεύων δικαιοῦται). That formulation echoes Hab. 2:4 (ὁ δὲ δίκαιος ἐκ πίστεώς μου ζήσεται), sharing its δικ- and πιστ- semantic fields, but many commentators have complained that Luke has not understood Paul's (supposed) teaching on justification. It is worth briefly commenting that

(a) recent work on Paul has refocused then realigned much of what once was assumed to be beyond dispute, and that

(b) Luke's echoing Hab. 2:4 immediately precedes his adaptation of Hab. 1:5, strengthening the probability that Habakkuk was one of the prophets favoured by Jesus-followers. Luke shared his interest in Habakkuk with Qumran,[1263] the author of Hebrews,[1264] and with Paul.[1265]

Psalm 142, manifestly of interest to Luke, was clear (Ps. 142:2) that in God's presence, no living person could be deemed δίκαιος. That verse implies

---

[1260] See Ch. 7B4i.

[1261] Luke 3:19–20; cf. Mark 6:17–29.

[1262] See, e.g., Luke 3:18–20; 7:18–35; 9:7–9; 13:31–35.

[1263] 1QpHab; as he did 2 Sam. 7; Amos and Ps. 2. We're looking at different groups' interpretations of their common scriptural pool.

[1264] Heb. 10:37–39.

[1265] Rom. 1:17; Gal. 2:15–16.

God's judgment (κρίσιν), an ultimate courtroom, so the sense of "innocent" is probably present. But the following verses echo the prayers of a righteous one:

> I think about (μελετάω) all your deeds […] I meditate [μελετάω] on the works of your hands […] my soul thirsts for you […] for in you I put my hope [ἐλπίζω …] make known [γνωρίζω] to me the way [ὁδός] I should go […] teach [διδάσκω] me to do your will, for you are my God […] let your good spirit [τὸ πνεῦμά σου τὸ ἀγαθὸν] lead [ὁδηγέω] me in straight country (Ps. 142:3–10).

This is the language of a psalmist who wants to be among those who are δίκαιος; his relationship with God transcends God's ultimate judgment, transforming his present existence – "for I am your servant" (142:12, cf. 10). A courtroom is not the only context for this word-group. Prayer, in the Temple, by a humble penitent before God the merciful, offers another perspective,[1266] one consonant with the psalmist's shift of context from God's judgment to God's being δίκαιος:

> ἔνεκα τοῦ ὀνόματός σου, κύριε, ζήσεις με,
> ἐν τῇ δικαιοσύνῃ σου ἐξάξεις ἐκ θλίψεως τὴν ψυχήν μου […]
> ὅτι δοῦλός σού εἰμι ἐγώ (Ps. 142:11–12).

David's story was filled with enemies, with τοὺς θλίβοντας τὴν ψυχήν μου; unsurprisingly, David's promised seed Jesus shared that experience.

ii. Luke-Acts, δίκαιος and conflict

Luke's identifying Jesus as the δίκαιος[1267] cast Luke-Acts into its conflict format where, on one hand, Luke characterized Jesus and his followers as faithful

---

[1266] Luke 18:9–14; this tax-gatherer was δεδικαιωμένος, unlike a professed strict observer of Torah who failed to love his neighbour as himself: Jesus' twice-cited *logion* – πᾶς ὁ ὑψῶν ἑαυτὸν ταπεινωθή-σεται, ὁ δὲ ταπεινῶν ἑαυτὸν ὑψωθήσεται – prioritizes that kind of love above comparative minutiae. See Luke 14:7–11 as expanded by 12–14.

[1267] Ac 3:14; 7:52; 22:6–16; anarthrously, Luke 23:47, see Doble (1996).

Jews; on the other, their opponents – especially the powerful, elite rulers – as impious, lacking the wisdom that the Wisdom of Solomon foregrounds.[1268]

At Luke 9:22 Luke retained tradition's persons – the elders, chief priests, and scribes – who with the High Priest constituted the Sanhedrin that secured Jesus' death. These were the Jesus movement's antagonists, who, as the Sanhedrin, engaged in a sequence of confrontations in Jerusalem: with Jesus;[1269] Peter and John;[1270] the apostles,[1271] and finally Stephen.[1272] Within this sequence Luke emphasized ways in which Jesus and his followers exemplified wisdom's characteristics, perhaps especially in their being filled with holy spirit;[1273] this is true especially of Stephen.[1274]

Luke's reference to the prophets who foretold the coming of the righteous one (Acts 7:52) deserves attention; given Luke's debts to Wisdom, there is much to be said for at least wondering whether those prophets might be extra-canonical and from among those holy souls whom Wisdom, in every generation, makes friends of God and prophets[1275] – significantly Luke-Acts knows of Christian prophets.[1276] Per contra, the Sanhedrin's groups[1277] plot,

---

[1268] Wis. 2:5–5:8 models the conflict.

[1269] Luke 22:63–23:25.

[1270] Acts 4:1–22.

[1271] Acts 5:17–42.

[1272] Acts 6:8–8:3; Paul's encounters with the Sanhedrin parallel this sequence, but have their own narrative development – from Acts 8:3 forward.

[1273] βουλὴν δέ σου τίς ἔγνω, εἰ μὴ σὺ ἔδωκας σοφίαν καὶ ἔπεμψας τὸ ἅγιόν σου πνεῦμα ἀπὸ ὑψίστων; cf. Ps. 142:10; Wis. 6–9:18.

[1274] Acts 6:3, 8; 7:55.

[1275] Wis. 7:27–28.

[1276] John is a prophet (Luke 7:24–30); but see especially Acts 13:1; 15:32; 19:6; 21:9 (Philip's daughters), 10. That Jesus is a prophet who fulfils the Moses' oracle (Deut. 18:15, 18) may reflect the same thought-world.

[1277] Named exceptions are Joseph (Luke 23:50–53) and Gamaliel (Acts 5:33–40).

293

scheme, encompass the death of good men; they are the "rulers" of Pss. 145, 117 and 2, so of Acts 4:1–28.[1278]

One aspect of Luke's thought-world is the Pharisee/Sadducee divide that probably emerged from Israel's post-Seleucid conflicts, complicated by Jesus' own conflict with Pharisees and scribes (of whichever sect (αἵρεσις). His is a thought-world discernible in the literature to which Luke appeals: the righteous and the impious divide sharply, with the latter oppressing the righteous – notably John, and Jesus. Both are wisdom's children – though radically different,[1279] as tradition had emphasized by the division crystallized in Luke 16:16,[1280] presaged in the Prologue's presentation of each of them. Each was distinctively wisdom's child. Their life-stories demonstrate how Wisdom discerned and taught the role of God's wisdom, God's spirit; but Jesus, not John, is the δίκαιος. Unsurprisingly, Luke's Paul concludes, "by [Jesus] everyone who entrusts himself (ὁ πιστεύων) to God is reckoned to be among the δίκαιοι."[1281]

2. Πίστις/Πιστεύω

This thread reaches back into pre-Lukan Jesus-tradition. In his first volume Luke shares two instances of his ἡ πίστις σου σέσωκέν σε[1282] with Mark and one with Matthew. Throughout this tradition, πίστις carries a sense of trust, often of entrusting oneself to another or to a conviction.[1283] Its verbal form, πιστεύω,

---

[1278] See Wis. 2:6–24, a passage addressed to "those who judge."

[1279] Luke 7:24–35.

[1280] This *logion* highlights Luke's approach to retelling Jesus' story: John is the forerunner; Jesus' many descriptors point to his climactic role in the issue of God's sovereignty, a key issue for Wis. (see, e.g., Wis. 6:3–5).

[1281] Cf. e.g., Wright, N.T. (2015: 91).

[1282] Luke 7:50; 8:48; 17:19; 18:42.

[1283] E.g., Luke 5:20; 7:9; 8:25; 17:5, 6; 18:8; 22:32.

reflects this sense.[1284] Notably, most appearances (75%) of this word-group fall in sayings attributed to Jesus; a link between trust and "saving" is rooted in Jesus' activity.

In Acts, trusting or believing is one response to the apostles' message: for example, those who welcomed Peter's message[1285] are characterized as "those trusting or being committed."[1286] Those who heard Philip believed him and were baptized.[1287] The "trust" dimension of πιστεύω is evident in 11:21, where the large number "turning to the Lord" belongs linguistically with "who believed" (ὁ πιστεύσας), committing themselves to life in the community gathered around Jesus' story (11:20). Similarly, at Athens a few responded to Paul's proclamation of Jesus' resurrection by "joining him" and "believed,"[1288] while at Corinth many who heard (ἀκούοντες), believed (ἐπίστευον) and were baptized.[1289] On the return leg of their "work" journey, Paul and Barnabas, revisiting Antioch,[1290] strengthen the disciples' souls, appoint elders in each church, and commit[1291] them "to the Lord in whom they had come to believe, to put their trust."[1292]

[1284] Luke 1:20, 45; 8:12, 13, 50; 16:11 (entrust); 20:15; 22:67; we defer discussion of 24:25 to Ch. 10. Cf. Wis. 1:2; 12:2; 16:26; 18:6; Pss. 26:13; 77:21–22; 105:12, 24; 115:1; 118:66.

[1285] Acts 2:41–2.

[1286] Acts 2:44; 5:14, οἱ πιστεύοντες; cf. 4:32, τῶν πιστευσάντων.

[1287] Acts 8:12–13.

[1288] Acts 17:34.

[1289] Acts 18:8.

[1290] Acts 13:50; 14:21–3.

[1291] Cf. Luke 23:46, echoing Ps. 30:5.

[1292] Acts 14:23, τῷ κυρίῳ εἰς ὃν πεπιστεύκεισαν.

iv. Cornelius and trusting (Acts 10:34–48)

The Cornelius episode both exemplifies that sense of πιστεύω sketched above, and sheds more light on Paul's Antioch sermon; this centurion is described as ἀνὴρ δίκαιος καὶ φοβούμενος τὸν θεόν.[1293] Significantly, Peter's conclusion, paralleling Paul's at Acts 13:38, is that "everyone who trusts in him (πάντα τὸν πιστεύοντα εἰς αὐτόν) receives forgiveness of sins through his name."[1294] a conclusion cohering with "the prophets."[1295] Luke notes the descent of the Spirit[1296] and agreement among the disciples with Peter that these Gentiles should be baptized in the name of Jesus Christ.

Peter later reminds the Jerusalem assembly[1297] that God had chosen him as the one through whom Gentiles would first "hear the message of the gospel and believe,"[1298] where "believe" apparently implies the whole complex of repentance, God's forgiveness, Spirit, baptism, and community with the followers of Jesus. Peter's resume concludes: "but through the grace of the Lord Jesus, we trust to be saved (πιστεύομεν σωθῆναι) in the same way as they."[1299] Luke's narrative thread about Peter and Cornelius has prepared readers for this crystallization of theology on the edge of a critical decision. Peter's account of initiating Gentiles into discipleship[1300] and Paul's reporting to Antiochene Jews and God-fearers his own understanding of what God had done in and through Jesus[1301] stand within a long, coherent Lukan trajectory.

[1293] Acts 10:22.

[1294] Acts 10:43.

[1295] Cf. Acts 13:40.

[1296] Cf. Luke 24:49.

[1297] Acts 15:6–21.

[1298] Acts 15:7, ἀκοῦσαι τὰ ἔθνη τὸν λόγον τοῦ εὐαγγελίου καὶ πιστεῦσαι.

[1299] Acts 15:11.

[1300] Cf. Acts 15:10.

[1301] Acts 13:38–9.

3. Summary

Luke's use of the πίστ-group follows a clear pattern. As in his first volume, trust leads to healing[1302] or entry into the new community;[1303] it also becomes, like δίκαιος, a descriptor of one characterized by the commitment that he exercises.[1304] By extension, ἡ πίστις occasionally seems to signify what is trusted in – an absolute use;[1305] in this sense it is not dissimilar to 20:21 or 24:24. Paul's vision crystallizes Luke's use:

> to open [Gentiles'] eyes so that they may turn from darkness to light and from the power of Satan to God, so that they may receive forgiveness of sins and a share among those who are sanctified by faith in me (Acts 26:18).

"Those who are sanctified by faith in me" sounds very like the righteous, and like the praying tax collector who, having entrusted himself to God, went home having become δίκαιος.[1306] By using ἐδόξασαν τὸν θεὸν[1307] in relation to these events, Luke relates them to God's plan revealed in scripture – although for Luke it is a plan substantially known only in retrospect.

I have argued elsewhere that this δόξ-phrase acts "as a clear Lukan signal for those moments when God's purposes to save people, purposes already revealed in scripture, are now being fulfilled in Jesus' activity."[1308] Those in Jerusalem who had first questioned Peter about the Cornelius incident,[1309]

[1302] Acts 3:16 bis; 14:9 15:9.

[1303] Acts 14:27; 20:20–21.

[1304] Acts 6:5; 11:24.

[1305] Acts 6:7; 13:8; 14:22; 16:5.

[1306] δεδικαιωμένος; Luke 18:14.

[1307] Acts 11:18.

[1308] Doble (1996: 53ff).

[1309] Acts 11:1–18.

impressed by his report of what God had done, were silenced, and glorified God. Later, Paul reported to James what God had been doing during his ministry to Gentiles and his hearers also "glorified God."[1310] Ascribing glory to God reflects a measured, wondering response to new events newly located in God's ordering of things: Jew and Gentile in one Abrahamic community.[1311] Unsurprisingly, then, Luke's Paul concludes, "by [Jesus] everyone who entrusts himself to God is reckoned to be among the δίκαιοι."[1312]

[1310] Acts 21:17–26; cf. "the People," who had been astonished by a lame man's changed life, "glorified God" for what had happened, unlike their rulers who tried to stifle news of it (Acts 4:16–18, 21).

[1311] See Acts 3:25–26; Ch. 5. On Luke's attitude to Jews, see, e.g., Brawley (1998: 279–96); idem. (1987); Morgan-Wynne (2014); Phillips (1998: 313–26) (for bibliography on topic); Sanders, J.T. (1998: 297–312); idem. (1987); Thompson (1998: 327–44); Wright, N.T. (2013). My own conclusion is that implied in James's quoting Amos – that God's act in Jesus was the rebuilding of David's house so that the nations might call on God; for Luke, the People of God is widened to include Jew and Gentile (cf. Acts 3:25–26).

[1312] The letter from the brothers in Jerusalem to the Gentile brothers in Antioch, Syria and Cilicia (Acts 15:23b–29 falls outside *Interpreter*'s remit, but for Luke-Acts' coherence we note the thread that makes Jesus-followers heirs of his Torah-fidelity: Acts 10:36–48; 11:4–18; 14:27; 15:4–21; cf. 3:25–26. The core Jerusalem issue was circumcision, not Torah.

D. Summary

This reading of Paul's sermon dissents from some recent readings in four key areas: in its method; in its underlying hypothesis; in its hermeneutical matrix consequent on that hypothesis; in its focus on Jesus' resurrection.[1313] But a reading produced by the synergy of these factors probably makes most sense of the evidence.[1314] In this chapter's distinctive re-reading, Paul's good news for Antioch is not only the sole example in Luke-Acts of Paul's synagogue preaching, but also coheres with Luke 1–3, both its Infancy Gospel (Luke's reference-frame) and John the Baptist traditions, its distinctively Lukan emphases meeting in Jesus – God has fulfilled ancient promises.[1315] Paul's midrash meets Theophilus's hypothesized need for security about the "things fulfilled among us"; Jesus' resurrection has its witnesses, and is also rooted in God's scriptural promises that comprise Israel's hope. This case is argued through midrash – we noted how central to Paul's activity is the ferment of debate around Israel's scriptures – revealing how his hermeneutic key, that God raised Jesus from the dead, allowed him to reinterpret a group of mutually illuminating scriptural passages that had been explored at Qumran, and later by the writer of Hebrews;[1316] Antioch's sermon builds on traditions found in the other Synoptic Gospels, in Paul's letters, but uniquely on Luke's distinctive subtext.

We have listened to a Jewish Paul, in a Diaspora synagogue, re-interpreting Israel's scriptures, and proclaiming "the things fulfilled among us."

[1313] E.g., Bock (2012); Johnson, L.T. (1991; 1992; 2013); Morgan-Wynne (2014); Parsons (2008); Pervo (2009). See Wright, N.T. (1992: 378–384).

[1314] Building (by abductive reasoning) on my approach to Stephen's speech (Doble, 2013), differing from *idem* (2006), sustaining their David-focus, especially their attention to psalms. See Moyise (2012: 34–36, 39–41).

[1315] Contra Conzelmann (1961: 18n1, 22n2, 24–5, 75n4, 172, 174n1, 193n5).

[1316] Building on Wright, N.T. (2003: 149, 277–374 on Paul, 647–660 on Luke).

But a mixed reception awaited Paul everywhere.[1317] Luke-Acts has made clear that activity in Jesus' name involves transformed personal biography (living) as much as verbal witnessing. Following Jesus is costly: his Son of Man descriptor, evoking Daniel's corporate model of the saints[1318] of the Most High, reinterprets Messiah, and for Luke, and Paul, Jesus is emphatically Israel's Messiah. The costliness of following him is a taking up a cross as those already condemned yet following in the conflict between the Kingdom of God and this present age. Peter had demonstrated its riskiness; Stephen had borne witness to its ultimate cost;[1319] Paul's letters glancingly tell of his own suffering.[1320]

This sermon contributes to dissolving Luke's alleged oxymoron at Luke 24:26, 46. Here we learn where it is written that the Messiah must be raised from the dead; here we discover how Luke's case may be argued from scripture. This unique example of Paul's synagogue preaching is clearly a hermeneutically significant passage in Luke's overall narrative that ultimately brings God's Kingship into focus in Rome in the "things about the Lord, Jesus Messiah" (Acts 28:31). Luke was not mistaken.

[1317] E.g., Acts 13:42–52; cf. 28:23–28.

[1318] In Acts, is δίκαιος reserved largely for Jesus, and "saints" for Jesus-followers? Both descriptors are corporate terms for Torah-focused Jewish reformists.

[1319] Acts 6:8–8:3.

[1320] Acts 9:10–18; cf. 2 Cor. 11:16–33; Phil. 1:12–14.

Part IV. Two Conclusions

Chapter 9. "It is written"

This chapter addresses the third of the issues we proposed in Chapter 1 as Luke's purpose for securing Theophilus's confidence (ἀσφάλεια): were Christian claims about Jesus truly grounded in Israel's scriptures? Luke's relationship with Israel's scriptures is structural; his retelling of Jesus' story is embedded within those scriptures and cannot be told without them. Its structure comprises a frame enclosing a narrative whose lexical palette is drawn from scriptural models or patterns, and whose purpose is to show how its events are "the things fulfilled among us" (Luke 1:1–4).

Interpreter addresses one focal problem: was Luke mistaken in twice affirming that "it is written" that the Messiah must suffer and be raised from the dead?[1321] Given that Luke's interpretative perspective was from his (Jewish) Weltanschauung-transforming event of God's raising Jesus from the dead, I have demonstrated in Parts I and II that he was not mistaken. For Luke, event governs interpretation.[1322]

Luke's triptych introduced Jesus,[1323] affirming that the subsequent narrative concerned the house of David and God's promises made about David's seed.[1324] Luke's introduction offers readers a roadmap through Luke's

---

[1321] Luke 24:25–27; 44–49; see Ch. 1; Doble (1996; 2000; 2004; 2006a; cf. 2013; 2014).

[1322] Chs 3–6.

[1323] Luke 1:26–38; 2:1–7; 8–20; see Ch. 2.

[1324] I will raise up – ἀναστήσω.

narrative,[1325] to its conclusion in Rome. There, Paul's encounter with its principal Jews re-affirmed those "things fulfilled among us" and their significance for his hearers. Luke's first-announced messianic descriptors, Saviour, Messiah and Lord (Luke 2:11), are also those of his narrative's closing scenes (Acts 28:28, 30–31), and the commonest throughout Jesus' story, where Christian proclamation was of Jesus, Lord and Messiah.

Further, by examining six of Jesus' witnesses' exegetical speeches I have shown:[1326]

(a) how their Jewish scriptural reasoning focused on explaining Jesus-*logia* (see chapters 4 to 6) or Lukan base-texts;[1327]

(b) where "it is written" that the Messiah "must suffer and be raised from the dead." Given *Interpreter*'s argument, this chapter crystallizes how Luke used scripture.

By understanding how Luke "used" Israel's scriptures, we can grasp what he probably understood by "fulfilment."[1328] Luke's narrative perspective is from the event of God's having raised Jesus from the dead; the principle of event controlling interpretation operates throughout Luke-Acts. Luke read his scriptures through this new, previously inconceivable lens and, as Acts' final scene makes plain, in his narrative this use remained disputable.[1329] "I will raise up" (ἀναστήσω) now carried two distinct meanings, both "fulfilled."[1330] Luke's retrospective reading became visible as his "using" scripture became clearer.

This chapter's five sections indicate the shape of this reading:

(A) a reference-frame encloses

[1325] See Ch. 1.

[1326] For Stephen's and Paul's exegetical speeches see Ch. 7 Ch. 8.

[1327] See section C.

[1328] Luke 1:1; see Dodd (1952: 27); Hays (2015; 2016).

[1329] Acts 28:23–31.

[1330] See Ch. 8.

(B) Luke-Acts continuous narrative, whose shaping is significant, and

(C) whose conflict narrative's exploiting of Jesus-descriptors

(D) forms part of a vigorous debate about scripture; and

(E) discusses resonances, evoked wholes, and labelling.

A. A reference-frame

I use "reference-frame" analogously.[1331] An acknowledged literary artist, Luke encloses his fulfilment-story about a Davidic-Jesus within his Prologue's Jesus-triptych and his narrative's final scene in Rome (Acts 28:17–31).[1332]

1. Memory and remembering

Interpreter accents this reference-framing because while both Matthew and John have forms of Prologue, Luke's is distinctively programmatic. One question implied by our research focus – what is Luke's concept of Messiah?[1333] – prompted a search from within his narrative. We identified his base-text (2 Sam. 7:8b–16) and its implications in his Prologue,[1334] concluding that Luke's concept underlay his narrative and was clarified by his account of Jesus' resurrection.[1335] Luke shared his interest in this base-text with 4Q174, and like its interpreter concluded that Amos 9:11–12 summarized the goal towards which the historically-failed David-promise still hopefully looked (Acts 15:13b–21).

James's summarizing of the Jerusalem debate again depends on his deploying the principle that event governs interpretation. His introductory "the words of the prophets agree with [Peter's report]" (Acts 15:15; contra NRSV *ad loc*) followed by γέγραπται presents his adaptation of Amos's oracle, Luke's final version of the David-promise. With both Stephen's speech focused on the bivalence of "He shall build a house for my name" and Paul's unpacking of "I

[1331] I.e. both structurally and pictorially.

[1332] See his Preface, Luke 1:1, for his fulfilment story: περὶ τῶν πεπληροφορημένων ἐν ἡμῖν πραγμάτων. See Ch. 2 for his Prologue's Jesus-triptych.

[1333] See Ch. 1.

[1334] Promises respecting David's seed (ἀναστήσω) and David's house (πιστωθήσεται).

[1335] See Ch. 3.

will raise up your seed after you" in mind, Luke's readers could recognize in James's evocation of the twice affirmed duo in Amos 9:11–12 – ἀναστήσω, ἀνοικοδομήσω – this prophet's echo from Nathan's oracle: ἀναστήσω τὸ σπέρμα σου followed by αὐτὸς οἰκοδομήσει μοι οἶκον and its accompanying assurance of the endurance of David's house.[1336]

Luke's Prologue is further distinguished by its embracing one oracle from Ezekiel 34 on renewal of the David-promise during the Babylonian Exile,[1337] an extension that offers Luke's first use of the term Messiah and a context for his distinctive understanding of Saviour and its related concepts,[1338] enriching and extending tradition's Isaianic understanding of John the Baptist's prophetic activity – "all flesh shall see God's salvation."[1339]

2. The frame's purpose

Luke-Acts' concluding exchanges in Rome encapsulate the kerygmatic ground of "this salvation of God" developed in the narrative to this point.[1340] Jesus is Paul's focus for scriptural understanding: the Kingdom of God and Jesus' relation to it are contained in Luke's "things about Jesus";[1341] Jesus as Israel's hope of a Messiah, the Lord raised up beyond mortality, are bound up in this Lukan shorthand. Luke-Acts' Prologue announced these goals through its two Jesus-annunciations. Reference-framing encloses a coherent narrative, shaping its development and controlling its interpretation of scripture. Luke's

---

[1336] See Ch.7 and Ch. 8.

[1337] Ezek. 34:2–31, esp. 23–24.

[1338] Ch. 2. See section B on Luke's structural *Exodus* thread.

[1339] Luke 3:4b–6 (Isa. 40:3–5 adapted); Mk 1:2b–3 (Mal. 3:1; Isa. 40:3; conflated; adapted); Mt. 3:3b (Isa. 40:3, adapted).

[1340] Acts 28:28; see, e.g., Luke 2:11 (Saviour); 3:6 (God's salvation); 19:10 (Son of Man); Acts 4:8b (σέσωται) -12 (σωτηρία, σωθῆναι); 13:23 (σωτῆρα), 26 (σωτηρίας), 37–39; etc.

[1341] Lukan shorthand: Acts 28:31, 23; cf. 18:25; Luke 24:19 (τὰ περὶ Ἰησοῦ), 27 (τὰ περὶ ἑαυτοῦ).

distinctive retelling of Jesus' story occupies the space within his clearly marked, traditional Davidic frame.[1342]

[1342] Cf. Rom. 1:1–6; Mt.1:1; Son of David, Mk 10:47–48, etc.

B. Luke's narrative shaping

The balanced proportions of Luke-Acts[1343] become clear in the analytical diagram that distributes blocks representing Luke's text across narrative-proportion and geographical axes. These proportions resemble a normal distribution where the conflict in Jerusalem – speaking truth to power – is focal, textually-central and volume-bridging. It is focal in that its events are Luke-Acts' dynamic, crystallized by *Interpreter*'s target verses. It is textually-central to Luke-Acts in that this Jerusalem-unit occupies roughly 25 percent of the total text, preceded in Luke by about 40 percent, of which the Prologue comprises 5 percent, and followed in Acts by around 36 percent. This narrative shaping goes beyond statistics into scriptural themes, highlighting just how scripturally focused Luke-Acts really is.

1. Exodus in Jerusalem

Speaking truth to power (Luke 19:41 – Acts 8:3) evokes a wide range of scriptural resonances, among which its Exodus shaping is formative, linking one journey narrative with a second.[1344] Timed during *Pesach* – whose festival focus is rich in Exodus symbols, story, events and food references – its place in the Lukan Jesus' life is central.[1345]

His ministry, especially its conflict, was his prophetic speaking truth to power. Jesus' witnesses continued that same prophetic ministry under their

---

[1343] See Ó Fearghail (1991).

[1344] From Galilee to Jerusalem (Luke 9:51–19:40) and from Jerusalem to Rome, beginning at Acts 8:4 (see Acts 1:8).

[1345] Luke 2:41–52; See Ch. 2, appended note. See also Luke 4:1–11; Acts 6:8–8:3.

exalted Lord,[1346] and both Peter and Stephen understood Jesus to be God's promised prophet like Moses,[1347] now raised up in both senses.

Interpreter has made much of Luke's multivalent Exodus.[1348] Luke-Acts is basically a trialogue among: its Deuteronomic norm;[1349] Luke's grasp of an Isaianic vision of a new Exodus from Babylon;[1350] his distinctive account of Jesus' twofold Exodus that he was to complete in Jerusalem – his death and post-mortem leadership of a renewed People obedient to God's rule. Throughout, this Jesus is principally Israel's Davidic Messiah.

Recall that Jesus spoke truth to power (Luke 19:41 – Acts 8:3).[1351] What truth, and to which power? Jesus' Galilee ministry announced the covenant's central affirmation that God alone is Israel's King. By proclaiming that Rule of God, Jesus recalled his hearers to covenantal fidelity, implicitly warning them of the dangers of forgetting Torah. In Jerusalem, the conflict-narrative's triggers addressed the city and its rulers who in practice had so ritualized Temple and scripture as to forget, like Solomon before them, the covenant's essential commands about idolatry and neighbourly love.[1352]

Jesus' cleansing of the Temple evoked both Jeremiah and Isaiah's recalling God's foundational acts (Jer. 7; Isa. 56); his "not one stone upon another" (Luke 21:6; 1 Kgs 9:1–9) evoked the solemn warnings of Solomon's

---

[1346] Chs 4–6; see Sleeman (2009) on Jesus' continuing Lordship.

[1347] Acts 3:17–23 (Peter); 7:37, 51–53 (See Ch. 7).

[1348] Luke 9:31: lit. "a going out" from Egypt or Babylon; metaphorically, death.

[1349] Esp. Deut. 5–10; cf. Luke 4:1–11.

[1350] Esp. Isaiah 55–66.

[1351] Ezekiel's oracle excoriated Israel's shepherds who plundered and were careless of their flock (Ezek. 34; Luke 2); Luke's Isaianic subtext (Isa. 55–66) to Luke's Exodus motif contrasted the righteous and the wicked (e.g., Isa. 57; 66:2b–4). Undergirding Luke's account of Peter's transformation, Psalm 145 celebrated Israel's God as the One to obey. Ps. 2:1–2 contrasted with Ps. 2:7–8. The Jerusalem-conflict was between those who "listened" and rulers who would not.

[1352] Highlighted by, but not limited to, Luke 16.

second theophany and probably memories of Shiloh (1 Kgs 9:1–9; Jer. 7:3–15).[1353] His vineyard parable, however, resonated not only with an early Isaiah's warnings (Isa. 5:1–7) but, by highlighting the rejection and killing of its owner's son and heir, echoed Luke's own narrative of Jesus' anointing.[1354] This central, bridging section of Luke-Acts is enclosed by two journey narratives. Together, they ensure that readers understand this conflict as Jesus' Exodus in Jerusalem.

2. Reading backwards from Jerusalem

Looking back from the Jerusalem towards which Jesus had firmly set his face Luke's distinctive interpretation of Jesus' story becomes clearer. It is what Luke has to say about his protagonist that gives his narrative its unity: his Transfiguration; his (Messiah's) mission; his (Messiah's) wilderness testing, and the Prologue's final scene form the core of Luke's pre-Jerusalem portrayal of Jesus.

What Luke does not say of Jesus should, however, also be clearly heard: he was indeed a true *Davidid*, but not via Solomon. Luke's Jesus-genealogy (Luke 3:23–38) spoke volumes to an age where Sirach's assessment of Solomon (Sirach 47:12–22; 1 Kgs 11:1–13) crystallized the reasons underlying Israel's continuing hope in the David-promise: Solomon's youthful wisdom, however famed, proved no guarantee of his ultimate Torah-fidelity.[1355] Luke-Acts implicitly contrasts Jesus' story with Solomon's.[1356] Jesus' witnesses finally recognized in this Son of David God's promised prophet like

---

[1353] See Ch. 7.

[1354] Luke 3:21–22; cf. Ps. 2:7b–8; see Doble (2014). Cf. Luke's Son of God thread (reversed): Luke 22:70; 9:35; 3:21–22; 1:32, 35. Cf. Paul, Acts 9:20.

[1355] On 1 Kgs 3–11 see Brueggemann (2005).

[1356] On Acts 7:47–53 see Ch. 7.

Moses,[1357] and affirmed his Torah-fidelity to his death – he was ὄντως δίκαιος;[1358] another Exodus colouring.

i. Transfiguration (Luke 9:28–36)

On the verge of Luke-Acts' first journey narrative[1359] this distinctive version of a shared story is an Exodus way-marker.[1360] On this mountain Moses and Elijah, recalling Sinai and Carmel, belong to a broader synoptic tradition. Distinctively Lukan, however, is its disclosure that these three prophets were discussing the Exodus that Jesus was to fulfil or complete in Jerusalem. Luke-Acts' later developments disambiguate ἔξοδος to be both his death and his leading a new Exodus to freedom to be God's People.

This unit's end-stress is on three apostles' Sinai-evoking experience of a *bat qol* speaking from a cloud, affirming for them Jesus' anointing: "this is my Son; listen to him."[1361] But readers had learnt earlier of Jesus' anointing commission: "you are my Son" (Luke 3:21–22) was God's purposeful anointing, clarified by Jesus' programmatic sermon at Nazareth.

ii. Jesus' Nazareth programme (Luke 4:16–30)

A Lukan distinctive, this account of Jesus' address draws upon Luke's Isaianic new Exodus base comprising Isaiah 55–66.[1362] From this base he later identified Jesus as the one promised as covenanting "David's holy things" (Isa.

[1357] Acts 3:13–26 (Peter, Ch. 4); 7:2–56 (See Ch. 7).

[1358] Luke 23:47; Acts 3:14 (Peter); 7:52 (Stephen); 22:14 (Ananias to Paul); cf. Wis. 2:18; 10:15–11:14.

[1359] Cf. Mk 9:2–18; Mt. 17:1–8.

[1360] Marked by its recalling Jesus-followers and crowds to the word of God and to neighbourly love.

[1361] Deut. 18:15, αὐτοῦ ἀκούσεσθε, cf. 18:18–19.

[1362] See Ch. 7.

55:3),[1363] equipped to proclaim the completion of Israel's incomplete return from Babylonian exile.[1364] Luke's Nazareth unit has two parts: the first identifies Jesus' commissioned ministry programme;[1365] the second deals with the role of signs in his ministry.

Luke presents Jesus as lector and interpreter in his home synagogue. The lection from Isa. 61:1–2 ends mid-sentence, probably an *aposiopesis* allowing hearers to recall what the Lord's "favourable year" entails. Significantly, this lector is that Jesus previously identified as David's promised seed, anointed by God and filled with the Holy Spirit, anointed as "my Son." Jesus identified his mission, according to the scriptures, as the new Exodus envisioned by Isaiah in one of a succession of oracles:

> The Spirit of the Lord is upon me,
> because he has anointed me
> to bring good news to the poor [...]
> to herald the year of the Lord's favour (Luke 4:19).[1366]

Jesus' programme starkly contrasted with Solomon's amassing riches by exploiting people; and with his hearers' own experience of Herodian rule under Roman suzerainty. Amazed by what they had heard from someone they knew – that God had anointed him to inaugurate this year – they wondered, "Is not this Joseph's son?"[1367]

This home-grown prophet knew, however, that his ministry (Isa. 55:1–5; cf. Acts 13:34b associated with Ps. 2:7) depended not on signs,[1368] but on his and his hearers' faithfulness to God's word; that this new Exodus (Isa. 55:6–

[1363] See Ch. 8.

[1364] On Luke's uses of Isa. 55–66 see Ch. 7.

[1365] See Doble (1996: 25–69).

[1366] κηρύξαι ἐνιαυτὸν κυρίου δεκτόν whose source-text continues καὶ ἡμέραν ἀνταποδόσεως, which, in the light of its context, is better understood as recompense in a good sense than as vengeance.

[1367] Cf. Luke 3:23; on Jesus' sonships see Ch. 2 and Ch. 9.

[1368] Luke 4:23; cf. Luke 11:29–32 (the sign of the Son of Man); 23:6–9 (a Herod hoped-for a sign).

13) was Israel's movement to an enlarged understanding of the people of God.[1369] Elijah and Elisha before him had brought signs only to aliens, a Sidonian and a Syrian. His refusal of a sign to validate his role in God's renewed Exodus plan was of a piece with Jesus' earlier wilderness testing.

iii. Wilderness testing (Luke 4:1–11)

Narratively, the newly-anointed Jesus was led by the Spirit into the wilderness, there reliving Israel's Exodus. His twofold γέγραπται – and parallel εἴρηται citing events from Deuteronomy 6–9, echoing Moses' own Exodus – affirm that David's later seed rejected the lures of power and institutional religiosity seducing Israel to forget the God-givenness of all that is.[1370]

Luke's distinctively ordered sequencing prepares readers for the radical conflict between this man who had humbled himself and those who had exalted themselves.[1371] His testing (a) began with the very heart of Torah; (b) faced the seductions that had made Israel a rebellious People; and (c) concluded with the possibility that both scripture and Temple remained potential, corruptible sources of testing. In Nazareth, Jesus publicly embraced an Isaianic vision; that newly-anointed Jesus had already undergone personal testing that established his faithfulness in the covenant community committed to live by Torah, serving God and loving neighbour. In the wilderness, each of Jesus' replies evoked Deuteronomy's wider context.[1372]

[1369] Isa. 56:1–8; cf. Luke's fuller citing of Isa. 40 – καὶ ὄψεται πᾶσα σὰρξ τὸ σωτήριον τοῦ θεοῦ (Luke 3:4–6).

[1370] The tempter's γέγραπται formed part of Jesus' testing: Torah carried more weight than a psalmist.

[1371] Luke 14:11; 18:14b; cf. Deut. 8:2–3, 11–16.

[1372] Esp. Deut. 5–10.

a. The Word of God (Luke 4:1–4; Deut. 8:1–5)

"Man shall not live by bread only" (Luke 4:4). For a Jew of Jesus' time his reply's unexpressed "but by every Word coming from the mouth of God" embraced not only Torah,[1373] but also creation.[1374] Among other sources, Pss. 30–36 are psalms of the righteous ascribed to David. See especially Ps. 32:6–12 with its affirmation:

> because [the Lord] it was who spoke, and [the universe] came to be;
>
> He it was who commanded, and they were created (Ps. 32:9).[1375]

Among the righteous, Torah-observant Israelites, human life is more than satisfying appetites; it is learning dependence on God for things created, and for Torah by which to live wisely and well.[1376] In God's creation stones are stones and bread is bread.

b. Neighbour-blind power corrupts (Luke 4:5–8; 16:13; Deut. 8:1–20)

By contrast, this test's imagery asserts that it is not God but the tempter in whose gift the world lies; here is the ultimate corruption underlying Jesus' vineyard parable and its echoing Ps. 2:7–8 – "if you are the Son of God."[1377] Again, differing from Matthew's version of this dual tradition, Luke's imagery includes no overt reference to a mountain, but his choice of verb, ἀνάγω, almost

---

[1373] Though quoted by Mt.4:4.

[1374] Gen. 1:1–31 "and God said"; cf. John 1:1–18; Proverbs 8:22–36; Wis. 9:1–4.

[1375] Ps. 32:9; note that the Lukan Jesus' final trusting word cited Ps. 30:6 (Luke 23:46); see Doble (1996).

[1376] Wis. 16:24–26; ἵνα μάθωσιν οἱ υἱοί σου, οὓς ἠγάπησας, κύριε, ὅτι οὐχ αἱ γενέσεις τῶν καρπῶν τρέφουσιν ἄνθρωπον, ἀλλὰ τὸ ῥῆμά σου τοὺς σοὶ πιστεύοντας διατηρεῖ.

[1377] Luke 3:21–22; 20:13–15a.

certainly evokes his understanding its presence. This Pisgah-like viewing is not of a Promised Land of neighbourly concern and human flourishing, but a corruption of Nebo, now promising world domination and exploitation.[1378] At its heart stands the lie: ὅτι ἐμοὶ παραδέδοται καὶ ᾧ ἐὰν θέλω δίδωμι αὐτήν, based on the fundamental corruption, σὺ οὖν ἐὰν προσκυνήσῃς ἐνώπιον ἐμοῦ, ἔσται σοῦ πᾶσα (Deut. 5:6–12). *Interpreter* has urged that Jesus' charge against Jerusalem's rulers, and others in Israel, was that their minds (seduced by selfish "accumulationitis": Πλεονεξία) and deeds (careless of their neighbours' needs) were idolatrous: he called their idol Mammon. Stephen's charge against the same rulers equated them with those who worshipped the golden calf at Sinai.

Systems that lust for riches and power placed, and still place, self-aggrandizement above gratitude for what is essentially gift; above reverence for its Giver, and above neighbourly love for fellow humans for whom also that gift was given. "Worship the Lord your God; and serve only him"; in God's creation neighbourly sharing is the service of the One who is alone to be worshipped; none can serve God and Mammon (Luke 16:13 / Mt.6:24) – not even Solomon with all his glory.[1379]

c. Trusting not testing (Luke 4:9–13; Deut. 6:16, within 6:4–25)

Luke's final image is of Jerusalem's Temple, the site of Jesus' ultimate tests of obedience,[1380] and of conflict ending in Stephen's death. Among a ruling elite who assumed the vineyard to be theirs to exploit, and on trial by them, Jesus answered their "who are you?" by reaffirming the descriptors in Luke 9:18–36

[1378] Parodying Deut. 34:1–5.

[1379] See Ch. 7.

[1380] Mount of Olives (Luke 22:39–46) before his interrogation by the Sanhedrin (Luke 22:66–71).

and acknowledging what they articulated,[1381] that he was David's successor and heir – Son of God.

What might validate this Messiah's anointing? What was the evidence for his authority? As a riposte to Jesus' γέγραπται the tempter offered his own test, citing a David psalm of trust, hope and deliverance:[1382] gain credence in your mission by performing this spectacular sign promised to David. Jesus' reply called upon a passage (Deut. 6:10–25) where "it has been said" (εἴρηται) that "you shall not put the Lord your God to the test," itself evoking a passage (Num. 20:1–13) where, to pacify complaining Israelites, Moses offered them a sign to assure them of God's presence among them. Forgetfulness of God is what Jesus' mission challenged. He refused any probatory signs save Torah-fidelity and the sign of Jonah, and something greater than Solomon was there – the Son of Man who had to suffer and be raised.[1383]

iv. Jesus' first Pesach (Luke 2:35–51)

In retrospect, the final scene in Luke's Prologue prepares readers for the drama about to unfold. In Jerusalem's Temple at *Pesach,* the young Jesus, Wisdom's child,[1384] was about his father's business,[1385] engaging in debate with those who were teaching. The Exodus setting for this boy's later conflict is clear. In an earlier essay I argued for further Solomonic parallels;[1386] Elliott (1972) has argued for resurrection hints. This boy is David's seed, the Messiah who is to

---

[1381] Luke 22:70 – ὑμεῖς λέγετε ὅτι ἐγώ εἰμι.

[1382] Ps. 90:11–12, adapted.

[1383] Luke 11:27–32; cf. Acts 4:13–19.

[1384] Luke 2:40, 52; cf. 7:33–35.

[1385] Luke 2:49 ἐν τοῖς τοῦ πατρός μου; see Ch. 2, appended note.

[1386] Doble (2000).

315

suffer and be raised from the dead; the one to right Solomon's wrong and be worthy of his father's throne.[1387]

v. Summary

At key moments in his narrative, Luke prepared his readers for that moment when they learned why Jesus' set his face to go to Jerusalem:

- from his Prologue's climax, portraying the boy Jesus' first Passover;
- through the newly-anointed Jesus' wilderness testing;
- then his public proclamation of his ministry's purpose

to complete the Exodus he had initiated at Nazareth and fulfil long-held hopes of freedom from tyrannies.[1388] His was a twofold Exodus: his death through lawless hands before his incorruptible reign as God's Messiah at the head of a reconstituted Israel.[1389] His death was not the end; Jesus and his followers looked beyond that.[1390]

3. Looking forwards

The Jerusalem conflict's finale is Stephen's retelling of Israel's Exodus and of Moses' role in it, a trialogue among Deuteronomic, Isaianic and Christian narratives. He enrolled his Torah-faithless hearers among both those calf-worshipping at Sinai and Isaiah's persisting ungodly. The continuity among Sinai and Jerusalem, Torah and Temple, Moses and David lay in the Ark, to replace whose tent Solomon built the Temple,[1391] the locus for Jesus' conflict with the city's rulers. Stephen's case was that their lawlessness continued to

---

[1387] Luke 1:32–33; Wis. 9:9–12, 17–18.

[1388] See Transfiguration above; Luke 9:3–31.

[1389] In this aspect, Deuteronomy and Isaiah feature most prominently, as at Qumran.

[1390] See Ch. 3.

[1391] Ps. 131; 1 Kgs 8:1–11.

threaten not only the Temple's existence but that of Israel also; by clearly alluding to Deuteronomy 10:16 he invoked its contextualizing Torah.[1392]

On the verge of a second journey narrative, from speaking truth to power in Jerusalem to *kerygma* in Rome, Luke placed a parallel to his earlier Transfiguration narrative: Stephen's telling this Sanhedrin of his vision (Acts 7:55–56) ensured his death at their hands.[1393]

The three apostles had remained silent about their seeing Jesus in glory (Luke 9:36b); Stephen instantly bore witness to his vision in which one Exodus dimension persists: Jesus' δίκαιος-descriptor evokes not only psalms of the righteous, but Wisdom's more developed model of the righteous among the ungodly (Wis. 2–5).[1394] That model stands in a Solomonic context of God's requirements of rulers. Solomon's prayer (Wis. 9) for Σοφία is followed by an account of her guiding the People of God from Adam to Moses.

Wisdom's account of the Exodus is of special interest to *Interpreter*. Echoing Wisdom's model in chapters 2–5, the Exodus is retold as a conflict between the righteous and the ungodly (Wis. 10:15–11:14). In that conflict, Moses is pre-eminent among the righteous (Wis. 11:1–14). Luke's Stephen echoed that conflict – with ungodly Israelites replacing Egyptians. He also implied what Peter had inferred (Acts 3:17–26),[1395] that by God's raising him from the dead, Jesus was also the promised Prophet like Moses and righteous one (Acts 7:51–53).

Stephen's vision of the exalted Jesus parallels earlier witnesses: "But God raised him from the dead." Jesus' word to the Sanhedrin at his trial had been fulfilled;[1396] fulfilled in the sense that this Moses-like Prophet had been

---

[1392] See Ch. 7.

[1393] See Doble (1985, 2013).

[1394] See Ch. 7.

[1395] See Ch. 5.

[1396] Luke 22:69; Acts 7:55–56.

317

raised from the dead.[1397] Fulfilled also in the sense that, post-exaltation, Jesus' *gezerah shewa'* (Luke 22:69) needed to be reinterpreted: this righteous Prophet was standing (ἑστῶτα),[1398] not seated as David had written and Jesus said,[1399] now proleptically fulfilling Wisdom's vision of God's vindicating the Righteous One in the presence of his oppressors.[1400] Jesus' Exodus was fulfilled.

4. Ἰησοῦς

Finally, we reflect on Jesus' name in Luke-Acts' Exodus context: is this prophet like Moses the Ἰησοῦς who is like Moses? His name was of interest to Matthew also, who in his distinctive Prologue played on its echoes of Hoshea:[1401] "She will bear a son, and you [Joseph] are to name him Ἰησοῦς, for he will save his people from their sins." That Mary's and Joseph's child, of David's house, was named Joshua by divine command is significant for both Prologues. Luke-Acts seems to have drawn its understanding of the Exodus largely from Deuteronomy that concludes:

> And there has not again arisen [ἀνέστη] a prophet in Israel like
> Moses whom the LORD knew face to face (Deut. 34:10).[1402]

In an earlier passage, however, sited in the Tent of Testimony, with God present in the Cloud at its entrance,[1403] Deuteronomy reported that God had commissioned Ἰησοῦς to complete the Exodus that Moses could not, as he

---

[1397] Deut. 18:15, 18, προφήτην ἀναστήσω αὐτοῖς ἐκ τῶν ἀδελφῶν αὐτῶν ὥσπερ σέ; paralleling the unexpectedness of meaning in Nathan's oracle.

[1398] Acts 7:55 ἑστῶτα ἐκ δεξιῶν τοῦ θεοῦ; 7:56, ἐκ δεξιῶν ἑστῶτα τοῦ θεοῦ.

[1399] Ps. 109:1, Εἶπεν ὁ κύριος τῷ κυρίῳ μου Κάθου ἐκ δεξιῶν μου, adapted by Jesus at Luke 22:29.

[1400] Wis. 4:16–5:23, esp. 5:1, Τότε στήσεται ἐν παρρησίᾳ πολλῇ ὁ δίκαιος κατὰ πρόσωπον τῶν θλιψάντων αὐτόν.

[1401] For Hoshea's renaming by Moses see Num. 13:16b.

[1402] Deut. 34:9–12 (NETS); its ἀνέστη recalls the now bivalent ἀναστήσω of Deut. 18:18.

[1403] Cf. 1 Kgs 8:10–12 for a paralleling of cloud (νεφέλη) with glory (δόξα) and God's "presence."

"commanded Joshua and said, "Be manly and strong, for you shall bring the sons of Israel into the land that the Lord swore to them; he will be with you."[1404]

Deuteronomy's Joshua fulfilled his Exodus commission and died in the Land. He was, however, neither a prophet nor reported to have known God face to face.

5. A cumulative argument

Luke's retelling of Jesus' conflict-story, per contra, concludes with Stephen's vision of the exalted Jesus beyond death, having completed the Exodus that he was to fulfil in Jerusalem. Luke does play on the "save" element of Jesus' name, but in resonance with Ezekiel's oracle of a new Exodus, a gathering and bringing home of Israel's plundered and lost sheep under the aegis of David *redivivus*: "Today, in David's city a Saviour has been born for you, who is Messiah, the Lord."

The root of Jesus' name; the clarity of Luke's angelic proclamation to shepherds (Luke 2:11); the circumcision and naming of Jesus (Luke 2:21), who, Luke was at pains to emphasize, was also that promised prophet like Moses, together hint that Luke's Exodus thread is more than a glance at Deuteronomy's final paragraphs. Its οὐκ ἀνέστη ἔτι is answered by the Jesus-witnesses' repeated ὃν ὁ θεὸς ἀνέστησεν (Acts 2:24 etc.).

Interpreter's focus, Jesus' central but problematic words, are "according to the scriptures." Listening to Luke's narrative revealed how deeply set these sayings are in Luke's trialogue among (a) his reinterpreted Jesus-story; (b) Torah's requirements disclosed primarily through Deuteronomy; and (c) Isaiah's continuing hope of their Exile's end by God's restoring Israel under a faithful

---

[1404] See Deut. 31:14–23 (NETS slightly adapted) – καὶ αὐτὸς ἔσται μετὰ σοῦ. Cf. Acts 10:38 – ὅτι ὁ θεὸς ἦν μετ᾽ αὐτοῦ.

David (Acts 13:34b / Isa. 55:3–4), thereby ending in Zion their new Exodus from an incomplete Exile. Luke's evocations, allusions and echoes of Israel's covenant belong as much to his "uses" of scripture as do labelled quotations. Further, Israel's foundation story, of which the David-promise forms part, links many of the Jesus-descriptors that Luke also uses.

C. Jesus-descriptors in the conflict narrative

The core of Luke's Jesus-story is his unique standpoint on how God raised Jesus from the dead and exalted him; his death resulted from a conflict over Torah-fidelity between Jesus and Jerusalem's rulers. To tell his story, Luke drew on Jesus-descriptors that richly demonstrated that "it was written" that the Messiah was to suffer and to be raised from the dead. For example, four descriptors within the conflict-narrative are scriptural models shaping Luke's Jesus-story, evoking the cultural memory of Luke's world.

1. Son of Man (primarily Dan. 7:2–27)

The unparalleled shift in Luke 24 from Son of Man to Messiah,[1405] both descriptors common to Christian tradition, defines Luke's understanding of both terms. A Son of Man who goes to suffering and betrayal with a kiss forms the heart of Luke's Supper narrative.[1406] The Son of Man who is to rise from the dead and come in glory reaches its climax in Luke-Acts' significant *inclusio* – Luke 22:69/Acts 7:56 – which is also a Jesus-*logion* fulfilled. Evoking Daniel's visionary model of God's ultimate vindication of the faithful, suffering saints of the Most High, Luke's distinctive use carries his Jesus-story from Galilee (Luke 9:7–27; cf. 24:1–7) to its climax in Jerusalem (Acts 7:51–56).[1407] Early Christian tradition received this imperial conflict model, echoing the Maccabean example of Torah-fidelity in the face of ruthless oppression.

[1405] See Ch. 3.

[1406] Luke 22:22, 48; for Luke 22:37 see section Ei.

[1407] See Ch. 7.

2. Righteous One (primarily Wis. 2–5)

A Lukan distinctive, indebted to psalms and to Wisdom, this model was associated with Wisdom's reflection on rulers, the Exodus and its mockery of idolatry.[1408] For Luke's story, we note the significance of one *inclusio*: a centurion, crystallizing the manner of Jesus' dying, said "This man was genuinely δίκαιος" (Luke 23:47). At the climactic end of the Jerusalem-conflict, Stephen accused his hearers of having murdered the δίκαιος (Acts 7:52). Echoing that descriptor, he conflated the climax of his Son of Man model with the climax of Wisdom's righteous one: the twofold ἑστῶτα at 7:55–56, melds Wisdom's "στήσεται" (Wis. 5:1) with Jesus' (and Ps.109:1) "sitting"; Stephen saw the vindicated Son of Man/Righteous One standing (ἑστῶτα) at God's right hand.

Luke embraced this conflict-model, with its appeal for Torah-fidelity in the face of ruthless oppression by the obdurate godless in Israel (e.g., Wis. 1:16–2:11); the righteous are quite other (Wis. 2:12–20). His vision is righteous Stephen's final word – except his prayer "Lord Jesus, receive my spirit" (Acts 7:60).

3. Lord (primarily Ps. 109:1; Luke 20:41–44)

Stephen's prayer reminds us that "Lord" belongs to tradition that Luke inherited, then made his own.[1409] One of Luke's principal three, it forms an *inclusio* with his concluding picture of Paul's witnessing in Rome: Luke's Jesus-triptych (esp. Luke 2:11; Saviour, Messiah, Lord) and his summarizing Paul's kerygmatic teaching (Acts 28:30–31) illustrate Luke-Acts' Davidic reference-frame.[1410]

[1408] See section B3.

[1409] See Hurtado (2003: 140, 176,179–184, 618).

[1410] This salvation from God (28:28; cf. 13:26) has come *via* the Lord Jesus Messiah.

What is distinctively Lukan is Peter's mirroring the *logion* Jesus riddled for scribes.[1411] In his Pentecost address expounding Joel's oracle,[1412] Peter argued that God's promise had been fulfilled: "everyone who calls on the name of the Lord shall be saved."[1413] He argued his case via the event of the resurrection – understood as God's fulfilling an oath sworn to David[1414] – and the outpouring of Spirit (Acts 2:32–33). Resolving Jesus' riddle to the scribes – David was dead; he had never been exalted – Peter proclaimed that God's raising Jesus from the dead had shown how David's son could be David's Lord: "God has made him both Lord and Messiah, this Jesus whom you crucified." So at the culmination of the Jerusalem conflict-narrative dying Stephen prayed as his Lord had taught him to pray for those who were persecuting him.

4. Prophet (Deut. 18:15, 18)

Johnson (2013: 145–161) makes "prophet" the key Christological category. I find that Luke has systematically argued for Jesus as the "prophet like Moses" within a Davidic-messianic context and via his *haruzin* on Deuteronomy's "I will raise up" (ἀναστήσω).[1415] "Prophet" thus evokes the ritual-cultural memory of Moses in Israel's founding story.

5. Servant?

Within *Interpreter*'s reading of Luke's narrative there is little, if any room for the much-touted Servant-motif. I have argued that Luke rightly affirmed that "it was

---

[1411] Luke 20:41–44; Ps. 109:1.

[1412] Acts 2:14b–36; see Ch. 4.

[1413] Acts 2:21, 38–40; cf. Joel 3.

[1414] Acts 2:24–31; 2:30–31 echoes Ps. 131:11–12.

[1415] Acts 3:18–23; cf. Luke 4:24; 7:16; 13:31–35; 24. 24:19; 7:52. See Ch. 4; cf. Ch. 7.

written" that "the Messiah must suffer and be raised,"[1416] provisionally side-lining the contras.[1417] During discussions, however, two contexts have consistently been advanced as putative evidence for the suffering servant model as Luke's scriptural source for the Messiah's suffering; each must be addressed.

i. The Passover meal (Isa. 53:12)

Bracketed by "this scripture must be fulfilled in me" and "what is written about me is being fulfilled," Jesus alluded to Isa. 53:12.[1418] Here, all depends on two factors: first, whether one judges that allusion in NA[28] to derive from a Hebrew or Greek source-text and how much of its co-text is in view. A Hebrew source qualifies "a righteous one" with "my servant" (Isa. 53:11, NRSV); but LXX has no qualifying "servant," leaving δίκαιος as the subject of the one "numbered among the lawless" (LXX; NETS).

Second, what weight should be given to Luke's distinctive Son of Man framework for his account of this meal? Luke-Acts offers its distinctive fulfilment of the earlier Lukan Son of Man sayings: "Judas, are you betraying the Son of Man with a kiss?" (Luke 22:47–53) completes the table-saying about the Son of Man's destiny and betrayal (Luke 22:21–22). On the cusp of Jesus' arrival in Jerusalem, Luke had prepared readers for this moment, itself an adaptation of pre-journey sayings in Luke 9: 21–22, 44–45:

> See, we are going up to Jerusalem, and everything that is written about the Son of Man by the prophets will be accomplished. For he will be handed over to the Gentiles; and he will be mocked and insulted and spat upon. After they have flogged him, they will kill him, and on the third day he will rise again (Luke 18:31–33).

[1416] In Parts I and II we have seen Luke's reconceptualizing the word Messiah, so this descriptor is assumed in section C.

[1417] See Ch. 1 n.6.

[1418] Luke 22:37 cf. Isa. 53:10–12.

Luke's distinctive framework, drawn from tradition's descriptor, reaches its culmination in Stephen's vision of the exalted Son of Man standing as the vindicated δίκαιος at God's right hand. The balance of evidence favours a Greek source for this allusion that then cohered with two of Luke's major descriptors.[1419]

ii. The Apostles' corporate prayer (Acts 4:27, 29)

At prayer the apostles twice speak of Jesus as "your holy servant."[1420] Their speaking also of David as "your servant" (Acts 4:25), combined with this narrative-unit's David framework,[1421] especially 4:25–28, make it probable that this is a wider reference to God's servants than to any specific Isaianic construct.[1422]

[1419] Contra, Holladay (2016: 190).

[1420] Acts 4:27, 29.

[1421] Acts 4:5–31, Peter's turning and strengthening his brothers (cf. Luke 22:31–34).

[1422] With Hooker (1959); contra Mallen (2008).

D. Narrative development and debating scripture

Beyond *Interpreter*'s strict research confines Luke-Acts offers evidence that Luke's narrative is consistent with our finding that Luke rightly claimed that scripture promised a suffering Messiah to be raised from the dead. Summaries of Paul's ministry, especially of his conflict with the Sanhedrin (Acts 22:30–26:32), confirm *Interpreter*'s account.

To frame *Interpreter*'s hypothesis for Luke's purposes in writing we drew on Luke-Acts' enigmatic ending;[1423] notably, this features debate about the scriptures (Acts 28:23–24). Luke highlights its great length,[1424] and its topic clearly coheres with Luke's principal concerns: the "Kingdom of God" and "the things about Jesus." Further, Paul's final word concerns God's salvation (Acts 28:28). From beginning to end, Luke-Acts needed to confirm that "It is written."

Luke reports a Paul whose consistent proclamation is that the Messiah is Jesus. In his Thessalonica synagogue debates he argued that case from scripture, interpreting and demonstrating that the Messiah had to suffer and be raised from the dead.[1425] Luke-Acts' sequence of synagogue debates offers its window on to Luke's understanding of debates around scripture in formal,[1426] and informal settings.[1427]

[1423] See Ch. 1A1.

[1424] Remember Eutychus (Acts 20:7–12); cf. Ch. 8; Luke probably condensed Paul's Antioch sermon.

[1425] διανοίγων καὶ παρατιθέμενος. Luke used a range of verbs signifying debating and interpretative processes; e.g., ἀνακρίνω (17:4); διαλέγω (Acts 17:2; 18:4); διακατελέγχομαι (18:28); ἐκδιηγέομαι (13:41); πείθω (18:4).

[1426] E.g., in synagogues: Acts 14:1–3; 17:1–4, 10–12, 16–17; 18:4–5, 19–21; 19:8–9.

[1427] E.g., Acts 18:7–8; 19:8–10; 28:23–25a; cf. tradition's account of Jesus' own appeal to scripture.

1. Formal (synagogue) settings

Luke's Jewish focus is best understood in the light of his own *apologia* before Agrippa and Festus.[1428] That specifies the grounds for Paul's journey to Rome as his own appeal to Caesar rather than any charge against him. More tellingly, it crystallizes the Lukan Paul's reflection on his life so far in bondage to the Spirit.[1429]

Reading backwards has many virtues – Paul's *captatio benevolentiae* (Acts 26:1–3) introduced his hope in promises particularized as his focus on the resurrection as the key to the remainder of this unit (Acts 26:4–8). His vision and commission are crucial to grasping the Lukan Paul's life and work (Acts 26:15b–18). "Forgiveness of sins" is probably shorthand for the now completed Exodus, and "among those sanctified by trust in me" echoes Jesus' commissioning of his witnesses (Acts 26:18; cf. Luke 24:45–48). Then Paul's summary of his *kerygma* (Acts 26:20–23) confirms its rootedness in Jesus' teaching and its coherence with the apostles' teaching: that the Kingdom of God calls for repentance and deeds consistent with that repentance. His own teaching was of only what Moses and prophets had said would happen – "the Messiah would suffer and be the first to be raised from the dead," *Interpreter's* focal issue.

2. Informal settings

Athens (Acts 17:16–34) and Miletus (20:17–38) offer Lukan insights into Paul among Gentiles and among "Christians" whom he styles as τοῖς ἡγιασμένοις, a term we encountered in Paul's *apologia*.[1430] Our sole reason for reaching

---

[1428] Acts 26; cf. Acts 28:17–22 on Paul's "innocence."

[1429] Cf. Acts 20:22–23; δεδεμένος ἐγὼ τῷ πνεύματι [...] τὸ πνεῦμα τὸ ἅγιον κατὰ πόλιν διαμαρτύρεταί μοι λέγον ὅτι δεσμὰ καὶ θλίψεις με μένουσιν. A punning inversion?

[1430] Acts 20:32; cf. 26:18; 1 Cor. 1:2.

beyond *Interpreter*'s limits is to indicate wider confirmation of Lukan coherence in the matter of its own thesis, that Luke was not mistaken. For example, at Athens, while idolatry was a major focus, Luke presented Paul's major perspective as Ἀνάστασις[1431] – thought by hearers to be a "foreign divinity," but according to Paul's own *apologia*, "light for Gentiles."[1432] Even here, however, his practice was "to the Jew first" (Acts 17:17).

Miletus has its own interesting secondary literature, and we note here only that it links well with Paul's *apologia* and with Luke-Acts' overall development. Recalling the Paul of the letters, his foundational activity among them had included "announcing my news to you" (ἀναγγέλλω) and teaching (διδάσκω) both publicly and house to house; bearing witness to Jews and Greeks about God-ward repentance and trusting fidelity (πίστις) towards our Lord Jesus (Acts 20:21–22); going about proclaiming (κηρύσσω) God's Kingship (Acts 20:25). This foundation picture accords well with Paul's activity in Luke-Acts; the remainder of his address to the Ephesian elders resonates with the pastoral nature of this man reflected in his canonical letters.

[1431] Acts 17:18; 30–32, ἀναστήσας αὐτὸν ἐκ νεκρῶν; ἀνάστασιν νεκρῶν.

[1432] Acts 26:23; Luke 2:29–32.

E. Reference-frame: objections, resonances and evocations

This note belongs to a very different scholarly world from that of even five years ago when the commonest objection to *Interpreter*'s case was "if Nathan's oracle is so important, why is it never cited?"[1433] Discussion has moved *Neutestamentlers'* discourse to a widened, less literary-focused understanding of Luke-Acts' Weltanschauung.[1434] The role of scripture's ἀναστήσω in Luke's Jesus-triptych, in Luke 24, then in the scriptural reasoning of Acts' exegetical speeches has confirmed that what was implied was often obvious to ritual-cultural memory.

A further objection, "then why does Luke cite and label Isaiah passages?" proved far more challenging. A twofold response lies in

- the distribution of Isaianic quotations or adaptations throughout Luke-Acts and
- Luke's clear interest in Isaiah's envisioned Exodus.

Luke's protagonist is the Davidic Messiah who fulfilled Israel's uncompleted *Exodus* from Babylon. As his distinctive introduction to John the Baptist's preaching exemplifies, Luke added Isaiah's hope (Isa. 55–66) to what he shared with tradition. The analytical diagram clarifies the sitings and contexts of his Isaianic Exodus thread at key stages in Jesus' story: Jesus' Nazareth programme moves towards his Transfiguration, whose distinctive *exodos-logion* culminates in Stephen's excoriating accusations against Jesus' opponents.

[1433] Ch. 2A3.

[1434] E.g., Hays (2015, 2016); Kirk, A. (2018); Dunn (2013a); Oropeza and Moyise (2016). Cf. Larry Hurtado's blog on early Christian bookishness: https://wp.me/pYZXr-2gE.

1. Narrative distribution

In Luke 2:29–32/Isa. 49:6,[1435] Simeon's song probably evokes Luke's underlying Isaianic exodus motif of salvation to earth's end. Sharing its theme of salvation with Luke-Acts' "Saviour" and Luke's form of John the Baptist's scriptural setting, the song's φῶς ἐθνῶν and the sense agreement of "before the face of all people" with "to earth's end" together offer strong support for this probability. Paul's citing (Acts 13:47), and later alluding to this passage confirm it as part of Luke's Isaianic subtext serving his and Luke's Davidic reference-frame. For the rest, it will help to follow the analytical diagram.

i. Galilee

In Luke 3:4–6/Isa. 40:3–5 (ὡς γέγραπται ἐν βίβλῳ λόγων Ἠσαΐου τοῦ προφήτου·), John the Baptist's setting in an Isaianic context belongs to the fourfold tradition. But Luke's citation is distinctive, leading to his broader vision of a restored People – all flesh shall see God's salvation.

In Luke 4:16–19/Isa. 61:1–2 (adapted) (βιβλίον τοῦ προφήτου Ἠσαΐου καὶ ἀναπτύξας τὸ βιβλίον εὗρεν τὸν τόπον οὗ ἦν γεγραμμένον·), the picture of Jesus in Nazareth's synagogue is a Lukan distinctive, rooting Jesus' programme scripturally. Jesus speaks as God's newly-anointed and tested Messiah, Son of God: this is his public declaration of who he "is" (Luke 4:21b). His widened vision of Israel's restoration within God's purposes provoked the antipathy Luke's Prologue envisaged.

[1435] See Koet (1989: 140, 144). On the issue of referencing-framing and labelled quotations, see Ch. 2C.

330

ii. Jerusalem

Luke 19:46/Isa. 56:7 (γέγραπται) is one element in tradition's compound quotation accompanying Jesus' cleansing of the Temple that precipitated his speaking truth to power.

Luke 22:37/Isa. 53:12 (τὸ γεγραμμένον δεῖ τελεσθῆναι ἐν ἐμοί,) is an allusion, not a citation, but is often appealed to in support of a Servant reading of Luke-Acts.[1436] For fuller discussion of this passage, see section C5.

In Acts 7:49–50/Isa. 66 (καθὼς ὁ προφήτης λέγει), "What kind of house will you build for me?" expects a very different answer from Jesus' earlier "a den of robbers."[1437] Closing his speaking truth to power, Stephen makes much of Isaiah's sense-unit (Isa. 65:17–66:1–16, 22–23) that envisions God's new, post-Exilic creation.

iii. Post-Jerusalem

Philip in Acts 8:30–35 / Isa. 53:7–8 (Φίλιππος ἤκουσεν αὐτοῦ ἀναγινώσκοντος Ἡσαΐαν τὸν προφήτην)[1438] undoes Deut. 23:1. Philip's proclaiming "Jesus" to this Ethiopian eunuch as good news echoes Isa. 56:1–8,[1439] the context of Jesus' "house of prayer" compound quotation (Luke 19:46b). This is a Lukan vision of the purpose of the New Exodus, from this renewed community none is debarred.

[1436] E.g., Holladay (2016: 190); Carroll (2012: 442).

[1437] See Ch. 7.

[1438] ἡ δὲ περιοχὴ τῆς γραφῆς: portion; summary? Cf. Wis. 2:12–20; Ps. 36:12–20.

[1439] Cf. Lev. 21:16–23.

iv. Paul

In Acts 13:34b/Isa. 55:3 (οὕτως εἴρηκεν),[1440] Paul appeals to Isaiah's promise of a Davidic covenant that implies God's ἀναστήσω,[1441] embedded in Luke's otherwise unrepresented crystallization of Paul's synagogue preaching; this differs from Jesus' Nazareth programme in that it proclaims the result of Jesus' Exodus in Jerusalem.

Acts 28:25/Isa. 6:9–13 (καλῶς τὸ πνεῦμα τὸ ἅγιον ἐλάλησεν διὰ Ἡσαΐου τοῦ προφήτου πρὸς τοὺς πατέρας ὑμῶν)[1442] is Luke-Acts' concluding citation. Tradition sets this passage in the co-text of the Sower.[1443] A prophet sows the word of God but some flourish, some do not; this prophet Paul persists.

2. Isaiah

Among the major Exilic prophets, Isaiah clearly held a special place for Luke, and so was labelled, signposting his Davidic theology of salvation as Luke-Acts unfolded.[1444] Luke's distinctive Isaianic quotations and allusions come principally from within his subtext (Isa. 55–66), governed by his Davidic-Messiah frame and developing his Exodus theme.[1445] Luke's debts to tradition tend to echo his source-text's labelling formula. In an age impatient for God's promised Messiah, Isaiah's hope-filled, broader vision spoke to early Christian tradition of the character of Jesus' bivalent Exodus focused on Jerusalem. As

---

[1440] While an antecedent subject is unclear, Luke's conviction that the Holy Spirit underlay prophet's speech accords well with Wisdom's view (Wis. 7:27–28).

[1441] Isa. 55:3 (incipit cf. the Bush); see Ch. 8.

[1442] Cf. Acts 7:51–53.

[1443] Cf. Luke 8:9–10 *et par* cf. 11–15.

[1444] For Qumran's discussions of Luke's base-text (2 Sam. 7; 4Q174) and his dominant Deuteronomy and Isaiah debts, see, e.g., Vermes (1994); Ulrich (1999).

[1445] Philip's encounter with the Ethiopian is anomalous. Tradition pointed Luke to his final extract from Isaiah (Acts 28:26–27; cf. Luke 8:10; Isa. 6:9–10 adapted).

Paul announced, God's Saviour (Acts 13:23; cf. Luke 2:11) was the agent of God's salvation (Acts 13:26; cf. Acts 28:28), fulfilling God's promises to David.[1446] Ezekiel's "David," scourge of self-aggrandizing shepherds (Ezek. 34:1–24), proved to be David's Torah-faithful son, Jesus, scourge of Jerusalem's unfaithful shepherds and restorer to wholeness of God's flock. Isaiah's wider vision was that "all flesh shall see the salvation of God" (Luke 3:6; Isa. 40:5), cohering with Abraham's covenantal promise – "by your seed shall all earth's families be blessed" (Acts 3:25b; Gen. 22:18).

F. Summary

The problem of *Interpreter* originated in the denial, overt or implied, that "it is written" that the Messiah must suffer and be raised. Parts I and II offered details of where and how it was so written, but Luke-Acts' whole systematic, two-volume narrative, with its allusions, evocations and descriptor-models, is its own vindication: Luke's Jesus-story is shaped "according to the scriptures."

As the analytical diagram makes clear, Luke's story of Jesus' suffering and resurrection/exaltation constitutes Luke's bridging conflict-narrative in Jerusalem – his narrative's dynamic. His distinctive transfiguration account indicates Jesus' Exodus as the reason for Luke-Acts' very long and detailed journey narrative to Jerusalem. But in the longer journey from Bethlehem to Rome we see unfold Lukan dialogues between Second Temple Davidic hopes and John the Baptist's,[1447] then Jesus' Isaianic hopes of salvation.[1448] For Luke,

---

[1446] Ch. 8. Cf. Acts 28:31; Luke 2:11; to Rome where Paul counter-culturally proclaimed God as King and Jesus as Saviour, Messiah and Lord.

[1447] Luke 3:6 (σωτήριον τοῦ θεοῦ) / Isa. 40:5; Acts 28:28 (σωτήριον τοῦ θεοῦ) / cf. Isa. 6:1–13.

[1448] Luke 4:18–19; Isa. 61:1–2 adapted also by 58:6b.

Jesus is primarily Israel's Saviour who is the Davidic Messiah and Lord;[1449] the δίκαιος who had been tested and found faithful in his wilderness.[1450]

In Luke's hopeful world, where cultural memory and vigorous scriptural debate dominated Second Temple Judaism's life, Luke-Acts' inner logic offered the ἀσφάλεια that Theophilus sought. Peter's exegetical activities were enriched by those of Stephen and Paul. Through Jesus, God had fulfilled the twofold David-promise – of a seed and a house. Through his Messiah, Jesus, God had completed in Zion the Babylonian Exodus, and "all flesh [was seeing] God's salvation." Luke doesn't "use" scripture; he interprets it dialogically and structurally.

[1449] Luke 2:11. Cf. Acts 13:23, 26, 32–33, 47.

[1450] Luke 4:1–11; cf. 23:47; Acts 7:52, etc.

Chapter 10. Luke the Interpreter

This final chapter (A) concludes one aspect of this study of Luke's work; (B) identifies some questions raised and needing discussion; (C) offers insights to post-graduate study of Luke-Acts and to study of first-century Jewish-Christian relations; to first-century literature and intertextuality; to interpretation theory and to the study of Christian Origins.

A. Completed business

This is essentially a single-issue volume: was it "written" that the Messiah must suffer and be raised from the dead as Luke twice wrote (Luke 24:26, 46)? Or did he, as many commentators claim or imply, understand Messiah to "mean" the suffering servant; the Prophet to come; the Son of Man, or one of the prophets? Like most problems, this could be addressed only by first asking what that issue really is – it needed to be problematized. At issue is Luke-Acts' narrative coherence.

Three inherent sub-problems became clear:

(a) what was Luke's concept of Messiah? Part I presented the evidence: Luke's narrative argument was that in and through the person of Jesus God fulfilled his promise to David of "a seed" who would reign "forever."[1451]

(b) How did Luke's perceived perspective affect his "problematic" *logia*? Was his focal problem the death of the Messiah, or was it resurrection? Luke's stance on this question has long plagued scholarship. It was often characterized as somehow his failure to grasp Paul's *theologia crucis*, producing instead a

---

[1451] 2 Sam. 7:12–16; cf. Ps. 88.

335

theologia gloriae that does not deal with what his critics see as the problem. After countless readings of the NA text of Luke-Acts, and discussions with colleagues, two matters became clearer: that for his age, Luke's major problem was Jesus' unique resurrection; that in "the things fulfilled among us" the David-promise contained the seed of Luke's unique contribution. It may well be the case that the writer we call Luke became acquainted with this "fulfilment" among Jesus-followers engaged with synagogues and critics. His appeal in Luke-Acts, however, to a fourfold ἀναστήσω, argues a coherent case: an appeal rooted in the Prologue's triptych;[1452] a case highlighted by his distinctive resurrection narrative;[1453] argued from within his witnesses' exegetical speeches,[1454] and reasoned from his perspective.

(c) Finally – which proved the most demanding sub-problem – how does Luke use Israel's scriptures? "Use" is the wrong word, but that is where the trail to Part III began. "Use" carries tones of manipulation that send all the wrong signals to a hearer-reader. The volume, and often density of references or allusions to Israel's scriptures, or echoes from them, demand explanation. I hypothesized three inter-related purposes for Luke's writing,[1455] implicitly characterizing him as at home in Israel's scriptures in their Greek version(s). His writing reveals him to be a skilled scriptural interpreter for whom events are to be understood in the context of scripture, especially of Torah.

The seminar that gathers annually at Gladstone's Library at Hawarden to discuss the multifaceted issues of intertextuality provides a rich source of

---

[1452] See Ch. 2.

[1453] See Ch. 3.

[1454] Parts II and III.

[1455] Ch. 1. See also Buckwalter (1996); I am indebted to long engagement with the work of Jenny Read-Heimerdinger, especially through the volumes of Rius-Camps and Read-Heimerdinger (2004; 2006; 2007; 2009).

insight and debate.[1456] It was among its members that one conviction underlying *Interpreter* emerged: Luke's "use" of scripture is essentially structural. Sustaining the principle that event controls interpretation, he aims to demonstrate both that the promised Davidic Messiah is Jesus and that through this Messiah God has completed Israel's Exodus; all flesh might now see God's salvation.[1457]

Modelling a problem helps display its essential character and dimensions: this book's analytical diagram helps display Luke-Acts' narrative dynamics. That diagram became central to the emergent conviction that ends the previous paragraph – Luke's distinctive Jerusalem conflict-narrative is Luke-Acts' bridging narrative, its narrative-fulcrum.[1458] The diagram developed over time and use, crystallizing Luke's narrative development. Spatially, Luke takes readers from Jerusalem to Rome; chronologically, from Jerusalem's temple priest, Zachariah, to Paul of Tarsus, waiting his appearance before the Emperor in Rome and still vigorously debating scripture (Luke 1:5–20; Acts 28:23–28). Chapter 7 has detailed Jesus' movement to Jerusalem, followed by the exalted Jesus' witnesses' movement from Jerusalem to Rome. There, in an *inclusio* that cannot escape notice, from the "leadership" of the Roman Tiberius (Luke 3:1–2) to Paul's proclaiming God's reign and the role of Jesus as Lord in that reign.[1459]

[1456] https://www.gladstoneslibrary.org/.

[1457] Either/or is a logico-philosophical blunder to be avoided wherever possible; Luke has affirmed a both/and. Ch. 7 has summarized the case for Luke's understanding that the Jesus of his Prologue's reference-frame (Ch. 1 and Ch. 2 on the promised Davidic Messiah), is that same Jesus who at Nazareth announced his mission programme (Luke 4:18–21) that was confirmed at his transfiguration (Luke 9:28–36), and finally proclaimed at the Roman Empire's heart – all flesh shall "see" God's salvation; Gentiles will listen (Luke 3:6; 4:24–30; Acts 28:28).

[1458] Luke 19:41-Acts 8:3; Luke 24:45–49; Acts 1:6–8.

[1459] Acts 28:30–31; proclaiming God's βασιλείαν, and teaching τὰ περὶ τοῦ κυρίου Ἰησοῦ, a Lukan summary for Jesus' story; its political dimensions are inescapable.

337

But, as the map is not the territory, so the model is not the text, which constantly demands dialogue. This modelling diagram and its contribution to answering *Interpreter's* research question has, however, been one way of organizing this reading of Luke's work and offering it to the scholarly community as a contribution to the discussion of Luke-Acts.

As with an earlier research work,[1460] it was radical dissent from accepted scholarly wisdom that prompted this very long-term engagement with Luke-Acts. Given current understanding of tradition's transmission among earliest Christian communities,[1461] if Luke was so clearly mistaken, as Chapter 1 reports, then how did his work ever circulate among earlier Christian communities and find itself in the NT canon? This book's approach to these sub-problems was to bracket out many current questions and to focus on Luke's text, listening to it in the Weltanschauung of Second Temple Judaisms. To make this dissent discussable with colleagues the commonly used, eclectic NA texts are provisionally held to report Luke's work.

Working abductively from that eclectic text, this work has focused on tracking Luke's narrative development. *Interpreter* is not a commentary and keeps minimal engagement with secondary literature, though the bibliography reveals the many years of close engagement with and reviewing of fellow *Neutestamentlers'* work. Listening and responding to Luke's text is *Interpreter's* key approach.

From his perspective the author of Luke-Acts is not mistaken. He has demonstrated for Theophilus how his narrative about Jesus of David's house is securely grounded in Israel's scriptures: the Messiah is Jesus who has suffered and been raised from the dead (Luke 24:25–27, 44–49).

[1460] Doble (1996).

[1461] E.g., Dunn (2013a); Kelber and Byrskog (2009); Kirk, A. (2018).

338

B. Unfinished business

That approach to Luke's text raised issues lying beyond this volume's remit, but on which *Interpreter* throws light.

1. Date, historicity, unity

How does Luke's Paul cohere with Paul of the commonly accepted letters? Earlier polarization of the two figures has not survived the revolution in Pauline studies. Lukan scholars have tended to keep in touch with the Paul debate, working through *Paul and the Faithfulness of God and* its ongoing discussion.[1462] Luke appears to have been as indebted as Paul to the eyewitnesses and servants of the message active in a nascent tradition.

How do *Interpreter's* exegetical speeches relate to "history," and how does an answer relate to the Westar Seminar's work?[1463] Luke's books of the acts of God demand God-talk, and centuries of discussion can obfuscate the interpretation of scripture. Luke-Acts is a work to be understood on its own terms: what had Luke to say? The time to pose further critical questions is when one has grasped that.

Do *Interpreter's* hypothesized purposes for Luke's writing, and its conclusions outlined in section A, point to a case made before the Jewish War? Discussion of Luke-Acts' probable date will continue, but on the current evidence, a date later than the imminence of the Jewish War seems unlikely for Luke's work.[1464] Now that we have begun to digest the newer insights into Christian tradition's early transmissions, the value of internal evidence from Luke-Acts is enhanced. A date between 57 and 62AD seems probable.

[1462] Wright (2013, 2015).

[1463] Smith and Tyson (2013).

[1464] See Dodd (1947); Robinson (1976); Ellingworth (1993: 29–33), whose comments on dating are pertinent also to Luke's work; Smith, S. (2017: 193–194).

Similarly, this work contributes to the Luke-Acts or Luke and Acts discussion. *Interpreter*'s analytical diagram originated when it grew clearer that the Jerusalem conflict-narrative was arguably a planned unity overlapping two scrolls, hence this work's Luke-Acts throughout – Parts I-II have argued that case. The argument that Luke is notably absent from second-century evidence, faces the counterchallenge that the absence of evidence is not evidence of absence. Remember Qumran. Theologically, *Interpreter* also contributes to discussions prompted by Dunn (e.g., 2004, 2010) and others of Jesus' "agency."[1465] On this, one issue must be highlighted, in the next subsection.

2. His son, born of David's seed

If Luke's Jesus-story is that of God's fulfilling the David-promise, then his Jesus must be David's genetic descendant.[1466] This conclusion contributes to theological discussion of Jesus' birth. Luke's attention to Joseph's being of the "house of David" strongly accents David's "seed" (τὸ σπέρμα σου) (Luke 1:27; 2:4–7).

Jesus' Davidic descent is overtly active in the scriptural reasoning of several Acts' exegetical speeches. For example, Peter's Pentecost reasoning requires that Jesus be "the fruit of David's loins."[1467] His reasoning in Solomon's Portico associates Jesus' resurrection and exaltation as Messiah with his being the fulfilment of God's promise of "seed" to Abraham.[1468] Crystallizing the issue underlying Stephen's speech, Sirach described Solomon's failure in relation to the Christological conditional as "you defiled your seed" but "the Lord will never

---

[1465] Hays (2015: 72–74; 2016); Hurtado (e.g., 2003, et al.); Lincoln (2013); Wright (e.g., 2003, 2013).

[1466] Rom. 1:1–6; see, e.g., Le Donne (2009: 185–189).

[1467] Acts 2:30 προφήτης οὖν ὑπάρχων καὶ εἰδὼς ὅτι ὅρκῳ ὤμοσεν αὐτῷ ὁ θεὸς ἐκ καρποῦ τῆς ὀσφύος αὐτοῦ καθίσαι ἐπὶ τὸν θρόνον αὐτοῦ, echoing Ps. 131 and its recalling Nathan's oracle.

[1468] Acts 3:25 ἐν τῷ σπέρματί σου [ἐν-]ευλογηθήσονται πᾶσαι αἱ πατριαὶ τῆς γῆς.

take away the seed of [David]" so "he gave a remnant to Jacob, and to David, a root out of him."[1469]

The Lukan genealogy, from which Luke plainly excluded Solomon, affirms Jesus' Davidic descent through Joseph (Luke 3:23–38). This genealogy immediately follows Luke's account of Jesus' anointing and precedes that of his temptation. In those accounts, the descriptor "Son of God" is either implied or basic to the narrative.[1470] The genealogy's much discussed "as was thought" (ὡς ἐνομίζετο) effectively realigns reader's thinking to note that this *Davidid*, descended from Abraham and, like every human, from Adam,[1471] had been anointed by God, and was now called Son of God, as Gabriel had promised.[1472]

Consequently, *Interpreter* links Son of God primarily with Luke's conceptual map of Messiah rather than with his Prologue's account of Jesus' conception and birth.[1473] "Son of God" is a Lukan descriptor, not an ontological statement. Of course it remains arguable that Luke 1:31 echoes Isa. 7:14, but in the context of his David-promise and its function as his reference-frame, it is probable that Luke's echoing God's good news according to Paul confirms that Luke's triptych poses questions that *Interpreter* provisionally brackets out,[1474] but towards which it contributes.[1475]

[1469] Sirach 47:20–22, emphasizing how God will never abandon his mercy (τὸ ἔλεος αὐτοῦ).

[1470] Luke 3:21–22; Acts 13:33. Luke 4:1–13; 9:35; in its "son and heir," Jesus' vineyard parable appears to depend on Ps. 2:7–8, basic to the David-story and to Jesus' anointing.

[1471] Luke, 3:23, 31, 34, 38; cf. 1 Cor. 15:22.

[1472] κληθήσεται υἱὸς θεοῦ (Luke 1:35); καὶ υἱὸς ὑψίστου κληθήσεται (1:32).

[1473] Diff. Hays (2015: 60–62). Cf. Moyise (2013: 78–101). LaCocque (2015: 276–277).

[1474] See, e.g., Brooke (2000a); Brown, R. E. (1979); Gerber (2008); Lincoln (2013); Moyise (2013); see also the commentaries cited in chs 1–3.

[1475] Rom. 1:1–3 περὶ τοῦ υἱοῦ αὐτοῦ τοῦ γενομένου ἐκ σπέρματος Δαυὶδ κατὰ σάρκα.

C. Prospects

Interpreter's unfinished business suggests further post-graduate research into Luke-Acts in a number of areas.

1. Luke among the world-shapers

One key area for continuing research is Luke's implied understanding of the "Kingdom of God" in his work's political, social and economic dimensions and its relation to Jesus' call for repentance (μετάνοια) (Luke 4:42–44; 5:27–32). The core of Luke's conflict-narrative that polarizes the worship of Mammon and the service of *HaShem* currently demands far more detailed study.[1476] The community gathered around Jesus was a multiply transformed society,[1477] committed to Israel's covenantal perspective on being human and on sharing the earth's givenness.[1478] Much work has already been done in this area, but changing understandings of key areas in human knowledge require sensitive, but firm reassessments of Luke-Acts.[1479]

2. Jewish-Christian relations

How does *Interpreter* throw light on the earliest Jewish-Christian relations? A major commentary, Pervo (2009: 192–193) highlights Luke's alleged anti-

---

[1476] See, e.g., Coleman (2019), a fine doctoral study that still demands explanation of why the Lukan lens is what it is. See Kathryn Tanner's forthcoming *Christianity and the New Spirit of Capitalism, resulting from her recent Gifford Lectures*. I am currently working on a study of *Luke among the Economists*.

[1477] E.g., Gal. 3:25–29.

[1478] See, e.g., Luke 10:25–27; 18:18–22; cf. Brueggemann (2017).

[1479] Political theology is a well-tilled field. Now that many economists are rethinking their field as political economy, there is much to be said for reframing questions concerning Luke's work into "socio-political-economic theology." Kate Raworth's *Doughnut Economics* (2017) offers a framework for re-thinking many "givens" in current discussions of politico-economic theology.

Semitism, following in a tradition represented by Jack T. Sanders (1987). The position revealed by *Interpreter* is quite other – of an inner, deep-rooted sectarian dispute that finally reached Rome, a dispute that concerned "Israel's hope" and the enlarging of Judaism's embrace to "all flesh."[1480] Luke's combining his Davidic reference-frame with the Baptist's Isaianic Exodus fulfilment motif reveals a moment within Jewish history, rather than any Jewish-Christian conflict of a very different order. Pervo and Sanders reached their conclusions by first disjointing Luke's work; *Interpreter* begins from its base-line that we have in Luke's work one developing narrative, an apologia for his own time, his interpretation of the still-fluid but recognizably similar traditions emerging around the Mediterranean.[1481] This throws light on the ethnonym *Ioudaios*, clarifying that synagogues might have Diaspora or Judaean roots or links. Whether Luke was or was not Jewish is a question outside *Interpreter*'s remit. Whether *Interpreter*'s case that Luke competently argues from Israel's scriptures and traditions is for specialists to comment. Interfaith relations remain an urgent, pressing question for humanity at present; Luke's stance is an important issue.

3. Interpretation theory

Interpreter will be scrutinized from many and diverse critical angles. Its purpose has been to listen and to try to understand what Luke wanted to say to his own time. But interpretation theory remains a complex area.[1482] Similarly the study of Christian Origins extends far beyond a *Neutestamentler*'s textual world, into

---

[1480] E.g., Acts 26:4–8; Luke 1:46b–55; Acts 28:23–28.

[1481] My indebtedness to, and differences from, Tannehill (1986, 1990) will be apparent to readers who know his work.

[1482] E.g., Grimshaw (2019); Oropeza and Moyise (2016).

the fascinating study of material culture.[1483] If Luke is indeed a major NT contributor to theological discussion, then how *Interpreter*'s findings fit into a larger picture of the first and second centuries becomes a concern for interdisciplinary discussion. But NT scholars the world over have access to the critically eclectic text that Luke calls a narrative and to which *Interpreter*'s author has listened, so as to enter into dialogue with other readers of this work in two scrolls.

D. Envoi

The longest single narrative in the NT canon, Luke-Acts constitutes more than a quarter of it, a coherent *apologia,* systematically answering Theophilus's implied questions while expounding Christian *kerygma,* and itself a potent socio-economic, so political declaration deeply rooted in Israel's covenantal life. Once we have dissolved *Interpreter*'s focal issue,[1484] Luke emerges as one of the NT's major creative theologians, taking his place at Caird's apostolic conference table alongside *Auct ad Heb,* John and Paul.[1485] Not mistaken, Luke was a major interpreter of Jesus' story and of Israel's scriptures.

[1483] It is, however, a world from which *Neutestamentler* readily learn and to which they often contribute. See, e.g., Hurtado (2006); Doble and Kloha (2014).

[1484] Luke 24:26, 46.

[1485] Caird (1994).

344

Bibliography

Adams, S. A. (2006), "Luke's Preface and its Relationship to Greek Historiography: a Response to Loveday Alexander," *Jnl Greco-Roman Christianity and Judaism*, 3, 177–91.

Adams, S. A. & Pahl, M. (eds) (2012), *Issues in Luke-Acts: Selected Essays*, Piscataway, NJ: Gorgias.

Adelman, R., (2014), "Can We Apply the Term "Rewritten Bible" to Midrash? The Case of Pirqe de-Rabbi Eliezer" in *Rewritten Bible after Fifty Years: Texts, Terms, or Techniques?* Leiden: Brill, 293–317.

Ahearne-Kroll, S. P. (2007), *The Psalms of Lament in Mark's Passion: Jesus' Davidic Suffering*, SNTSMS 142, Cambridge: Cambridge University Press.

Aletti, J-N. (1989), *L'art de raconter Jésus Christ*, Paris: Éditions du Seuil.

Aletti, J-N. (1998), *Quand Luc raconte. Le récit comme théologie*, Paris: Cerf.

Alexander, L. C. (1993), *The Preface to Luke's Gospel: Literary Convention and Social Context in Luke 1:1– 4 and Acts 1:1*, SNTSMS 78, Cambridge: Cambridge University Press.

Alexander, L. C. (1998), "Fact, Fiction and the Genre of Acts," *NTS* 44:3, 380–399.

Alexander, L. C. (1999), "Formal Elements and Genre," in Moessner, D. P. (ed.), *Jesus and the Heritage of Israel,* 9–26, Harrisburg: TPI.

Alexander, L. C. (2001), "Acts," in Barton, J. & Muddiman, J. (eds) *The Oxford Bible Commentary,* 1028–1061, Oxford: Oxford University Press.

Alexander, L. C. (2005), *Acts in its Ancient Literary Context,* London: T&T Clark International.

Alexander, P. S. (1988), "Retelling the Old Testament," in Carson, D. A. & Williamson, H. G. M. (eds), *It is Written: Scripture Citing Scripture,* Essays in Honour of Barnabas Lindars, 99–121, Cambridge: Cambridge University Press.

Alexander, P. S. (2000), "Yeshu/Yeshua ben Yosef of Nazareth: Discerning the Jewish Face of Jesus," in Brooke, G. J. (ed.), *The Birth of Jesus: Biblical and Theological Reflections,* 9–22, Edinburgh: T&T Clark.

Alexander, P. S. (2001), "Post-Biblical Jewish Literature," in *Oxford Bible Commentary,* 792–829, Oxford: Oxford University Press.

Alexander, P. S. (2015), "Rabbinic and Patristic Bible Exegesis as Intertexts: Towards a Theory of Comparative Midrash," in McLay, R. T. (ed.) *The Temple in Text and Tradition,* LSTS 83, 71–97, London/New York: Bloomsbury.

Allen, D. (2018), *According to the Scriptures: the Death of Christ in the Old Testament and the New,* London: SCM.

Allen, L. C. (1968), "The Old Testament Background of (pro)ori/zein in the New Testament," *NTS* 17, 104–108.

Anderson, R. W. & Harrelson, W. (eds) (1962), *Israel's Prophetic Heritage: Essays in Honor of James Muilenberg,* New York: Harper & Bros.

Anderson, R. (1997), "Theophilus: A Proposal," *EvQ* 69:3, 195–215.

Anderson, R. (1999), "The Cross and Atonement from Luke to Hebrews," *EvQ* 71:2, 127–49.

Anderson, R. (2002), "A la Recherche de Théophile," in "Saint Luc, évangéliste et historien." *Dossiers d'Archéologie* 279, 64–71.

Arnal, W. (2011), "The Collection and Synthesis of 'Tradition' and the Second-Century Invention of Christianity," *Method & Theory in the Study of Religion,* 23(3–4), 193–215.

Arnold, B. T. (1996), "Luke's characterizing use of the Old Testament in the Book of Acts," in Witherington, B. (ed.) *History, Literature and Society in the Book of Acts,* 300–323, Cambridge: Cambridge University Press.

Baban, O. D. (2006), *On the Road Encounters in Luke-Acts,* Paternoster Biblical Monographs, Milton Keynes: Paternoster.

Bammel, E. & Moule, C. F. D.(eds) (1984), *Jesus and the Politics of His Day,* Cambridge: Cambridge University Press.

Barbour, R. S. (ed.) (1993), *The Kingdom of God and Human Society,* Edinburgh: T & T Clark.

Barenboim, D. & Said, E. (2004), *Parallels and Paradoxes,* London: Bloomsbury.

Barker, M. (2008), *Christmas: The Original Story*, London: SPCK.

Baron, L. & Oropeza, B. J. (2016), "Midrash," in Oropeza, B. J. & Moyise, S. (eds) *Exploring Intertextuality: Diverse Strategies for New Testament Interpretation of Texts,* 63–80, Eugene, OR: Cascade Books.

Barrett, C. K. (1959), "The Background of Mark 10:45," in Higgins A. J. B. (ed.) *New Testament Essays: Studies in Memory of T. W. Manson,* 1–18, Manchester: Manchester University Press.

Barrett, C. K. (1988), "Luke/Acts," in Carson, D. A. & Williamson, H. G. M. (eds) *It is Written: Scripture Citing Scripture,* Essays in Honour of Barnabas Lindars, 231–244, Cambridge: Cambridge University Press.

Barrett, C. K. (1961), *Luke the Historian in Recent Study*, London: The Epworth Press.

Barrett, C. K. (1994), *Acts* Vol I I – XIV, ICC, Edinburgh: T & T Clark.

Barrett, C. K. (1998), *Acts* Vol II XV – XXVIII, ICC, Edinburgh: T & T Clark.

Barrett, C. K. (1999), "The Historicity of Acts," *JTS* 50:2, 515–34.

Bartholomew, C. G., Green, J.B. & Thiselton, A.C. (eds) (2005), *Reading Luke: Interpretation, Reflection, Formation," Scripture and Hermeneutics Series,* Vol. 6, Grand Rapids: Zondervan.

Barton, J. (1994) "Why does the Resurrection of Christ Matter?", in Barton, S. & Stanton, G. (eds) *Resurrection* [*FS* Leslie Houlden], 108–115, London: SPCK.

Barton, J. and Muddiman, J. (eds) (2001), *The Oxford Bible Commentary,* Oxford: Oxford University Press.

Barton, S. and Stanton, G. (eds) (1994), *Resurrection* [*FS* Leslie Houlden], London: SPCK.

347

Bauckham, R. (1996), "James and the Gentiles (Acts 15:13 – 21)," in Witherington, B. (ed.) *History, Literature and Society in the Book of Acts,* 154–84, Cambridge: Cambridge University Press.

Bauckham, R. (2006), *Jesus and the Eyewitnesses,* Grand Rapids, MI/Cambridge: Eerdmans.

Bayer, H. F. (1994), "Christ-Centered Eschatology in Acts 3:17–26," in Green, J.B. & Turner, M. (eds) *Jesus of Nazareth: Lord and Christ, FS Howard Marshall,* 236–50, Grand Rapids: Eerdmans.

Beale, G. K. & Carson, D. A. (eds) (2007), *Commentary on the New Testament Use of the Old Testament,* Grand Rapids/Nottingham: Baker/Apollos.

Bechard, D. P. (2000), *Paul Outside the Walls: A Study of Luke's Socio-geographical Universalism in Acts 14:8 – 20,* AnBib 143, Rome: Pontifical Biblical Institute.

Beers, H. (2015), *The Followers of Jesus as the "Servant": Luke's Model from Isaiah for the Disciples in Luke-Acts,* London: T&T Clark.

Bellinger, W. H. (1984), *Psalmody and Prophecy,* JSOTSup 27, Sheffield: JSOT Press.

Bellinger, W. H. & Farmer, W. R. (eds) (1998), *Jesus and the Suffering Servant: Isaiah 53 and Christian Origins,* Harrisburg: TPI.

Bellinzoni, A. J. (1998), "The Gospel of Luke in the Second Century CE," in Thompson, R. P. & Phillips, T. E. (eds), *Literary Studies in Luke-Acts,* [FS J. B. Tyson], 59–76, Macon: Mercer University Press.

Ben-Chorin, S. (2001), *Brother Jesus: The Nazarene through Jewish Eyes,* Athens: University of Georgia.

Best, E. (1965), *The Temptation and the Passion: the Markan Soteriology,* SNTSMS 2, Cambridge: Cambridge University Press.

Bird, M. F. (n.d.), *Jesus and the Origins of the Gentile Mission,* Library of New Testament Studies (JSNTSup) 331, London: T & T Clark International.

Bird, M. F. (2007a), "The Unity of Luke-Acts in Recent Discussion," *JSNT* 29:4, 425–48.

Bird, M. F. (2007b), "Jesus is the "Messiah of God": Messianic Proclamation in Luke-Acts," *RefTheolRev* 66:2, 69–82.

Bock, D. L. (1987), *Proclamation from Prophecy and Pattern*, JSNTSup 12, Sheffield: JSOT Press.

Bock, D. L. (1994), "The Son of Man Seated at God's Right Hand and the Debate over Jesus' 'Blasphemy,'" in Green, J. B. and Turner, M. (eds) *Jesus of Nazareth: Lord and Christ, FS Howard Marshall,* 181–191, Grand Rapids: Eerdmans.

Bock, D. L. (1998), "Scripture and the Realization of God's Promises," in Marshall, I. H. & Peterson, D. (eds) *Witness to the Gospel: the Theology of Acts,* 41–62, Grand Rapids: Eerdmans.

Bock, D. L. (2012), *A Theology of Luke and Acts,* Grand Rapids: Zondervan.

Bockmuehl, M. (2001a), "Resurrection," in Bockmuehl, M. (ed.) *The Cambridge Companion to Jesus,* 102–18, Cambridge: Cambridge University Press.

Bockmuehl, M. (ed.) (2001b), *The Cambridge Companion to Jesus,* Cambridge: Cambridge University Press.

Bockmuehl, M. (2005), "Why Not Let Acts Be Acts? In Conversation with C. Kavin Rowe," *JSNT* 28:2, 163–66.

Bockmuehl, M. (2006), *Seeing the Word: Refocusing New Testament Study,* Studies in Theological Interpretation, Grand Rapids: Baker Academic.

Bockmuehl, M. (2012), *Simon Peter in Scripture and Memory,* Grand Rapids: Baker Academic.

Borgman, P. (2006), *The Way according to Luke: Hearing the Whole Story of Luke-Acts,* Grand Rapids/Cambridge: Eerdmans.

Bovon, F. (1978), *Luc le Théologien. Vingt-cinq ans de recherches (1950 – 1975),* Le Monde de la Bible, Neuchatel: Paris.

Bovon, F. (1987), "The Interpretation of the Old Testament," in Bovon, F. & McKinney, K. (eds) *Luke the Theologian. Thirty-three Years of research (1950 – 1983),* Allison Park: Pickwick Publishing.

Bovon, F. (1996), *"L'Évangile selon Saint Luc 9,51 – 14,35,* Commentaire du Nouveau Testament 2.IIIb, Genève: Labor et Fides.

Bovon, F. (2001), *L" Évangile selon Saint Luc 15,1 – 19,27,* Commentaire du Nouveau Testament 2.IIIc, Genève: Labor et Fides.

Bovon, F. (2005), "The Reception and Use of the Gospel of Luke in the Second Century," in Bartholomew, C. G., Green, J.B. & Thiselton, A.C. (eds) (2005), *Reading Luke: Interpretation, Reflection, Formation,"* Scripture and *Hermeneutics Series,* Vol. 6, 379–400, Grand Rapids: Zondervan.

Bovon, F. (2006), *Luke the Theologian: Fifty-five Years of Research (1950 – 2005),* Waco: Baylor.

Bovon, F. (2009), *L'Évangile selon Saint Luc 19:28–24:53,* Commentaire du Nouveau Testament 2.IIId, Genève: Labor et Fides.

Bovon, F. & McKinney, K. (eds) (1987), *Luke the Theologian. Thirty-three Years of research (1950 – 1983),* Allison Park: Pickwick Publishing.

Bowker, J. W. (1967), "Speeches in Acts: A study in Proem and Yellammadenu form," *NTS* 14:1, 96–111.

Brawley, R. L. (1987), *Luke-Acts and the Jews: Conflict, Apology, and Conciliation,* SBLMS 33, Atlanta: Scholars Press.

Brawley, R. L. (1990), *Centering on God: Method and Message in Luke-Acts,* Louisville: Westminster/JKP.

Brawley, R. L. (1995a), *Text to Text Pours Forth Speech: Voices of Scripture In Luke-Acts,* Bloomington: Indiana University Press.

Brawley, R. L. (1995b), "Resistance to the Carnivalization of Jesus: Scripture in the Lucan Passion Narrative," *Semeia* 69–70, 33–60.

Brawley, R. L. (1998), "The God of Promises and the Jews in Luke-Acts," in. Thompson, R. P & Phillips, T. E. (eds) *Literary Studies in Luke-Acts,* [FS J B Tyson], 279–96, Macon: Mercer University Press.

Brawley, R. L. (1999), "The Spirit, the Power and the Commonwealth in Acts," *BibToday* 37:5, 268–275.

Brink, G. van den (2008), "How to speak with intellectual and theological decency on the resurrection of Christ? A comparison of Swinburne and Wright." *SJT* 61:4, 408–419.

Brodie, T. L. (2000), *The Crucial Bridge: the Elijah-Elisha Narrative as an Interpretive Synthesis of Genesis-Kings and a Literary Model for the Gospels*, Collegeville, MN: Liturgical Press.

Brodie, T. L. (2006), *Proto-Luke: The Oldest Gospel Account,* Limerick: Dominican Biblical Institute.

Brooke, G. J. (1995), "Luke-Acts and the Qumran Scrolls: the Case of MMT," in Tuckett, C M (ed.), *Luke's Literary Achievement: Collected Essays,* JSNTSup 116, 72–90, Sheffield: Sheffield Academic Press.

Brooke, G. J. (1998), "Shared intertextual interpretations in the Dead Sea Scrolls and the New Testament," in *Biblical Perspectives: Early Use and Interpretation of the Bible in Light of the Dead Sea Scrolls*, 35–57, Leiden/Boston: Brill.

Brooke, G.J. (2000a), "Qumran: The Cradle of the Christ?", in Brooke, G. J. (ed.), *The Birth of Jesus: Biblical and Theological Reflections,* 23–34, Edinburgh: T&T Clark.

Brooke, G. J. (ed.) (2000b), *The Birth of Jesus: Biblical and Theological Reflections,* Edinburgh: T&T Clark.

Brooke, G. J. (2004), "The Psalms in Early Jewish Literature," in Moyise, S. & Menken, M. J. J. (eds) *Isaiah in the New Testament,* 5–24, London & New York: T & T Clark International.

Brown, J. K. (2016), "Metalepsis" in Oropeza, B.J. & Moyise, S. (eds) *Exploring Intertextuality: Diverse Strategies for New Testament Interpretation of Texts,* 29–41, Eugene, OR: Cascade Books.

Brown, R. E. (1979), *The Birth of the Messiah,* Garden City, NY: Image/Doubleday.

Brown, R. E. (1994), *The Death of the Messiah*, Anchor Bible Reference Library, 2 Vols, New York, London, etc: Doubleday.

Brown, S. (1978), "The Role of the Prologues in Determining the Purpose of Luke-Acts," in Talbert, C. H. (ed.) *Perspectives on Luke-Acts*, 99–111, Edinburgh: T & T Clark.

Bruce, F. F. (1952), *The Acts of the Apostles,* London: Tyndale Press.

Bruce, F. F. (1974), "The Speeches In Acts Thirty Years After," in Banks, R. (ed.) *Reconciliation and Hope. New Testament Essays on Atonement And Eschatology, FS* L.L. Morris, 53–68, Carlisle: The Paternoster Press.

Bruce, F. F. (1978), "The Davidic Messiah in Luke-Acts," in Tuttle, G. A. (ed.) *FS W. S. LaSor, Biblical and Near Eastern Studies, Essays in Honor of William Sanford LaSor*, 7–17, Grand Rapids: Eerdmans.

Bruce, F. F. (1984), "Render to Caesar," in Bammel, E. & Moule, C. F. D. (eds) *Jesus and the Politics of His Day,* 249–63, Cambridge: Cambridge University Press.

Bruce, F. F. (1987), "Paul's Use of the Old Testament in Acts," in *Tradition and Interpretation in the New Testament,* [FS Earle Ellis], 71–79, Grand Rapids: Eerdmans.

Brueggemann, W. (1998), *Isaiah 40 – 66,* Westminster Bible Companion, Louisville: W/JKP.

Brueggemann, W. (2005), *Solomon: Israel's Ironic Icon of Human Achievement*, Columbia: University of South Carolina Press.

Brueggemann, W. (2016), *Money and Possessions,* Louisville, KY: WJK.

Brueggemann, W. (2017), *God, Neighbour, Empire: the Excess of Divine Fidelity and the Command of Common Good*, London: SCM.

Brunson, A. C. (2003), *Psalm 118 in the Gospel of John: An Intertextual Study on the New Exodus Pattern in the Theology of John,* Tübingen: Mohr Siebeck.

Burger, C. (1970), *Jesus als Davidssohn,* FRLANT 98, Göttingen: Vandenhoeck & Ruprecht.

Buckwalter, H. D. (1996), *The character and purpose of Luke's Christology,* SNTSMS 80, Cambridge: Cambridge University Press.

Burridge, R. A. (2011), "The Genre of Acts – Revisited," in Walton, S. (ed.) *Reading Acts Today: Essays in Honour of Loveday C.A. Alexander*, LNTS 472; 3–28, London: T&T Clark.

Cadbury, H. J. (1922), "Commentary on the Preface of Luke," in Foakes-Jackson, F. J. & Lake, K. (eds) *The Beginnings of Christianity: Part I, The Acts of the Apostles*, Vol. 2, 489–510, London: Macmillan.

Cadbury, H. J. (1933a), "The Titles of Jesus in Acts," in Foakes-Jackson, F. J. & Lake, K. (eds), *The Beginnings of Christianity: The Acts of the Apostles:* Vol. 5. edited by Lake, K. & Cadbury, H. J., Additional notes to the commentary, 354–75, London: Macmillan and Co.

Cadbury, H. J. (1933b), "The Speeches in Acts," in Foakes-Jackson, F. J. & Lake, K. (eds), *The Beginnings of Christianity: The Acts of the Apostles:* Vol. 5. edited by Lake, K. & Cadbury, H. J., Additional notes to the commentary, 402–27, London: Macmillan and Co.

Cadbury, H. J. (1933c), "The Summaries in Acts," in Foakes-Jackson, F. J. & Lake, K. (eds), *The Beginnings of Christianity: The Acts of the Apostles:* Vol. 5. edited by Lake, K. & Cadbury, H. J., Additional notes to the commentary, 392–402, London: Macmillan and Co.

Cadbury, H. J. (1958), *The Making of Luke-Acts,* London: SPCK.

Caird, G. B. (1963), *Saint Luke,* London: Penguin.

Caird, G. B. (1980), *The Language and Imagery of the Bible,* London: Duckworth.

Caird, G. B. (1994), *New Testament Theology,* Oxford: Clarendon Press.

Campbell, W. S. (2007), *The "We" Passages in the Acts of the Apostles: The Narrator as Narrative Character*, Studies in Biblical Literature 14, Atlanta: SBL.

Carroll, J. T. & Green, J. B. et al. (1995), *The Death of Jesus in Early Christianity,* Peabody, MA: Hendrickson.

Carroll, J. T. (2012), *Luke: a Commentary,* NTL, Kentucky: WJK.

Carson, D. A. & Williamson, H. G. M. (eds) (1988), *It is Written: Scripture Citing Scripture,* Essays in Honour of Barnabas Lindars, Cambridge: Cambridge University Press.

Casey, M. (2007), *Solution to the "Son of Man" Problem,* LNTS 343, London/New York: T & T Clark International.

Cassidy, R. J. & Scharper, P. J. (eds) (1983), *Political Issues in Luke-Acts,* Orbis Books.

Catchpole, D. (2000), *Resurrection People: Studies in the Resurrection Narratives of the Gospels*, London: DLT.

Catto, S. K. (2007), *Reconstructing the First-Century Synagogue: A Critical Analysis of Current Research*, LNTS 363, London: T&T Clark.

Charlesworth, J. H. (ed.) ([1983] 2016), *The Old Testament Pseudepigrapha,* Vol. 1 (Peabody, MA: Hendrickson.

Charlesworth, J. H. (ed.) ([1983] 2016), *The Old Testament Pseudepigrapha,* Vol. 2, Peabody, MA: Hendrickson.

Chen, D. G. (2006), *God as Father in Luke-Acts,* Studies in Biblical Literature 92, New York: Peter Lang.

Chilton, B (1982), "Jesus ben David: reflections on the *Davidssohnfrage" JSNT* 14, 88–112.

Christopherson. A., Claussen, C., Frey, J. & Longenecker, C. (eds) (2002), *Paul, Luke, and the Graeco-Roman World, FS A. J. M. Wedderburn*; JSNTS 217, Sheffield: Continuum.

Clark, A. C. (2001), *Parallel Lives: The Relation of Paul to the Apostles In the Lucan Perspective,* Carlisle: Paternoster.

Clarke, A. D. (1999), "Barrett and Fitzmyer on Acts," *ExpTim* 110:10, 333.

Clarke, W. K. L. (1922), "The Use of the Septuagint in Acts", in Foakes-Jackson, F. J. & Lake, K. (eds) *The Beginnings of Christianity: The Acts of the Apostles*, Vol. 2. *Prolegomena II: Criticism*, 66–105, London: Macmillan and Co.

Clines, D. J. A. (1976), *He, We and They: A literary Approach to Isaiah 53,* JSOTSup 1, Sheffield: JSOT Press.

Coleman, R. L. (2019), "The Lukan Lens on Wealth and Possessions," *Biblical Interpretation Series*, 180, Leiden, Netherlands/Boston, Mass: Brill.

Collins, J. J. (2000) "The Nature of Messianism in the Light of the Dead Sea Scrolls," in Lim, T. H. et al. *The Dead Sea Scrolls in their Historical Context,* Edinburgh: T&T Clark.

Conzelmann, H. (1960), *The Theology of Saint Luke,* London: Faber & Faber.

Conzelmann, H. (1987), *The Acts of the Apostles,* Hermeneia, Philadelphia: Fortress Press.

Coloe, M. L. & Thatcher, T. (eds) (2011), *John, Qumran, and the Dead Sea Scrolls,* Early Judaism and its Literature, SBL 32, Atlanta: SBL.

Cosgrove, C. H. (1984), "The Divine Δεῖ in Luke-Acts: Investigations into the Lukan Understanding of God's Providence," *NovT* 26, 168–90.

Creed, J M. (1950), *The Gospel According to St. Luke*, London: Macmillan.

Cullmann, O. (1963), *The Christology of the New Testament,* London: SCM.

Culpepper, R. A. (2005), "Designs for the Church in the Gospel Accounts of Jesus' Death," *NTS* 51:3, 376–92.

Cunningham, S. (1997), *Through Many Tribulations,* JSNTSup 142, Sheffield: Sheffield Academic Press.

Dahl, N. A. (1968), "The Story of Abraham in Luke-Acts," in Keck, L. E. & Martyn, J. L. (eds) *Studies in Luke-Acts*, 139–158, London: SPCK.

Dahl, N. A. (ed. Juel, D. H.) (1991), *Jesus the Christ: The Historical Origins of Christological Doctrine,* Minneapolis: Fortress Press.

Daly-Denton, M. (2000), *David in the Fourth Gospel: The Johannine Reception of the Psalms,* Leiden: Brill.

Danker, F W, (ed.) (2000), *A Greek-English Lexicon of the New Testament and Other Early Christian Literature,* DBAG, Chicago and London: University of Chicago Press.

Davies, P. R. (2000) "Judaisms in the Dead Sea Scrolls: the Case of the Messiah," in Lim T. H. et al. *The Dead Sea Scrolls in their Historical Context,* Edinburgh: T&T Clark.

D'Costa, G. (1996), *Resurrection Reconsidered,* Oxford: Oneworld.

D'Costa, G. (1997), "Theology of Religions" in Ford, D. F. (ed.), *The Modern Theologians,* 638, Oxford: Blackwell; 1997.

Denova, R. I. (1997), *The Things Accomplished Among Us: Prophetic Tradition in the Structural Pattern of Luke-Acts,* JSNTSup 141, Sheffield: Sheffield Academic Press.

Derrett, J. D. M. (1978), "The Stone that the Builders Rejected," in Derrett, J. D. M. *Studies in the New Testament*, Vol. 2, *Midrash in action and as a literary device 2*, 60–67, Leiden: Brill.

Dibelius, M. (1956), *Studies in the Acts of the Apostles,* London: SCM.

Dibelius, M. (ed. Hanson, K. C.) (2004), *The Book of Acts*, Augsburg: Fortress.

Dicken, F. (2012), "The Author and Date of Luke-Acts: Exploring the Options," in Adams, S. A. & Pahl, M. *Issues in Luke-Acts: Selected Essays,* 7–26, Piscataway, NJ: Gorgias.

Dillon, R. J. (1978), "From Eyewitnesses to Ministers of the Word," AnBib 89, Rome: Biblical Institute Press.

Doble, P. (1985), "The Son of Man Saying in Stephen's Witnessing: Acts 6:8 – 8:2," *NTS* 31, 68–84.

Doble, P. (1996), *The Paradox of Salvation*, SNTSMS 87, Cambridge: Cambridge University Press.

Doble, P. (2000), "Something Greater than Solomon: An Approach to Stephen's Speech," in Moyise (ed.) *The Old Testament in the New Testament,* JSNTS 189, 181–207, Sheffield: Sheffield Academic Press.

Doble P. (2002a), "The Stone-saying and a Community Prayer: Acts 4:1–31, Unpublished Hawarden paper, cited by Marshall, I. H. (2007: 603).

Doble, P. (2002b), "Use of the Psalms in Luke-Acts: Towards Understanding Paul's Sermon at Pisidian Antioch", Unpublished paper, cited by Marshall, I. H. (2007: 603).

Doble, P. (2004), "The Psalms in Luke-Acts," in Moyise, S. & Menken, M. J. J. (eds) *The Psalms in the New Testament*, 83–117, London & New York: T&T Clark International.

Doble, P. (2006a), "Luke 24:26, 44 – Songs of God's Servant: David and his Psalms in Luke-Acts," *JSNT* 28:3, 267–83.

Doble, P. (2006b), "Listening to a Prophet Like Moses (Acts 3:22–23)," Unpublished paper; cited Marshall, I. H., (2007: 603).

Doble, P. (2013) ""Are these things so?" (Acts 7:1): A narrative-intertextual approach to reading Stephen's speech," in Koet, Moyise & Verheyden (eds) *The Scriptures of Israel in Jewish and Christian Tradition: Essays in Honour of Maarten J.J. Menken,* 95–113, Leiden: Brill.

Doble, P. (2014), "Codex Bezae and Luke 3:22 – Internal Evidence from Luke-Acts," in Doble, P. & Kloha, J. (eds) *Texts and Traditions: Essays in Honour of J. Keith Elliott,* New Testament Tools, Studies and Documents 47, 175–199, Leiden: Brill.

Doble, P. & Kloha, J. (eds) (2014), *Texts and Traditions: Essays in Honour of J. Keith Elliott,* New Testament Tools, Studies and Documents 47, Leiden/Boston: Brill.

Docherty, S. E. (2009) *The Use of the Old Testament in Hebrews: A Case Study in Early Jewish Interpretation,* WUNT II, Tübingen: Mohr Siebeck.

Docherty, S. (2014), *The Jewish Pseudepigrapha,* London: SPCK.

Dodd, C. H. (1936), *The Apostolic preaching and its Developments,* London: Hodder & Stoughton.

Dodd, C. H. (1947), "The Fall of Jerusalem and the 'Abomination of Desolation,'" *Journal of Roman Studies* 37:1–2, 47–54.

Dodd, C. H. (1952), *According to the Scriptures: The Substructure of New Testament Theology,* London: Nisbet.

Doeve, J. W. (1954), *Jewish Hermeneutics in the Synoptic Gospels and Acts,* Assen: Van Gorcum.

Donahue, J. R. (1994), "Redaction Criticism: Has the *Hauptgasse* become a *Sackgasse?*", in Malbon, E. S. & McKnight, E. V. (eds), *The New Literary Criticism and the New Testament,* 27–57, Sheffield: Sheffield Academic Press.

357

Downing, F. G. (1981), "Ethical Pagan Theism and the Speeches in Acts" *NTS* 27, 544–563.

Downing, F. G. (1982), "Common Ground with Paganism in Luke and in Josephus" *NTS* 28, 546–559.

Downing, F G. (1995), "Theophilus's First Reading of Luke-Acts" in Tuckett, C. M. (ed.) *Luke's Literary Achievement: Collected Essays,* JSNTSup 116, Sheffield: Sheffield Academic Press.

Draisma, S. (1989), *Intertextuality In Biblical Writings,* [FS Bas van Iersel], Kampen: Kok.

Drury, J. (1976), *Tradition and Design in Luke's Gospel,* London: DLT.

Dumais, M. (2000), *Communauté et Mission. Une Lecture des Actes des Apôtres,* Paris: Bellarmin. Les Editions Fides.

Dungan, D. L. (2006), *Constantine's Bible: Politics and the Making of the New Testament,* London: SCM.

Dunn, J. D. G. (2002), "Beyond the Historical Impasse? In Dialogue with A.J.M. Wedderburn," in Christophersen et al. (eds) *Paul, Luke, and the Graeco-Roman World, FS A. J. M. Wedderburn*; JSNTSup 217, 250–264, Sheffield: Continuum.

Dunn, J. D. G. (2003), *Jesus Remembered,* Christianity in the Making, Vol. 1, Grand Rapids: Eerdmans.

Dunn, J. D. G. (2004), "Was Jesus a Monotheist? A Contribution to the Discussion of Christian Monotheism," in Stuckenbruck, L. T. and North, W. E. S (eds), *Early Jewish and Christian Monotheism,* JSNTSup 263, 104–119, London and New York: T & T Clark International.

Dunn, J. D. G. (2006), "Living Tradition," in McCosker, P. *What is it that the Scripture Says?,* LNTS (JSNTSup) 316, 275–89, London: T & T Clark.

Dunn, J. D. G. (2009), *Beginning from Jerusalem. Christianity in the Making,* Vol. 2, Grand Rapids: Eerdmans.

Dunn, J. D. G. (2010), *Did the first Christians worship Jesus?,* London: SPCK.

Dunn, J. D. G. (2011), "Luke's Jerusalem Perspective" in Walton et al. (eds) *Reading Acts Today, FS* L. C. A. Alexander, LNTS 427, 120–136, London: Bloomsbury T&T Clark.

Dunn, J. D. G. (2013), *The Oral Gospel Tradition,* Grand Rapids/Cambridge: Eerdmans.

Dunn, J. D. G. (2015), *Neither Jew nor Greek.* Christianity in the Making, Vol. 3, Grand Rapids: Eerdmans.

Dunn, J. D. G. ([1996] 2016), *The Acts of the Apostles,* Grand Rapids: Eerdmans.

Dupont, J. (1953), "L'utilisation apologétique de l'Ancient Testament dans les discours des Actes," *Ephemerides théologicae lovanienses* 29, 298–327.

Dupont, J. (1959), "Le salut des gentils et la signification théologique du livre des Actes," *NTS* 6, 132–55.

Dupont, J. (1967), *Études sur les Actes des Apôtres,* LD 45, Paris: Cerf.

Dupont, J. (1979), *The Salvation of the Gentiles: Essays on the Acts of the Apostles,* New York: Paulist Press.

Dupont, J. (1984), *Nouvelles Études sur les Actes des Apôtres,* LD 118, 57–511, Paris: Cerf.

du Plessis, I. J. (1994), "The Saving Significance of Jesus and his Death on the Cross in Luke's Gospel – Focussing on Lk 22:19b–20," *Neot* 28, 523ff.

Eaton, J. (2005), *The Psalms: A historical and Spiritual Commentary with An Introduction and New Translation,* London and New York: Continuum.

Ehrman, B. D. (1993), *The Orthodox Corruption of Scripture: The Effect of Early Christological Controversies on the Text of the New Testament,* New York/Oxford: Oxford University Press.

Eissfeldt, O. (1962), "The Promise of Grace to David in Isaiah 55:1–5," in Anderson & Harrelson (eds), 196–207.

Ellingworth, P. (1993), *The Epistle to the Hebrews,* Carlisle/Grand Rapids: Paternoster/Eerdmans.

Ellingworth, P. (1994a), "Acts 13:38 – a Query," *Bible Translator*, 242–3.

Ellingworth, P. (1994b), "Christology: Synchronic or Diachronic?", in Green, J. B. & Turner, M. (eds) *Jesus of Nazareth: Lord and Christ, FS Howard Marshall*, 489–499, Grand Rapids: Eerdmans.

Elliott, J. K. (1972), "Does Luke 2:41 – 52 anticipate the Resurrection?", ExpT 83 (1971 – 2), 87–89.

Elliott, J K. ([1993] 1999), *The Apocryphal New Testament*, Oxford: Oxford University Press.

Elliott, J. K. (2001), "Extra-canonical early Christian literature," in Barton, J. & Muddiman, J. (eds), *The Oxford Bible Commentary*, 1306–30, Oxford: Oxford University Press.

Elliott, J. K. (2010), *New Testament Textual Criticism: The Application of Thorough-Going Principles*, NovTSup 137, Leiden/Boston: Brill.

Elliott, M. (2005), "Review of Moyise, S. & Menken, M. J. J. (eds) (2004), *The Psalms in the New Testament*," London: T & T Clark, JSNT 27:5, 25–6.

Ellis, E. E. (1974), *The Gospel of Luke*, New Century Bible, London: Oliphants.

Enslin, M. S. (1943), "Luke and the Samaritans," HTR 36, 278–97.

Esler, P. F. (1987), *Community and Gospel in Luke-Acts*, SNTSMS 57, Cambridge: Cambridge University Press.

Evans, C. A. & Sanders, J. A. (eds) (1993), *Luke and Scripture: The Function of Sacred Tradition in Luke-Acts*, Minneapolis: Fortress Press.

Evans, C. A. & Sanders, J. A. (eds) (1997), *Early Christian Interpretation of the Scriptures of Israel: Investigations and Proposals*, JSNTSup 148, Sheffield: Sheffield Academic Press.

Evans, C. A. & Porter, S. E. (eds), (2000), *Dictionary of New Testament Background*, Downers Grove: InterVarsity.

Evans, C. A. (2011), *Ancient Texts for New Testament Studies*, Grand Rapids, MI; Baker Academic.

Evans, C. F. (1967), "The Central Section of St Luke's Gospel," in Nineham, D. E. (ed.), *Studies in the Gospels,* Oxford: Blackwell.

Evans, C. F. (1990), *Saint Luke,* London: SCM/TPI.

Farris, S. (1985), *The Hymns of Luke's Infancy Narratives,* JSNTS 9, Sheffield: JSOT Press.

Ferreira, J. (1999), "The Plan of God and Preaching in Acts," *EvQ* 71:3, 209–215.

Fitzmyer, J. A. (1968), "Jewish Christianity in Acts in the Light of the Qumran Scrolls," in Keck, L. E. & Martyn, J. L. (eds), *Studies in Luke-Acts*, 233–257, London: SPCK.

Fitzmyer, J. A. (1978), "The Composition of Luke, Chapter 9," in Talbert, C. H. (ed.) *Perspectives on Luke-Acts,* 139–52, Edinburgh: T & T Clark.

Fitzmyer, J. A. (1981), *The Gospel According to Luke I – IX,* Anchor Bible 28, New York: Doubleday.

Fitzmyer, J. A. (1985), *The Gospel According to Luke X – XXIV*, Anchor Bible 28A, New York: Doubleday.

Fitzmyer, J A. (1989), *Luke the Theologian: Aspects of his Teaching,* London: Geoffrey Chapman.

Fitzmyer, J A (1998), "The Use of the Old Testament in Luke-Acts," in Fitzmyer, J.A. *To Advance the Gospel: New Testament Studies*, 295–313, Grand Rapids:Eerdmans[2]

Fitzmyer, J. A. (1998a), *To Advance the Gospel: New Testament Studies,* Grand Rapids:Eerdmans.

Fitzmyer, J. A. (1998b), *The Acts of the Apostles,* Anchor Bible 31, New York: Doubleday.

Flichy, O. (2000), *L'oeuvre de Luc. L'Évangile et les Actes des Apôtres,* Cahiers Evangiles, Paris: Cerf.

Foakes-Jackson, F. J. (1930) "Stephen's Speech in Acts," *JBL* 49, 283–86.

Foakes-Jackson, F J (1931), *The Acts of the Apostles,* Moffatt New Testament Commentary London: Hodder and Stoughton.

Foakes-Jackson, F. J. & Lake, K. (eds) (1920), *The Beginnings of Christianity: The Acts of the Apostles,* Vol I. *Prolegomena I: The Jewish, Gentile and Christian backgrounds*, London: Macmillan.

Foakes-Jackson, F. J. & Lake, K. (eds) (1922), *The Beginnings of Christianity: The Acts of the Apostles,* Vol. II. *Prolegomena II: Criticism*, London: Macmillan.

Foakes-Jackson, F. J. & Lake, K. (eds) (1926), *The Beginnings of Christianity: The Acts of the Apostles,* Vol. III, *The text of Acts*, by Ropes, J. H., London: Macmillan.

Foakes-Jackson, F. J. & Lake, K. (eds) (1933a), *The Beginnings of Christianity: The Acts of the Apostles, Vol. IV. English translation and commentary*, edited by Lake, K. & Cadbury, H. J.

Foakes-Jackson, F. J. & Lake, K. (eds) (1933b), *The Beginnings of Christianity: The Acts of the Apostles,* Vol. V. *Additional notes to the commentary*, edited by Lake, K & Cadbury, H. J.

Ford, D. F. (ed.) (1997), *The Modern Theologians,* Oxford: Blackwell.

Ford, D. F. (2007), *Christian Wisdom: Desiring God and Learning in Love,* Cambridge: Cambridge University Press.

Ford, D. F. & Stanton, G. (eds) (2003), *Reading Texts, Seeking Wisdom,* London: SCM.

Forrester, D. B. (1989), "Christianity and Politics," in Wainwright, G. (ed.) *Keeping the Faith: Essays to mark the centenary of Lux Mundi*, 250–273, London: SPCK.

Foster, P. (2005), review of Litwak, K. D. (2006), *Echoes of Scripture in Luke-Acts*, London & New York: T & T Clark International,, *ExpTim* 118:3, 153.

Foster, P. (2015), "Echoes without Resonance: Critiquing Certain Aspects of Recent Scholarly Trends in the Study of the Jewish Scriptures in the New Testament," *JSNT* 38:1, 96–111.

Franklin, E. (1975), *Christ the Lord: A Study in the Purpose and Theology of Luke-Acts,* London: SPCK.

Franklin, E. (2001), "Luke," in Barton, J. & Muddiman, J. (eds) *The Oxford Bible Commentary,* 922–5, Oxford: Oxford University Press.

Fuller, M. E. (2006), *The Restoration of Israel: Israel's Re-gathering and the Fate of the Nations in Early Jewish Literature and Luke-Acts.* BZNW 138, Berlin & NY: de Gruyter.

Funk, R. W. (1988), *The Poetics of Biblical Narrative,* Sonoma, California: Polebridge.

Gaston, L. (1980), *No Stone on Another: studies in the significance of the fall of Jerusalem in the synoptic gospels,* NovTSup 023, Leiden: Brill.

Gaventa, B. R. (2003), *The Acts of the Apostles,* Abingdon New Testament Commentaries, Nashville: Abingdon Press.

George, A. (1978), *Études sur l'oeuvre de Luc,*.Paris: Gabalda.

Gerber, D. (2008), *Il vous est né un Sauveur: La construction du sens sotériologique de la venue de Jésus en Luc-Actes,* Genève: Labor et Fides.

Gignilliat, M. (2008), "Who is Isaiah's Servant? Narrative identity and Theological Potentiality," *SJT* 61:2, 125–36.

Glombitza, O. (1959), *Akta xiii.15 – 41. Analyse einer lukanischen Predigt vor Juden, NTS* 5:4, 306–317.

Goodacre, M. (2002), *The Case Against Q,* Harrisburg: TPI.

Goulder, M. D. (1978), *The Evangelists' Calendar,* London: SPCK.

Grangaard, B. R. (1999), *Conflict and Authority in Luke 19:47 to 21:4,* SBL 8, New York: Peter Lang.

Grayston, K. (1990), *Dying, We Live,* London: DLT.

Green, J. B. (1988), *The Death of Jesus: Tradition and Interpretation in the Passion Narrative,* WUNT 2:33, Tübingen: Mohr.

Green, J. B. (1990), "The Death of Jesus, God's Servant," in Sylva, D.D. (ed.), *Reimaging the Death of the Lukan Jesus,* BBB 73, 1–28, Frankfurt: Hain.

Green, J. B. (1994a), "The Problem of a Beginning: Israel's Scriptures in Luke 1 – 2," Bulletin for Biblical Research 4, 61–85.

Green, J. B. (1994b), "Good News to Whom? Jesus and the "Poor" in the Gospel of Luke," in Green, J. B. & Turner, M. (eds) *Jesus of Nazareth: Lord and Christ, FS Howard Marshall*, 59–74, Grand Rapids: Eerdmans.

Green, J. B. (ed.) (1995a), *Hearing the New Testament: Strategies for Interpretation,* Grand Rapids/Carlisle: Eerdmans/Paternoster.

Green, J. B. (1995b), *The Theology of the Gospel of Luke,* Cambridge: Cambridge University Press.

Green, J. B. (1997), *The Gospel of Luke,* NICNT, Grand Rapids: Eerdmans.

Green, J B. (1998), "Salvation to the End of the Earth (Acts 13:47): God as the Saviour in the Acts of the Apostles," in Marshall, I. H. & Peterson, D. (eds) *Witness to the Gospel: the Theology of Acts,* 41–62, 83–106, Grand Rapids: Eerdmans.

Green, J. B. (2005), "Learning Theological Interpretation from Luke," in Bartholomew, C. G., Green, J.B. & Thiselton, A.C. (eds) *Reading Luke: Interpretation, Reflection, Formation," Scripture and Hermeneutics Series,* Vol. 6, 55–78, Grand Rapids: Zondervan.

Green, J. B. & Turner, M. (eds) (1994), *Jesus of Nazareth: Lord and Christ, FS Howard Marshall,* Grand Rapids: Eerdmans.

Gregory, A. (2005a), "Looking for Luke in the Second Century," in Bartholomew, C. G., Green, J. B. & Thiselton, A. C. (eds), 401–15, *Reading Luke: Interpretation, Reflection, Formation,* Vol. 6. Grand Rapids: Zondervan.

Gregory, A. (2005b), "Prior or Posterior? *The Gospel of the Ebionites* and the Gospel of Luke," *NTS* 51:3, 344–60.

Gregory, A. (2007), "The Reception of Luke and Acts and the Unity of Luke-Acts," *JSNT* 29:4, 459–72.

Grimshaw, J. P. (ed.) (2019), *Luke-Acts,* texts@contexts, London/New York: T&T Clark.

Haenchen, E. (1968), "The Book of Acts as Source Material for the History of Early Christianity," in Keck, L. E. & Martyn, J. L. (eds) *Studies in Luke-Acts*, 258–78, London: SPCK.

Haenchen, E. (1971), *The Acts of the Apostles,* Oxford: Basil Blackwell.

Hahn, S. W. (2005), "Kingdom and Church in Luke-Acts: From Davidic Christology to Kingdom Ecclesiology," in Bartholomew, C. G., Green, J. B. & Thiselton, A. C. (eds), 401–15, *Reading Luke: Interpretation, Reflection, Formation*, Vol. 6, 294–326, Grand Rapids: Zondervan.

Halpern, B. (2001), *David's Secret Demons: Messiah, Murderer, Traitor, King,* Grand Rapids: Eerdmans.

Hansen, G W. (1998), "The Preaching and Defence of Paul," in Marshall, I. H. & Peterson, D. (eds) *Witness to the Gospel: the Theology of Acts*, 295–306, Grand Rapids: Eerdmans.

Hanson, A. T. (1983), *The Living Utterances of God: The New Testament Exegesis of the Old,* London: DLT.

Harrington, J. M. (2000), *The Lukan Passion Narrative. The Markan Material in Luke 22,54–23:25: A Historical Survey, 1891 –1997,* NTTS XXX, Leiden: Brill.

Harris, S. (2016), *The Davidic Shepherd King in the Lukan Narrative,* LNTS(JSNT), 558, London: Bloomsbury.

Hart, H. St J. (1984), "The coin of 'Render unto Caesar,'" in Bammel, E. & Moule, C. F. D. (eds) *Jesus and the Politics of His Day,* 241–8, Cambridge: Cambridge University Press.

Hartsock, C. (2008), *Sight and Blindness in Luke-Acts: the Use of Physical Features in Characterization,* Leiden / Boston: Brill.

Hastings, A. (1958), *Prophet and Witness in Jerusalem: A Study of the Teaching of Saint Luke,* London: Longmans, Green.

Hay, D. M. (1973), "Glory at the Right Hand: Psalm 110 in Early Christianity," *SBLMS* 1973, 70–72.

Hays, R. B. (1989), *Echoes of Scripture in the Letters of Paul,* New Haven/London: Yale University Press.

Hays, R. B.(1997), *The Moral Vision of the New Testament: A Contemporary Introduction to New Testament Ethics,* Edinburgh: T & T Clark.

Hays, R.B. (2015), *Reading Backwards,* London: SPCK.

Hays, R. B. (2016), *Echoes of Scripture in the Gospels,* Waco: Baylor.

Hays, R. B. & Green, J. B. (1995), "The Use of the Old Testament by New Testament Writers," in Green, J. B. (ed.), *Hearing the New Testament: Strategies for Interpretation,* 222–238, Grand Rapids/Carlisle: Eerdmans/Paternoster.

Hays, R. B., Alkier, S. & Huizenga, L. A. (eds) (2009), *Reading the Bible Intertextually,* Waco: Baylor.

Hengel, M. (1983), *Between Jesus and Paul,* London: SCM.

Hengel, M. (2002), *The Septuagint as Christian Scripture,* Edinburgh: T & T Clark.

Hickling, C. (1994) "The Emmaus Story and its Sequel," in Barton, S. & Stanton, G. (eds) *Resurrection* [*FS* Leslie Houlden], 21–33, London: SPCK.

Higgins, A. J. B. (ed.) (1959), *New Testament Essays: Studies in Memory of T. W. Manson,* Manchester: Manchester University Press.

Hoegen-Rohls, C. (2002), "Κτίσις and καινὴ κτίσις in Paul's Letters," in Christopherson A., et al. (eds) *Paul, Luke, and the Graeco-Roman World, FS A. J. M. Wedderburn*; JSNTS 217, 108–110, Sheffield: Continuum. 102–122.

Holladay, C. R. (2016), *Acts: a Commentary,* NTL, Louisville, KY: WJK.

Hooker, M. D. (1959), *Jesus and the Servant,* London: SPCK.

Hooker, M. D. (1967), *The* Son of Man *in Mark*, London: SPCK.

Hooker, M. D. (1991), *The Gospel According to St Mark*, London: A & C Black.

Hooker, M. D. (1994), *Not Ashamed of the Gospel,* Carlisle: Paternoster Press.

Horrell, D. (1998), *The Epistles of Peter and Jude*, Peterborough: Epworth Press.

Horrell, D. (ed.) (1999), *Social-Scientific Approaches to New Testament Interpretation,* Edinburgh: T & T Clark.

Horsley, R. A.(2001), *Hearing the Whole Story: the Politics of Plot In Mark's Gospel,* Louisville: WJK.

Hurtado, L. (1999), *At the Origins of Christian Worship,* Carlisle: Paternoster.

Hurtado, L. W. (1988), *One God, One Lord,* London: SCM.

Hurtado, L. W. (2003), *Lord Jesus Christ: Devotion to Jesus in Earliest Christianity*, Grand Rapids: Eerdmans.

Hurtado, L W. (2006), *The Earliest Christian Artifacts: Manuscripts and Christian Origins,* Grand Rapids/Cambridge: Eerdmans.

Hurtado, L. W. (2014), "God or Jesus? Textual Ambiguity and Textual Variants in The Acts of the Apostles," in Doble, P. & Kloha, J. (eds) *Texts and Traditions: Essays in Honour of J. Keith Elliott*, New Testament Tools, Studies and Documents 47, 239–254, Leiden: Brill.

Jantzen, G. M. (2000), Nativity and Natality," in Brooke, G.J. (ed.), *The Birth of Jesus: Biblical and Theological Reflections,* 111–121, Edinburgh: T&T Clark.

Jeremias, J. (1969) *Jerusalem in the Time of Jesus* London: SCM.

Jeremias, J. (1972), παῖς θεοῦ, *TDNT*, Vol. 5, 673–77, Grand Rapids: Eerdmans,

Jervell, J. (1972), *Luke and the People of God,* Minneapolis, Minnesota: Augsburg.

Jervell, J. (1996), *The Theology of the Acts of the Apostles,* Cambridge: Cambridge University Press.

Jipp. J. W. (2010), "Luke's Scriptural Suffering Messiah: A Search for Precedent; a Search for Identity," *CBQ* 72:2, 255–274.

Johnson, L. T. (1991), *The Gospel of Luke,* Sacra Pagina 3, Minnesota: Michael Glazier.

Johnson, L. T. (1992), *The Acts of the Apostles,* Sacra Pagina 5, Minnesota: Michael Glazier.

Johnson, L. T. (2008), "Narrative Criticism and translation: the Case of Luke-Acts and the NSRV," in Gray, P. & O'Day, G. R, (eds) *Scripture and Traditions,* 387–410. Leiden: Brill

Johnson, L. T. (2013), *Contested Issues in Christian Origins and the New Testament: Collected Essays,* Leiden/Boston: Brill.

Johnson, S. E. (1968), "The Davidic-Royal Motif in the Gospels," *JBL* 87, 136–50.

Jones, G. H. (1991), *The Nathan Narratives*, JSOTSup 80, Sheffield: JSOT.

Jonge, M. de (1986), "The Earliest Christian Use of Christos: Some Suggestions," *NTS* 32, 321–343.

Jonge, M. de (1989), "Jesus, Son of David and Son of God," in Draisma (ed.) *Jewish eschatology, early Christian Christology and the Testaments of the twelve Patriarchs*, 95–104, Leiden: Brill.

Joyce, P. (1993), "The Kingdom of God and the Psalms," in Barbour (ed.) *The Kingdom of God and Human Society,* 42–59, Edinburgh: T & T Clark.

Just, A. A. (1993), *The Ongoing Feast: Table Fellowship and Eschatology at Emmaus*, Pueblo: The Liturgical Press.

Kaiser, W. C. (1980), "The promise to David in Psalm 16 and its Application in Acts 2:25 – 33 and 13:32 – 37," *JETS* 23, 219–229.

Keck, L. E. & Martyn, J. L. (eds) (1968), *Studies in Luke-Acts*, London: SPCK.

Kee, H. C. (1990), *Good News to the Ends of the Earth: The Theology of Acts,* London/Philadelphia: SCM/TPI.

Kennedy, G. A. (1984), *New Testament Interpretation through Rhetorical Criticism,* Chapel Hill: University of North Carolina Press.

Kelber, W. H. and Byrskog, S. (eds) (2009), *Jesus in Memory: Traditions in Oral and Scribal Perspectives,* Waco, TX; Baylor University Press.

Kilgallen, J. J. (1998), "Your Servant Jesus Whom You Anointed (Acts 4,27)," RB 105:2, 185–201.

Kilgallen, J. J. (2001), "The Use of Psalm 16:8–11 in Peter's Pentecost Speech," *ExpTim* 113:2, 47–50.

Kilgallen, J. J. (2013), *Major Events in Luke's Gospel and the Acts of the Apostles,* Lampeter, Ceredigion: Edwin Mellen Press.

Kilpatrick, G. D. (1942), "A Theme of the Lucan Passion Story and Luke xxiii.47," *JTS* 43, 34–36.

Kimball, C. A. (1994), *Jesus' Exposition of the Old Testament in Luke's Gospel,* JSNTSup 94, Sheffield: Sheffield Academic Press.

Kinman, B. (1995), *Jesus' Entry into Jerusalem: In the context of Lukan Theology and the Politics of His Day,* Leiden: Brill.

Kittel, G. & Friedrich, G. (eds) (1964–), *Theological Dictionary of the New Testament* (trans. Geoffrey W. Bromiley), 10 vols, Grand Rapids: Eerdmans.

Kirk, A. (2018), *Memory and the Jesus Tradition,* The Reception of Jesus in the First Three Centuries, 2, London, et al.: Bloomsbury T&T Clark.

Kirk, J. R. D. (2016), "Narrative Transformation" in Oropeza, B.J. & Moyise, S. (eds) *Exploring Intertextuality: Diverse Strategies for New Testament Interpretation of Texts,* 165–175, Eugene, OR: Cascade Books.

Klein, R. W. (1983), *1 Samuel*, WBC10, Waco: Word Books.

Knox, J. (1968), "Acts and the Pauline Letter Corpus," in Keck, L. E. & Martyn, J. L. (eds) *Studies in Luke-Acts*, 279–87, London: SPCK.

Koet, B. J. (1989), *Five Studies on Interpretation of Scripture in Luke-Acts,* Leuven: Leuven University Press.

Koet, B. J. (2006), *Dreams and Scripture in Luke-Acts,* Leuven: Peeters.

Koet, B. J. (2006b), "Isaiah in Luke-Acts," in idem. *Dreams and Scripture in Luke-Acts,* 51–79, Leuven: Peeters.

Koet, B. J., Moyise, S. & Verheyden, J. (eds) (2013), *The Scriptures of Israel in Jewish and Christian Tradition, Essays in Honour of Maarten J. J. Menken,* NovTSup 148, Leiden/Boston: Brill.

Kohlenberger, J. R. III (1991), *The NRSV Concordance Unabridged,* Grand Rapids: Zondervan.

Kraus, H-J. (1986), *Theology of the Psalms,* Minneapolis: Augsburg.

Kraus, T. J. (1999), "'Uneducated,' 'Ignorant,' or even 'Illiterate'? Aspects and Background for an Understanding of ἀγράμματοί (and ἰδιῶται) in Acts 4:13," *NTS* 45:3, 434–45.

Krodel, G. (1986), *Acts,* Augsburg Commentary on the New Testament, Minneapolis: Augsburg.

Kugel, J. L. (1994), *In Potiphar"s house: The Interpretive Life of Biblical Texts,* Cambridge, Mass/London: Harvard University Press.

Kurz, W. S. (1993), *Reading Luke-Acts: Dynamics of Biblical Narrative,* Louisville: WJK.

LaCocque, A. (2015), *Jesus the Central Jew: His Times and His People,* Atlanta, GA: SBL.

Lampe, G. W. H. (1984), "The Two Swords (Luke 22:35–38)," in Bammel, E. & Moule, C. F. D. (eds) *Jesus and the Politics of His Day,* 335–51, Cambridge: Cambridge University Press.

Lane, A. N. S. (ed.) (1997), *Interpreting the Bible: Historical and Theological Studies, FS* D. F. Wright, Leicester: Apollos.

Larkin, W. J. (1974), *Luke's Use of the Old Testament in Luke 22–23,* University of Durham: PhD Thesis.

Le Donne, A. (2009), *The Historiographical Jesus: Memory, Typology, and the Son of David,* Waco, TX: Baylor University Press.

Leaney, A. R. C. (1966), *The Gospel According to St Luke,* London: A & C Black.

Lee, A. H. I. (2005), *From Messiah to Preexistent Son: Jesus' Self-Consciousness and Early Christian Exegesis of Messianic Psalms,* WUNT II/192, Tübingen: Mohr-Siebeck.

Lentz, J. C. (1993), *Luke's Portrait of Paul,* SNTSMS 77, Cambridge: Cambridge University Press.

Levinskaya, I. (1996), *The Book of Acts in its Diaspora Setting,* The Book of Acts in its First Century Setting: Vol. 5, Grand Rapids/Carlisle: Eerdmans/Paternoster.

Liberto, D. (2003), "To Fear or Not to Fear? Christ as "Sophos" in Luke's Passion Narrative," *ExpTim* 114, 219–23.

Lieu, J. (1994), "The Women's Resurrection Testimony," in Barton, S. & Stanton, G. (eds) *Resurrection [FS* Leslie Houlden], 34–44, London: SPCK.

Lim, T. H. et al. (2000), *The Dead Sea Scrolls in their Historical Context,* Edinburgh: T&T Clark.

Lim, T. H. (2004), "The Origins and Emergence of Midrash in Relation to the Hebrew Scriptures," in Neusner, J. & Avery-Peck, A. J. (eds) *The Midrash. An Encyclopaedia of Biblical Interpretation in Formative Judaism,* 595–612, Leiden: Brill Academic Publishers.

Lincoln, A. T. (2013), "Luke and Jesus' Conception," *JBL* 132:3 , 639–658.

Lindars, B. (1961), *New Testament Apologetic,* London: SCM Press.

Litwak, K. D. (2005), *Echoes of Scripture in Luke-Acts: Telling the History of God's People Intertextually,* London & New York: T&T Clark International.

Litwak, K. D. (2012) "The Use of the Old Testament in Luke-Acts: Luke's Scriptural Story of the 'Things Accomplished Among Us,'" in Adams & Pahl (eds) *Issues in Luke-Acts: Selected Essays,* 147–169, Piscataway, NJ: Gorgias.

Lohse, E. (1972), "υἱός Δαυΐδ," *TDNT,* Vol. 8, 478–88, Grand Rapids: Eerdmans.

Longenecker, B. (2004), "Lukan Aversion to Humps and Hollows: The Case of Acts 11:27–12:25," *NTS* 50, 185–204.

371

Longenecker, B. (2005), *Rhetoric at the Boundaries: The Art and Theology of New Testament Chain-link Transitions,* Waco: Baylor.

Longenecker, R N. (1970), *The Christology of Early Jewish Christianity,* SBT (Second Series 17), London: SCM.

Longenecker, R. N. (1999), *Biblical Exegesis in the Apostolic Period,* Grand Rapids/Vancouver: Eerdmans/Regent College.

Louw, J. P. & Nida, E. A. (eds) (1988), *Greek-English Lexicon of the New Testament based on Semantic Domains,* Vol. 1: *Introduction and Domains,* New York: United Bible Societies.

Louw, J. P. & Nida, E. A. (eds) (1988), *Greek-English Lexicon of the New Testament based on Semantic Domains,* Vol. 2: *Indices,* New York: United Bible Societies.

Lövestam, E. (1961), *Son and Saviour: a Study of Acts 13,32–37, with an appendix, "Son of God" in the Synoptic Gospels,* Coniectanea Neotestamentica 18, Lund: C. W. K. Gleerup.

Lüdemann, G. (2005), *The Acts of the Apostles,* Amherst, NY: Prometheus Books.

MacAdam, H. I. (2000), "The True and Lively Word: the Acts of the Apostles at the end of the twentieth Century," a review article; in memoriam Colin J. Hemer (19??-1987). *Theological review,* 21:2, 170–212.

McComiskey, D. S. (2004), *Lukan Theology in the Light of the Gospel's Literary Structure,* Milton Keynes/Waynesboro, GA: Paternoster.

McLay, R. T. (2003), *The Use of the Septuagint in New Testament Research,* Grand Rapids/Cambridge: Eerdmans.

McLay, R. T. (ed.) (2015), *The Temple in Text and Tradition,* LSTS 83, London/New York: Bloomsbury.

McNicol, A. J. (1998), "Rebuilding the house of David: The Function of the Benedictus in Luke-Acts," ResQ 40 25–38.

Mahfouz, H. (2003), *La Fonction Littéraire et Théologique de Luc 3,1–20 dans Luc-Actes,* Jounieh, Liban: Kaslik.

Malbon, E. S., & McKnight, E. V. (eds) (1994), *The New Literary Criticism and the New Testament,* Sheffield: Sheffield Academic Press.

Malina, B. J. & Pilch, J. J. (2008), *Social-Science Commentary on the Book of Acts,* Minneapolis: Fortress.

Mallen, P. (2008), *The Reading and Transformation of Isaiah in Luke-Acts,* LNTS (JSNTS) 367, London: T&T Clark International.

Mann, J. (1971), *The Bible as read and preached in the old synagogue: a study in the cycles of reading from Torah and Prophets, as well as from Psalms, and in the structure of the Midrashic homilies,* New York: Ktav Publishing.

Mann, J. L. (2016), *What is opened in Luke 24:45, the Mind or the Scriptures?,* JBL 135:4.

Manson, W. (1930), *The Gospel of Luke,* London: Hodder and Stoughton.

Marcus, J. (1992), *The Way of the Lord: Christological Exegesis of the Old Testament in the Gospel of Mark,* Edinburgh: T & T Clark.

Marcus, J. (1995), "The Role of Scripture in the Gospel Passion Narratives," in Carroll, J. T. & Green, J. B. et al. *The Death of Jesus in Early Christianity,* 205–33, Peabody, MA: Hendrickson.

Marguerat, D. (1999a), "Luc-Actes entre Jérusalem et Rome. Un procédé lucanien de double signification," *NTS* 45:1, 70–87.

Marguerat, D. (1999b), The Enigma of the Silent Closing of Acts (28:16–31)," in Moessner, D. P. (ed.) *Jesus and the Heritage of Israel,* 284–304, Harrisburg: TPI.

Marguerat, D. (2002), *The First Christian Historian: Writing the Acts of the Apostles,* SNTSMS 121, Cambridge: CUP.

Marguerat, D. (2007), *Les Actes des Apôtres, (1 – 12),* Commentaire du N T Va (Deuxième Série), Genève: Labor et Fides.

Marguerat, D. (2008), "Paul après Paul: une histoire de réception," *NTS* 54:3, 317–37.

373

Marshall, I. H. (1970) "The Resurrection in the Acts of the Apostles," W. Ward Gasque & Ralph P.Martin, eds., *Apostolic History and the Gospel, FS* F.F. Bruce, 92–107, Exeter: The Paternoster Press.

Marshall, I. H. (1978), *The Gospel of Luke,* Exeter: Paternoster.

Marshall, I. H. (1980), *Acts,* Leicester: IVP.

Marshall, I. H. (1988a), *Luke – Historian and Theologian,* Exeter: Paternoster.

Marshall, I. H. (1988b), "An assessment of recent developments," in Carson, D. A. & Williamson, H. G. M. (eds), *It is Written: Scripture Citing Scripture,* Essays in Honour of Barnabas Lindars, 1–21, Cambridge: Cambridge University Press.

Marshall, I. H. (1991), "Luke and his 'Gospel," in Stuhlmacher, *Gospels*, 272–92.

Marshall, I. H. (1993), "Acts and the 'Former Treatise,'" in Winter, B. W. & Clarke, A. D. (eds), *The Book of Acts in its First Century Setting,* Vol 1: *Ancient Literary Setting*, 163–182. Grand Rapids: Eerdmans.

Marshall, I. H. (1999), "'Israel' and the Story of Salvation: One Theme in Two Parts," in Moessner, D. P. (ed.), *Jesus and the Heritage of Israel,* 340–57, Harrisburg: TPI.

Marshall, I. H. (2005), "Political and Eschatological Language in Luke," in Bartholomew, C. G., Green, J.B. & Thiselton, A.C. (eds) *Reading Luke: Interpretation, Reflection, Formation," Scripture and Hermeneutics Series,* Vol. 6, 157–77, Grand Rapids: Zondervan.

Marshall, I. H. (2007), "Acts," in Beale G. K. & Carson D.A. (eds) *Commentary on the New Testament Use of the Old Testament*, 513–606, Grand Rapids/Nottingham: Baker/Apollos.

Marshall, I. H. & Peterson, D. (eds) (1998), *Witness to the Gospel: the Theology of Acts,* Grand Rapids: Eerdmans.

Matera, F. J. (1999), *New Testament Christology,* (Louisville: Westminster/John Knox)

Matson, M A (2001), *In Dialogue with Another Gospel? The Influence of the Fourth Gospel on the Passion Narrative of the Gospel of Luke,* SBLDS 178, Atlanta: SBL.

Mays, J. L. (1994), *The Lord Reigns: A Theological Handbook to the Psalms,* Louisville: WJK Press.

McCarter, P. K. (1980), *1 Samuel,* AB8, New York: Doubleday.

McCosker, P. (2006), *What is it that the Scripture Says?,* LNTS (JSNTSup) 316, London: T & T Clark.

McLay, R. T. (2003), *The Use of the Septuagint in New Testament Research,* Grand Rapids: Eerdmans.

Meeks, W. A. (1983), *The First Urban Christians: the Social World of the Apostle Paul,* New Haven & London: Yale.

Menken, M. J. J. (2004), *Matthew's Bible,* BETL CLXXIII, Leuven: Peeters.

Metzger, B. M. (1971), *A Textual Commentary on the Greek New Testament,* London: United Bible Societies.

Metzger, B. M. (1994), *A Textual Commentary on the Greek New Testament,* Stuttgart: Bibelgesellschaft.

Minear, P. S. (1968), "Luke's Use of the Birth Stories," in Keck, L. E. & Martyn, J. L. (eds) *Studies in Luke-Acts,* 111–30, London: SPCK.

Mitchell, M. M. (2005), "Patristic Counter-Evidence to the Claim that 'The Gospels Were Written for All Christians,'" *NTS* 51:1, 36–79.

Mittman-Richert, U. (2008), *Der Sühnetod des Gottesknechts: Jesaja 53 im Lukasevangelium,* WUNT 220, Tübingen: Mohr Siebeck.

Miura, Y. (2007), *David in Luke-Acts,* WUNT 2:232, Tübingen: Mohr Siebeck.

Moessner, D. P. (1986), "'The Christ Must Suffer: New Light on the Jesus-Peter, Stephen, Paul Parallels in Luke-Acts," *NovT* XXVIII, 220–256.

Moessner, D. P. (1996), "The 'Script' of the Scriptures in Acts: suffering as God's 'plan' (βουλή) for the world for the 'release of sins,'" in Witherington III, B. *History, Literature and Society in the Book of Acts,* 218–50, Cambridge: Cambridge University Press.

Moessner, D. P. (1998), "Two Lords 'at the Right Hand'? The Psalms and An Intertextual Reading of Peter's Pentecost Speech (Acts 2:14 – 36)," in Thompson R. P. & Phillips, T. E. (eds), *Literary Studies in Luke-Acts,* [*FS* J B Tyson], 215–32, Macon: Mercer University Press.

Moessner, D. P. (1989), *Lord of the Banquet: The Literary and Theological Significance of the Lukan Travel Narrative,* Minneapolis: Fortress.

Moessner, D. P. (ed.) (1999), *Jesus and the Heritage of Israel,* Harrisburg: TPI.

Moessner, D. P. (2005), "Reading Luke's Gospel as Ancient Hellenistic Narrative: Luke's Narrative Plan of Israel's Suffering Messiah as God's Saving 'Plan' for the World," in Bartholomew, C. G., Green, J.B. & Thiselton, A.C. (eds) (2005), *Reading Luke: Interpretation, Reflection, Formation, Scripture and Hermeneutics Series,* Vol. 6, 125–54, Grand Rapids: Zondervan.

Moessner, D. P. (2016), *Luke the Historian of Israel's Legacy, Theologian of Israel's Christ,* BZNW 182 Berlin/Boston: de Gruyter.

Morgan, J. (2013), "Luc-Actes: un tour de force littéraire et théologique," *Hokhma: revue de réflexion théologique* 103, 9–29.

Morgan-Wynne, J. E. (2014), *Paul's Pisidian Antioch Speech (Acts 13),* Cambridge: James Clarke & Co.

Morgan, R. (2003), "Jesus Christ, the Wisdom of God (2)" in Ford, D. F. & Stanton, G., *Reading Texts, Seeking Wisdom,* 22–37, London: SCM.

Morgan, T. (2015) *Roman Faith and Christian Faith:* Pistis *and* Fides *in the Early Roman Empire and Early Churches,* Oxford, Oxford University Press.

Moule, C. F. D. (1968), "The Christology of Acts," in Keck, L. E. & Martyn, J. L. (eds) *Studies in Luke-Acts,* 159–85, London: SPCK.

Moulton, H. K. (1957), *The Acts of the Apostles,* The Christian Students' Library 12, Madras: CLS.

Moyise, S. (ed.) (2000a), *The Old Testament in the New Testament,* JSNTSup 189, Sheffield: Sheffield Academic Press.

Moyise, S. (2000b), "Intertextuality and the Study of the Old Testament in the New Testament," in Moyise, S. (ed.), *The Old Testament in the New Testament,* JSNTS 189, 14–41, Sheffield: Sheffield Academic Press.

376

Moyise, S. (2001), *The Old Testament in the New: An Introduction,* London and New York: Continuum.

Moyise, S. (2008) *Evoking Scripture: Seeing the Old Testament in the New,* London: T&T Clark Continuum.

Moyise, S. (2009), "Intertextuality and Historical Approaches to the Use of Scripture in the New Testament," in Hays, R. B., Alkier, S. & Huizenga, L. A. (eds), *Reading the Bible Intertextually,* 3–21, Waco: Baylor.

Moyise, S. (2012) *The Later New Testament Writers and Scripture,* London: SPCK.

Moyise, S. (2013), *Was the Birth of Jesus According to Scripture?,* London: SPCK.

Moyise, S. & Menken, M. J. J. (eds) (2004), *The Psalms in the New Testament,* London & New York: T & T Clark.

Moyise, S. & Menken, M J. J. (eds) (2005), *Isaiah in the New Testament,* London & New York: T & T Clark International.

Muller, M. (1996), *The First Bible of the Church: A Plea for the Septuagint,* JSOTSup 206, Sheffield: Sheffield Academic Press.

Munck, J. (1967) *The Acts of the Apostles,* Anchor Bible 31 New York: Doubleday.

Neagoe, A. (2002), *The Trial of the Gospel: An Apologetic Reading of Luke's Trial Narratives,* SNTSMS 116, Cambridge: Cambridge University Press.

Neyrey, J. (1985), *The Passion According to Luke,* New York: Paulist Press.

Nineham, D. E. (ed.) (1967), *Studies in the Gospels,* Oxford: Blackwell.

Nolland, J. (1989), *Luke 1 – 9:20,* World Biblical Commentary Vol. 35A, Dallas, TX: Word Books.

Nolland, J. (1993a), *Luke 9:21 – 18:34,* World Biblical Commentary Vol. 35B, Dallas, TX: Word Books.

Nolland, J. (1993b), *Luke 18:35 – 24:53,* World Biblical Commentary Vol. 35C, Dallas, TX: Word Books.

North, J. L. (2000), "KAINA KAI PALAIA: An Account of the British Seminar on the Use of the Old Testament in the New Testament," in Moyise, S. (ed.), *The Old Testament in the New Testament,* JSNTSup 189, 278–81, Sheffield: Sheffield Academic Press.

North, J. L. (2004), "Jesus and Worship, God and Sacrifice," in Stuckenbruck, L. T. and North, W. E. S. (eds) *Early Jewish and Christian Monotheism,* JSNTSS 263,186–202, London and New York: T & T Clark International.

North, J. L. (2014) "1 Corinthians 8:6: From Confession to Paul to Creed to Paul," in Doble, P. & Kloha, J. (eds) *Texts and Traditions: Essays in Honour of J. Keith Elliott,* New Testament Tools, Studies and Documents 47, 175–199, Leiden: Brill.

North W. E. S. (2015), *A Journey Round John*, London: Bloomsbury.

Novakovic, L. (2014), *Raised from the Dead According to Scripture: the Role of Israel's Scripture in the Early Christian Interpretations of Jesus' Resurrection,* JCTS 12, London: Bloomsbury.

Oakes, P. (2001), *Philippians: From People to Letter,* SNTSMS 110, Cambridge: Cambridge University Press.

Oakes, P. (2009) *Reading Romans in Pompeii: Paul's Letter at Ground Level,* London/Minneapolis: SPCK/Fortress.

Oakes, P. (2015) *Galatians,* Grand Rapids, MI: Baker Academic.

Ó Fearghail, F. (1991), *The Introduction to Luke-Acts: A Study of the Role of Lk 1:1–4:44 in the Composition of Luke's Two-Volume Work*, AnBib: Investigationes Scientificae in Res Biblicas, Vol. 126, Rome: Editrice Pontificio Istituto Biblico.

Oliver, H. H. (1963), "The Lucan Birth Stories and the Purpose of Luke-Acts," *NTS* 10 (1963–4), 202–26.

O'Neill, J. C. (1970), *The Theology of Acts in its Historical Setting,* London: SPCK.

O'Toole, R. F. (2004), *Luke's Presentation of Jesus: A Christology,* Subsidia Biblica 25, Rome: Editrice Pontificio Istituto Biblico.

Oropeza, B.J. & Moyise, S. (eds) (2016), *Exploring Intertextuality: Diverse Strategies for New Testament Interpretation of Texts,* Eugene, OR: Cascade Books.

Paffenroth, K. (1997), *The Story of Jesus According to L,* JSNTSup 147, Sheffield: Sheffield Academic Press.

Pao, D. W. (2000), *Acts and the Isaianic New Exodus,* Tübingen: J. C. B. Mohr.

Pao, D. W. & Schnabel, E. J. (2007), "Luke," in Beale, G. K. & Carson, D. A. (eds) *Commentary on the New Testament Use of the Old Testament,* 251–414, Grand Rapids/Nottingham: Baker/Apollos.

Parsons, M. C. (2006), *Body and Character in Luke-Acts,* Grand Rapids: Baker.

Parsons, M. C. (2007), *Luke, Storyteller, Interpreter, Evangelist,* Peabody, MA: Hendrickson.

Parsons, M. C. (2008), *Acts,* Paideia Commentaries, Grand Rapids: Baker.

Parsons, M. C. (2015), *Luke,* Paideia Commentaries, Grand Rapids: Baker.

Parsons, M. C. & Pervo, R. I. (1999), *Rethinking the Unity of Luke and Acts,* Minneapolis: Fortress.

Peacocke, A. (2000), "DNA of our DNA," in Brooke, G.J. (ed.) *The Birth of Jesus: Biblical and Theological Reflections,* 59–67, Edinburgh: T&T Clark.

Pelikan, J. (2006), *Acts.* London: SCM.

Penner, T. & Vander Stichele, C. (eds) (2003), *Contextualizing Acts: Lukan Narrative and Greco-Roman Discourse,* SBL Symposium Series 20, Atlanta: SBL.

Perry, P.S. (2016), "Relevance Theory and Intertextuality" in Oropeza, B. J. & Moyise, S. (eds) *Exploring Intertextuality: Diverse Strategies for New Testament Interpretation of Texts,* 207–221, Eugene, OR: Cascade Books.

Perry, T. A. ([2008] 2014), *Wisdom in the Hebrew Bible: God's Twilight Zone,* Peabody, MA: Hendrickson.

Pervo, R. I. (1987), *Profit with Delight: the Literary Genre of the Acts of the Apostles,* Philadelphia: Fortress.

Pervo, R. I. (2008), *The Mystery of Acts: Unraveling its Story,* Santa Rosa: Polebridge.

Pervo, R I. (2009), *Acts: a commentary,* Hermeneia, Minneapolis: Fortress Press.

Pfister, M. (1989), "Konzepte der Intertextualität," in Broich, U. & Pfister, M. (eds) *Intertextualität, Formen, Funktionen, anglistiche Fallstudien,* 29, Tübingen: Niemeyer.

Phillips, T. E. (1998), "Subtlety as a Literary Technique in Luke's Characterisation of Jews and Judaism," in Thompson, R. P. & Phillips, T. E. (eds), *Literary Studies in Luke-Acts,* [FS J. B. Tyson], 313–26, Macon: Mercer University Press.

Phillips, T. E. (2008), "'Will the Wise Person Get Drunk?': the Background of the Human Wisdom in Luke 7:35 and Matthew 11:19," *JBL* 127:2, 385–96.

Phillips, T. E. (2009a), *Acts Within Diverse Frames of Reference,* Macon: Mercer University Press.

Phillips, T. E. (2009b) *Paul, His Letters, and Acts,* Peabody, MA: Hendrickson.

Phillips, T. E. (ed.) (2009c), *Contemporary Studies in Acts,* Macon, GA: Mercer.

Pietersma, A. (2000), *A New English Translation of the Septuagint and Other Greek Translations Traditionally Included under That Title: The Psalms,* Oxford/New York: Oxford University Press.

Plummer, A. (1922), *The Gospel According to S. Luke,* ICC, Edinburgh: T&T Clark.

Porter, S. E. (1997), "The Use of the Old Testament in the New Testament: A Brief Comment on Method and Terminology," in Evans, C. A. & Sanders, J. A. (eds) *Early Christian Interpretation of the Scriptures of Israel: Investigations and Proposals,* JSNTSup 148, Sheffield: Sheffield Academic Press.

Powell, M. A. (1995), "Narrative Criticism," in Green, J. B. (ed.) *Hearing the New Testament: Strategies for Interpretation,* 239–55, Grand Rapids/Carlisle: Eerdmans/Paternoster.

Praeder, S. M. (1981), "Luke-Acts and the Ancient Novel," in Richards, K. H. (ed.), SBL Seminar Papers, 20. 269–292, Chico: Scholars Press.

Rahlfs, A. (1979), *Septuaginta,* Stuttgart: Bibelgesellschaft.

Ramsey, A. M. (1949), *The Glory of God and the Transfiguration of Christ,* London: Longmans, Green & Co.

Rapske, B. (1994), *The Book of Acts and Paul in Roman Custody,* The Book of Acts in its First Century Setting: Vol. 3, Grand Rapids/Carlisle: Eerdmans/Paternoster.

Ravens, D. (1995), *Luke and the Restoration of Israel,* JSNTSup 119, Sheffield: Sheffield Academic Press.

Read-Heimerdinger, J. (1997), "The 'Long' and the 'Short' Texts of Acts: a Closer Look at the Quantity and Types of Variation," Revista catalana de teología, 22:2, 245–61.

Read-Heimerdinger, J. (1998), "Barnabas in Acts: A Study of his Role in the Text of Codex Bezae," *JSNT* 72, 23–66.

Read-Heimerdinger, J. (2002), *The Bezan Text of Acts: A Contribution of Discourse Analysis to Textual Criticism,* JSNTSup 236, London: Sheffield Academic Press.

Read-Heimerdinger, J. & Rius-Camps, J. (2002), "Emmaous or Oulammaous? Luke"s Use of the Jewish Scriptures in the Text of Luke 24 in Codex Bezae," *RcatT* XXVII/1, 23–42.

Reasoner, M. (1999), "The Theme of Acts: Institutional History or Divine Necessity in History?," *JBL* 118:4, 635–59.

Rese, M. (1969), *Alttestamentliche Motive in der Christologie des Lukas,* Gütersloh: Gütersloher Verlagshaus G. Mohn.

Riesenfeld, H. (1947), *Jésus transfiguré: l'arrière-plan récit évangélique de la transfiguration do Notre-Seigneur,* [Acta Seminarii Neotestamentici Upsaliensis; 16], Kobenhaven: E Munksgaard.

381

Riesner, R. (1994), "James's Speech (Acts 15:13–21), Simeon's Hymn (Luke 2:29–32), and Luke's Sources," in Green, J. B. & Turner, M. (eds) *Jesus of Nazareth: Lord and Christ, FS Howard Marshall*, 263–78, Grand Rapids: Eerdmans.

Rius-Camps, J. & Read-Heimerdinger, J. (2004), *The Message of Acts in Codex Bezae: A Comparison with the Alexandrian Tradition,* Vol. 1: *Acts 1:1 – 5:42: Jerusalem,* JSNTSup 257, London: T&T Clark International.

Rius-Camps, J. & Read-Heimerdinger, J. (2006), *The Message of Acts in Codex Bezae: A Comparison with the Alexandrian Tradition,* Vol. 2: *Acts 6:1 – 12:25: From Judaea and Samaria to the Church in Antioch,* LNTS JSNTSup 302, London: T&T Clark International.

Rius-Camps, J. & Read-Heimerdinger, J. (2007), *The Message of Acts in Codex Bezae: A Comparison with the Alexandrian Tradition,* Vol. 3: *Acts 13:1–18:23: The Ends of the Earth: First and Second Phases of the Mission to the Gentiles,* LNTS JSNTSup 365, London: T&T Clark International.

Rius-Camps, J. & Read-Heimerdinger, J. (2009), *The Message of Acts in Codex Bezae: A Comparison with the Alexandrian Tradition,* Vol. 4: *Acts 18:24–28:31: Rome,* LNTS 415, London: T&T Clark International.

Robb, J. E. (2003), "The Prophet like Moses: Its Jewish Context and Use in the Early Christian Tradition," Unpublished PhD Thesis; London University.

Robinson, J. A. T. (1956), "The Most Primitive Christology of All?," *JTS* 7 (1956), 177–79.

Robinson, J. A. T. (1962), *Twelve New Testament Studies,* London: SCM Press.

Robinson, J. A. T. (1976), *Redating the New Testament,* London: SCM.

Rodd, C. S. (2001), "Psalms," in Barton, J. & Muddiman, J. (eds) *The Oxford Bible Commentary,* 355–405, Oxford: Oxford University Press.

Rösel, M. (2018) *Tradition and Innovation: English and German Studies on the Septuagint;* Septuagint and Cognate Studies 70, Atlanta: SBL Press.

Roth, D. T. (2008), "Marcion's Gospel and Luke: The History Of Research in Current Debate," *JBL* 127:3, 513–27

Roth, D. T. (2015), *The Text of Marcion's Gospel,* Leiden: Brill.

Rowe, C. K. (2005), "History, Hermeneutics and the Unity of Luke-Acts," *JSNT* 28:2, 131–57.

Rowe, C. K. ([2006] 2009), *Early Narrative Christology: The Lord in the Gospel of Luke,* Grand Rapids: Baker Academic.

Rowe, C. K. (2007a), "Literary Unity and Reception History: Reading Luke-Acts as Luke and Acts," *JSNT* 29:4, 449–57.

Rowe, C. K. (2007b), "Acts 2:36 and the Continuity of Lukan Christology," *NTS* 53:1, 37–56.

Rowe, C. K. (2009), *World Upside Down: Reading Acts In the Graeco-Roman Age,* Oxford: Oxford University Press.

Rowland, C. (2004), "Scripture: New Testament," in Scott, P. & Cavanaugh, W. T. (eds) *The Blackwell Companion to Political Theology,* 31, Oxford: Blackwell.

Rylaarsdam, J. C. (ed.) (1968), *Essays in Divinity 6,* Chicago: University of Chicago Press.

Sanders, J. T. (1987), *The Jews in Luke-Acts,* London: SCM.

Sanders, J. T. (1998), "Can Anything Bad Come out of Nazareth, or Did Luke Think that History Moved in a Line or in a Circle?," in Thompson, R. P. & Phillips, T. E. (eds), *Literary Studies in Luke-Acts,* [FS J. B. Tyson], 297–312, Macon: Mercer University Press.

Sanders, J. A. & Evans, C. A. (eds) (1993), *Luke and Scripture: The Function of Sacred Tradition in Luke-Acts,* Minneapolis: Fortress.

Sanders, E. P. (1992), *Judaism: Practice and Belief 63BCE-66CE,* London/Philadelphia: SCM/TPI.

Sanders, E. P. (2000), "The Dead Sea Sect and Other Jews: Commonalities, Overlaps and Differences," in Lim, T. H. et al. *The Dead Sea Scrolls in their Historical Context,* Edinburgh: T&T Clark.

Sawyer, J. F. A. (1996), *The Fifth Gospel: Isaiah in the History of Christianity,* Cambridge: Cambridge University Press.

Scaer, P. J. (2005), *The Lukan Passion and the Praiseworthy Death,* Sheffield: Sheffield Phoenix Press.

Schubert, P. (1957), "The Structure and Significance of Luke 24," in *Neutestamentliche Studien fur Rudolf Bultmann,* BNZW 2, 165–86, Berlin: Topelmann.

Schubert, P. (1968a), "The Place of the Areopagus Speech in the Composition of Acts," in Rylaarsdam (ed.) *Essays in Divinity 6,* 235–61, Chicago: University of Chicago Press.

Schubert, P. (1968b), "The Final Cycle of Speeches in the Book of Acts," *JBL* 87, 1–16.

Schweizer, E. (1968a), "Concerning the Speeches in Acts," in Keck, L. E. & Martyn, J. L. (eds) *Studies in Luke-Acts,* 208–16, London: SPCK.

Schweizer, E. (1968b), "The Concept of the Davidic "Son of God" in Acts and its Old Testament Background," in Keck, L. E. & Martyn, J. L. (eds) *Studies in Luke-Acts,* 186–93, London: SPCK.

Schweizer, E. (1993), *Das Evangelium nach Lukas,* NTD Band 3, Göttingen: Vandenhoeck & Ruprecht.

Scott, P. & Cavanaugh, W. T. (eds) (2004), *The Blackwell Companion to Political Theology,* Oxford: Blackwell.

Selwyn, E. G. (1952), *The First Epistle of St. Peter,* London: Macmillan.

Senior, D. (1989), *The Passion of Jesus in the Gospel of Luke,* Collegeville, MN: Liturgical Press.

Shuve, K. (2012), "The Patristic Reception of Luke and Acts: Scholarship, Theology, and Moral Exhortation in the Homilies of Origen and Chrysostom," in Adams, S. A. & Pahl, M. *Issues in Luke-Acts: Selected Essays,* 171–193, Piscataway, NJ: Gorgias.

Simon, U. (1953), *A Theology of Salvation,* London: SPCK.

Simonetti, M. (1994), *Biblical Interpretation in the Early Church: An Historical Introduction to Patristic Exegesis,* Edinburgh: T & T Clark.

Sleeman, M. (2009), *Geography and the Ascension Narrative in Acts,* SNTSMS 146, Cambridge: CUP.

Smallwood, E. M. (1962), "High Priests and Politics in Roman Palestine," *JTS* 14–34.

Smallwood, E. M. (1976), *Jews under Roman Rule from Pompey to Diocletian,* Leiden: Brill.

Smith, D. E. (2000), "Introducing the Acts Seminar," The Fourth R (Santa Rosa CA), 13:3, 6–10.

Smith, D. E. & Tyson, J. B. (eds) (2013), *Acts and Christian Beginnings,* Westar Institute: Polebrige Press.

Smith, S. (2017), *The Fate of the Jerusalem Temple in Luke-Acts,* LNTS 553, London: Bloomsbury, T&T Clark.

Soards, M. L. (1987), *The Passion According to Luke,* JSNTSup 14, Sheffield: JSOT Press.

Soards, M. L. (1994), *The Speeches in Acts: Their Content, Context and Concerns,* Louisville: Westminster/Knox.

Spencer, F. S. (2019) *Luke,* THNTC, Grand Rapids, MI: Eerdmans.

Spencer, P. E. (2007), "The Unity of Luke-Acts: a Four-Bolted Hermeneutical Hinge," *Currents in Biblical Research* 5:3, 341–66.

Squires, J. T. (1993), *The Plan of God in Luke-Acts,* SNTSMS 76, Cambridge: Cambridge University Press.

Squires, J. T. (1998), "The Function of Acts 8:4 – 12:25," *NTS* 44:4, 608–17.

Stanford, T. J. F. (2014), *Luke's People,* Eugene, OR: Wipf & Stock.

Stanley, C. D. (1992), *Paul and the Language of Scripture,* SNTSMS 74, Cambridge: Cambridge University Press.

Stanton, G. N. (1974) *Jesus of Nazareth in New Testament Preaching,* SNTSMS 27, Cambridge, Cambridge University Press.

Stec, D. M. (2004) *The Aramaic Bible: The Targum of Psalms,* Collegeville, MN: the Liturgical Press.

Stegemann, E. W. & Stegemann, W. (1999), *The Jesus Movement: A Social History of its First Century,* Edinburgh: T & T Clark.

Sterling, G. E. (1999), "'Opening the Scriptures': The Legitimation of the Jewish Diaspora and the Early Christian Mission," in Moessner, D. P. (ed.) *Jesus and the Heritage of Israel,* 199–225, Harrisburg: TPI.

Sterling, G. (2001), "Mors philosophi: the Death of Jesus in Luke," HTR 94, 383–402.

Steyn, G. J. (1999), "ἐκχεῶ ἀπὸ τοῦ πνεύματός... (Acts 2:17, 18): What is being poured out?," Neotestamentica 33:2, 365–71.

Strange, W. A. (1992), The Problem of the Text of Acts, SNTSMS 71, Cambridge: Cambridge University Press.

Strange, W. A. (2000), "The Jesus Tradition in Acts," *NTS* 46:1, 59–74.

Strauss, M. L. (1995), *The Davidic Messiah in Luke-Acts: the Promise and its Fulfillment in Lukan Christology,* JSNTS 110, Sheffield: Sheffield Academic Press.

Strelan, R. (2000), *Recognizing the Gods (Acts 14:8 – 10), NTS* 46:4, 488–503.

Stuckenbruck, L. T. & North, W E S, (eds) (2004), *Early Jewish and Christian Monotheism,* JSNTSS 263, London and New York: T & T Clark International.

Stuhlmacher, P. (ed.) (1991), *The Gospel and the Gospels,* Grand Rapids: Eerdmans.

Sylva, D. D. (1990), *Reimaging the Death of the Lukan Jesus,* BBB 73, Frankfurt: Hain.

Talbert, C. H. (1974), *Literary Patterns, Theological Themes and The Genre of Luke-Acts,* Missoula: SBL/Scholars Press.

Talbert, C. H. (ed.) (1978), *Perspectives on Luke-Acts,* Edinburgh: T & T Clark.

Talbert, C. H. (1984a), "Prophecy and Fulfillment in Lucan Theology," in idem. *Luke-Acts: New Perspectives from the Society of Biblical Literature Seminar,* 91–103, New York: Crossroad.

Talbert C. H. (ed.) (1984b), *Luke-Acts: New Perspectives from the Society of Biblical Literature Seminar,* New York: Crossroad.

Talbert, C. H. (1988), *Reading Luke,* New York: Crossroad.

Tannehill, R C. (1986), *The Narrative unity of Luke-Acts: A Literary Interpretation,* Volume one: *The Gospel according to Luke,* Fortress Press.

Tannehill, R. C. (1990), *The Narrative unity of Luke-Acts: A Literary Interpretation,* Volume two: *The Acts of the Apostles,* Minnesota: Fortress Press.

Tannehill, R. C. (1996), *Luke,* ANTC, Nashville: Abingdon.

Tannehill, R. C. (1998), "Freedom and Responsibility in Scripture Interpretation, with Application to Luke," in Thompson, R. P. & Phillips, T. E. (eds), *Literary Studies in Luke-Acts,* [FS J. B. Tyson], 265–78, Macon: Mercer University Press.

Taylor, J. (1998), "St Paul's Mission field: the World of Acts 13 – 28," *ProcIrBibAssoc* 21, 9–24.

Taylor, J. (1990), "The Making of Acts: A New Account," *RB* 97:4, 502–24.

Taylor, V. (1952), *The Gospel According to St Mark*, London; Macmillan.

Taylor, V. (1953), *The Names of Jesus,* London: Macmillan.

Taylor, V. (1955), "The Origin of the Markan Passion Sayings," *NTS* 1:3, 159–67.

Taylor, V. (1966), *The Person of Christ in New Testament Teaching,* London: Macmillan.

Taylor, V. (1970), *New Testament Essays,* London: Epworth.

Taylor, V. (1972), *The Passion Narrative of St Luke*, SNTSMS 19, Cambridge: Cambridge University Press.

Thompson, R. P. & Phillips, T. E. (eds) (1998), *Literary Studies in Luke-Acts,* [*FS* J B Tyson], Macon: Mercer University Press.

Thompson, R. P. (1998), "Believers and Religious Leaders in Jerusalem: Contrasting Portraits of Jews in Acts 1 – 7," in Thompson, R. P. & Phillips, T. E. (eds), *Literary Studies in Luke-Acts,* [*FS* J. B. Tyson], 327–344, Macon: Mercer University Press.

Tiede, D. L. (1980), *Prophecy and History in Luke-Acts,* Philadelphia: Fortress.

Tobin, T. H. (1990), "The Prologue of John and Hellenistic Jewish Speculation," *CBQ* Vol. 52 no. 2, 252–269.

Tomson, P. J. (2001), *"If this be from Heaven": Jesus and the New Testament Authors in their Relationship to Judaism,* Sheffield: Sheffield Academic Press.

Trites, A. A. (1978), "The Prayer Motif in Luke-Acts," in Talbert, C. H. (ed.) *Perspectives on Luke-Acts,* 168–186, Edinburgh: T & T Clark.

Tuckett, C. M. (ed.) (1995), *Luke's Literary Achievement: Collected Essays,* JSNTSup 116, Sheffield: Sheffield Academic Press.

Tuckett, C. M. (1997), *The Scriptures in the Gospels,* BETL 131, Leuven: Leuven University Press, Peeters.

Turner, M. (1996), *Power from on High: the Spirit in Israel's Restoration and Witness in Luke-Acts,* Sheffield: Sheffield Academic Press.

Tyson, J. B. (1986), *The Death of Jesus in Luke-Acts,* Columbia SC: University of South Carolina.

Tyson, J. B. (1987), "The Gentile Mission and the Authority of Scripture in Acts," *NTS* 33, 619–631.

Tyson, J. B. (1992), *Images of Judaism in Luke-Acts,* Columbia, SC: University of South Carolina Press.

Tyson, J. B. (2006), *Marcion and Luke-Acts: a Defining Struggle,* Columbia, SC: University of South Carolina Press.

Ulrich, E. (1999) *The Dead Sea Scrolls and the Origins of the Bible,* Grand Rapids, MI: Eerdmans; Leiden: Brill.

Unnik, W. C. van (1960), "The "Book of Acts" – the Confirmation of the Gospel," *NovT* IV, 26–59.

Unnik, W. C. van (1968), "Luke-Acts, A Storm Center in Contemporary Scholarship," in Keck, L. E. & Martyn, J. L. (eds) *Studies in Luke-Acts*, 15–32, London: SPCK.

Vanhoozer, K. J. (1995), "The Reader in New Testament Interpretation," in Green, J.B. *Hearing the New Testament: Strategies for Interpretation,* 301–328, Grand Rapids/Carlisle: Eerdmans/Paternoster.

Verheyden J. (2012), "The Unity of Luke-Acts: One Work, One Author, One Purpose?," in Adams, S. A. & Pahl, M. *Issues in Luke-Acts: Selected Essays,* 27–50, Piscataway, NJ: Gorgias.

Vermes, G. (1993), *The Religion of Jesus the Jew,* London: SCM.

Vermes, G. (1994), *An Introduction to the Complete Dead Sea Scrolls,* London: SCM.

Vesco, J. L. (2012) *Le Psautier de Jésus: les Citations des Psaumes dans le Nouveau Testament, II,* Paris: Cerf.

Vielhauer, P. (1968), "On the "Paulinism" of Acts," in Keck, L. E. & Martyn, J. L. (eds) *Studies in Luke-Acts*, 33–50, London: SPCK.

Vinzent, M. (2014), *Marcion and the Dating of the Synoptic Gospels,* Studia Patristica: Supplements 2, Leuven: Peeters.

Waaler, E. (2016), "Multidimensional Intertextuality," in Oropeza, B. J. & Moyise, S. (eds) *Exploring Intertextuality: Diverse Strategies for New Testament Interpretation of Texts,* 222–241, Eugene, OR: Cascade Books.

Wagner, J. R. (1997), "Psalm 118 in Luke-Acts: Tracing a Narrative Thread," in Evans, C. A. & Sanders, J. A. (eds) *Early Christian Interpretation of the Scriptures of Israel: Investigations and Proposals,* 154–178, JSNTSup 148, Sheffield: Sheffield Academic Press.

Wainwright, A. W. (1977), "Luke and the Restoration of the Kingdom of Israel," *ExpTim* 89, 76–9.

Wainwright, G (ed.) (1989), *Keeping the Faith: Essays to mark the centenary of Lux Mundi,* London: SPCK.

Walasky, P. W. (1983), *"And So We Came to Rome": the Political Perspective of St Luke,* SNTSMS 49, Cambridge: Cambridge University Press.

Walker, W. O. (1998), "Acts and the Pauline Corpus Revisited: Peter's Speech at the Jerusalem Conference," in Thompson, R. P. & Phillips, T. E. (eds), *Literary Studies in Luke-Acts,* [FS J. B. Tyson], 77–86, Macon: Mercer University Press.

Wall, R. W. (2000), "Intertextuality, Biblical," in Evans, C. A. & Porter, S. E. (eds), *Dictionary of New Testament Background,* 541–551, Leicester: IVP.

Walton, S. (2000), *Leadership and Lifestyle: the Portrait of Paul in the Miletus Speech and 1 Thessalonians,* Cambridge: Cambridge University Press.

Walton, S. (2008), "The Acts – of God? What is the 'Acts of the Apostles' All About?," *EvQ* 80:4, 291–306.

Walton, S, Phillips, T. E., Pietersen, L. K., Scott Spencer, F. (eds) (2011), *Reading Acts Today,* LNTS 427 FS L. C. A. Alexander, London: Bloomsbury T&T Clark.

Wassen, C. (2016), "The Use of the Dead Sea Scrolls for Interpreting Jesus's Action in the Temple," *Dead Sea Discoveries*, 23:3, 280–303.

Watson, A. (1996), *The Trial of Stephen*, Athens, GA: University of Georgia Press.

Watson, F. (1994), "'He is not here': Towards a Theology of the Empty Tomb," in Barton, S. & Stanton, G. (eds) *Resurrection* [FS Leslie Houlden], 95–107, London: SPCK.

Watson, F. (2004), *Paul and the Hermeneutics of Faith,* London, New York: T & T Clark International.

Wedderburn, A. J. M. (1999), *Beyond Resurrection,* London: SCM.

Weiser, A. (1962), *The Psalms,* London: SCM.

Weren, W. J. C. (1989), "Psalm 2 in Luke-Acts: an Intertextual Study," in Draisma, S. *Intertextuality In Biblical Writings,* [FS Bas van Iersel], Kampen: Kok.

White, V. (1991), *Atonement and Incarnation,* Cambridge: Cambridge University Press.

Whitsett, C. G. (2000), "Son of God, Seed of David: Paul's Messianic Exegesis in Romans 1:3–4," *JBL* 119:4, 661–681.

Whybray, R. N. (1978), *Thanksgiving for a Liberated Prophet: An Interpretation of Isaiah, Chapter 53,* JSOTSup 4, Sheffield: Sheffield Academic Press.

Whybray, R. N. (1983), *The Second Isaiah,* Sheffield: Sheffield Academic Press.

Wiefel, W. (1988), *Das Evangelium nach Lukas,* THzNT 3, Berlin: Evangelische Verlagsanstalt.

Wilckens, U. (1968), "Interpreting Luke-Acts in a Period of Existentialist Theology," in Keck, L. E. & Martyn, J. L. (eds) *Studies in Luke-Acts,* 60–83, London: SPCK.

Williams, C. S C. (1964), *The Acts of the Apostles,* Black's New Testament Commentaries, London: A & C Black.

Witherington III, B. (1998a), *The Acts of the Apostles: A Socio-Rhetorical Commentary,* Eerdmans/Paternoster.

Witherington III, B. (1998b), *The Paul Quest: The Renewed Search for the Jew of Tarsus,* 304–31, Downers Grove/Leicester: IVP.

Witherington III, B (ed.) (1996), *History, Literature and Society in the Book of Acts,* Cambridge: Cambridge University Press.

Wolter, M. (2016) *The Gospel According to Luke,* Vol. I (Luke 1–9:50), Waco TX: Baylor University Press.

Wolter, M. (2017), *The Gospel According to Luke* Vol. II (Luke 9:51–24), Waco TX: Baylor University Press.

Woods, E. J. (2001), *The "Finger of God" and Pneumatology in Luke-Acts,* JSNTSup 205, Sheffield Academic Press.

Wright, N. T. (1992), *The New Testament and the People of God, Christian Origins and the Question of God,* Vol. 1, London: SPCK.

Wright, N. T. (1996), *Jesus and the Victory of God,* Christian Origins and the Question of God, Vol. 2, London: SPCK.

Wright, N. T. (1998), "The Servant and Jesus: the Relevance of the Colloquy for the Current Quest for Jesus," in Bellinger, W. H. & Farmer, W. R. (eds), *Jesus and the Suffering Servant: Isaiah 53 and Christian Origins,* 281–97, Harrisburg: TPI.

Wright, N. T. (2003), *The Resurrection of the Son of God,* Christian Origins and the Question of God, Vol. 3, Minneapolis: Fortress Press.

Wright, N. T. (2013), *Paul and the Faithfulness of God,* Christian Origins and the Question of God, Vol. 4; Parts I-IV London: SPCK.

Wright, N. T. (2015), *The Paul Debate: Critical questions for Understanding the Apostle,* Texas: Baylor University Press.

Wright, R. (2007), *The Psalms of Solomon: A Critical Edition of the Greek Text,* Jewish and Christian Texts in Contexts and Related Studies, 1, London/New York: T&T Clark.

Wright, T. (2018), *Paul: a Biography,* London: SPCK.

Yoder, J. H. (1972), *The Politics of Jesus,* Carlisle/Grand Rapids: Paternoster/Eerdmans.

Yoder, J. H. (ed. Cartwright, M. G.) (1994), *The Royal Priesthood: Essays Ecclesiological and Ecumenical,* Grand Rapids: Eerdmans.

Ziesler, J. A. (1979), "The Name of Jesus in the Acts of the Apostles," *JSNT* 4, 28–41.

Zimmerli, W & Jeremias, J. (1957), *The Servant of God, SBT* 20, London: SCM.

Zwiep, A. W. (1997), *The Ascension of the Messiah in Lukan Christology,* Leiden: Brill.

Index of Biblical References

Note to the index:
To aid legibility, the page references do not differentiate between the main text and footnotes. Thus, a reference to a chapter or verse may be anywhere on the page. Entries in bold represent general references to a chapter.

398

399

401

405

Index of Authors

Phillips, T. E. (ed.) (1998)   299
Plummer, A. (1922)   1, 12

Rahlfs, A. (1979)   1, 12, 127
Ramsey, A. M. (1949)   204
Raworth, K. (2017)   343
Read-Heimerdinger, J.   3, 337
    (2002)   16, 98
Rese, M (1969)   274
Rius-Camps, J.   337
    (2002)   16, 98
Robinson, J. A. T. (1976)   340
Roth, D. T.
    (2008)   44
    (2015)   44
Rowe, C. K.   35
    (2007a)   85

Said, E. (2004)   217
Sanders, E. P.   344
    (1992)   223, 228
    (1993)   215
Sanders, J. T.
    (1987)   299, 344
    (1998)   299
Scaer, P. J. (2005)   175
Schnabel, E. J. (2007)   69, 86, 141
Schubert, P. 1957   85
Schweizer, E. (1993)   1, 12
Sleeman, M. (2009)   85, 108, 144,
    309
Smith, D. E. (ed.) (2013)   340
Smith, S. (2017)   340
Soards, M. L. (1994)   14, 279
Stanford, T. J. F. (2014)   120, 167,
    183
Stanton, G. (ed.) (1994)   85
Stanton, G. N. (1974)   269
Strauss, M. L. (1995)   1, 8, 12, 20,
    35, 39, 42, 75,
    86, 141, 263, 266

Talbert, C. H. (1988)   1, 12
Tannehill, R. C.
    (1986)   344
    (1990)   165, 183, 344
    (1996)   1, 12
Taylor, V. (1953)   1, 13, 169
Thompson, R. P. (ed.) (1998)   299
Tobin, T. H. (1990)   65
Tomson, P. J. (2001)   124, 223
Tyson, J. B.
    (2006)   43
    (2013)   340

Ulrich, E. (1999)   333

Vermes, G. (1994)   333
Vesco, J. L. (2012)   266, 272, 275
Vinzent, M. (2014)   44

Wedderburn, J. M. (1999)   85
Weren, W. J. C. (1989)   275
Whitsett, C. G. (2000)   15, 27, 44, 52,
    61, 257, 277
Wiefel, W. (1988)   1, 12
Wolter, M. (2017)   1, 12
Wright, N. T.
    (1992)   215, 223, 228, 259, 260,
    300
    (2003)   24, 25, 36, 85, 124, 263,
    271, 277, 300,
    341
    (2013)   290, 299, 340, 341
    (2015)   291, 295

Author biography

Peter Doble (1929-2023) read Economics at the University of Wales, followed by Theology and New Testament Studies at Cambridge University. He was awarded a PhD by the University of Leeds, which was later published as *The Paradox of Salvation*.[1486] Peter's Lukan research continued long after retiring from his final appointment as Senior Fellow in the Department of Theology and Religious Studies at the University of Leeds.

A member of the *SNTS, BNTS, SBL*, and the Hawarden seminar on the uses of the Old Testament in the New, he regularly reviewed for the *Journal for the Study of the New Testament*, and occasionally reviewed for *Novum Testamentum*, and for *Expository Times*. Ordained a presbyter in the Church of South India, he also served in the UK and the USA as indivisibly both Methodist minister and Anglican presbyter. Until his death in January 2023, he remained actively engaged in the wider life of scholarly research and of Christian communities, particularly in relation to the socio-economic-political dimensions of faith – especially of *Luke-Acts*.

[1486] SNTSMS 87, Cambridge University Press, 1996.

Printed in Great Britain
by Amazon

2b76c0a3-a15e-4286-9855-4b7b719abcc5R01